Four Hundred Years of Gun Control

Why Isn't It Working?

Howard Nemerov

CONTRAST MEDIA PRESS

Published by CONTRAST MEDIA PRESS
P.O. Box 6195 - Lakewood, California 90714

First published May 5th, 2008

ISBN-13   978-0-9817382-2-2

Please contact the Author for interviews or other interest at www.ContrastMediaPress.com or email the author: hnemerov@netvista.net

DISCLAIMER: The contents of this book are opinion, an analysis of findings and facts on the topic appearing on the public record, sourced as same, which opinion and analysis of the author and CMP are furnished as clarification in the public interest, and in no way constitute medical, tactical, ethical, moral, business, accounting, legislative, or legal advice. For any such advice, the reader is urged to consult the appropriate licensed professional.

To my wife Grace, beloved, partner, and editor:
Thanks for making this a book.

To Dave Kopel:
Thank you for vetting Chapter 3 and making it more accurate and effective.

To Marilyn Kamelgarn, editor extraordinaire:
Thanks for confirming the value of three years of effort.

Critical Acclaim for Howard Nemerov's Writings

Howard's always a great guest on NRA News. He's become our unofficial Investigative Analyst because of his exceptional ability to go out, gather the data, and report the truth about gun control. Howard crunches the numbers and puts his data out there like no one else I've seen. He's truly one of a kind! – Cam Edwards, Host of NRA News

Howard's writing creates clear, objective analysis on the subject of gun control and its affects on people. It is a most striking rebuttal of the false claims, and inaccurate and twisted data, used by the anti-self-defense crowd. Well done! – Jerry Patterson, Texas Land Commissioner

I have watched Howard Nemerov come out of 'nowhere' to become a regular and impressive contributor to pro-gun-rights literature. His writing enhances our vital knowledge base in the fight to preserve the Second Amendment. I have included it in my column in Guns & Ammo's Handguns magazine. – Don Kates

Anyone interested in the gun control debate can learn a lot by reading this wide-ranging book filled with interesting facts and data. – Dave Kopel, Research Director, Independence Institute

I've read your work often, and while I disagree with you on policy, I think you're a very good writer. – Peter Hamm, Brady Campaign to Prevent Gun Violence

Table of Contents

Preface

Gun control laws are nothing new. The concept of limiting civilian access to firearms has been touted as a useful policy since their invention. What has changed the most about gun control is how it is employed in modern times. Where it was initially used to deal with specific groups of people, these days it is now often considered a policy to be applied to the general public as a way to improve safety and security.

The question of whether gun control is a policy that benefits the general public often evokes intensely emotional responses from proponents on both sides of the issue. When the topic is broached, it can devolve into a contest of stubbornness, rhetoric, and volume, with both groups walking away feeling misunderstood and more convinced than ever that they are right.

I want to make it clear that I do not now support gun control, but before you close this book in dismay you should know that, in the recent past, I supported complete civilian disarmament. My profession involves helping people. I believed anything that could cause as much human damage as a firearm was a very bad object to have floating around in public. Though not autobiographical, this book explains why and how I reevaluated my position on gun control. After reviewing the history of gun control and its consequences, I concluded that in real life, gun control doesn't benefit honest law-abiding people like you and me; instead, it puts us at more risk than you can imagine. If you swim along the surface of this very deep and complex subject wanting only good for others, it is easy to miss the undertow of unintended consequences.

Gun control is a very successful policy, depending on which side of the muzzle you stand (Chapter 1). The basic postulates of gun control are that guns are unnecessary in modern, civilized society (Chapter 2), that guns are dangerous consumer products that cause more harm than good (Chapter 3), that politicians who want to disarm us are doing so for the common good (Chapter 4), and that removing guns from society will make it a safer place for all of us (Chapters 2-6, from different perspectives). Chapter 7 examines the data and criteria used by gun control organizations to prove all these premises. Chapter 8 attempts to determine exactly how efficient the U.S. and state criminal justice systems are in prosecuting and convicting those who commit violent crimes. This information is an important aspect to keep in mind when considering the idea that we should "let the professionals" take care of personal security.

What really happened after various gun control policies were enacted by well-meaning governments? Did violent crime diminish, including crimes of opportunity against those who are physically less able to fend off a violent attacker, such as women? Did murder and suicide rates drop when fewer guns were available? What about civil and political rights? Did the reduction of civilian firearms result in more freedom and increased civil rights? And what about the origins of gun control? Was it always intended as a democratic tool to promote public safety? Is there a darker side to the history of gun control that many today want to ignore? The purpose of this book is to answer these questions with data from sources on all sides of the issue.

I hope by the time you finish this book, you will have a better understanding about this extraordinarily critical issue.

Howard Nemerov
April 2008

Chapter 1
A Brief History of Gun Control

Gun control can be very beneficial to those administering the laws, especially when there is a population group that they consider "different" and therefore suspect. You can justify gun control as a method to remain safe from the threat of attack from those "others." In this chapter, we will look at a few historical examples where gun control successfully accomplished the two interrelated goals of safety and control of others.

Native Americans and Early American Colonists

Arriving in an untamed new land, far from civilization and organized governmental protection, and with no commercial infrastructure to provide food, shelter, or clothing, the colonists were truly on their own. They had nothing but their faith in God and their own abilities to pull together, survive, and thrive in the New World.

John Winthrop, the first governor of the Massachusetts Bay Colony, wrote a sermon while still in transit to America called the *City on the Hill*, stating his belief that "Puritan colonists emigrating to the New World were members of a special pact with God to create a holy community."[1] He called upon the colonists to help and support one another in all things, even if it means another in need would be unable to repay a loan. He based this unity upon the religious beliefs that "true Christians are of one body in Christ." Winthrop concluded his sermon with this admonishment:

> I shall shutt upp this discourse with that exhortation of Moses, that faithfull servant of the Lord, in his last farewell to Israell, Deut. 30. Beloued there is now sett before us life and good, Death and evill, in that wee are commanded this day to loue the Lord our God, and to loue one another, to walke in his wayes and to keepe his Commandements and his Ordinance and his lawes, and the articles of our Covenant with him, that wee may liue and be multiplied, and that the Lord our God may blesse us in the land whither wee goe to possesse it. But if our heartes shall turne away, soe that wee will not obey, but shall be seduced, and worshipp and serue other Gods, our pleasure and proffitts, and serue them; it is propounded unto us this day, wee shall surely perishe out of the good land whither wee passe over this vast sea to possesse it;

> Therefore lett us choose life that wee, and our seede may liue, by obeyeing His voyce and cleaveing to Him, for Hee is our life and our prosperity.[2]

The two main points of the sermon were:

- Colonists were to walk the straight-and-narrow if they were to survive.

- As proper Christians, they were sailing across the ocean to "possess" (defined by the Oxford English Dictionary as: "Hold as property"[3]) a new land.

Out of this second belief sprang a philosophy that was termed "manifest destiny" by the mid-1800s:

It was the nation's manifest destiny to overspread and to possess the whole of the continent which Providence has given us for the development of the great experiment of liberty and federated self-government entrusted to us.[4]

At the beginning, the colonists ran into a few difficulties in possessing the New World. One problem was the fact that there were already people living here, and there were more of "them" than there were colonists. One way to favorably control the balance of power was to find some technological superiority which gave them an advantage against overwhelming odds; they did this by striving to ensure that firearms remained only in the hands of the colonists. Thus we have gun control in America right from the beginning of European habitation.

In 1629, the Massachusetts Colony enacted a law that anyone who would "sell munitions, guns, or other furniture, to arm the Indians against us, or teach them the use of arms" would be arrested and sent to prison in England "where they will not escape severe punishment."[5]

Maybe that law had some loopholes, or else some enterprising folks decided the profits were worth the risk, because the Indians did obtain firearms. (This may be the first evidence of illegal gun smuggling in America, and this is an important point examined further in Chapter 6: Prohibition creates overwhelmingly tempting financial gain for those with the proper mix of greed and disdain for law.) By 1637, Massachusetts law evolved to include those who might offer to fix a gun owned by an Indian or sell them ingredients for making ammunition:

It is ordered, that no man within this jurisdiction shall, directly or indirectly amend, repair, or cause to be amended or repaired, any gun, small or great, belonging to any Indian, nor shall endeavor the same, nor shall sell or give to any Indian, directly or indirectly, any such gun or gunpowder, or shot, or lead…[6]

So even back then, gun control proponents knew that they could not stop restricted persons from owning guns, but if they could restrict access to ammunition, the gun would be useless, creating the equivalent of a gun ban.

Nor was this an issue unique to Massachusetts. The very first page of the Colonial Connecticut Records stated: "It is ordered from henceforth none within the jurisdiction of this court shall trade with the natives or Indians any piece or pistol or gun or powder or shot…[7]" By 1642, Connecticut law was identical to the earlier Massachusetts law.[8]

Clayton Cramer, in his paper *The Racist Roots of Gun Control*, follows early Connecticut gun control through its evolution, chronicling how they passed additional laws when the original didn't work, hoping that the next one would finally fix all the loopholes.

For example, by October 25, 1644, it was clear that "Dutch and French do sell and trade to the Indians guns, pistols, and warlike instruments."[9] To control these foreign entrepreneurs, it was then ordered that colonists "shall at any time hereafter sell neither gun nor pistol, nor any instrument of war, neither to Dutch or French men..." in an effort cut off this smuggling pipeline to the Indians.[10] Finally, on April 9, 1646 they banned ammunition sales to Indians, just like their neighbors in Massachusetts.[11]

On September 18, 1649 the General Court of Hartford noted:

> Whereas the French, Dutch, and other foreign nations do ordinarily trade guns, powder, and shot, etc. with the Indians, to our great prejudice, and the strengthening and animating of the Indians against us...Whereas the French, Dutch, etc. do prohibit all trade with the Indians within their respective jurisdictions...[12]

As a result of empowering the Indians to revolt against the colonists, all trade with Indians was now prohibited within the jurisdiction of Connecticut, regardless of the goods being sold. This threatened the livelihoods of French and Dutch traders who had no dealings in firearms: Such a blanket ban had the effect of hurting those with lawful intentions.

Back up a bit and consider colonial gun control from another perspective: Was there another desired outcome of these trade bans and gun control regulations? The early New England Colonists befriended and supported a tribe called the Wampanoag against rival tribes such as the Narragansett, forcing the Narragansett to abandon their war against the Wampanoag who were now too strong an enemy by virtue of their alliance with colonists, who had technologically superior means of offense and defense.

Later, while the Narragansett were distracted by fighting the Mohawk, the early colony of Plymouth became firmly established. Then the Puritans arrived, bringing with them a more intolerant view of anybody not Puritan. These colonists began their westward expansion, possessing what land they wanted.

During the war with the Dutch, both the New England Colonists and the Dutch used Indian tribes as pawns, weakening the Indians through war-related attrition. By the end of this period, the English were the undisputed power in the area, and they continued their expansion: The Indians were merely in the way. Further depredations of disease, Puritan missionary work, and war permanently removed the Indians as a power in southern New England.[13] The colonists practiced the old game of divide and conquer, diminishing the Indians as a threat to colonial expansion. Disarming the Indians was the final ingredient to ensure they had no means to resist the expansion of colonial settlers.

Over a century later, American Revolutionary writer Thomas Paine would observe: "Arms discourage and keep the invader and plunderer in awe, and preserve order in the world." The colonists believed in their own religious and racial superiority, their divinely inspired manifest destiny, and a practical strategy involving gun control to establish and preserve the order of colonial rule.

Black Disarmament: Colonial to Post-Civil War

> I became curious about the history of the Buffalo Soldiers. I started reading everything I could lay my hands on. What I learned filled me with pride at the feats these black men had achieved and with sadness at the injustices and neglect they had suffered. Blacks had fought in just about all of America's wars. They served to prove themselves the equal of white soldiers, which was precisely why some whites did not want blacks in uniform. My reading led me to the words of Howell Cobb, a Confederate general, who advised Jefferson Davis against arming blacks. "Use all the negroes you can for…cooking, digging, chopping and such," Cobb said. "But don't arm them. If slaves will make good soldiers," he warned, "our whole theory of slavery is wrong." Frederick Douglas put it another way: "Once you let the black man get upon his person the brass letters 'U.S.,' let him get an eagle on his button and bullets in his pocket, and there is no power on earth which can deny he has earned the right to citizenship in the United States."–Colin Powell, U.S. Secretary of State and Chairman of Joint Chiefs of Staff, retired[14]

There were many Black disarmament laws on the colonial books, such as the following gun control statutes compiled by Cramer.[15]

A Virginia law from 1640 explained the colony's support of the militia, but excluded Blacks: "All persons except negroes to be provided with arms and ammunition or be fined at pleasure of the Governor and Council."[16] This law was expanded in 1723 to include other people besides Blacks: "no negro, mulatto, or Indian whatsoever; (except as hereafter excepted) shall hereafter presume to keep, or carry any gun…"[17] There was one interesting exception in this law: "That every free negro, mulatto, or Indian, being a housekeeper, or listed in the militia, may be permitted to keep one gun…"[18] Thus, free persons of color were given limited rights in exchange for their willingness to fight and die for those with full rights: They could bear arms only if they were willing to defend property, though this property could only belong to citizens, meaning white people.

In 1700, the colony of Pennsylvania enacted a similar statute:

> That if any negro shall presume to carry any guns, swords, pistols, fowling pieces, clubs or other arms or weapons whatsoever, without his master's special license for the same, and be convicted thereof before a magistrate, he shall be whipped with twenty-one lashes on his bare back.[19]

In 1715, Maryland enacted their own colonial statute:

> No Negro or other slave, within this province, shall be permitted to carry any gun or any other offensive weapon, from off their Master's land without license from their Master.[20]

During the Revolutionary War and early republic eras, the new states continued to enact more detailed Black disarmament laws. Sometimes, this had negative consequences even for those passing the laws.

Presuming that patriotic fervor would provide plenty of enlistments for the Continental Army during the Revolution, Black slaves and freemen were not allowed to enlist. But once it became clear that there would not be enough volunteers, George Washington became more conciliatory and gave Blacks permission to join the army.[21]

Even after the war, this desire to keep Blacks out of the military persisted. For example, the Militia Act of 1792 allowed only whites to enroll:

> [E]ach and every free able-bodied white male citizen of the respective States, resident therein, who is or shall be of age of eighteen years, and under the age of forty-five years... shall severally and respectively be enrolled in the militia...every citizen, so enrolled and notified, shall, within six months thereafter, provide himself with a good musket or firelock...[22]

By the middle of the 19th Century, gun control efforts began to focus upon disarming all Blacks, usually by stripping them of "personhood" in order to justify what most state constitutions considered a right of all persons to keep and bear arms. These laws were primarily intended to keep slaves from having the wherewithal to stage a successful revolt. Understanding that freedom in early America was often obtained or defended at the end of a gun, it was a simple matter of controlling guns in order to control who was free. As Cramer notes:

> It is not surprising that the first North American English colonies, then the states of the new republic, remained in dread fear of armed blacks, for slave revolts against slave owners often degenerated into less selective forms of racial warfare. The perception that free blacks were sympathetic to the plight of their enslaved brothers, and the dangerous example that 'a Negro could be free' also caused the slave states to pass laws designed to disarm all blacks, both slave and free.[23]

In *Jurisprudence of the Second and Fourteenth Amendments*, Stephen Halbrook explains how the revolutionary experience taught people a thing or two about the relationship between guns and freedom:

> Having won their national independence from England through armed struggle, it became increasingly demonstrative to pre-Civil War Americans that the technological development of the gun had egalitarian propensities. It likewise was clear to both proponents and opponents of slavery that an armed black population meant the abolition of slavery...[24]

Black disarmament laws increased following Nat Turner's rebellion of 1831, where Black slaves revolted in Southampton County, Virginia, killing about sixty Whites.[25] By 1834, Black gun bans began appearing in state constitutions. Cramer notes that Article XI, 26 of the 1796 Tennessee Constitution was revised from: "That the freemen of this State have a right to keep and to bear arms for their common defense" to: "That the *free white men* of this State have a right to keep and to bear arms for their common defense."[26] [Emphasis added]

In 1843, the North Carolina Supreme Court ruled:

The bill of rights in this State secures to every man indeed, the right to "bear arms for the defense of the State."[27]

But by 1844, the same court decided it was okay to disarm Blacks:

The Act of assembly passed in 1840, ch 30, entitled 'an act to prevent free persons of color from carrying fire arms,' is not unconstitutional.[28]

The original Act referred to in this decision was included in its entirety in the court's findings:

Be it enacted, etc. That if any free negro, mulatto, or free person of color, shall wear or carry about his or her person, or keep in his or her house, any shot gun, musket, rifle, pistol, sword, dagger or bowie-knife, unless he or she shall have obtained a license therefore from the Court of Pleas and Quarter Sessions of his or her county, within one year preceding the wearing, keeping or carrying therefore, he or she shall be guilty of a misdemeanor, and may be indicted therefore.[29]

The court got around the right to bear arms mentioned in 1843 by reinterpreting the state constitution in order to redefine who was a citizen of the state: "Free people of color in this State are not to be considered as citizens."[30]

Black disarmament did not end after the Civil War. As Cramer notes: "the various Black Codes adopted after the Civil War required blacks to obtain a license before carrying or possessing firearms…"[31]

The Mississippi Black Code of 1865 declared: "no freedman, free Negro, or mulatto not in the military service of the United States government, and not licensed so to do by the board of police of his or her county, shall keep or carry firearms of any kind…[32]

The Black Codes kept freed slaves living in a state as close to slavery as possible, within the new laws of the Reconstruction. Besides limiting firearms ownership, the Codes restricted access to courts, forced Blacks into indentured servitude, forbade Black/White marriage, and severely restricted relations between Blacks and Whites in public.[33] Another source notes: "South Carolina's code reflected the white obsession with controlling the former slaves. It banned black people from possessing most firearms…"[34]

As a result of these codes, Congress enacted the Civil Rights Act of 1866, so that by "abolishing the badges of slavery, the bill would enforce fundamental rights against racial discrimination in respect to civil rights…"[35] Furthermore, in order to rejoin the Union, ex-Confederate states were required to ratify the Fourteenth Amendment, which forbade states to deny any citizen the rights acknowledged under federal law.[36]

Considering this history of economic and social repression enforced by racial disarmament, it is curious that one long-term goal of the National Association for the Advancement of Colored People is to reduce their constituents' access to firearms by "pursuing legal actions against the gun industry" for the criminal use of guns, potentially putting manufacturers out of business and thereby reducing supply.[37] (This subject is examined further in Chapter 4).

As Cramer notes: "In the last century, the official rhetoric in support of such laws was that 'they' were too violent, too untrustworthy, to be allowed weapons."[38] Now it appears that many Black leaders have accepted this hypothesis as true, and tacitly agree they are unworthy of the freedom and responsibility of self-determination, including self-defense, as if many Blacks do indeed prefer to live under the Black Codes.

WASHINGTON – Secretary of State Condoleezza Rice, recalling how her father took up arms to defend fellow blacks from racist whites in the segregated South, said Wednesday the constitutional right of Americans to own guns is as important as their rights to free speech and religion.

In an interview on CNN's "Larry King Live," Rice said she came to that view from personal experience. She said her father, a black minister, and his friends armed themselves to defend the black community in Birmingham, Ala., against the White Knight Riders in 1962 and 1963. She said if local authorities had had lists of registered weapons, she did not think her father and other blacks would have been able to defend themselves.

Rice said the Founding Fathers understood "there might be circumstances that people like my father experienced in Birmingham, Ala., when, in fact, the police weren't going to protect you."[39]

An Early British Experience with Gun Control

As a young boy, King Charles Stuart II watched his royal world disintegrate:

In 1642, when he was twelve years old, the three kingdoms of his father Charles I, England, Scotland, and Ireland, dissolved into civil war. His father was eventually imprisoned, and then executed in 1649.[40]

After the collapse of the interim republic following the civil war, Charles II was restored as the king of England, Scotland, and Ireland. Facing financial difficulties as the result of an unsatisfactory settlement with the Parliament, Charles II also inherited a country whose unified Church of England was shattered by the war:

The Restoration settlements made this situation considerably worse as, much against Charles's will, his Parliament decided on a narrowly defined Church based on hierarchy and ceremony, and expelled from it everybody who preferred a broader-based and more austere one, with a greater emphasis on preaching. This created a major new problem of nonconformity, as several new groups of Protestants formed alongside and outside the national one. The Parliament's answer was to try to persecute them out of existence, but their own courage and tenacity, and the negligence and good nature of local officials, meant that they survived. The government was therefore left with a mass of religious dissenters that could neither be wiped out nor reconciled to the Church.[41]

The new king and his administration confronted another major challenge:

A third challenge for the restored monarchy was the obvious fact that it returned to a land in which old enmities still lingered among the former parties of the civil wars, and that care would have to be taken in the employment and management of royal ministers.[42]

In response to a politically volatile and religiously divisive political environment, they enacted many gun control measures to disarm anybody considered a threat to the newly restored crown. These laws included:

- Disarming and disbanding the army that had welcomed Charles II home,

- A series of royal proclamations to disarm all those who ever fought against the Stuarts, and

- A new militia act which authorized unwarranted search and seizure of arms in the possession of any person considered a threat to the state.

They created a firearm registry, where gunsmiths had to record the number of guns made and sold each week, with a list of their customers. The Parliament enacted a law that "for the first time prohibited the possession and use of a firearm for all persons unqualified to hunt."[43]

This last law forms the template for the modern day "sporting use" argument advanced by gun control organizations and governments: A gun must have a role in hunting or target shooting, or it should not be sold to civilians. Carrying this forward into the current era, once this door was opened in Parliament, the United Kingdom created a rationale for increasingly restrictive gun control laws and increasing police power to restrict and confiscate private firearms, resulting in the UK gun ban today. Even sporting uses are not protected anymore: The UK Olympic pistol shooting team must train outside the country, as their firearms are banned; now hunting is being curtailed as well.[44]

Learning his life's lessons well, Charles II consolidated his power by disarming those he considered a threat to his crown.

Disarming American Immigrants

In 1911 state senator Timothy Sullivan of New York promised that if New York City outlawed handgun carrying, homicides would decline drastically. The year the Sullivan law took effect, however, homicides increased and the New York Times pronounced criminals "as well armed as ever."[45]

In the first three years of the Sullivan Law, 70% of those arrested had Italian surnames. In *Gun Control and Economic Discrimination: The Melting-Point Case-In-Point*, Funk highlights the media's elitist, exclusionary attitudes that led to enactment of the law, noting the *New York Tribune* complaint in 1903 that police were finding pistols mostly in the pockets of "ignorant and quarrelsome immigrants of law-breaking propensities," and the *New York Times* writing about the affinity of "low-browed foreigners" for handguns.

The Sullivan Law was a pre-emptive, victimless crime law that turned law-abiding citizens into criminals with the stroke of a pen. Counter to our legal system's presumption of innocence, this law assumed anybody with a handgun was a criminal or intended to commit a crime. As the judges noted in the New York State Appeals Court in 1913:

There had been for many years upon the statute books a law against the carriage of concealed weapons. No court in this country, so far as I know, has ever declared such a law in violation of the Constitution or the Bill of Rights. It did not seem effective in preventing crimes of violence in this state. Of the same kind and character, but proceeding a step further with the regulatory legislation, the Legislature has now picked out one particular kind of arm, the handy, the usual, and the favorite weapon of the turbulent criminal class, and has said that in our organized communities, our cities, towns, and villages where the public peace is protected by the officers of organized government, the citizen may not have that particular kind of weapon without a permit, as it had already said that he might not carry it on his person without a permit. If he has it in his possession, he can readily stick it in his pocket when he goes abroad.[46]

Even though they admit the law against concealed carry "did not seem effective in preventing crimes of violence," the court supported the law's restrictions anyway, ignoring the fact that the very features which made a handgun the "favorite weapon of the turbulent criminal class" also made it the tool of choice for the law-abiding citizen seeking to protect their lives and livelihoods from this same criminal class. Instead, the court sought to reassure us (or them?) that the "public peace is protected by the officers of organized government." This is very curious, because United States higher court rulings have consistently concluded the police are under no legal obligation to provide protection to any particular citizen.[47] The most recent ruling was from the Supreme Court in 2005, proof that the courts are remaining consistent in supporting this legal position:

[June 27, 2005] WASHINGTON (AP) - The Supreme Court ruled Monday that police cannot be sued for how they enforce restraining orders, ending a lawsuit by a Colorado woman who claimed police did not do enough to prevent her estranged husband from killing her three young daughters.

Jessica Gonzales did not have a constitutional right to police enforcement of the court order against her husband, the court said in a 7-2 opinion.

Gonzales contended that police did not do enough to stop her estranged husband, who took the three daughters from the front yard of her home in June 1999 in violation of a restraining order.

Hours later Simon Gonzales died in a gun fight with officers outside a police station. The bodies of the three girls, ages 10, 9 and 7, were in his truck.[48]

The Supreme Court concluded:

- A temporary restraining order "imposed no duty on police" and

- "It does not follow that respondent had 'a legitimate claim of [police] entitlement.' "[49]

This seems like schizophrenic reasoning. On the one hand, the government wants to limit what you may do to protect yourself from violent criminals in public; on the other hand, it will not accept responsibility in picking up the slack between what you are allowed to do and what the criminal–who doesn't care about laws–is willing to do. How then do you propose to avail yourself of 24/7 protection, when the government won't guarantee protection and yet limits the options to do it yourself?

World War II Disarmament Examples

One way to control people is to register them in order to keep tabs on their movements. During World War II, America used such a "people registry" to control movements of Japanese living on the West Coast. After this registry was in effect, the gun portion of the control began.

On January 4, 1942, the United States War Department began implementing plans to exclude and relocate "enemy aliens" from strategically sensitive areas like the West Coast, under the command of General John L. DeWitt. Less than one month later, registration of "enemy aliens" began. By February 15, officials began moving "enemy aliens" out of restricted military zones. On February 24, all of Northern California was declared a "strategic area." Shortly after, the evacuation of "Axis aliens" began to ramp up, with internment camps beginning operation by March 31, 1942.[50]

General DeWitt issued a proclamation reported by the San Francisco News on March 24, 1942, that stated in part:

The proclamation also extended the ban on possession of firearms, war materials, short-wave radio receiving and transmitting sets and other contraband to Japanese-Americans. Enemy aliens already had been forbidden to have such articles.[51]

Once again, the same story plays out: A particular group of people becomes socially isolated, disarmed, and stripped of their rights. Found guilty without trial and unable to defend themselves, Japanese Americans became unwanted *things*, an unpleasant daily reminder of a faceless enemy on the other side of the ocean, and a target for racial fear and hatred. As the United States Department of Justice recently admitted:

As a result of the war with Japan, many people in the U.S. did not trust people of Japanese ancestry. Even Japanese-Americans who were born in this country were mistakenly thought to be loyal to Japan. There was no proof that they were disloyal to America...

Most [Japanese-American] people did not have time to store or sell their household goods at a fair price. Some people moved to other states, but the majority went to internment camps. They were only allowed to take few belongings with them, and many families lost virtually everything they owned except what they could carry.[52]

A disarmed population was easier to round up and deport to internment camps. Nor was this disarmed population able to protect their personal property, livelihoods, or estates. As noted by Polsby and Kates:

On May 15, 1942, a proclamation was issued on the orders of Lieutenant General J.L. DeWitt of the Northern California Sector of the Western Defense Command that required one hundred thousand American citizens of Japanese descent to report to depots for transfer to detention camps. As a result of doing so, they lost, along with their freedom, property with a value in the billions of dollars–all their businesses, virtually all their personal property of any importance, and much of their realty.[53]

Perhaps even more uncomfortable to the modern American conscience is the fact that during the same time period, another government, one that was just as much our sworn enemy as Japan, was practicing a similar strategy of marginalization, dehumanization, confiscation, and condemnation.

Hitler's attacks against Jews began soon after winning the Chancellorship of Germany, beginning with a one-day boycott of Jewish shops in 1933. In 1935, the Nuremberg Laws were passed, stripping Jews of German citizenship. On the nights of November 9 and 10, 1938, the Nazis manufactured a "spontaneous" uprising of Germans against the Jews, called "Kristallnacht." A day later, new regulations were published that forbade Jews to own firearms. One day after this, the top Nazi leadership met to decide what to do about the "Jewish question." In a twist of logic made enforceable because the Nazis wielded absolute power, they blamed the crime victims, declaring that Kristallnacht was the Jews' fault, and instead of the Jews filing for damages with their insurers, the Nazis fined the Jews one billion marks.[54,55] Hermann Goering, German national police chief, called the Jews "usurers" and declared them outside police protection.[56]

Dehumanized, disenfranchised, and disarmed, the Jewish people were set up for the beginning of the Holocaust: the sweeping away of an unarmed population. It may be true that even had the Jews been armed, they could not have successfully taken on the might of the Nazi War machine. However, the point here is that governments and autocratic leaders have a clear understanding of the importance of first disarming those whom they wish to control or eliminate.

Conclusion

American gun control began with the fear that armed Indians would exterminate small, vulnerable colonial settlements. It escalated with plantation owners fearing that armed Blacks would rebel against them. In the Twentieth Century, those in power continued to expand their policies of disarming those not directly loyal to them, considering all others a threat to their power base, regardless of race or economic status.

History consistently verifies the efficacy of gun control. One group believes in its superiority, either from its belief in eminent domain or perceived religious, philosophical, or political nobility of purpose. Mix in a little "fear of those who are different." Add disarmament, and one group gains the ability to control others. Numerous population groups in America, as well as those who fought on the other side during the restoration of England's royalty, experienced disarmament as part of being controlled, and the governments who did this knew exactly what they were doing and why. As George Santayana said: "Those who cannot remember history are condemned to repeat it." By the same token, those who study history sometimes intend to repeat it in order to acquire more power. The question is: Who is doing the disarming, and who will suffer for it next? Should we register and disarm Muslims because some have turned commercial airplanes into guided missiles? Would you like to live in a society where the freedom of many is restricted because of the actions of a few? Where people are presumed guilty because those in power fear them?

With gun control, guns don't evaporate: Those in power always keep their guns or have armed forces to protect their prerogatives. If you happen to end up being one of the "others" during some cycle of religious or political power, what will you do — what *can* you do — to protect your civil and political rights?

Stephen Halbrook eloquently sums up this government-sanctioned, elitist attitude towards gun ownership:

It is ironic that espousal of second amendment rights is dismissed as reactionary; on the contrary, it is arguable that those who would restrict access to firearms by those who are not members of the ruling class espouse the "reactionary" view.[57]

Examining the history of gun control reveals civilian disarmament as a time-honored policy for those seeking control of others. People in modern society like to talk about their "rights." Does gun control make us safer? Is it working? If these two premises are true, is the right to own a firearm now superfluous? Chapter 2 will begin to answer these questions.

Chapter 2
Modern Experiments in Gun Control

Gun control advocates promote the theory that limiting public access to guns will enhance public safety. In their paper *Australia: A Massive Buyback of Low-Risk Guns*, Reuter and Mouzos state:

> The hypothesized link between buybacks and violent crime is straightforward. By making the most lethal weapons (firearms) less available, the number of violent crimes will fall and the average lethality of those crimes will also decline.[1]

To stop violence is a noble goal supported by all persons of conscience. But can it be proven beyond a reasonable doubt that disarming the law-abiding public will increase public safety, save lives, and enhance or preserve our civil rights? And if not, is it worth risking possible negative consequences by implementing this concept as a national policy? Furthermore, if a government begins to make policy decisions based on a legal standard other than "beyond reasonable doubt," will such an ideological disconnect by such a powerful entity result in the erosion of other civil rights? And once initiated, could this process gradually shift the government's attitude towards citizens to that of being "guilty until proven innocent?"

On the other hand, can the "competing" hypothesis of placing firearms into the hands of law-abiding citizens accomplish the same goal of enhancing public safety, and is there any way to prove this?

It seems reasonable, when deciding which theory to support, that a person would perform their own analytical research to determine the veracity of each claim. A simple litmus test could be to examine actual crime statistics in countries similar to ours that have recently disarmed the public, and see if there have been any resulting changes in crime rates since they removed firearms from civilian ownership.

In the mid-1990s, two westernized countries, Britain and Australia, instituted national gun control laws, each following a mass murder where mentally ill men used firearms to commit the crimes. Both countries are English-speaking democracies with a bicameral legislature, similar enough to the United States for our litmus test. In addition, both are island countries, which theoretically should make it easier to control gun smuggling.

The UK instituted their ban in 1997, banning all handguns and severely limiting ownership of rifles and shotguns. As Joyce Lee Malcolm notes in her book *Guns and Violence: The English Experience*:

> The Firearms Act (No. 2) 1997, a measure unprecedented in a democratic country, initiated a newly complete ban on handguns. Owners of pistols were ordered to hand them in. The penalty for possession of an illegal handgun was ten years in prison.[2]

Australia enacted a slightly less rigorous ban in 1996. The Australian government reacted to the mass murder by effectively banning all semi-automatic firearms. You could apply for a license to own a gun, but Reuter and Mouzos note:

15

In order to own a firearm, an individual was required to show a legitimate purpose and fitness of character ("genuine reason and need for owning, possessing or using a firearm"), conform to stringent safe storage requirements, and undertake safety training if a new licensee.[3]

Thus, the government had the final say over whether you were appropriate for gun ownership or not. Semi-automatic rifles, shotguns and "handguns of .22 caliber or higher" were prohibited.[4]

If the gun control thesis is the correct one, then it should follow that by removing a factor that incites or enhances criminal behavior — in this case handguns and semiautomatic weapons — violent crime rates (murder, rape, robbery, and assault) should drop.

The International Crime Victimization Surveys

To avoid any possible hyperbole surrounding both sides of the gun control issue, one needs to locate consistently similar statistics from multiple sources in order to ensure the reliability of their findings. Since the consequences of drawing the wrong conclusion regarding self-defense versus government-only crime protection is a matter of life and death, it is important to consider only fact-based knowledge and avoid emotional rhetoric that feels good.

To align the facts, establish a pre-ban baseline and compare it to similar research post-ban to determine crime trends. Two respected references, the *International Crime Victimization Surveys* of 1992 and 2000, compare violent crime rates between Australia, the United Kingdom, and the United States. In the 1992 version, van Dijk and Mayhew of the Netherlands Ministry of Justice referenced interviews of over 55,000 people living in 20 different countries.[5] The 2000 version, by del Frate and van Kesteren of the United Nations Office on Drugs and Crime, included national samples from nine countries of over 2,000 persons per country, approximately the same average sample size per country as the 1992 version.[6]

The 1992 survey showed there was more violent crime in the United States than the United Kingdom in all categories:

- The U.S. had double the rate of assault and robbery, and

- five times England's rate of "sexual assault," which includes rape, attempted rape, and indecent assault.[7]

In the same 1992 survey, Australia's overall violent crime rate was higher than the U.S. in two of three categories:

- sexual assault and assault were about 25% higher in Australia, but

- robbery rates were about 50% higher in the U.S.[8]

In the 2000 survey, over three years after the British and Australian gun bans, researchers combined the three violent crimes of robbery, sexual assault, and assault into one category entitled "Selected Contact Crime." Comparing the trends between the two surveys shows that between 1992 and 2000, violent crime rates in the United Kingdom increased 56% to become nearly twice the rate of the United States, which saw a drop in violent crime during the same time period.[9]

Australia saw a 30% drop in violent crime, but remained more violent than the UK and the U.S. The United States, with its continued availability of civilian firearms, had about a 67% drop in violent crime. In spite of its limited availability of civilian firearms, Australia's overall violent crime rate went from just 7% higher than the U.S. in 1992 to over twice the U.S. rate by the year 2000.[10]

While Australia's survey shows lower levels of victimization over time, possibly indicating a benefit from partial civilian disarmament, this is more than cancelled by the United Kingdom's greater increase. According to crime trends derived from data in the International Crime Victimization Surveys, there is no proof that civilian disarmament reduces violent crime.

Crime Trends Based Upon Police Statistics

Surveys have potential shortcomings. Respondents may not remember an incident, or may be unwilling to discuss a victimization experience with strangers, especially if the event was emotionally traumatic, such as a rape. There may also be what is called sampling error: The subset of the selected population in the survey may not reflect the experience of the total population. For instance, if too large a percentage of respondents live in areas where crime rates are higher than the national average, it may make the national crime rate appear higher.

Actual police statistics, recording all crimes reported to police, is another method of measuring relative crime rates and trends. Of course, they also carry a potential downside, in that not all victims report the crimes committed against them. Victims don't always trust that the police can or will do anything. So the police may never know about a crime.

These concepts are supported by research. In *Australian Crime: Facts and Figures 2003*, the Australian Institute of Criminology notes:

> It is well known that not all crime is reported to the police, and rates of reporting vary depending on the type of offence. In addition, not all crimes that are reported to the police are recorded by them in official statistics.[11]

Australian Crime: Facts and Figures 2003 shows a general correlation between how personal the incident was and police reporting rates. This means that motor vehicle theft, a less-intimate property crime, had reporting rates nearing 100%. Robbery, more personal, was reported about 50% of the time, and assault, even more personal and traumatic, about 31%. Sexual assault of women dropped from about 30% in 1998 to 20% of all incidents reported to police in 2002, the lowest rate of any reported crimes.[12] (This reporting rate was confirmed in the 2005 edition.[13]) Regarding the low reporting rates for the most personal crimes, the report says:

> The main reasons given by victims of assault for not reporting to police were that the matter was too trivial, it was a personal matter the victim would take care of themselves, the police would be unable or unwilling to do anything to help, and fear of reprisal from the offender.[14]

Therefore, women who were raped were victimized the most intimately and traumatically, and were the most convinced that there was nothing the police could do, or they were afraid that having been brutally assaulted once it could easily happen again if they tried to prosecute the offender. This would make sense, as 66% of female sexual assaults were perpetrated by persons known to the victim, thus making it easier for the perpetrator to locate the victim for purposes of revenge.[15]

The British Home Office report, *Crime in England and Wales 2002/2003*, corroborates this tendency for victims to report more personally traumatic crimes less often. Vehicle theft was reported 97% of the time, the non-confrontational crime of burglary 87%, the more personal contact crime of robbery 53%, and the more traumatic crime of common assault was reported 34%.[16]

Mirroring Australians' reason for not reporting incidents to police, the Home Office report states:

> For most crimes the main reason for not reporting was that the incident was too trivial, there was no loss or the victim believed the police could not do much about it (69% for all comparable crime), followed by the incident being considered a private matter and dealt with by the victim (28% of comparable crime).[17]

The most recent U.S. Department of Justice survey reports similar trends in how victims report crimes, noting that motor vehicle theft was reported to police 84.8% of the time, aggravated assault 64.2%, simple assault 44.9%, and rape/sexual assault 35.8%.[18]

These relative levels of incident reporting correspond closely with the U.S. Federal Bureau of Investigation's hierarchy rules of reporting crime, with rape rated second highest, after homicide, and motor vehicle theft lowest.[19] This means that the more personal and traumatic the crime, the higher it rates in the FBI hierarchy.

The point here is to show the consistency of behavior in all three countries: Respondents reported non-intimate property crimes more often than violent attacks, and the more personal the crime the less often it was reported. This similarity makes comparisons of police statistics between these countries more reliable when determining whether or not civilian disarmament limits violent crime among the general population.

Drawing from most recent sources of final data available, as well as earlier sources, garners enough data to determine trends in crime rates (per 100,000 population) over a ten-year period, starting from before the Australian and British gun bans and comparing these trends with the United States.

Starting in 1995 (pre-ban) and ending in 2006, homicide trends in the three countries show:

- Australia has seen a 21.8% decrease.
- The UK has seen an 1.7% decrease.
- The U.S. has seen a 30.6% decrease.

During this time period, robbery trends show:

- Australia's rate is up 3.6%.
- The UK's rate is up 38.1%.
- United States' rate is down 32.4%.

Not to be an exception, trends in the crime of assault show:

- Australia's rate is up 46.7%.
- The UK's rate is up 19.4%.
- The U.S. rate is down 31.3%.[20]

In fairness, we should note that compared to the United States, Australia and the United Kingdom have had traditionally low homicide rates. Since a difference of even 10 murders can have a large effect upon either country's homicide rate, it can easily vary significantly from year to year. While there may be cultural factors that make murder less likely "over there," this does not seem to be the case for other violent crimes. On the other hand, the U.S. not only has seen a significant drop in its homicide rate, there has been a large numerical reduction (4,572) in murders between the years of 1995 (21,606) and 2006 (17,034).[21] Finally, Australia and the United Kingdom used to be generally less violent across the board than the United States, but in recent years, they have overtaken the U.S. in the categories of sexual assault and assault, and the UK now has a higher rate of robbery.

Gun Control's Impact on Women

Peace Movement Aotearoa is an example of an organization that believes gun confiscation has a positive impact upon crime. They call themselves a "national networking organization…interested in peace and social justice."[22] An article posted on their site is entitled *Sharp Drop in Gun Crime Follows Tough Australian Firearm Laws*.[23] Indeed, there is evidence that the number of homicides and robberies involving a firearm has dropped since the Australian gun ban went into effect.[24] But has violence against women increased or decreased since the gun ban? Gun control organizations allege that guns are a catalyst in violence towards women:

Two campaigns - Control Arms and Stop Violence Against Women: "Those two campaigns have now come together to bring the strength of both communities, the disarmament community, and the women's rights communities together in order to stop armed violence against women, recognizing that the disarmament conversation, too often does not involve women, and that the women's rights movement has too often not realized the importance of taking away the weapons."[25] – Rebecca Peters, director of International Action Network on Small Arms (IANSA)

Therefore, gun control should diminish the incidence of rape/sexual assault.

Conversely, one of the beliefs of gun-rights proponents is that women, who are smaller and therefore less capable of physically fending off a sexual predator, stand to gain a significant benefit from being armed for their own self-defense. Which theory more effectively nurtures women's right to live in a society which respects them?

One report, *Australia: Crime Fact and Figures 2002* states: "In 2000-2001, 99% of all sexual assault offenders were male,"[26] while the 2003 version of the same report says: "Females consistently recorded higher rates of sexual assault than males irrespective of age."[27] So there is a documented link between male predators and female victims.

Australia and the United Kingdom have both seen an increase in sexual assault (their category that includes rape) since enactment of their gun ban. More telling is the comparison of rates of recorded sexual crimes between Australia, the U.K. and the U.S. from 1995 and 2006:

- The United Kingdom: increased 76.5%
- Australia: increased 21.4%
- United States: decreased 16.8%.[28]

Compared to the United States, where there has been no nationally-instituted civilian gun ban:

- British women are now raped and sexually assaulted over twice as often. (Before the ban, Britain's rate was comparable to the United States.)
- Australian women are now raped and sexually assaulted nearly three times as often. (Before the ban, women were raped about twice as often as in the U.S.)

Perhaps there is no way to positively conclude that banning civilian firearms led directly to this increasing violence against women in Australia and the United Kingdom. But considering the diverging trends between those two countries and the United States, these findings support the idea that women are indeed being disadvantaged in self-defense. These statistics fail to prove that civilian disarmament has improved personal safety for women. The reality is:

- There is no statistic that proves removing guns alters the behavior of aberrants who prey upon women, and

- In two countries where firearms are banned for self-defense, women are now at greater risk of violent attacks than they were before.

Peace Movement Aotearoa's article about a "sharp drop in gun crime" merely reprises the misleading concept of gun ban organizations that gun control works if the amount of gun-involved crime diminishes, regardless of the fact that overall violent crime increases. Such a claim is irrelevant: If guns didn't exist, there would be no "gun crime," but there would still be crime. The only relevant question is: Would levels of violent crime increase or decrease? Even the head of Australia's Bureau of Crime Statistics and Research, Don Weatherburn, has acknowledged the gun ban had no significant impact even on the amount of gun crime, thoroughly discrediting Peace Movement's grandstanding headline:

There has been a drop in firearm-related crime, particularly in homicide, but it began long before the new laws and has continued on afterwards. I don't think anyone really understands why. A lot of people assume that the tougher laws did it, but I would need more specific, convincing evidence …

There has been a more specific … problem with handguns, which rose up quite rapidly and then declined. The decline appears to have more to do with the arrest of those responsible than the new laws. As soon as the heroin shortage hit, the armed robbery rate came down. I don't think it was anything to do with the tougher firearm laws.[29]

Weatherburn also acknowledges that the best crime measure consists of "the arrest of those responsible" rather than gun control laws.

Of greatest concern is the delusion of those whose ideologically-driven agenda justifies the risk of putting women in danger as long as their narrowly-defined outcome is attained. Considering that overall violent crime levels are rising since the gun ban, their vision of "peace and social justice" through gun control is illusionary.

With the exception of Australia's murder rate, violent crime in Australia and the United Kingdom is increasing, while violent crime in the United States has decreased across the board since 1995. At best, availability of guns has nothing to do with these trends; at worst, unavailability of guns has everything to do with increasing levels of violence. Australia's top crime statistician, Weatherburn, concluded: "I would need to see more convincing evidence than there is to be able to say that gun laws have had any effect."[30]

NEW YORK (AP) — Margaret Johnson might have looked like an easy target.

But when a mugger tried to grab a chain off her neck Friday, the wheelchair-bound 56-year-old pulled out her licensed .357 pistol and shot him, police said.

Johnson said she was in Harlem on her way to a shooting range when the man, identified by police as 45-year-old Deron Johnson, came up from behind and went for the chain.

"There's not much to it," she said in a brief interview. "Somebody tried to mug me, and I shot him."

Deron Johnson was taken to Harlem Hospital with a single bullet wound in the elbow, police said. He faces a robbery charge, said Lt. John Grimpel, a police spokesman.

Margaret Johnson, who lives in Harlem, has a permit for the weapon and does not face charges, Grimpel said. She also was taken to the hospital with minor injuries and later released.[31]

Australian Redux

The Sydney Morning Herald exposed another flaw in Australia's gun buyback program:

A NETWORK of firearms dealers has rorted [an Australian word for a fraudulent practice] the $600 million national guns buyback scheme, and weapons supposedly destroyed years ago have resurfaced in criminal hands in [New South Wales].

"Thousands" of the 650,000 civilian firearms confiscated under the buyback program were sold on the black market instead of being destroyed:

But thousands of the guns were never destroyed. The man largely responsible for the rort is Frank Curr, a licensed firearms dealer and pawn shop owner from Wacol in Queensland.

Curr paraded as a civic-minded dealer concerned about drugs and violence in his neighbourhood while secretly arming criminals across the border with an estimated 2000 guns he had been paid to destroy or render inoperable. Only 50 of the weapons have been recovered.[32]

Reuter and Mouzos noted at the beginning of this chapter: "the hypothesized link between buybacks and violent crime is straightforward." Agreed: The buyback led, in a straightforward manner, to a ready supply of guns for criminal use.

The British Crime Survey and 'Funny Business'

There are pronounced inconsistencies in British Home Office crime reporting, which are vitally important to address in order to understand why there are two sets of conflicting data about the United Kingdom's crime trends. These are important because in the United Kingdom, "government reports" show the crime rate has been dropping since the gun ban went into effect.

Home Office crime reports consist of two distinct sections. The first section relies on the new British Crime Survey, a government-run program that selects a group of respondents and asks them questions about crime victimization. Simmons and Dodd state: "Crime measured by the BCS has fallen in every survey since the peak in 1995"[33] and "BCS violence has fallen by 19 per cent since 1999 and by 24 per cent since 1997…"[34]

Yet the authors also throw in a confusing comment that reverses their previous statements about falling crime:

> Of those crimes recorded by the police in 2002/03, 23.5 per cent were detected. The number of detections in 2002/2003 was eight per cent higher than in 2001/2002, though the detection rate was similar…[35]

This means police reporting was no more efficient than the previous year and the police recorded more crime during the current year, but crime is falling anyway. In effect, the report claims that crime is decreasing even though the police data indicates it is increasing. The way they get around this apparent contradiction is by combining all crime. Property crime constituted 79.6% of all reported crime for 2003.[36] This is a non-confrontational activity where the ability of the victim to actively resist is irrelevant. So if property crime drops a little, it can make the overall crime rate drop even if violent crime goes up, because property crimes are committed four times as often.

As for the Crime Survey's claim that "violence" has fallen since 1997, this is based upon two factors which place this claim in doubt.

Factor One: Slicing and Dicing Their Definitions

First, the Survey results show an overall drop in the number of respondents who reported being violently victimized.[37] But this is a curious outcome when compared to their explanation as to why the new recording standards have "inflated" crime numbers reported by police. The new National Crime Recording Standard was developed to "promote greater consistency between police forces," and to take a more "victim-oriented approach to recording crime," a process of "recording based more on the victim's perception of a crime occurring rather than the police satisfying themselves that a crime had indeed taken place."[38] This last comment defines the recording criterion the Survey itself uses, as the interviewers are taking the respondent's word that a crime has occurred, and not "satisfying themselves that a crime had indeed taken place." So now the authors are saying: "Even though the Survey and the police use the same 'victim-oriented' standard when recording a crime, the police results are wrong and ours are right." The authors then attempt to dodge around this additional inconsistency by claiming that violent crime recorded by police was impacted heavily by the new National Crime Recording Standard, inflating the number of violent crimes reported to police in 2003 by 23%.[39]

For discussion's sake, we will take the Home Office at their word: The police inflated their statistics because of a previous inability to accurately and consistently identify what was a crime. Recalculating the numbers using police crime statistics with the authors' 23% inflation claim, we find that for the period 1995-2003:

- Murder increased 36.3%. (This statistic remains unaffected. Police can't mistake a dead body, and this statistic is not effected by how the victim might "perceive" this crime being committed. Nor can you interview the victim in a survey to determine if he or she is telling the truth.)

- Rape increased 24.2%.

- Robbery increased 18.9%.

- Assault increased 16.7%.[40]

Given their best-case scenario, despite the Home Office's claim about the impact of the new crime reporting standards, the United Kingdom remains a more violent place than it was before the gun ban: It remains more violent than the United States in the categories of rape, robbery, and assault, and it is gradually but inexorably catching up in the murder rate as well.

But why does the same recording standard result in two wildly different outcomes? If the respondent tells the Survey interviewer "I was assaulted" it is recorded as an assault. If a person walks into the police station and says "I was assaulted" it is recorded by the police as an assault. Yet the survey claims violent crime is dropping, while police statistics show a dramatically opposite trend. Couple this with the fact that yet another victimization survey, the International Crime Victimization Survey discussed earlier in this chapter, also shows a significant increase in violent crime in the UK, and the British Crime Survey, with all its verbal dodges and weaves, becomes highly suspect.

They also fudge their definition of who qualifies to be interviewed for the Survey, which introduces sampling bias. The Survey does not include offenses against businesses, persons who are institutionalized, or victims under age 16.[41] For example, 10% of 2003 robberies occurred on business property.[42] Twenty percent of the United Kingdom population is under age 16.[43] As of November, 2003, there were 74,547 people in custody, 74,057 of whom were in prison, accounting for about 0.1% of the population.[44] None of this is considered valid information when the surveyors look about the kingdom to determine how much the people are suffering. The British Crime Survey results do not reflect the entire population's experiences with crime victimization.

Factor Two: British Bobbies, Pencils and Paper

The second issue deals with the crime detection rate, or the percentage of all crime that is recorded by the police. For example, if the police record 100 robberies in a year, and the detection rate is 75%, then the actual number of robberies for that year is 133. If the detection rate drops to 50% for a reported 100 robberies, then the actual number of robberies is 200.

The British Crime Survey states that detection rates for violence against the person and sexual offenses dropped from a high of 75% in 1997 for both, to 60% and 50% by 2003, respectively.[45] This means that while the total number of violent crimes recorded by police has been rising since 1997, the UK is even more violent than recorded crime rates make it appear.

The authors of British Crime Survey keep digging themselves in deeper, claiming that crime is dropping, yet every additional commentary they add indicates otherwise. This is reinforced by recent reports from the British Broadcasting Corporation. The first article, from July 2004, states: "Police in England and Wales recorded a 12% jump in violent crime over the past year..." Shadow Home Secretary David Davis said: "We're facing over a million violent crimes a year for the first time in history."[46] An article from July 2005 mirrored these findings: Violent crime increased another 7% from 2004, and gun crime increased 6%, despite the now-nine-year-old ban on guns.[47] This trend does not appear to be slowing. A *London Times* article from January 2006 notes:

MUGGINGS and violent attacks on people soared by more than 10 per cent in the third quarter of last year as the police struggled to contain street crime, according to figures published yesterday.

Street robbery is rising at its fastest since Tony Blair demanded action three years ago by the Home Office and police to tackle the issue.

The increase in violent crime came as rising numbers of people expressed concern at the extent of antisocial behaviour, including public drunkenness and drug dealing in their neighbourhoods. Homicides of people under 16 rose by a quarter in the year to the end of September 2005.[48]

The article noted that "Overall crime recorded by the 43 police forces in England and Wales fell by 1 per cent..." However, one must remember the property crime influence, because the same article also notes that violent crime in these jurisdictions rose 4% in just the third quarter of 2005, while robbery increased 11% during that period. Remembering that it is illegal for a civilian to own firearms, it is notable that "gun crime" rose 1% during the year's reporting period ending September 2005, and "serious injuries from gun crime rose by 18 per cent..." Meanwhile, property offenses of burglary and "car crime" continued a long-term decline. (This is an interesting counter-trend in property crime which gets examined later in this chapter.) Finally, criminals released early from jail are increasingly likely to return to a life of crime:

In a separate report published today, it was disclosed that record numbers of prisoners released early are being sent back to jail after returning to a life of crime or breaking the terms of their supervision. The figures, in a report by Anne Owers, the Chief Inspector of Prisons, show a 250 per cent increase in the number of prisoners recalled to jail in the past five years.[49]

Another *Times* article notes the increasing use of firearms among youth:

BOYS as young as 12 are carrying firearms in areas of South London where arguments that begin in the playground are ending in shoot-outs.

Senior police officers are increasingly concerned about the young age of children walking the streets with guns tucked in their trouser waistbands. Scotland Yard has directed its latest anti-gun advertising campaign at the 11-16 age group.

The pattern of youthful gunmen is being repeated across Britain with police forces reporting the growing involvement of children in shootings. The weapons are displayed as a show of street credibility and bravado, or are obtained by children on the periphery of drug gangs because they feel that they need protection.[50]

There is even dissension among government organizations regarding the veracity of the British Crime Survey. The *BBC* notes that members of the Office for National Statistics as well as the Home Secretary are "concerned":

The Statistics Commission said last year that the Home Office should be stripped of the task of compiling and processing the crime figures.

An independent panel of opposition party nominees and other experts will suggest new methods of calculating the data which is "transparent, understood and trusted", the Home Office said.

"I have been concerned for some time that Home Office crime statistics have been questioned and challenged," Home Secretary Charles Clarke said.

"Most people seem confused about what is happening to crime in this country."[51]

Losing Trust in the Criminal Justice System

Another challenge to the Home Office's claim that crime is dropping has to do with how the BCS report contradicts respondents' perception of crime. Seventy-three percent of respondents believed that crime had risen in the two years prior to their interviews. Also, there has been a drop in respondents' confidence in the British criminal justice system. Only 30% believe the system meets crime victims' needs, 31% believe it is effective in reducing crime, and 39% believe criminals are effectively brought to justice.[52] All of these percentages are down from the previous survey. Conversely, the only question getting a more favorable response was the belief that the system respects the rights of the accused and treats them fairly; 77% believe this, up 1% from the prior survey.[53] When law-abiding people have failing confidence in the justice system's ability to effectively deal with crime, how can one believe that same system is honest when they claim to be reducing crime? When criminals know their chance of being arrested, tried, and sentenced is decreasing, they become more confident in their pursuits, and crime rates will rise.

To summarize:

- The British government's crime survey claims that crime is dropping, even though police statistics show otherwise.

- The Home Office obfuscates the country's growing violent crime problem by hiding it inside the overall crime numbers, of which violent crime is about 20% of the total.

- The British Crime Survey attempts to explain the contradiction between the Survey's and police reports by claiming that the police statistics are "inflated" due to new reporting standards, yet when we factor in this inflation factor, violent crime rates remain higher post-gun ban.

- The Survey excludes significant parts of the population, producing results that do not reflect crime rates among the entire population. (Sampling error)

- Police detection rates are falling even as reported incidents are rising, indicating a hidden explosion in violent crime that is not officially acknowledged because that very lack of detection conceals it.

- People's confidence in the criminal justice system is falling, the government will not allow people to defend themselves, and criminals are emboldened because the system is becoming more lenient towards them.

Is it any wonder the United Kingdom has become more violent?

Ashgar Jilow used to sell stab-proof vests to nightclub bouncers and security guards at his London military surplus store. Now his clients are kids as young as 10 who fear they're going to be knifed at school or on the street.

"Some of them are so tiny the vests don't even fit under their school uniforms," said Jilow, 55, who sells about three of the 120-pound ($230) vests a week. "Parents don't know what to do to keep their kids safe."

Every week in London 52 teenagers are victims of knife crime, according to the Metropolitan Police. A child is stabbed to death in Britain every two weeks and knife killings outnumber gun homicides three to one, said Norman Brennan, a police officer and director of the Victims of Crime Trust.

"Knife crime is out of control and kids carry them like fashion accessories," Brennan said. The youngest child to be suspended from school for brandishing a blade was just five...

Statistics indicate that more children are reaching for blades as gang culture spreads. Some 42 percent of boys aged between 11 and 16 in state-funded schools admit to having carried a knife, according to the Youth Justice Board, which oversees punishment of child offenders.[54]

More recently, the *London Times* declared that firearms are readily available on the streets and that "a growing number of teenagers in big cities are becoming involved in gun crime."[55]

The age of victims and suspects has fallen over the past three years as the availability of firearms in some cities has risen. Liverpool and Manchester are the cities where illegal guns are most readily available, with criminals claiming that some weapons are being smuggled from Ireland. Sawn-off shotguns are now being sold for as little as £50, and handguns for £150.[56]

(Note: As of this writing £50 equaled about $102 and £150 equaled $307.)[57]

The *Times* went on to note that despite the 1997 ban on handguns, their use in crime had almost doubled by 2006. This reflects a general trend:

Official figures show that although Britain has some of the toughest anti-gun laws in the world, firearm use in crime has risen steadily...

"Illegal firearms have become increasingly accessible to younger offenders who appear more likely to use these firearms recklessly," a report on gun crime commissioned by the Home Office cautioned last year.[58]

Moreover, official data shows that both victims and offenders are getting younger:

Figures from the Metropolitan Police show that the average age of gun crime victims in London fell from 24 to 19 between 2004-06 and that there was a similar trend among suspects charged in connection with shootings.[59]

A recent *Time* article does not paint a rosy picture for England's youth:

[I]n 2003, according to the Institute for Public Policy Research (IPPR), 27% of British 15-year-olds had been drunk 20 times or more, compared to 12% of young Germans, 6% of Netherlands youth and only 3% of young French. British kids were also involved more frequently in fights (44% in the U.K. to 28% in Germany). They are more likely to try drugs or start smoking young. English girls are the most sexually active in Europe. More of them are having sex aged 15 or younger, and more than 15% fail to use contraception when they do — which means that Britain has high rates of both teen pregnancy and sexually transmitted diseases. Small wonder, then, that a 2007 UNICEF study of child wellbeing in 21 industrialized countries placed Britain firmly at the bottom of the table.

Drunkenness and promiscuity are not all that afflict British children. The article notes: "Violent offenses by British under-18s rose 37% in the three years to 2006."[60]

The Substitution Effect as an Indicator of Effective Self-Defense

In his book *The Bias Against Guns,* John Lott discusses the substitution effect. When criminals believe more citizens are armed, they switch from crimes where they come into direct contact with their victims to crimes where there is no contact. So instead of robbery, where they confront the intended victim, they wait until people leave home and commit burglary. As Lott describes it:

> If you make something more difficult, people will be less likely to engage in it. This well-known principle applies to products: When the price of apples rises relative to oranges, people buy fewer apples and more oranges.

> [I]t may appear cold to compare apples to human victims. But just as grocery shoppers switch between different types of produce depending on costs, criminals switch between different kinds of prey depending on the cost of attacking. Economists call this, appropriately enough, "the substitution effect."[61]

This substitution effect appears to be occurring in the UK, where the property crime rate decreased 5.9% between 1998 and 2005, while violent crime rose 89.8%.[62] As victims present less potential threat due to the loss of self-defense capabilities, criminals need not spend the extra effort necessary to plan burglaries in order to avoid confrontations, corroborating the *Times* report above which noted an increase in robbery (confrontational) while burglary (non-confrontational) was falling.

Australia has witnessed a more pronounced substitution effect: The property crime rate decreased 29.1% during the period of 1995 through 2005, while the violent crime rate increased 37.4%.[63] Such similar but opposite trends make it almost appear that criminals who used to perpetrate property crime have switched to violent crime.

In the United States, both property crime and violent crime rates have trended downwards during the same time frame, with violent crime leading the way, decreasing 31.5% while property crime dropped 25.3%.[64] United States crime trends also seem to confirm Lott's principle. Since American citizens are more likely to be armed, non-confrontational property crime would be a safer career choice for criminals: therefore, it dropped more slowly.

After U.S. crime rates peaked in 1991-1992, over 50 million more firearms were sold through 1999.[65] The U.S. population grew about 21 million in the 1990s, which means that firearm purchases occurred at over double the population growth rate. Yet both violent crime and property crime rates steadily dropped during this period. Meanwhile, Australia and the United Kingdom severely curtailed ownership of firearms and are now experiencing violent crime rates far greater than the U.S., and far greater than they did before the gun bans. In those countries, law-abiding citizens are also more at risk of losing their property, usually through force or the threat of physical violence.

There may be another type of substitution effect occurring here. As the capability for law-abiding self-defense diminishes, more people may be embracing a career in crime. It offers quicker, low-risk financial gain and greater return than toiling at a job. The criminals can choose their own work environment and hours. They get a choice of benefits from a broad array of personal and material categories. And they don't have to obey onerous gun laws, placing them in a distinctly advantageous negotiating position in their "business" dealings.

Does Gun Control Lead to Further Erosion of Civil Rights?

Gun rights supporters claim that gun control contains a "slippery slope" that gradually but inexorably results in erosion of civil rights. They point to historical examples of totalitarian dictatorships where civilian disarmament preceded government-sponsored genocide against the people living in those countries.

In early 2005, the British government enacted The Criminal Justice Act of 2003, which allows a previously acquitted person to be retried if "new and compelling" evidence is produced. Citing the unresolved sexual assault/murder of a young woman in 1989, the government claimed the new law will enable them to retry the accused "if evidence such as DNA material, new witnesses or a confession came to light." A Home Office spokesperson said, "It is important the public should have full confidence in the ability of the criminal justice system to deliver justice."[66]

The Act also allows hearsay evidence, including situations where the witness is unavailable to appear in court or has fears about appearing.[67] Thus, the accuser is no longer required to face the accused, and the defense attorney has limited ability to cross-examine and perhaps create reasonable doubt as to the veracity of the witness's testimony.

The Act was the government's response to claims that the Blair government failed in its campaign promise to crack down on crime. In an article from 2002, the government claimed that part of the problem was an out-of-date criminal justice system:

> Mr. Blair promised the first major overhaul of the British criminal justice system in more than a century in an attempt to balance the rights of defendants with more rights for victims.[68]

The Blair government also cited delays and inefficiencies in the judiciary and greedy trial lawyers as contributing factors in a breakdown of the criminal justice system.[69] It would seem that the government tacitly admits there are systemic shortcomings that limit it's ability to administer justice, but the cure may be worse than the symptom: Removing double jeopardy eradicates the very motivation necessary for an inefficient system to reform itself, instead placing the emotional and financial onus upon individuals who are hauled into court a second time because of poor investigative work or prosecutorial incompetence.

It is curious that the government expresses a need to dismantle an 800-year-old legal precedent to fix a supposed problem within the criminal justice system, when at the same time their British Crime Survey claims that crime is dropping. This indicates another inconsistency with the Home Office in reconciling police records against the British Crime Survey: Why would the government need to retract such an important foundation stone of modern legal doctrine, if their present policy of civilian disarmament and their present approach to criminal justice is effectively reducing crime?

As a result of what is happening in Britain, the government of New South Wales in Australia is also considering double jeopardy reform, which would:

[G]rant the prosecution a new power to apply for an acquittal to be quashed and a retrial ordered where fresh evidence emerges in a case of murder, manslaughter or a crime punishable by life imprisonment, and other conditions are met. The prosecution would also be able to appeal against directed verdicts of acquittal and have greater scope to appeal certain judicial rulings during a trial.[70]

The Council for Civil Liberties at University of New South Wales went on record against such reform. They cite national and international laws such as the United Nations International Covenant on Civil and Political Rights, Article 14(7) which states:

No one shall be liable to be tried or punished again for an offence for which he has already been finally convicted or acquitted in accordance with the law and penal procedure of each country.[71]

In 2004, the Australian Attorney General's Department convened a committee to discuss submissions they received regarding a national proposal to rescind double jeopardy protections. The committee heard "some very articulate and committed opposition to the general principle of meddling with the double jeopardy principle at all," but "was unpersuaded by it." In other words, their minds were made up before they convened their hearing. The committee was apparently more concerned about the government, rather than the defendant, getting a "fair trial." The wording of their working document said, "An order for the retrial of a person is not in the interests of justice if the Court of Criminal Appeal is satisfied that a fair trial is unlikely..."[72]

Does a "fair trial" mean "finding him guilty" the next time? Since the government holds all the cards in this matter, changing law to suit their whims, "fair trial" ends up meaning anything they desire. For example, the committee decided that allowing only two days to file an application for appeal was insufficient time. Therefore, they proposed a modification from their original draft:

"Recommendation 6: The time for lodging an application should be increased from 2 to 10 business days with power to apply to extend."[73] Since they get to write all the rules, and are "unpersuaded" by arguments that don't fit their agenda, why not extend the window of appeal to 30 days, or three months, or even three years?

The concern here is the trend away from personal liberty towards greater government dominance in determining guilt or innocence. Volokh and Newman explained the concept of this "slippery slope" as it affects the evolution of the legal system:

> Many people think of slippery slopes as most applicable to judicial decisions, where judges are supposed to follow precedent and one decision is legally supposed to lead to others... Voters and legislators aren't legally obligated to take for granted the policy judgment embedded in past legislative and judicial decisions. Still, they often do, because they find it rational to rely on past judgments in order to save the time and effort needed to think through the matter on their own. And so long as this happens—so long as our support of one political or legal decision today can change people's attitudes and thus lead them to enact another decision later—we have to take this sort of mechanism into account when deciding on an initial proposal.[74]

Don Kates presents the issue from the perspective of a flawed governmental approach to fighting crime:

> Governments impose gun control, as England banned handguns, because they are at their wit's end to deal with skyrocketing crime. But gun control does not work: it does not solve the increasing crime problem. So the government has to add more and more curtailments of other civil rights. Thus gun control goes hand in hand with infringement of other rights even though it may not be the direct cause.[75]

There seems to be a presumption of guilt behind this evolving legal revisionism: Dissatisfied with an acquittal, the government wants to haul the alleged offender back into court until it is satisfied that it got what it wanted, since the acquittal was not acceptable. "We lost; that wasn't fair." This reflects the government's presumption that the accused is guilty and must prove his innocence. Also, there is an indication of the government's bias against its citizens: The government does not trust the law-abiding citizen with the responsibility of firearms; now it appears the government does not trust law-abiding citizens to handle the responsibility of a jury in order to come up with a "fair" verdict.

The following two stories contrast the differences in perspective between similar burglary incidents, one happening in Britain and one in the United States. They highlight the disparity between legal perspectives and the resulting loss of civil rights in the UK:

> [Britain] A farmer who opened fire on two burglars who broke into his remote farmhouse has been found guilty of murder.

Tony Martin, 55, was sentenced to life at Norwich Crown Court for murdering 16-year-old Fred Barras by a majority verdict of 10 to two.

Chief Inspector Martin Wright, who led the investigation, said he took no satisfaction from the outcome of the case.

"It has been a tragedy from start to finish," he said.

"Burglary is without doubt one of the most despicable crimes there is but I would stress to everybody it is up to the police to resolve it and this very tragic case when there has been no winners shows that is the case."[76]

Martin killed Barras, a market trader from a Gypsy traveling family based in Newark, Nottinghamshire, last August during a late-night incident at his farm. The teenager, who had a number of convictions, was on his "first big job" to burgle Martin's home, Bleak House.

Norwich crown court heard that Martin...had been repeatedly burgled and that he had laid booby traps and lookout posts for anyone who came onto his property.

Peter Tidey, the chief crown prosecutor for Norfolk, said: "Actions such as that taken by Tony Martin cannot be tolerated in a civilised society. When people break the law it is for the law to punish them, not for individuals to take the law into their own hands, whether acting out of revenge or their own individual system of justice."[77]

[United States] A 79-year-old man armed with a .357 magnum revolver shot two men after they broke into his home overnight...

Police answering a call about a break-in and burglary found two men shot outside a home...in Grant County.

The homeowner told police the two men kicked in his back door just before 5 a.m. Saturday. They tried to flee after being shot.

"It bothers me because we have children. It bothers me that anybody would intrude into your home," [a neighbor] said.

[Another neighbor] had a message for anybody thinking about breaking into somebody's home.

"Yeah, don't pick the wrong door."[78]

Infringing upon the legal tradition of double jeopardy means that additional power is designated to the government by the government, creating its own body of legal precedent beginning with the diminished protection of double jeopardy in order to "bring justice" to past victims, and ending with altering legal doctrine to create a presumption of guilt in all cases. This supports the "slippery slope" theory that once disarmed, the government proceeds to find reasons to rescind additional civil rights, always justifying it in a reasonable way. The final outcome is not just loss of civil rights, but loss of liberty, a reality that is in stark opposition to the stated goals of a government continually assuming more power in order to "promote justice" or "maintain the peace," as anybody who actively defends themselves becomes a competitor — thus a threat — to government authority, as shown by what happened to Tony Martin.

Meanwhile, On the Other Side of the Law...

A series of reports expose the continued increase in violent crime in Britain, the resulting overload of the criminal justice system, and the consequences of these two factors which favor criminals. One article noted that violent crime, including the use of firearms during commission, continued to rise in 2005:

> There were 315,800 violent incidents in the three months to September, compared with 304,300 in the same period in 2004.
>
> The number of robberies recorded by police leapt to 23,500, but total recorded crime fell one per cent to 1,376,200 incidents in the period.
>
> In the year to the end of September, gun crime rose one per cent to 11,110 incidents, compared with 10,950 in the previous 12 months.
>
> Violence against the person rose four per cent overall, although more serious cases including homicide, threats to murder and serious woundings fell by ten per cent.
>
> Offences in a lower category involving crimes such as less serious woundings rose by ten per cent.
>
> The Home Office's firearms data showed the number of serious injuries from gun crimes rose by 18 per cent to 470, and slight injuries leapt 35 per cent to 3,600 in the year.[79]

As a result of this increased criminal activity, one police force–and perhaps many more–decided they had to focus their overworked resources on racist or homophobic crimes. This change in policy was described by one divisional commander as becoming common in Britain.

> A police force has stopped investigating less serious crimes unless they are racist or homophobic.
>
> Theft, criminal damage, common assault, harassment and non-domestic burglary are among offences being "screened out" due to manpower shortages.
>
> But officers are allowed to make an exception for any such incident judged to be motivated by race or gay hatred. It would then classify as "aggravated" and qualify for more serious treatment by police and the courts...

Police chiefs on Humberside insisted their officers no longer had time to solve minor crimes..

The architect of the policy is Chief Superintendent Sean White, divisional commander for Hull. Incredibly, while he introduced it last December his boss, Chief Constable Tim Hollis has only recently been told about it.

Chief Superintendent White defended the approach yesterday and insisted similar measures were in place across the country.

'It is the only way you can match resources to work,' said the 40-year-old police chief. 'We were set targets by the Home Office to cut the backlog of old cases of robbery, burglary, vehicle crime and violent crime, and we had to make this decision back in December.

'This is unusual for Humberside, but in terms of the rest of the country I would say it's not an extreme example of a screening policy.' [80]

Another new policy instituted by Britain's Home Office entails letting perpetrators off with a "caution" rather than arresting them:

Burglars will be allowed to escape without punishment under new instructions sent to all police forces. Police have been told they can let them off the threat of a court appearance and instead allow them to go with a caution.

The same leniency will be shown to criminals responsible for more than 60 other different offences, ranging from arson through vandalism to sex with underage girls.

New rules sent to police chiefs by the Home Office set out how seriously various crimes should be regarded, and when offenders who admit to them should be sent home with a caution.

A caution counts as a criminal record but means the offender does not face a court appearance which would be likely to end in a fine, a community punishment or jail.

Some serious offences - including burglary of a shop or office, threatening to kill, actual bodily harm, and possession of Class A drugs such as heroin or cocaine - may now be dealt with by caution if police decide that would be the best approach.

And a string of crimes including common assault, threatening behaviour, sex with an underage girl or boy, and taking a car without its owner's consent, should normally be dealt with by a caution, the circular said. [81]

For those perpetrators who actually go to prison, an evolving new policy is aimed at promoting inmates' "human rights".

Thousands of prisoners are being given keys to their cells in the latest farce to hit the criminal justice system.

They can roam in and out virtually at will under a scheme designed to give them more "respect and decency"…

It also emerged that some youth prisons now call offenders 'trainees' or 'residents'.[82]

It appears that the British criminal justice system has been strained beyond its capacity to handle crime. In order to avoid placing greater strain on the system, many offenders will now be sent home without needing to appear in court. Other police departments are retrenching in order to focus only on crimes they consider the highest priority, either to reduce investigative backlogs or to avoid such backlogs in the future. For those convicted of crimes, prisons are being turned into hotels, according to some sources, in order to avoid injuring the prisoners' self-esteem. This is all a curious double standard when compared to what happened to Tony Martin, a farmer who defended his home against repeat offenders after having been repeatedly burglarized and receiving no protection from the local police.

Dazed and Confused

Perhaps the saddest testament to Britain's inverted approach to crime comes from two reports by the *BBC*. After the third teenager was shot within a two-week period in south London, a police advisor said guns are becoming a fashion accessory among youth:

Reacting to Billy's death, Claudia Webbe, who is vice chair of the independent advisory group to the Metropolitan Police's Operation Trident, said youngsters want to be seen with weapons.

"Guns have gone from the domain of the crack cocaine dealers to now being an everyday accessory, a fashionable accessory, that young people want to be seen with," she said.

"It's become a lifestyle choice… part of a culture to be part of a gang.

"I think that's what's motivating young people, where a gun has become almost a status symbol demanding respect and power." [83]

Another person quoted in the article used the same language employed by U.S. gun control organizations to justify more gun control laws:

Jennifer Blake, a local community worker, said the main problem was "easy access" to guns and a breakdown of communication between the youths and their parents.

"Parents need to know more about, and understand more about, where these things are coming from.

"There's a concern with parents because they want to know where these guns are coming from and how easy to access they are." [84]

Her quote serves as proof of how ineffective civilian gun bans are: The United Kingdom has already banned civilian ownership for over a decade; criminals, by their very nature, will ignore laws and gain access to firearms regardless of the obstacles in their way.

Another *BBC* article noted the success of a police program which focused on priority areas suffering the most crime. Unfortunately, crime increased again after the program ended:

> The government's Street Crime Initiative targeted the 10 worst-hit areas and reduced offences by almost a third between 2002 and 2004-5.
>
> But since the £81m programme ended last April, street crime has increased.[85]

Of the greatest concern is the reason given by government sources for the rise in assaults:

> The Metropolitan Police has said the main factor behind a rise in muggings in London is the increasing number of hi-tech goods being carried by people such as the new generation of mobile phones and MP3 players.[86]

The Metropolitan Police place the blame for crime on "hi-tech goods" rather than criminals. When placed in the context of not wanting to arrest offenders and treat them gently should perpetrators actually get incarcerated, this makes perfect sense. Do the police think a ban on cell phones will help?

Conclusion

Civilian disarmament benefits those who seek to gain advantage from the law-abiding being defenseless. When implemented as a government policy under the guise of reducing crime or even just violent crime, it has failed. The Australian and English experiences show that guns and violence have an insufficient correlation to justify civilian disarmament. Do we in the U.S. want to go down the same road when the resulting evidence is so alarming? When the consequences could be so tragic and economically destructive?

This begs answers to a most important set of questions that arise as a result of the issues discussed here: Who else might benefit from civilian disarmament, since the common folk do not? Would not a benevolent government be alarmed at the crime wave resulting since implementation of gun control, and seeing no benefit in crime reduction, return the means of daily self-defense to its besieged citizens? Gun control must offer some other benefit, or else it would not be such a hot topic of discussion at all levels of government all over the world. If gun control had no benefit to government, more countries would simply allow civilians to be armed without so much as a license. Yet the fact remains that only a handful of countries allow civilian firearms ownership. Is it because governments do not trust the people, as may be indicated by the continued loss of civil rights after disarmament?

Chapter 3
Product Defect or Defective Policy?

A new approach to gun control is to promote it as "gun safety". The theory is that:

- guns have a series of defects that make them unpredictably dangerous,

- firearms manufacturers operate in an unregulated environment that makes them irresponsible and insensitive to the need for more safety,

- guns should contain certain features that would make them safer, and

- more regulatory oversight is required to assure these safety features are implemented to protect us from these unethical manufacturers.

Gun rights advocates respond that placing the "safety" devices on guns would render them inoperable in an emergency, and therefore the gun safety movement is just another ploy to disarm the civilian population. Guns perform their greatest utility in an unforeseen moment of need, say the gun rights proponents, and criminals will not abide by laws requiring safer guns. If the proposed safety features make it more difficult to defend against a sudden attack — because deactivating mandatory trigger locks or computerized biometric locks would take so much time — are they really about safety? If the end result endangers law-abiding gun owners, only criminals have increased safety. Gun-rights advocates also claim that thorough training and education is the most effective way to avoid or reduce accidents.

Gun safety advocates counter that guns are inherently dangerous; safety training alone does not work, and guns need further regulation by a government agency whose sole purpose is to protect consumers from dangerous products.

Enter the Consumer Federation of America

The Consumer Federation of America is an organization comprised of "some 300 nonprofit organizations from throughout the nation with a combined membership exceeding 50 million people" which, according to CFA, "enables CFA to speak for virtually all consumers."[1]

In early 2005, CFA released a study entitled *Buyer Beware: Defective Firearms and America's Unregulated Gun Industry*. The study makes a case that "every year many gun owners and bystanders are killed or injured by defective or hazardously-designed gun."[2] In *Buyer Beware*, CFA states:

> The gun lobby maintains that unintentional shootings generally occur as a result of carelessness on the part of the gun owner. Firearms industry marketing is replete with messages about "responsibility" that emphasize the importance of owner behavior without mentioning the potential dangers of the product.[3]

CFA continues:

> While consumer education does play an important role in injury prevention, no amount of user instruction can eliminate the risks associated with product defects in design or manufacture.[4]

Consumer Federation of America makes a very good point, which we will discuss later in this chapter when we look at how consistently CFA applies this standard to manufacturers of another major consumer product. For now, we will consider 10-year trends in the rates (per 100,000 population) of various unintentional causes of death. From 1994-2004 (the latest data available):

- There was a small decrease in the motor vehicle death rate of 5.3%.
- Drowning deaths decreased 24.8%.
- Poisoning rates more than doubled, up 108.7%.
- Accidental suffocation rates increased as well, up 27.4%.
- Accidental firearms deaths decreased 57.1%.

By 2004, the rate of accidental death involving a firearm was 0.22 per 100,000 population, less than one accidental death per 400,000 people. Compare this to the rates for the other causes:

- Poisoning – over 7 persons per 100,000, or 32.3 times the firearms rate.
- Drowning – over 1.1 per 100,000; 5.1 times the firearms rate.
- Motor Vehicle – 15.3 per 100,000; 69.2 times the firearms rate.
- Suffocation – 2 per 100,000; 9.1 times the firearms rate.[5]

CFA's "Product Safety" and "Child Safety" web pages contain no studies, brochures, or publications regarding deadly household products such as household chemicals, swimming pools, and plastic bags.[6]

Buyer Beware continues:

> Despite the fact that firearms kill nearly twice as many Americans as all household products combined, no federal agency has the necessary authority to ensure that guns do not explode or unintentionally discharge when they are dropped or bumped. This is unique.

> Exactly how many victims are killed or injured each year by defective firearms is unknown.[7]

The claim that "firearms kill nearly twice as many Americans as all household products" is true only if one narrowly defines exactly what can be considered a household product, and only if one broadly interprets "kill." Also, mixing intentional and unintentional deaths confuses the reader by linking firearms homicide — a violent, intentional crime — with firearms accidents.

For the year 2004, the National Center for Injury Prevention and Control reports there were 49,796 homicide and suicide injury-related deaths; of these 28,374, or 57%, occurred through use of a firearm. So guns do result in more than half of all injury-induced homicides and suicides. But these are intentional deaths, which means that they are either criminal or purposefully self-inflicted, and not the result of product defect. Indeed, you can make the case that these deaths prove that guns function as designed; criminals certainly think so, or they would not use guns as a tool of their trade.

However, if one adds in unintentional injury-related deaths, firearm-related death drops to 17.9% of the total. If one looks at only unintentional injury-related deaths, firearms represented 0.6% percent of the total. Meanwhile, motor vehicles comprise 40.1% of all unintentional deaths, and 27.9% of the total number of murder, suicide, and unintentional deaths: over 55% more than firearms.[8]

Because CFA does not differentiate between intentional self-harm and accidental death, they sidestep the question of how altering civilian firearm accessibility might impact suicide rates. Nor do they ask if a person intent on self-harm would simply find the most convenient tool available. For example, Australia and the United Kingdom saw slight increases in their suicide rates the four years following their gun restrictions, while the U.S. suicide rate dropped 12.6% despite increasing numbers of civilian firearms.[9]

The blurring of the lines between accidents, intentional violence, and self-inflicted injury encourages a perspective in which personal responsibility is no longer a consideration. Such a perspective encourages a legal environment in which the manufacturer of any inanimate product becomes the target of wrongful death suits. (This attitudinal/legal trend will be further addressed in Chapter 4.)

CFA also sidesteps the question of whether criminals would stop killing people if guns were made "safe." As Dr. Martin L. Fackler, a leading firearms wound ballistics expert, notes:

> When anti-gun activists list the number of deaths per year from firearms, they neglect to mention that 60 percent of the 30,000 figure they often use are suicides. They also fail to mention that at least three-quarters of the 12,000 homicides are criminals killing other criminals in disputes over illicit drugs, or police shooting criminals engaged in felonies. Subtracting those, we are left with no more than 3,000 deaths that I think most would consider truly lamentable.[10]

Since CFA mentions the word "safety" 344 times in *Buyer Beware*, we will address the issue of safety, but first, keep in mind that a person of evil intent could use many "household products" to kill another human being. In 2004, over 3,000 murders were attributed to cutting instruments, drowning, fire, poison, and suffocation.[11] Thus, accident prevention or safety concerns are irrelevant when the intention is homicidal, as the criminal will avoid or circumvent any and all safety features to accomplish his or her goal. Safety concerns are only an issue when considering unintentional (accidental) deaths that arise from the use of a product assumed to be non-defective.

What is the Consumer Federation of America doing to address the imminent and omnipresent dangers of the "household products" that are causing the highest numbers of accidental deaths?

Is Motor Vehicle Safety Being Properly Addressed?

The National Center for Injury Prevention and Control lists firearms as the 16th leading cause of unintentional death. Poisoning is the second leading cause, suffocation fifth, fire/burn sixth, and drowning seventh, with motor vehicle accidents topping the list.[12]

In 2004, motor vehicles caused a total of 45,113 deaths. Fifty-one of these were homicide and 108 suicide, leaving 21 deaths of undetermined intent.[13] This means that there were 44,933 unintentional, or accidental, deaths. Since Consumer Federation of America's stated concern is to curtail sales of potentially defective, commonly-used products that result in unintentional death, motor vehicles fall under this criteria. The CFA links to an associated site called Regulate Guns, which discusses the need for the Consumer Product Safety Commission (CPSC) to have oversight on firearms. Regulate Guns states:

> More than 30 years ago, the United States made prevention of deaths from motor vehicles injuries a national priority. As a result, the death rate from motor vehicle crashes was cut nearly in half.[14]

The claim is correct: According to the National Highway Traffic Safety Administration, between 1966 to 2004 (latest NHTSA data available) the motor vehicle traffic fatality rate decreased 43.9%.[15] But when we compare motor vehicle death and injury rates to those from firearms accidents, using the earliest and latest data available online from the Centers for Disease Control, we find that between 1979 and 2004:

- Accidental deaths from motor vehicles dropped 36%, but
- Accidental deaths from firearms dropped 75.3%.

Between 1993 and 2004:

- Accidental injuries from motor vehicles dropped 22.3%, but
- Accidental injuries from firearms dropped 86.1%.[16]

Firearm safety has improved at a far faster rate than motor vehicle safety, despite CFA's claim of the government making it a priority to prevent motor vehicle deaths. This does not encourage confidence that a government program could do any better with gun safety, since voluntary safety education is shown to be more successful than federal regulation. Nor do these statistics bode well for "gun safety" advocates. Since CFA is content that safety issues have been properly addressed with motor vehicle regulation, it should follow that because accidental firearm death has decreased over twice as fast, and accidental firearm injury nearly 4 times as fast, as the corresponding motor vehicle rates, there is even less of a need for more firearms regulation.

The CPSC admits on its own web site that the National Highway Traffic Safety Administration (NHTSA) is the government agency with jurisdiction over motor vehicles.[17] Thus, CFA is implicitly declaring that despite not being regulated by the CPSC, having a different government organization dedicated to the product's oversight is a satisfactory assurance that consumer safety concerns are being properly addressed. CFA's satisfaction is borne out by the fact that there is only one reference to motor vehicles listed on their site,[18] as opposed to about 50 for guns.[19] The main point to remember is this: If the CPSC says another government agency is sufficient for oversight on a product, this is acceptable to the Consumer Federation. Later in this chapter, current governmental regulatory and oversight agencies under which firearms manufacturers operate are examined.

The NHTSA, overseer of the automotive industry's safety standards, confirms that motor vehicle crashes are the leading non-disease cause of death in 2003,[20] and are the leading cause of death for children and young people:

> In 2003, motor vehicle traffic crashes were the leading cause of death for the age group 4 through 34. Because of the young lives consumed, motor vehicle traffic crashes ranked third overall in terms of the years of life lost, i.e., the number of remaining years that the person is expected to have lived had they not died, behind only cancer and diseases of the heart.[21]

NHTSA estimated there were 6,181,000 motor vehicle crashes in 2004,[22] with 42,636 people losing their lives, and an estimated 2,831,000 people injured, with 308,000 injuries resulting in incapacitation.[23] In alcohol-related crashes, 16,694 persons were killed and 248,000 injured, 39.2% and 8.8%, respectively, of the victim totals.[24]

Drunk driving could be considered an intentional or premeditated crash, as the driver must spend time and money getting drunk prior to getting into the vehicle and operating it, knowing that such behavior is dangerous. Drunks with cars killed 79% more people in 2004 than did criminals with firearms, as the FBI reports there were 9,326 intentional firearm murders that year.[25]

In terms of non-fatal injuries in 2004, the CDC reports there were 46.7 times more motor vehicle injuries (intentional plus accidental) as all firearm injuries, and over 181 times the unintentional firearms injuries. Firearms accounted for 0.2% of all injuries, while motor vehicle injuries accounted for over 10%.[26]

CFA-Approved Regulation Does Not Eradicate Product Defects

No matter who is in charge of regulating automobile safety, many dangerous vehicles slip through the regulatory net. Here is a partial list of recent automobile recalls, all covering issues which had the potential for causing injury or death:

Ford has announced a safety recall for a part that could cause fires underneath the hoods of several popular Ford pickup trucks and SUVs. But consumer advocates and lawyers representing several Texans whose vehicles were destroyed say the problem extends beyond the models recalled.[27,28]

Ford is recalling nearly 360,000 Ford Focus cars to fix a potential problem with their rear door latches. The problem involves about 358,857 vehicles from the 2000-2002 model years and stems from a build-up of corrosion around the rear door latches which can eventually prevent them from ensuring the doors are secure.

"If not latched properly, the door may open while the vehicle is in motion," NHTSA said.

The Focus has set new recall records since its introduction. This is the tenth safety recall conducted in the U.S. There have also been several defect investigations.[29]

General Motors is recalling 717,000 minivans because of a problem with the power sliding door. Passengers could hurt their arms or wrists, the automaker said.[30]

General Motors Corp. is recalling 155,465 pickups and sport utility vehicles – including the Hummer H2 – because of possible brake malfunctions, the automaker and federal safety regulators said Thursday.

NHTSA said a pressure accumulator in the braking system could crack during normal driving and fragments could injure people if the hood was open. The crack also could allow hydraulic fluid to leak, which could make it harder to brake or steer and could cause a crash.[31]

The National Highway Traffic Safety Administration said the North American division of problem-plagued Mitsubishi was recalling 65,436 of its mid-sized Endeavor SUVs, built between 2004 and 2005, because their parking brakes may fail.

NHTSA also said the Chrysler group was recalling 43,180 of its Pacifica SUVs because some may experience intermittent or eventual total failure of their halogen headlamps.[32]

Despite regulatory oversight by the NHTSA, including the CFA's much-touted ability to issue recalls, hundreds of thousands of dangerously defective automobiles are sold each year. Sometimes these defective products result in litigation for wrongful death and injury. Despite the CFA-acceptable regulation, motor vehicle crashes result in far more deaths and injuries than firearms. The high death rate exists notwithstanding mandatory consumer education (drivers' education) and ongoing anti-drunk-driving advertising. Nevertheless, Consumer Federation of America is satisfied that motor vehicles are properly regulated, and has not called upon the Consumer Protection Safety Commission for additional regulation.

Firearms Regulation Under the Consumer Product Safety Commission

Currently, the Consumer Product Safety Commission is forbidden by federal law to impose restrictions on firearms. The CPSC is comprised of three politically-appointed administrators who, if they were anti-gun, could regulate civilian gun ownership out of existence by creating product safety standards so stringent as to make it impossible for civilians to own functioning firearms.

Consider what happened when the CPSC got involved with air guns. In 1993, CPSC initiated an investigation into two of Daisy Manufacturing's air rifles, based upon a complaint that there were dangerous defects. Ten years later, after rancorous and expensive litigation, both parties reached a settlement. There were four basic points in the settlement to which Daisy and CPSC agreed:

1. "Add warnings related to the hazards associated with these air guns, including misfeeding and failure to load BBs as part of its $1.5 million safety campaign."

2. "All BBs manufactured by Daisy will contain a label or insert on the package, which will be apparent to all users accessing BBs."

3. "Submit performance issues to the appropriate ASTM [American Society for Testing and Materials] committee for the purpose of developing standards related to the propensity of air guns to fail to load, feed or fire BBs."

4. "Submit the issue of age appropriateness for air guns that fire projectiles in excess of 350 feet per second to the appropriate ASTM standards committee."[33]

Point 1 of the agreement actually forced Daisy to accept responsibility for extreme, intentional consumer misuse of their product. In a dissenting opinion, Mary Sheila Gall, one of the commissioners, stated:

Even Complaint Counsel's expert could induce lodging in the magazine of the Model 880 air rifle only by using BBs that were grossly out of specification in their dimensions or by loosening a screw in the receiver of the Model 880.

Similarly, a laboratory modification to a gun in order to induce lodging is of interest only if the modification is reasonably likely to occur when such guns are in the hands of consumers. Even Complaint Counsel's expert concluded that the experiment in screw loosening that led to BB lodging in the laboratory was unlikely to occur in the hands of consumers. Therefore, like the issue of out-of-specification BBs, the laboratory example of BB lodging is simply irrelevant in the Commission's determination over whether the Model 880 is a substantial product hazard. Without evidence of BBs lodging in the magazine in a manner likely to be encountered by consumers, the Commission cannot find that this characteristic of the Model 880 constitutes a substantial product hazard.[34]

In other words, in order to demonstrate the gun's defect, basic product design considerations had to be willfully ignored, or the gun had to be partially disassembled prior to use, another willfully malicious act intended to make the air rifle unsafe.

Point 2 is interesting because the first two parts of the safety insert are "1) Always point the gun in a safe direction; (2) Always treat every gun as if it were loaded..."[35] The first safety rule is copied verbatim from the National Rifle Association's safety rule 1, while the second is another NRA safety rule.[36] The NRA is an independent, non-regulatory organization that, through its extensive education program, strongly and consistently promotes responsible use, and its gun safety rules are considered the industry standard.[37]

Points 3 and 4 are particularly interesting, as the CPSC creates a standard that acknowledges certain issues are best left to independent experts. In this case, the CPSC relies on the American Society for Testing and Materials, a voluntary standards development organization whose mission is to promote public health and safety and help produce more reliable products.[38] The mission is accomplished via participation of their international membership:

> Standards developed at ASTM are the work of over 30,000 ASTM members. These technical experts represent producers, users, consumers, government and academia from over 100 countries.[39]

Therefore, by promoting the CPSC, the CFA effectively supports the CPSC policy of relying upon an independent group of experts to help create safe design standards. This concept, that the Consumer Federation's prize regulatory organization (CPSC) can designate independent organizations to create safety standards, is also a very important point to remember when covering the existing regulatory standards for firearms later in this chapter.

There are some other issues in this settlement which should concern the firearms industry as well as gun owners. Hal Stratton, Chairman of the CPSC, wrote:

> Based upon the evidence adduced in the case, I am not at all sure the CPSC complaint counsel would prevail on the merits of the case. Should the complaint counsel fail in their efforts to prove their case, consumers would obtain no benefit from a long and costly legal proceeding...

> Although I do not consider it determinative in itself, I have also taken Daisy's financial condition into consideration. From a review of the extensive financial documentation that we requested and received from Daisy, it is clear that Daisy is in a "precarious

financial" condition as alleged. It is less clear to me the role this proceeding has played in Daisy's financial condition. I believe the CPSC action may now be a factor in Daisy's financial condition, but I do not believe it is the only factor. Nevertheless, when considered with the other reasons to settle this matter, a settlement would provide certain immediate benefits to consumers, which they would not receive if Daisy becomes insolvent or this litigation drags on for years.[40]

This is an acknowledgement by the CPSC that litigation is expensive for firearms manufacturers, to the point that it may place them in a "precarious financial condition." Litigation has the potential to quickly bankrupt such businesses, causing job loss that spreads into local economies like a rock thrown into a pool. (This point will be explored in greater detail in Chapter 4.)

Returning to the CPSC statement, Chairman Stratton stated:

Throughout its 30-year history, the Commission consistently found that regulating this product would not enhance safety. Rather, the Commission has continuously made the determination to work with voluntary standards organizations to improve the safety standards of these products...

The Commission has never found that air rifles, or any model of air rifle, constitute a substantial product hazard.[41]

It is curious that the CPSC admits a "consistent" history of finding air rifles safe, and that voluntary standards have been sufficient to keep the rifles safe. Commissioner Gall also noted:

The Commission's actions have done serious and unjustified damage to the reputation and business prospects of a company whose product represents no substantial product hazard.[42]

Finally, Chairman Stratton stated in his Analysis of Facts:

Loading, feeding, and firing problems may not be best addressed by singling out a particular air gun or air guns for a corrective action, but by submitting these issues to the appropriate ASTM Subcommittee for the development of voluntary standards.

Even though BB lodging may occur, the link between lodging and injuries is not at all clear... It is apparent that if BB lodging injuries occur, they are relatively rare, which goes to the issue of whether the defects alleged in the complaint, as a legal matter, constitute a substantial product hazard.

All of the injuries that can be attributed to the guns at issue in this case were preventable. They all involved either someone pointing the gun at someone and pulling the trigger or playing with the gun in an inappropriate manner—all in violation of widely known and accepted safety rules for the use of guns.[43]

There are three important points being made here:

- The CPSC call for voluntary standards is repeated.

- Chairman Stratton admitted that grounds for pursuing litigation for alleged defects are weak, as there is no clear proof that there is a "substantial product hazard."

  - He admitted that all of the injuries in this case were in fact the responsibility of the gun owner, and that if consumers followed "accepted safety rules" they would have prevented these injuries.

These points — voluntary standards, no clear proof of substantial product defect, and user error — are exactly the ones that the Consumer Federation of America condemns firearm manufacturers for promoting; CFA alleges that the points are merely a cover for a tacit admission that guns are inherently, dangerously defective.

A Few Cases or a Vast Conspiracy?

The Consumer Federation of America released another report claiming: "Many firearms contain defects in design or manufacture making them likely to unintentionally discharge."[44] The report actually unwittingly proves that the existing structures of industry regulation and product liability litigation work.

For example, the report discusses a Sturm, Ruger single action revolver considered dangerous for its unintentional discharges. The manufacturer voluntarily stopped making the revolver in 1972 and replaced it with an upgraded model designed to prevent such accidental discharges. They document how the manufacturer saw a design flaw and corrected it over 20 years ago.

CFA discusses another model of single-action revolver that accidentally discharged after falling out of the holster and hitting a rock. The case resulted in a court settlement. The Excam Derringer is another pistol considered by the Consumer Federation to be "of poor construction and therefore prone to unintentional discharge." The Consumer Federation reports the company has been successfully sued for this defect. Lorcin Pistols is also reported to have been manufacturing "junk guns" that accidentally discharged. The report states: "In 1996 Lorcin announced it was filing for bankruptcy to protect itself from at least 18 pending liability suits." A Remington hunting rifle was reported to be defective, resulting in unintentional discharge. The report states: "In 1994 a Texas jury awarded $15 million in punitive damages to a hunter who shot himself in the foot when a Remington Model 700 rifle discharged without the trigger being pulled."

The above examples all prove that the legal system works in cases where the gun was proven to be defective, and that manufacturers who produce substandard products will be held accountable.

The report ends with an analysis report of Glock pistols, and an incident in which "the 3-year-old daughter of a District of Columbia police officer unintentionally shot and killed herself with her father's service pistol." The sad attempt at using tragedy to further the cause of gun control should embarrass the CFA: Had the officer been practicing all the safe gun handling and storage procedures he was taught in Police Academy, his daughter never would have had access to a firearm, loaded or not.

Consumer Federation of America prefers to intentionally group product defects together with user errors, rather than point out that professionals who have been trained in gun handling and safety do not always behave responsibly. As we saw with automobiles, owner irresponsibility is a far greater danger than real or alleged product defects.

Far from demonstrating the need for further regulation of firearms, the case studies show that a responsible manufacturer will discontinue manufacturing a questionable design to avoid the risk of customer injury and expensive product liability judgments, while irresponsible manufacturers end up in court, all as it should be.

Are Guns Unregulated?

Consumer Federation of America alleges that firearms are insufficiently regulated, and as a result, they present a substantial hazard to consumers and the public at large. Continuing with CFA's *Buyer Beware*:

> Pro-gun organizations such as the Sporting Arms and Ammunition Manufacturers Institute, Inc. (SAAMI) suggest that focusing on user education is all that is needed to reduce firearm accidents…

> Although the federal Bureau of Alcohol, Tobacco, Firearms and Explosives (ATF) licenses manufacturers, dealers, and importers, it has no general safety authority, such as the power to set safety standards or institute recalls.[45]

The CFA has one point, in that the ATF has only the authority to "to ensure that the firearms dealers are complying with the requirements of the Gun Control Act of 1968 and other federal firearms laws."[46] However, as to CFA's reliance on issuing recalls as a way to improve design safety, there are two points to remember:

- Automobiles may be recalled after hundreds of thousands of dangerously defective units have been released into the general population. This hardly shows how the regulatory ability to recall has made cars safer.

- CFA and other "safety" organizations have provided no evidence that there is any significant number of defective firearms sold, dubious justification when clamoring that we need a regulatory agency with the authority to recall guns.

It is hard to consider CFA's firearms safety claim when another government agency is not satisfactorily performing its job. The CFA's own criteria are in play here: They promote the Consumer Product Safety Commission as the solution to dangerous products. The CPSC operates according to three important guidelines:

- The CPSC does not need to act when another government agency provides sufficient oversight on a product.

- Independent expert organizations can create satisfactory safety standards.

- Voluntary standards are an essential part in creating safe products.

Therefore, by supporting the CPSC, Consumer Federation implicitly supports CPSC decision-making processes for determining proper safety standards.

The ATF has certain regulatory authority that is greater than the NHTSA, as its powers can be exercised without notice. The ATF can enter a retailer's establishment unannounced, and the business owner has no right of refusal either on the premises or in their home, should the ATF wish to inspect their private residence. As one retailer wrote in an email interview:

> "Persons who hold FFL's [Federal Firearms License, required by ATF for any firearms business] give up their Fourth Amendment rights to search and seizure. The authorities can knock at my [home] door, come to my business, my car or any other property I own and search same without a warrant."[47]

The ATF also has the authority to perform unannounced audits and inspections on distributors and manufacturers.[48] An ATF public information officer confirmed that the Bureau can perform one unannounced site inspection per year under normal circumstances, but may show up unannounced at any time if a criminal investigation is under way.[49] Thus, suspected violations of federal law involving manufacturing or sales can be investigated immediately, any time, with no legal right of refusal for the business owner.

NHTSA inspections are limited to probable cause related to "an occurrence associated with the maintenance or operation of a motor vehicle or motor vehicle equipment resulting in personal injury, death, or property damage."[50] The NHTSA's authority is strictly reactive, responding to a suspected defect infraction which resulted in injury, death, or property damage. This means that, regarding federal regulations, firearms manufacturers are already held to a tougher inspection standard than the CFA-approved automobile regulation.

This partially satisfies CFA's first criterion: Another government agency is sufficient for oversight on a product. Further control over product quality comes from a coalition of private standards and inspection organizations, plus market-induced pressures from government law enforcement agencies.

The Consumer Federation of America report disparages the Sporting Arms and Ammunition Manufacturers Institute (SAAMI) for emphasizing user education and responsible use.[51] The SAAMI web site's main technical page states: "SAAMI is an accredited Standards Developer for the American National Standards Institute (ANSI)."[52] The technical page elaborates:

> As an accredited standards developer, SAAMI's standards for industry test methods, definitive proof loads, and ammunition performance specifications are subject to ANSI review and various ANSI criteria.

> According to the American National Standards Institute, "Approval of an American National Standard requires verification by ANSI that the requirements for due process, consensus, and other criteria for approval have been met by the standards developer."[53]

So it is not the firearms manufacturers who set product quality standards, but an independent organization. Also, there are opportunities for input from many other agencies during the standards development process. Part of the ANSI standards process involves approval by the U.S. Customs Service, the Federal Bureau of Investigation, the National Institute of Standards & Technology, the Royal Canadian Mounted Police, and the Association of Firearms & Tool Mark Examiners.[54] These organizations together satisfy CFA's second criterion: Independent expert organizations can create satisfactory safety standards. Nor are standards set once and forgotten. As SAAMI states:

> It is ANSI and SAAMI policy that every five years the standards be revised or reaffirmed. Even if the standards remain the same, they must go through the approval process outlined above. Simply stated, the standards accepted by ANSI and promulgated by SAAMI are reviewed and accepted by outside experts, and every five years the validity of the standards are re-affirmed.[55]

ANSI also schedules audits with the participating manufacturer.[56] Furthermore, if a firearms manufacturer wants to do business with the government, the manufacturer must adhere to the SAAMI/ANSI standards:

> The U.S. military, the Federal Bureau of Investigation, and many other state and local agencies frequently require that their suppliers manufacture to SAAMI specifications. SAAMI is the only trade association whose member companies manufacture and set standards for high-performance law enforcement ammunition.[57]

These lucrative government contracts provide incentive to satisfy the rest of CFA's first criterion by virtue of being large, influential consumers.

It should also be noted that other government regulatory agencies rely upon ANSI to create safety standards for other products. For example, the National Institute for Occupational Safety And Health worked with ANSI to develop "a new voluntary standard for preventing motor vehicle crashes" for vehicle fleets in the workplace.[58] The Bureau of Labor Statistics notes that in 2005, there were 1,428 workplace deaths from "highway incidents" and 564 workplace homicides.[59]

Voluntary safety standards are sufficient when dealing with other, more lethal, products than firearms, making CFA's attempt to promote firearm regulation even more questionable.

The Association of Firearms & Tool Mark Examiners (AFTE) is "an international organization dedicated to the advancement of one of the finest disciplines of Forensic Science...Firearm & Toolmark Identification."[60] The organization began in 1969 with a core group of 35 police and civilian forensics experts. It conducts annual training seminars, and now has about 850 members.[61] AFTE explains:

> The organization is formed exclusively for charitable, scientific, educational, and testing for public safety purposes; and to improve and elevate the quality, integrity, and public image of the scientific crime laboratories... (Emphasis added)

One of the specific goals of the AFTE is "To engage in the testing of firearms, components, ammunition and examiners for the benefit of public safety."[62] The AFTE code of ethics states:

> It is the duty of any person practicing the profession of firearms and toolmark examination to serve the interests of justice to the best of his ability at all times. He will use all of the scientific means at his command to ascertain all of the significant physical facts relative to the matters under investigation. Having made factual determinations, he must then interpret and evaluate his findings. In this he will be guided by experience and knowledge which, coupled with a serious consideration of his analytical findings and the application of sound judgment, may enable him to arrive at opinions and conclusions pertaining to the matter under study. These findings of fact and his conclusions and opinions should then be reported with all the accuracy and skill of which the examiner is capable.
>
> In carrying out these functions, the examiner will be guided by those practices and procedures which are generally recognized within the profession to be consistent with a high level of professional ethics. The motives, methods and actions of the examiner shall at all times be above reproach, in good taste and consistent with proper moral conduct.[63]

The Shorter Oxford English Dictionary (OED) defines "integrity" as:
- "The condition of having no part or element taken away or lacking; undivided state; completeness" and

- "The condition of not being marred or violated; unimpaired or uncorrupted condition; original state; soundness."

OED defines "defect" as: "The absence of something essential to completeness; a lack, a deficiency." These two words — "integrity" and "defect" — are antonyms; i.e., conceptual opposites. Therefore, when the AFTE inspects "testing of firearms, components, ammunition," AFTE is looking to detect and eradicate defects, and thus ensure that proper manufacturing standards are employed to produce properly-working products.

If a firearms manufacturer wants to remain profitable, to be free from meritorious negligence and product defect litigation, and to have access to lucrative government contracts, the manufacturer must maintain the highest standards of product quality. The manufacturing standards and processes must be transparent to all parties involved with the development of standards and processes. The gun maker must be open to inspections and participate in regular reviews of manufacturing standards and processes by a number of different types of organizations. This is multi-layered quality control:

- A government organization dedicated to enforcing federal firearms laws, plus a number of powerful, interested government law-enforcement organizations who represent lucrative business opportunities for the gun-makers. (CFA's criterion 1)

- Three independent non-governmental standards oversight organizations; (CFA's criterion 2);

- Voluntary participation by the manufacturer (CFA's criterion 3);

The Utility Argument

When pointing out the differing regulatory results and safety records between cars and guns, you will likely get a response along the lines of: "But automobiles are useful; guns just kill people. Cars help us in our everyday life."

Those who need a firearm to protect themselves during an attack find it extremely useful. In *Guns and Crime: Handgun Victimization, Firearm Self-Defense, and Firearm Theft*, an analysis of crime victimization surveys, Rand concluded that there was a benefit from owning firearms, finding that from 1987-92, 75% of victims who resisted with a firearm did so during a violent crime, and that victims who resisted with other weapons suffered injury 2.5 times as often as those who resisted with a firearm.[64]

In *Armed Resistance to Crime*, Kleck and Gertz address the issue of the usefulness of firearms, concluding that "gun defenders appear to face more difficult circumstances than other crime victims, not easier ones."[65] This was based upon their defensive gun use survey, where they found:

Although the gun defenders usually faced unarmed offenders or offenders with lesser weapons, they were more likely than other victims to face gun-armed criminals. This is consistent with the perception that more desperate circumstances call forth more desperate defensive measures. The findings undercut the view that victims are prone to use guns in "easy" circumstances which are likely to produce favorable outcomes for the victim regardless of their gun use.[66]

While victims face multiple offenders in only about 24% of all violent crimes, the victims in our sample who used guns faced multiple offenders in 53% of the incidents.[67]

Kleck and Gertz estimated firearms were used defensively 2.1-2.5 million times a year, based upon a one-year recall period for survey respondents.[68] Their estimates of annual defensive gun use over a five year period reflect findings of similar surveys, where the number of defensive gun uses ranged from 1.5-1.8 million per year.[69]

When asked about their perceived likelihood that a victim would have died had they not used a gun for protection, 14.2% responded that somebody "probably would have," while 15.7% said somebody "almost certainly would have" died.[70] Using the more conservative estimates above of 1.5 to 1.8 million defensive gun uses per year, this means it was likely that between 235,500 and 282,600 lives "almost certainly" were saved annually by defensive gun use and another 213,000 to 255,600 lives were "probably" saved. This may sound extreme, but as Kleck and Gertz note:

> If even one-tenth of these people are accurate in their stated perceptions, the number of lives saved by victim use of guns would still exceed the total number of lives taken with guns.[71]

In their survey, Kleck and Gertz found that 5.5% of defenders were injured during a violent encounter with their attackers. The U.S. Department Of Justice 2003 Crime Victimization Survey estimated that in the period of 2002-3, 38.5% of robbery victims were injured and 32.4% of aggravated assault victims were injured.[72] Compared to defensive gun users, the overall injury rate for robbery victims was seven times greater, and the aggravated assault injury rate was almost six times greater. This translates to a potential of over 280,000 (140,711 aggravated assault plus 91,832 robbery) injuries avoided annually for the 2002-2003 period.

In *Victim Costs and Consequences*, Miller, Cohen, and Wiersema of the National Institute of Justice spent two years studying the financial costs (in 1993 dollars) of various crime categories. They concluded:

> Personal crime is estimated to cost $105 billion annually in medical costs, lost earnings, and public program costs related to victim assistance.[73]

Beyond tangible costs such as medical care, the authors found:

> Including pain, suffering, and the reduced quality of life increases the cost of crime to victims to an estimated $450 billion annually.[74]

Using the study's average costs per incident, defensive gun use during an assault has the potential for saving over $3.8 billion in annual medical costs, lost productivity, public services, property loss, and quality of life, while defensive gun usage during a robbery would have saved another $1.9 billion.[75] These amounts assume each crime incident where a defensive firearm was successfully deployed is downgraded from a completion plus injury to an attempt with no injury. If, in certain cases, defensive gun use downgrades the crime to no interaction at all, the savings would be greater.

It is also interesting to note that the authors of *Victim Costs and Consequences* consider drunk driving to be a violent crime, stating:

> Drunk driving is illegal. This study considers it a violent crime when a drunk driver maims or kills innocent victims or damages their property.[76]

Using the DOJ estimates, the costs to society for DWI-caused deaths in 2004 was nearly $69.3 billion. Compared to the estimated costs of firearm-related death — mostly intentional murder by criminals — at $35.8 billion, drunk driving fatalities cost us over $33 billion more in 2003.[77] To put this amount in perspective, $32 billion was roughly equivalent to the gross national product of the 65th wealthiest country in the world.[78]

There is significant social utility in civilian ownership of firearms, not only in lives saved and injuries avoided, but in a massive reduction in the cost of crime to society in terms of productivity and quality of life.

Women, Rape Prevention, and Self-Defense

There is one category of violent crime that is unique in its ability to completely violate, humiliate, and dehumanize a person. The costs to society in terms of lost work, medical care, and social services can be calculated in a sterile vacuum of hard numbers, but the hidden costs of damage to the human spirit and family relationships are incalculable. Would not any reasonable person be willing to do anything legally and morally possible to reduce the incidents of rape?

In *Determinants of Completing Rape and Assault*, Lizotte sought to determine if rape had unique properties that differentiated it from other forms of assaultive violence. He analyzed data from the National Crime Survey, compiling over 13,000 cases of rape and assault that occurred in 26 cities from 1972 through 1975. By comparing rape to assault, he was able to create a more definitive qualitative analysis of the crime of rape. He found that resisting assault was not a successful strategy:

> The data suggest that the best method of resisting assault is not to resist with force. Men and women who resist assault with force seem to fare much worse than those who do nothing to resist and those who resist without force.[79]

However, his findings on resisting rape were opposite that of assault:

> Resisting rape with force decreases the probability of a completed victimization. For assaults, resisting without force and doing nothing are equivalent: on average they neither raise nor lower the probability of completion.
>
> For rape, however, resistance without force is better than doing nothing at all. In other words, for rape, resisting with force and resisting without force both decrease the

probability of victimization. Further, women who resist rape with a gun or knife dramatically decrease their probability of completion.[80]

In *Rape and Resistance*, Kleck and Sayles sought to continue this research by examining stranger rape incidents recorded in the National Crime Surveys from 1979 to 1985. They concurred that the most effective method for lowering rape completion rates was for the victim to resist with a weapon,[81] and that such resistance did not create "any significant additional risk of other injury." On the other hand, they found some correlation between additional injury and "unarmed forceful resistance or threatening or arguing with the offender."[82] In other words, if you are going to resist, use a weapon to support your intention.

In *Judged Effectiveness of Common Rape Prevention and Self-Defense Strategies*, Furby, Fischhoff, and Morgan surveyed comparably-sized groups of women, men, and rape experts to determine effective preventative strategies, and for self-defense strategies once an assault was initiated. They stated this was the first such study to attempt to quantify exactly how different types of strategies might reduce risk or completion of rape. They concluded:

> Consensually effective strategies included threatening the man with a gun, poking the assailant's eyes, kicking him in the groin, and screaming, in roughly that order.

> Women, men, and experts all attributed greater effectiveness to physically assertive strategies than to less assertive ones.[83]

Both women and men respondents rated defensive gun use as the most effective strategy once the assault was under way. The only physical resistance strategy rape experts rated higher than defensive gun use was poking the assailant's eyes.[84] While this sounds good in theory, it means the assailant is already in physical contact, and since men are generally bigger and stronger than women, the assailant will most likely be in control of the situation at that point. This reflects on Rand's findings, that those who resist with other weapons — stiffened fingers in this case — fare worse than those who resist with firearms. Dramatic increases in rape in both Australia and the United Kingdom also give credence to this conclusion.

Rape experts surveyed in *Judged Effectiveness of Common Rape Prevention and Self-Defense Strategies* also agreed that the three most effective prevention strategies are for a woman to appear confident and strong (63.3% reduction), stay vigilant (64.1%), and participate in frequent public awareness programs (60%).[85] The authors calculate an enormous fiscal savings even if the three least effective rape-prevention strategies are employed by women:

> Pursuing the three strategies judged by the experts to be least effective should reduce the risk of assault by 73% (i.e., $1 - [(1 - .326)(1 - .365)(1 - .374)]$.[86]

Using their formula, the three *most* effective strategies, all of which come from training in defensive gun use, would reduce the risk of sexual assault 94.7%. Again, one could argue that all three prevention strategies are developed in martial arts training, but fighting off a violent predator with no social mores — who holds no value for a woman's life — at close quarters is far different than sparring with fellow students under the watchful eye of a teacher. Combine these behavioral strategies with a tool that can halt the assault outside of grappling and striking distance, and it appears that rape could be effectively and dramatically reduced.

Using the same calculations from the analysis of the costs of aggravated assault and robbery, we find that by employing the successful strategies outlined in *Judged Effectiveness of Common Rape Prevention and Self-Defense Strategies*, there would have been an additional $11.5 billion saved annually in medical costs, lost productivity, public services, property loss, and quality of life, during the 2002-2003 period.[87]

There is a belief among many gun control proponents that using physical means of resistance during a sexual assault only provokes the attacker to greater levels of violence. For instance, the U.S. State Department recommends "It may be more advisable to submit than to resist and risk severe injury or death."[88]

Quinsey and Upfold found, "victims resisted more strongly when they were being injured. There was, in fact, no association of victim resistance and the probability of later injury."[89]

After examining the 1984 Victim Risk Supplement, Kleck and Sayles examined the sequence of events in assaults and robberies, finding that only in a small minority of cases did the victim resist before being injured. They concluded:

In short, the time sequence of injury and resistance in the overwhelming majority of assaults and robberies is inconsistent with the resistance-provokes-attack thesis...[90]

They then referred back to the issue of resisting during attempted rape, concluding:

Taking into account the evidence concerning the causal/temporal order of injury and self-protection, the findings are consistent with the view that injury to the victim can provoke her to take self-protection action...[91]

Kleck and Sayles also found:

Completion rates for all specific forms of self-protection are substantially lower than for nonresistance, with the lowest rate, 0 percent, associated with resistance with a gun or knife.[92]

Guns not only save lives, they save money, they save families, they save relationships, and they save the sanity of our society. As Dr. Fackler notes:

Consider the implications of the fact that firearms save many more lives than they take. That means decreasing the number of firearms would actually cause an increase in violent crime and deaths from firearms.[93]

This inverse relationship between civilian firearms ownership and violent crime has been reinforced by the experiences of both Australia and the United Kingdom, where rape and other violent crime increased since their respective gun bans.

Is There a Political Motive for Promoting 'Gun Safety'?

Consumer Federation of America posted surveys on its website dealing with questions on firearms regulation and politics. The first survey, published in April, 2000, lists in its Executive Summary a number of findings that seem to indicate popular support for more gun control. Three of its conclusions were:

- Most people oppose permissive, shall-issue, concealed-carry laws.

- Pro-gun-control candidates have a voting edge over "anti-gun-control" politicians.

- A greater number of people favor the more pro-gun-control position of the Democrats over the more anti-gun-control stance of the Republican party.[94]

Let us take a look at the first point, that "most people" oppose right-to-carry laws. Between 1995 and 2004, 17 states enacted right-to-carry laws, bringing the total to 36 states with such laws.[95] They all passed right-to-carry laws in their respective legislatures, where duly elected representatives of the people voted in two separate houses to enact them. The laws then had to be signed by the duly elected governor, or in the rare case of a veto, passed again by the legislature with a super-majority (usually two-thirds) to override the veto. This process provided ample time for "most people" who opposed "permissive, shall-issue, concealed-carry-laws" to rise up and put a stop to it. Could it be because most people actually support the right to carry?

Now let us examine points 2 and 3 in the 2000 survey on the CFA web site, citing statistics to verify if "most people" support pro-gun-control candidates:

In 2000, NRA-PVF was involved in 275 campaigns for the U.S. House and Senate, winning in 237 of those races. NRA-PVF endorsed thousands of candidates running in state legislative races and achieved a 82% success rate in those elections.[96]

The National Rifle Association endorses candidates during each election cycle, regardless of party affiliation. The NRA "won" 86% of the federal races in 2000. Considering national elections a reasonable substitute for a comprehensive national survey, it is easy to conclude that a majority of the American people favor the more pro-gun stance of the Republican party over the gun-control stance of most Democrats.

Undeterred by the 2000 election cycle, CFA posted another survey on the assault weapons ban in March, 2004, which declared:

Sixty-seven percent said they favored renewing the ban, including 57 percent who strongly favor its renewal. A solid majority of gun owners, 56 percent, support renewing the ban, with 45 percent strongly supporting renewal.[97]

As with 2000, the 2004 election, which occurred after the assault weapons ban sunset earlier that September, saw solid gains by "pro-gun" candidates:

In the U.S. Senate, we saw a net gain of four pro-gun votes, with victories in Florida (Mel Martinez), Louisiana (David Vitter), North Carolina (Richard Burr), South Carolina (Jim DeMint) and South Dakota (Thune), and a loss in Colorado. In fact, 13 of the 14 Senate candidates we profiled in the November NRA magazines won their races. Of the 251 candidates endorsed by NRA-PVF in U.S. House of Representatives races, 241 won, for a 96% winning percentage!

Roughly 7,000 state legislative races were held November 2, and your NRA-PVF was involved in more than half. NRA-PVF-endorsed candidates won 86% of their races. Pro-Second Amendment gubernatorial candidates supported by NRA-PVF won 9 of 11 elections, with the Washington race still too close to call. In state Attorneys General races, all of our candidates carried the day.[98]

When renewal of the assault weapons ban came up in the Senate, Senators Graham (Florida), Breaux (Louisiana), Daschel (South Dakota), and Edwards (North Carolina) all voted to renew.[99] In the 2004 elections, pro-gun candidates replaced these Senators: Martinez replaced Graham; Vitter replaced Breaux; and Burr replaced Edwards. Thune replaced Daschle, who led the charge to renew the ban as Senate minority leader. The 2004 elections resulted in a net loss of four Senate seats for those supporting renewal of the ban. Likewise, those supporting renewal of the ban lost ground in the House. The people, in most state majorities, voted on how they felt about those trying to renew the ban. The NRA, as a representative of a large body of gun owners, also shows how unlikely it was that the CFA survey accurately reflected gun owners' attitudes about renewing the ban.

If the CFA survey represented the "solid majority", then why was George W. Bush re-elected over John Kerry? The national "survey," called an election, endorsed the pro-gun-rights agenda put forth by the Department of Justice under the Bush administration: that the Second Amendment guarantees an individual right to keep and bear arms.[100] This begs the question: Did the CFA want to use these "opinion surveys" as social engineering to influence voters?

Conclusion

Gun controllers give lots of credence to gun fatalities that are almost all suicides or homicides to make their case that guns are too dangerous to remain among the general population. But to look at firearm-related deaths outside any statistical context makes it impossible to determine just how dangerous guns are. The Consumer Federation of America pays little notice to motor vehicle deaths, which produce a far greater mortality rate than guns. Nor do they acknowledge the benefits of civilian gun ownership in terms of lives saved and injuries avoided. If they really cared about unnecessary death and suffering, why this slanted coverage?

The Consumer Federation of America has defined its criteria for requiring the Consumer Product Safety Commission to regulate a product: It must be dangerous to the average user, and even with proper use it can accidentally cause death and injury. With so many defective motor vehicles and dangerous automobile drivers on the road, why does the CFA not demand CPSC oversight, in order to "properly regulate" automobile safety? The CFA's own criteria condemn the NHTSA as ineffective. Even with dedicated NHTSA oversight, hundreds of thousands of defective motor vehicles are sold and driven in public each year, adding to accidental deaths and injuries. Why doesn't CFA lobby for ignition-defeating breathalyzers in cars? Like a gun in the hands of a criminal, a car driven by a drunk is a weapon aimed at innocent victims. The Consumer Federation of America remains curiously silent on this topic, preferring to focus its lobbying efforts on resolving an "unknown" number of firearms injuries and deaths that are many times fewer than those caused by motor vehicles. CFA insists on this regulation despite the fact that firearms are already more successfully and safely government- and self-regulated than cars are by a CFA-approved government agency; despite the fact the Consumer Product Safety Commission believes that safe handling education is the best way to reduce firearms injuries; and despite the fact the CPSC admits in its own investigations that user errors, not product defects, are the real culprit. Why does CFA not demand that private ownership of automobiles be restricted or outlawed? After all, many lives might be saved if people went to work using public transportation or bicycles.

These inconsistencies in its demands make the Consumer Federation of America look like an anti-gun political organization hiding behind the façade of people who "care about safety." When an organization puts a political agenda ahead of objective safety standards, they themselves become a danger to society.

Chapter 4
The Politics of Gun Control

The purpose of this chapter is not to report current events but to examine the story behind the story. Tort reform regarding the ability of private individuals and municipalities to sue firearms manufacturers is a settled issue in Congress: The Protection of Lawful Commerce in Arms Act was passed and signed into law in the fall of 2005. However, the reason it was an issue in the first place, the reason why it was a rancorous process for Congress to decide to pass tort reform, and the reason it remains a threat to firearms manufacturers, is a most interesting tale. In other words, why did some members of Congress fight so vehemently against tort reform?

During 2004 and 2005, Congress debated the legality of suing firearms manufacturers when criminals intentionally misuse a legally-sold, non-defective product. Both chambers in Congress introduced legislation to curtail such lawsuits.

Numerous court cases were filed in previous years for the purpose of holding manufacturers liable for private criminal behavior. In Chapter 3, we examined a case study of a gun control organization averring that the court system is the only way to address product defects. In this chapter we see that gun control proponents want it both ways: They willingly use courts for law suits against the gun industry when the issue is neither product defect nor manufacturer negligence.

We also examined a case study of a years-long legal battle between Daisy Manufacturing and the Consumer Product Safety Commission, and how legal expenses almost sent Daisy into bankruptcy. Can firearms manufacturers withstand an all-out onslaught of litigation like the tobacco industry did? Are there other hidden motivations for such law suits? Is there a link between special interests and political decision-making that may create a bias towards law suits?

A Modest Industry Whose History is Entwined with Our Own

Most firearm manufacturers are small-to medium-sized businesses. In 2002, only 12% of all manufacturers produced more than 10,000 units. At the other end, 56% of all manufacturers are little more than family-owned businesses, producing less than 100 guns annually.[1]

Some of the larger manufacturers have a long history that is intertwined with our country's. Springfield Armory was created under the leadership of George Washington. When he was commander of the Continental Army during the Revolutionary War in 1777, his Chief of Artillery, Colonel Henry Knox, established the armory in Springfield, Massachusetts. It was originally used to store weaponry for the war effort, but in 1794 Springfield was selected by President Washington as one of two federal armories to manufacture firearms for the military. The U.S. National Park Service notes: "In 1794 the new Federal government decided to manufacture its own muskets so that the Nation would not be dependent on foreign arms." Over the next century and three-quarters, Springfield Armory became a major provider of innovative new firearms to the U.S. Military, until the government closed it in 1968 for budgetary reasons.[2] In 1974, the name and many of the designs were resurrected when a private family opened a modern version of the armory.[3]

Colt's Manufacturing Company began in 1836, when Samuel Colt received the patent for his revolver. He got his first break when the Mexican War began in 1846, receiving a government contract for 1,000 revolvers. During the Civil War, Colt supplied only the Union Forces. Colt's firearms were used by the U.S. military in both World Wars, and Colt continues to supply the military to this day.[4]

Smith & Wesson was founded in 1856, specializing in their patented revolver with the first fully self-contained cartridge. The company later developed the revolver which "has been used by virtually every police agency and military force around the world."[5]

Why the Democratic Party Should Support Firearms Ownership

It may seem that the following discussion disparages one political party more than another: Such is not the intent. There are exceptions on "both sides of the aisle" for and against gun rights, and history has proven time and again that no mere human can easily resist the siren song of absolute power, the seeking of which usually brings ruin to all involved — including, perhaps especially — the people. At this point in the larger political cycle, the Democratic party is more firmly in favor of gun control, so we ended up focusing on them for now.

The New Shorter Oxford English Dictionary defines *politics* as: "Activities concerned with the acquisition or exercise of authority or status."[6] It defines *power* as: "(Possession of) control or authority over others."[7] Thus, political power is the activity of acquiring and possessing control over others. Once power is acquired, it seems a small and natural step to want to believe in one's own righteousness of thought, and the attitude ensues that what the one in power wants is what is best for all. Thus, the needs of those in power come to symbolize the country's needs. As Lord Acton said: "Power tends to corrupt and absolute power corrupts absolutely."

It also seems true, as shown in Chapter 2, that a criminal can more easily acquire and exercise power over another when he is assured of their inability to exercise any counterbalancing power. If the data presented in this book are any indication, then civilian disarmament provides such a criminal incentive.

Part of the Democratic Party's agenda declares: "The Democratic Party is committed to keeping our nation safe and expanding opportunity for every American."[8] Their civil rights page states: "Democrats are unwavering in our support of equal opportunity for all Americans."[9] Reviewing how gun control has resulted in loss of opportunity for minorities and women, it seems reasonable that the Democratic Party would want to support these historically disadvantaged population groups in the basic right of self-defense.

Eleanor Roosevelt, wife of Democractic President Franklin Roosevelt, understood this. In 1958, at age 74, she traveled to Tennesee to speak at a civil rights workshop. Having heard from the FBI that the Ku Klux Klan had placed a bounty on her head, she nevertheless attended, driving from the airport to the school with a loaded pistol on the seat next to her.[10]

Democratic President John F. Kennedy wrote to the NRA:

On the occasion of Patriots Day, I wish to offer my congratulations and best wishes to the National Rifle Association of America which over the past years has done credit to our country by the outstanding achievements of its members in the art of shooting.

Through competitive matches and sports in coordination with the National Board for the Promotion of Rifle Practice, the Association fills an important role in our national defense effort, and fosters in an active and meaningful fashion the spirit of the Minutemen.

I am pleased to accept Life Membership in the National Rifle Association and extend to your organization every good wish for continued success.[11]

President Kennedy's reference to the Minutemen is especially interesting, as the Minutemen were comprised of farmers and craftsmen who were selected from a town's militia to be a "small hand-picked elite force which were required to be highly mobile and able to assemble quickly." This democratic, "everyman" military organization was our form of homeland security from as early as the mid-1600s to the Revolutionary War.[12]

The Democratic Party, often considered the party of the little people, would do well to consider that the little people sometimes need to be able to defend their families from harm as part of their "equal opportunity" to pursue the American Dream. While Democratic Senators and Representatives reside in their legislative chambers, protected by dedicated security details, they need to remember that those of more modest means, whose hard-earned tax dollars pay for those private police forces, are unable to afford the same protection for their families, and that the police often cannot arrive in time to avert tragedy. Thus, the right of self-defense supports the pursuit of happiness. The Democratic party would be more in keeping with the spirit of their stated goals if their actions supported this fact.

Tort Reform: Follow the Money

To get a better idea of the undercurrents of the tort reform issue, it is helpful to look at campaign contributions and see how they relate to the "return on investment" effect by influencing congressional votes. According to Center for Responsive Politics, lawyers and law firms contributed heavily to congressional and presidential races in 2004, more than any other industry, spending a total of $184,297,231 on federal candidates and parties.[13] Of the victors in the 2004 election cycle, 16 of the top 20 Senate campaign contribution recipients from law firms were Democrats.[14] Sixteen of the top 20 House recipients were likewise Democrats.[15] Of all candidates, 18 of the top 20 law firm campaign contribution recipients in the

Senate races,[16] and 19 of the top 20 in the House races, were Democrats.[17] Also, 74% of all lawyer/law firm contributions went to Democrats. This trend of favoring Democrats dates back at least to 1990. The highest percentage ever donated in an election cycle to the Republicans is 31% in 1990.[18]

The top individual legal organization in 2004 was the Association of Trial Lawyers of America — since renamed the American Association for Justice — contributing $2,588,332, over twice as much as the second-highest donor, with 92% of their money going to Democrats.[19] Compare this to gun rights organizations, which contributed $1,324,324 for the 2004 election cycle, less than 1% of what lawyers gave.[20] The National Rifle Association contributed $1,151,130 to federal candidates and parties in 2004.[21]

The purpose here is not to derogate any political party or attorneys, but to open the discussion of the relationship between campaign contributions and congressional voting records. One should pause to consider whether it benefits regular folk, who comprise the vast bulk of society, to have one special interest group with so much influence in a Congress which debates laws that can result in great financial return for that industry. This is a fair topic of consideration, as gun control groups use the same standard in their complaints about special interests on the other side of the issue.

For example, a press release by the Brady Campaign to Prevent Gun Violence called the current tort reform bill a "transparent gift to the NRA."[22] Another article claimed:

> Politicians in Washington are poised to give unprecedented freedom to the gun industry – and they're so beholden to the NRA they're allowing potential terrorists to buy weapons over the counter.[23]

The picture above this second article displays a vending machine dispensing handguns, despite the fact that the Brady Law, promoted by the Brady Campaign, requires all handgun sales by federally licensed dealers to be directed through the national background check system before being approved.

Investing in Congressional candidates to maintain a favorable legal environment for further high-return litigation is partly historical and partly a long-term game plan. The legal profession received billions of dollars in contingency fees from the tobacco litigation of the 1990s, in which manufacturers were held liable for the deliberate actions of consumers. One Texas attorney was awarded $260 million for his part in the tobacco settlement in 1999.[24] A study by the Cato Institute found that:

> Private attorneys in Texas, Mississippi and Florida made out like bandits, fleecing tobacco companies, smokers and taxpayers for $8.2 billion in legal fees – billions more than the lawyers themselves had demanded![25]

After the tobacco settlement, lawyers and law firms more than tripled the amount of total political contributions to federal candidates and political parties, from $59 million in 1998 election cycle to over $184 million in 2004. Considering that "soft money" contributions were banned in 2004 by the Bipartisan Campaign Finance Reform Act following the 2002 elections, the 2004 figure is even more compelling.[26]

What happened to the rest of tobacco settlement money will be most interesting to those of us who work hard, only to see a sizable amount of our efforts drained off as taxes. In California, state legislators grabbed the first $562 million installment for the settlement payment, placing it in the general fund and thwarting those who wanted the money to directly fund public health programs. In fairness, the legislature intended to fund state public health programs via government spending increases for health and human services.[27]

In 2002-3, nearly $1 billion of the Texas settlement went to health and human services, including education and enforcement programs requiring more bureaucrats, buildings and maintenance, and even debt service on capital improvement bonds for one hospital. Another $90 million went for higher education programs such as nursing.[28]

These expenditures may actually be what the people of those states wanted. However, the point here is the behavior of state governments in directing this money to projects involving government programs and institutions. The Shorter Oxford English Dictionary defines the word "tax" as: "A contribution to State revenue, compulsorily levied on people, businesses, property, income, commodities, transactions, etc."[29] In this case, state governments imposed a form of eminent domain on the money, effectively turning the tobacco settlement into a compulsory levy.

The financial damages were not exactly punitive to the tobacco companies: You may be unpleasantly surprised to learn where the settlement money is coming from. Tobacco companies are often part of conglomerates, allowing them to raise prices on products unrelated to smoking in order to pay the settlement. For example, Phillip Morris, one of the tobacco companies involved in the settlement, is owned by Altria Group,[30] which also owns Kraft Foods.[31] Settlement payments thus become part of Altria's liabilities on their balance sheet. In 2002, under "Liabilities: Consumer Products, Accrued liabilities" is a line item entitled "Settlement charges" which cost Altria over $3 billion annually for 2001 and 2002.[32]

R.J. Reynolds owns a subsidiary called RJR Packaging, which produces packaging used on many food products for both human and pet consumption.[33] They also produce packaging for many medical devices and over-the-counter medications, as well as personal care, coffee, and confectionary products.[34]

In order to remain in business, a company must be profitable. In order to remain profitable in the face of extensive, long-term compulsory levies by state governments via the tobacco settlement, the costs of products must go up so that income remains higher than expenses. Thus, Altria can raise prices on their Kraft food products you buy in order to pay off their tobacco settlement. R.J. Reynolds can pass along the cost by raising packaging costs for manufacturers of many different types of consumer products, who pass the increased production costs along to you.

As for the future of this type of litigation, it may seem that going after a relatively small industry would give the lie to any accusation that lawyers are only in it for the money. Surely they have public safety in mind and are just being good corporate citizens, right? In human affairs, things do not always progress in a simple, linear fashion. In the legal field, part of how new cases are decided is based upon "case law," what the Law Encyclopedia defines as: "Law established by previous decisions of appellate courts, particularly the United States Supreme Court."[35] Thus, any judgments that are accepted by a higher court can be compelling reasons to find for plaintiffs in future cases. Because of their politically incorrect products, firearms manufacturers may be the perfect set-up for the longer-term goal of creating case law that justifies suing manufacturers for the misuse of their non-defective products. The fact that the firearms industry does not enjoy the deep pockets of tobacco companies to fund expensive litigation and judgments is largely irrelevant. Once proper case law exists, lawyers can go after juicier targets such as automobile or clothing manufactures. After all, criminals can wear Levis and Nikes and use Chevrolets as getaway vehicles after robbing a bank. These companies know this is true, yet they continue to manufacture their products in sufficient quantities that some fall into the hands of criminals. Why not sue them for the criminal misuse of their products if it was allowable for firearms manufacturers?

Such a hypothesis is not so far-fetched. This is why the U.S. Chamber of Commerce supported tort reform for the firearms industry. In a letter to Congress, R. Bruce Josten, Executive Vice President of Government Affairs for the Chamber, said:

> The U.S. Chamber is greatly concerned about the growing trend of litigation being filed against entire legal industries with the goal of either raising government revenue or achieving policy goals outside the constraints of the political process. This dangerous trend began in the state lawsuits against the tobacco industry to recover Medicaid funds and, as the Chamber predicted, has now spread to other industries – including the firearm industry.[36]

John Engler, President and CEO of The National Association of Manufacturers, had this to say in his letter to the full House:

The NAM normally does not take a position on industry-specific legislation, and it does not have a position on the desirability of laws and regulations limiting or expanding the use of firearms. The NAM is concerned, however, about "regulation through litigation," whereby courts are misused to impose public policy objectives that are best left to the legislative and executive branches working in a transparent, democratic process.[37]

Both organizations understand that using the courts to create policy is not democratic, but it is clear from the tobacco litigation that once such policies are in place, they can be very profitable for lawyers filing suits under those policies, no matter the industry being targeted.

The tobacco settlement money went to lawyers and to governments, which effectively turned the money into a tax and then spent it on state bureaucracy. Regular folk did not receive any tax refund checks, nor did we see lower health insurance premiums, but we did pay more for everyday products not related to smoking. This means we are, in effect, paying billions of dollars in additional tax besides the billions in legal fees because of the tobacco settlement, as well as funding the next legal campaign to collect another large pay-day in contingency fees. It is very interesting to note during the tobacco suit that, while claiming various individuals were being victimized, or medical costs were mounting from misleading advertising or dishonest business practices, it was lawyers and governments, not the people nor their insurance companies, that collected all the loot. This the type of litigation did nothing to improve your life and it raised your cost of living.

Politicians Who Support Firearms Lawsuits

Senator Charles Schumer of New York has gone on record as supporting restrictive gun control laws such as the "assault weapons" ban. He believes President Bush is pandering to the National Rifle Association:

Unless the President personally intervenes here, it looks like terrorists are going to have an even easier time avoiding detection by law enforcement. The President has a choice: He can give the NRA a Christmas present and make it easier for an Al-Qaeda operative to avoid the police, get a gun and shoot up a mall.[38]

Senator Schumer is the 7th highest Senate recipient of donations from law firms, receiving $1,207,868 during his 2004 re-election cycle.[39] Through 2006, he received $2,363,373 from lawyers.[40]

Senator John Kerry received over $22.4 million from law firms during his presidential campaign in 2004, the most of any candidate running for any office.[41] This does not include the $1.4 million that law firms contributed to his successful 2002 senate race.[42] Senator Kerry believes: "Terrorists can now come to America, go to a gun show and, without a background check, buy an assault weapon."[43]

There has been, to date, no terrorist attack using "assault weapons" on U.S. soil. Furthermore, all firearms dealers who sell firearms in retail stores or at gun shows must perform background checks on prospective buyers, submitting personal information on the prospective buyer to the National Instant Criminal Background Check System to determine if the buyer has a criminal record that would preclude him from owning firearms.[44]

There is much confusion as to what an assault weapon really is. Most people think of automatic weapons, such as machine guns. Such firearms were outlawed for general civilian ownership in 1934. While it is theoretically possible for a civilian to own an automatic weapon, they must apply for a special license directly to the Bureau of Alcohol, Tobacco, and Firearms.[45] This entire process is simply too prohibitive for a terrorist, and would likely blow his cover during the background investigation process required for the ATF to approve his application. This is why no terrorist has used any automatic assault weapon purchased in the United States to date.

It also strains credulity that terrorists, who are primarily residents of the Middle East, would want to come to an American gun show to buy guns that are relatively useless as weapons of war, when they can buy all the military-grade weaponry they want near home. The country of Yemen sports a large arms bazaar where the discerning terrorist can buy whatever his heart desires:

At an arms bazaar outside Sanaa, an ambitious shopper could easily arm a militia group, or even a small army.

Machine guns, landmines, hand grenades, rocket launchers and a plethora of light firearms are spread out on blankets or sold in stalls.[46]

The Tamil Tigers, a group the U.S. considers a terrorist organization, and other groups are quite adept at purchasing everything they need without visiting an American gun show:

These are some of the weapons in the arsenal of the Tamil Tigers, the guerrilla army waging a war for an independent state on the island nation of Sri Lanka: surface-to-air missiles from Cambodia, assault rifles from Afghanistan, mortar shells from the former Yugoslavia and Zimbabwe, and 60 tons of explosives from Ukraine…

"The Tigers are on the cutting edge of arms trafficking," said Rohan Gunaratna, an authority on the Tigers who is at the Center for the Study of International Terrorism at St. Andrews University in Scotland.

Mr. Gunaratna, who has good access to Sri Lanka's intelligence services, said the Tamil Tigers have bought arms from dealers in Hong Kong, Singapore, Lebanon and Cyprus; from corrupt military officers in Thailand and Burma, and directly from governments, including Ukraine, Bulgaria and North Korea.

These are the same venues where other insurgencies and terrorist groups shop. Favorite arms bazaars are the states of the former Soviet bloc, like Ukraine, Bulgaria, Slovakia and

Kazakhstan, countries that are long on weapons and poorly paid officials, and short on cash and law enforcement. War zones gone quiet, like the former Yugoslavia, Cambodia, Afghanistan and Mozambique, are other places where arms traders look for wares.[47]

None of the aforementioned military-grade weapons are sold in American gun shops or gun shows. For a politician to imply that gun shows are shopping malls for terrorists, or that the NRA supports legislation that will arm terrorists, is ludicrous at best and dangerously misleading at worst.

Senator Barbara Boxer is the 6th highest recipient of donations from law firms, receiving $1,280,125 in 2004.[48] She has gone on record supporting gun control such as the "assault weapons" ban.[49] She also wants all guns to be sold with trigger locks.[50]

Senator Hillary Clinton is the 12th highest recipient of donations from law firms, receiving $686,975 in 2004.[51] Through 2006, she received $4,167,226 from lawyers.[52] She supports many forms of gun control, such as licensing all gun owners and registering all handgun sales in a national registry. Senator Clinton believes that children and guns do not mix. She told the National Education Association:

> We have to do everything possible to keep guns out of the hands of children, and we need to stand firm on behalf of the sensible gun control legislation that passed the Senate and then was watered down in the House. It does not make sense for us at this point in our history to turn our backs on the reality that there are too many guns and too many children have access to those guns — and we have to act to prevent that.[53]

As noted in Chapter 2, Australia severely restricts gun ownership and has a licensing system in place, yet rates of rape and other violent crimes are higher since these laws went into effect. Once again, gun control measures touted as crime-fighting tools — in this case, licensing — do not work.

All four senators, considered Democratic leaders in the Senate, voted against the Lawful Protection of Firearms Act in 2004,[54] even though it had been amended to include a renewal of the 1994 assault weapons ban and to require child safety locks for all handguns being sold.[55] Both of these amendments were priorities for the senators. Thus, it was more important to them to defeat the tort reform law than it was to get their pet gun control legislation passed as amendments to the bill.

It is very interesting to note that the United States Senate has a Sergeant at Arms who is "charged with maintaining security in the Capitol and all Senate buildings, as well as protection of the members themselves."[56] It is also most curious that women senators would promote legislation that places American women — who have no access to such a private security detail — at risk.

A Timeout for the Children

We are going to take a little break in our discussion of tort reform to highlight another gun control gambit employed by politicians who seek to use heart-breaking tragedy to promote legislation of dubious value, while concealing their greater agenda to enact laws which benefit their financial sponsors. Senators Boxer and Clinton both proclaim a desire to make children safe from guns. However, what they really do is manipulate or manufacture "statistics" to scare parents into supporting gun control. In her "Kids Corner," Senator Boxer writes that she believes child safety locks on every handgun would reduce crime.[57]

During the 2004 firearms manufacturers' tort reform bill debate, Senator Boxer co-sponsored an amendment to require safety locks on all handguns sold in the United States, in order to "help stop children from accidentally shooting themselves with handguns they find inside the home." Senator Boxer's claims were referenced in an article:

> "If we were to pass this legislation and it become the law of the land, the number of children involved in the number of accidental shootings would go way down," said Boxer, who cited FBI statistics showing a child killed by a firearm every three hours.[58]

How does Senator Boxer arrive at 8 "children" killed daily? Before we descend on Washington D.C. to demand a halt to civilian firearms ownership, it would be prudent to study the actual statistical record.

Citing 2003 FBI statistics available on the Internet — the latest data available at the time of Senator Boxer's speech — it is impossible to determine where the estimate of eight children per day comes from. The FBI determined there were 599 firearm murder victims in 2003 under the age of 18, an average of 1.6 per day. They do note that 2,330 people under the age of 22 were murdered in 2003, an average of 6.4 per day, and that the total firearms deaths up to age 24 is 3,751, or 10.3 per day. The FBI does not count suicide or accidental deaths in this report, so this source does not appear to be the basis for Senator Boxer's estimate.[59] Using data from the Centers for Disease Control, we find that in 2003 there were 2,849 firearm deaths for persons ages zero to 19, including murder, suicide, legal intervention, accidents, and undetermined intent. This total averages out to 7.8 deaths each day, close to her estimate.[60] But this does not have any bearing on her desire to reduce accidental shootings, because legal intervention, murder, and suicide are not accidental. There are also some basic conceptual problems regarding her claims.

First, let us clarify what a child is. The Supreme Court defines an adult to be age 18 or older. In a recent decision, the Court abolished capital punishment for juvenile offenders, considered to be under 18.[61] Already, Senator Boxer includes at least one year of invalid mortality data. If we reduce the age range at the CDC web site by that one year, we end up with a total of 2,018 shooting deaths, or 5.5 per day, for all causes.[62] Oxford English Dictionary defines the word "childhood" as: "The state or stage of life as a child...the time from birth to puberty."[63] Oxford defines "puberty" as: "The period during which adolescents reach sexual maturity and become capable of reproduction, distinguished by the appearance of secondary sexual characteristics."[64] In terms of age, there seems to be general agreement that this ability to procreate occurs by the age of 15.[65] Thus, true children are ages 0-14. Comparing Boxer's definition of children to the accepted standard, we see there was an average of slightly more than one child killed with a firearm daily.[66] This is still a tragedy, but Boxer's mathematical and/or ethical standards must be called into question for making an eight-fold statistical error in order to promote her gun control agenda. She greatly inflates her figures in order to make it sound more tragic, using statistically invalid public statements to instill fear in a trusting but insufficiently informed populace.

Second, Senator Boxer's "belief" that her trigger lock law would reduce firearms accidents and crime is not supported by available research. In *Firearms and Violence, A Critical Review*, a research council of the National Academy of Sciences studied laws requiring safety locks or otherwise aimed at reducing children's access to firearms. They concluded that it was impossible to know if such laws helped:

In general, we find that the scientific bases for understanding the impact of different technologies on the rates of injury is sorely lacking. The existing research outlines a number of interesting hypotheses, but, in the end, the extent to which different technologies affect injury remains unknown.[67]

From 2000-2002, the CDC studied child access laws, which require the owner to store the gun locked and/or unloaded, to determine their effectiveness for preventing violence. The CDC could not conclude that child access laws had any significant impact one way or another.[68] John Lott compared the rate of accidental firearm deaths in states with safe storage laws to those without such laws. He found that while the rate was lower in the safe storage states, they already had lower accidental death rates prior to the laws being enacted, indicating that residents of those states may already have been more safety conscious of their own volition. The result was no significant improvement in safety.[69]

Third, suicide is not related to the availability of guns. Lott also compared suicide rates between states with safe storage laws to states without such laws. Again, he found that states with safe storage laws began with lower rates of suicide and ended with similar rates, resulting in no significant improvement of suicide rates due to safe storage laws. More important, he found that non-gun suicides increased over a four-year period following enactment of safe-storage firearm laws.[70] It would appear that those intent on self-inflicted harm simply found another means.

Nation Master rates the U.S. 27th overall in suicide, below many countries with far greater restrictions on civilian firearms ownership, such as Japan and Australia.[71] Greenwood collated information from a 1997 United Nations report and found no positive correlation between gun ownership and higher levels homicide or suicide. He found that many emerging eastern European countries have relatively low levels of gun ownership and high levels of suicide: Belarus, Czech Republic, Estonia, Hungary, Poland, and Slovakia. Other countries with similar rates of low gun ownership and high suicide include Singapore, Trinidad and Tobago, and the United Kingdom.[72] Suicide appears to be a cross-cultural phenomenon that is a far more complex issue than whether a gun is available or not. If we exclude suicides, we arrive at 306 children — less than one each day — dying in 2003 due to gunshot-related violence and accidents.

Fourth, it is questionable whether most homicides should be included. Children, being smaller, more trusting, and less physically able to run away or defend themselves, can be killed by many other means. All it takes is a determined larger person. Greenwood also found no relationship between homicide and levels of gun ownership: The same U.N. study showed that ten of the 33 countries surveyed had low rates of firearms ownership and high rates of homicide; another eight countries had relatively high rates of firearms ownership and low homicide rates.[73] In 2003, the FBI noted that out of 9,638 firearms murders, 797 were committed by juvenile gangs, another 2,477 were committed during arguments, and another 90 during brawls while under the influence of drugs or alcohol.[74] While it does not break out the data by age, the FBI reports that 268 sons and 193 daughters were murder victims of the offenders, with 71 of them killed during arguments.[75] Therefore, firearms deaths that theoretically might have been prevented by gun control laws are likely much closer to the number of accidental shootings. This reduces the average to 0.15 children per day.

Fifth, we must put gun-related deaths into a contextual perspective: Without analyzing these numbers in relation to other mortality rates, and without looking at firearms mortality trends, we will rush to erroneous conclusions. The CDC rates firearm homicide as the sixth leading cause of death in children, after unintentional motor vehicle traffic, suffocation, drowning, unspecified homicidal causes, and unintentional fire fatalities. Children were 9.2 times more likely to die in a traffic accident, 3.7 times more likely to die from suffocation, 3.3 times more likely to drown, and 16% more likely to die from burns than they were to be murdered by a criminal using a firearm.[76] If we use the same ratio of drunk driver fatalities to overall fatalities from Chapter 3, we can estimate that drunk drivers account for about 943 of the child traffic fatalities, over four times the rate of firearm homicides, which explains why vehicular manslaughter is considered a felony when committed by a drunk driver.[77]

The U.S. Health and Human Services estimates that in 2004, 1,490 children died as a result of abuse and neglect, with more than 80% younger than four years old, and 97% younger than 12.[78] Since this report includes dependents up to 17, we will halve the 3% of the 12-17 age range. This brings the estimated total of abuse fatalities for children ages 0-14 to around 1,468, or 4 per day, 6.5 times the rate of firearm homicides in 2004 (226).[79] The report states that 79% of the perpetrators were parents.[80]

Sixth, let us examine the value of education in reducing the number of preventable deaths from firearms accidents. The NRA program called Eddie Eagle has taught gun safety to children since 1988.[81] In conjunction with the focus on safety discussed in Chapter 3, we can begin to determine if safety education has impacted rates of accidental shootings. Examining the 1990-2004 trend in various unintentional causes of death for children under 15 we see that while there has been a significant decrease in the motor vehicle death rate for children, it has dropped less than half as much as the rate of fatal firearm accidents. Poisoning deaths decreased at a similar rate to motor vehicles, accidental drowning deaths decreased a bit faster, and accidental suffocation rates actually increased. The fatal firearms accident rate for children decreased 77.3%.[82]

During the same time period, accidental shooting deaths for all ages dropped 61.4%.[83] Between 1990 and 2004, accidental shooting deaths for children fell even faster than the rate for the general population. Keep in mind that during this period, the ATF estimates that an average of 4.5 million new firearms were sold each year.[84] It would seem that Senator Boxer is making dubious claims regarding her safety lock legislation, as "the number of accidental shootings" has already been going "way down."

Lott studied cases where children under age ten accidentally shot another child under ten. He found that these incidents were extremely rare:

> Of the fifty-six accidental gun deaths involving children under ten in 1998 and the thirty-one in 1999, only eight and six, respectively, were shot by another child or themselves. The same statistic for 1997 was only five.[85]

The CDC notes that in 1990, there were 90 accidental gun deaths for children under age ten, 0.24 per 100,000 children.[86] This fell to 28 in 2004, a rate of 0.07, representing a rate drop of over two-thirds. Either safety education or voluntary safety measures, or some combination of both, has already created a much safer environment for children around guns.

Each child's death, no matter the cause, is a tragic event, and a reasonable person would want to avert it if at all possible. However, Senator Clinton's claim that we need to "keep guns out of the hands of children" and Senator Boxer's concern that eight children are being slaughtered daily seem superfluous or misleading. If they truly want to create the biggest influence on preventing unnecessary deaths among children, their efforts would be more productive by pressing for more safety regulation for users of household chemicals, swimming pools, plastic bags, and training for prospective parents and automobile drivers.

Nor should we ignore the beneficial results when children are trained to properly respect and handle firearms, and that children's lives may be saved by firearms. In the fall of 2006, the *Corpus Christi Caller-Times* reported on such an incident:

A 57-year-old man who was shot and killed by his 14-year-old hostage Monday at a home on Ocean Drive had been released from jail Friday and had committed several other burglaries, including a similar home invasion, according to police and court records.

Capt. John Houston said the man, who police identified through fingerprinting Tuesday as James Slaughter, had been involved in criminal activities since 1967 and was in and out of the prison system on several occasions.

"His (method of operation) was to break into homes. If someone was there, he'd tie them up," Houston said.

Police reported that when the boy and his mother arrived home after she picked him up from school, they were confronted by Slaughter, who threatened to kill her with his knife. He took them both upstairs to the master bedroom, and bound them both. After freeing herself and her son, she retrieved her husband's revolver from a security box under the bed and gave it to her son. (Note that the firearm was secured from child access, according to Texas state law. Had the parent not been home and the boy was alone when Slaughter broke in, the outcome would have been different.) She then locked the bedroom doors. When Slaughter tried to force his way in, the boy "aimed the pistol at the space between the partially open doors and fired one shot..."

What is interesting is that Slaughter was sentenced to 45 years in prison in 1984 for a previous break-in. In that incident, police "were forced to shoot him twice when he raised a rifle and pointed it at them." He was paroled in 2000 and then arrested again in June for violating his parole and sent back to jail, but this habitual criminal was again released.

Local residents at the nearby H-E-B on Alameda Street and Robert Drive commended the teenager for his actions.

"I would have done the same thing. I'm glad (Slaughter) won't be able to do it again," said Tanya Brandon, the mother of a 6-year-old girl. "He was protecting his family."

Yvette Contreras, who lives on Grossman Drive, said the recent burglary has made her reconsider keeping a gun in her home.

"They probably would have been killed if he hadn't shot him," Contreras said. "Nowadays, it seems like it's happening everywhere."[87]

A grand jury Thursday [the same week as the incident] decided a 14-year-old boy who shot and killed an intruder in his home Monday acted in self-defense and no charges were necessary.

"I guess, as far as we're concerned, this was a completely justified shooting," said District Attorney Carlos Valdez.

Valdez said details of the Ocean Drive shooting were presented to the grand jury for consideration in the same manner as any other case, which ensured fairness.

"Any time there's a shooting involving the death of one citizen at the hands of another it is our policy to present it to the grand jury," he said.[88]

If it saves one life, it's worth it, right?

Tort Reform – Truth or Fiction?

Whether trying to mislead the public about children and guns, or trying to sell the public on the need to sue firearms manufacturers, there is a distinct lack of fact-checking and editorial standards. It would be helpful to compare some of the public statements about tort reform to the Congressional Record to determine the statement's veracity. The *Los Angeles Times* ran an editorial entitled "Remember Gun Control", which discussed what it called a firearms manufacturers' "immunity bill":

[G]un owners can't sue if poorly made handguns explode in their hands or fire unintentionally. In many instances, the bill would shield gun dealers who allow criminals to buy a firearm, by severely weakening the ATF's ability to shut down unscrupulous dealers.[89]

The Brady Campaign also took issue with the proposed legislation. A form letter which they urged people to send to congressional representatives discussed three cases where negligence on the part of dealers was a factor in the criminal use of firearms.[90]

Brady had another press release on the legislation which also included examples of alleged criminal behavior and negligence on the part of persons involved in the firearms industry. It then quoted bereaved parents who were afraid they would not receive justice because they believed the tort reform bill gave blanket immunity to the industry.[91]

The *Protection of Lawful Commerce in Arms Act* (Senate Bill 397) represented the final version of the legislation. While civil liability suits are banned due to injuries and damages resulting from strictly criminal abuse, the bill specifically stated that litigation could proceed where:

- damages have resulted from unlawful firearms transfers;
- an action is brought against a seller for negligence;

- a manufacturer or retailer knowingly violated a State or Federal statute applicable to the sale or marketing of the product;

- there is breach of contract or warranty;

- death, physical injuries or property damage resulted directly from a defect in design or manufacture of the product, except where a criminal offense was determined to be the cause.[92]

The Brady Campaign misrepresentation was self-serving: They started an organization called the Legal Action Project, which has spearheaded a campaign of litigation against gun manufacturers. The Brady Campaign has invested much money, personnel, and political capital in holding the industry accountable for the actions of criminals.[93] When the Senate's version of the tort reform bill passed, Michael Barnes, then President of the Brady Campaign, was quoted as saying: "This is a day in America when the little guy lost out to powerful special interests."[94]

This is a very curious statement from someone we should know more about before we accept his claim of representing the "little guy." Michael Barnes is a Washington insider, having been a congressman from 1979-1987. As a lawyer, he has had an association with the Washington, D.C. law firm of Hogan & Hartson.[95] Hogan and Hartson donated $615,748 during the 2004 election cycle.[96] As a member of the Washington Lawyers' Committee for Civil Rights and Urban Affairs, Hogan & Hartson supports the Committee's filing of *District of Columbia, et al. v. Beretta U.S.A. Corp., et al.* which "contends that gun manufacturers should be liable for negligently permitting — through illegal sales and distribution channels — guns to illegally enter the District." Through this association, Hogan & Hartson supports the idea that manufacturers are responsible for criminals importing and using guns illegally. The Center to Prevent Handgun Violence, part of the Mr. Barnes's Brady Campaign, is a co-counsel on this case.[97]

Getting back to the $184 million in campaign contributions in 2004, a perusal of those who voted "Nay" (against reform) on the tort reform bill is a Who's Who of senators who received this campaign money.

The 31 senators who voted "Nay" received nearly as much law firm money ($20,025,128) as the 65 who voted "Yea" ($23,845,052). The 65 "Yea" voters received an average of $366,847 per senator, while the 31 "Nay" voters received $645,972 per Senator, 73.4% more.

For 31% of those who voted "Yea," lawyers were the number one industry contributor, while among those who voted "Nay," lawyers were number one for 74%. For those voting in favor of tort reform, in terms of the biggest contributor, lawyers' average ranking was 3.4 (between the third and fourth largest donor industry). For those who voted against tort reform, lawyers averaged 1.4.[98] Of the "Nay" voters, 93.5% were Democrat.[99]

Those senators voting against tort reform are clearly more influenced by campaign contributions from lawyers. Thus, we have a series of direct links between Michael Barnes and a gun control organization, the heavily-vested interests of wealthy law firms, and anti-gun politicians, all interested in maintaining these frivolous liability suits for financial reasons.

Mr. Barnes complains of "powerful special interests" having undue influence on the decision-making processes in Congress. In a sense, he is absolutely correct. In 2002, there were about 695,000 lawyers in the United States.[100] Their campaign contributions for that year's election cycle was $95,478,421, or $137 per lawyer.[101] During the same cycle, the National Rifle Association contributed $2,027,889.[102] Since the NRA had about 3 million members,[103] this averages out to 68 cents per member. Rather than avail themselves of readily-available monetary wealth to influence votes, the organization practices the democratic undertaking of voter activism:

As former Clinton spokesman George Stephanopoulos said, "Let me make one small vote for the NRA. They're good citizens. They call their Congressmen. They write. They vote. They contribute. And they get what they want over time."[104]

While lawyers contributed their $184 million during the 2004 election cycle, the NRA's contributions dropped to $1,151,130,[105] or about 38 cents per member. According to Mr. Barnes's criteria, this is "powerful special interests," but 700,000 lawyers, donating about $260 each, is not.

Baron & Budd, supporter of gun manufacturer liability lawsuits like the Beretta case mentioned above, contributed $1,269,222 during the 2004 election cycle, more than the entire NRA, and they are only the third-highest law firm contributor. Ninety-seven percent of their campaign contributions went to Democrats.[106] Since Baron & Budd employs "over 80 attorneys,"[107] this averages out to about $15,000 in campaign contributions per attorney. According to Mr. Barnes, this level of contribution by lawyers, seeking to maintain a favorable legal environment for potentially valuable tort litigation, merely symbolizes "the little guys" trying to fend off special interest manipulation in Congress.

Senate Bill 397 as written seems like reasonable tort reform: A model that can be applied to any product, regardless of one's opinions of the product in question. For example, in July, 2003, an 86-year-old man drove his car through a crowded farmers' market in Santa Monica, killing 10 people, including a seven-month-old baby.[108] In the rush of litigation following the tragedy, eleven lawsuits were filed against the driver and the city of Santa Monica, seeking damages for two of the people killed and nine of those injured.[109] There was no reported litigation against the auto manufacturer. According to the Brady Campaign criteria, had the man been wielding a gun with equally irresponsible or incompetent recklessness, a lawsuit against the manufacturer would have been desirable.

Of more concern is the fact that many of the law suits against gun manufacturers are initiated by government entities, meaning that resources and tax money which could be spent on criminal justice are instead funding legal activities of dubious benefit to tax payers, much like tobacco litigation.

In his testimony before the House Subcommittee on Commercial and Administrative Law, Lawrence G. Keane of the National Shooting Sports Foundation stated:

> The shuttering of the firearm industry will hit states—especially rural states—especially hard. Each year hunters and shooters spend $21 billion generating 366,344 jobs that pay more than $8,896,623,900 in salaries and wages and provide $1,223,049,215 in state tax revenue.[110]

He also said: "The firearm industry taken together would not equal a Fortune 500 company."[111] The costs of tort litigation risks the entire industry, and risks closing a major source of our military and law enforcement firearms.

Tort Reform in the House – Confirming the Senate Findings

On October 20, 2005, the House of Representatives passed Senate Bill 397, and President Bush signed it into law on October 26, 2005. To be fair, the financially-induced voting preferences in the Senate might be an aberration, so we should look at campaign contributions in the House to see if lawyers were trying to buy favors there as well.

Of the 283 representatives who voted "Yea" on the bill, 14 either received no money from lawyers, or received so little that the amounts were not listed in the representative's top 20 industry donor lists, making it impossible to determine exact contribution amounts on the Open Secrets web site. Of the remaining 269 representatives, lawyers contributed $13,305,711, or an average of $49,464 apiece. Of the 144 who voted "Nay" (against tort reform) only one received little or no campaign contributions from lawyers. The remaining 143 received $10,688,135, or an average of $74,742 apiece, 51% higher than those voting for tort reform. For those voting in favor of tort reform, lawyers averaged between the 6th and 7th biggest donor industry. For those voting against tort reform, lawyers averaged the 3rd largest donor industry. Similar to the Senate vote, over 97% of the "Nay" voters were Democrats.[112] The big-money bias we found in the Senate replicated itself in the House: more law firm money, more support for continued lawsuits against gun manufacturers when a criminal shoots somebody.

The Missing Link In Tort Cases

If you still doubt that firearms litigation is motivated by the same greed involved in the tobacco suits, a 2005 editorial by Senator Mark Dayton of Minnesota provides the necessary connection. He claimed firearms and tobacco are "the only two consumer products to be exempted from federal Consumer Product Safety laws and regulations." He continues with his linking of the two industries:

> How the manufacturers and sellers of two inherently dangerous products, guns and tobacco, were given the only two exceptions from our country's product safety requirements is incomprehensible and indefensible. It demonstrates, however, their extraordinary political and financial powers over a majority of members of Congress.[113]

Lawyers were Senator Dayton's second biggest industry contributor in his 2000 election race,[114] so he surely understands the "disgraceful disregard for the public interest in order to serve the demands of a powerful special interest."[115] Nevertheless, in his public display of sour grapes, he has tipped the hand of the powerful special interest lobby of the law firms who planned to do with the firearms industry what they accomplished with the tobacco industry: make money in contingency fees while creating additional legal precedent showing that the manufacturer of any product is liable for the criminal use of that product. This prepares the ground for yet another cycle of litigation as lawyers set their sights on the next target, and the next, all while enriching themselves, which in turn gives them additional seed money to buy more influence in Washington, D.C. No wonder they spend so much money on campaign contributions!

The Trend Continues

Between 2001 and 2006, the latest Senate election cycle, lawyers contributed over $403 million dollars to federal elections, while gun rights organizations contributed just over $5 million, or 1.3% the amount spent by lawyers.[116,117] Over $295 million of the attorney money landed in senatorial coffers, with 73.2% of it going to Democrats.[118] It should be no surprise that Democrats averaged over 2.3 times the amount of lawyer contributions received by Republican senators or that Democrats continue to be the primary source of anti-gun votes.

It is also interesting to note that when separated by right-to-carry (RTC) status, senators from non-RTC states averaged 84% more in lawyer contributions than senators from RTC states, and all 20 non-RTC senators are Democrats.[119]

Between 2005 and 2006, the latest House election cycle, lawyers contributed over $121 million dollars to federal elections,[120] while gun rights organizations contributed about $1.3 million, or 1% the amount spent by lawyers.[121] Nearly $30 million of the attorney money went to representatives' campaign funds. Democrats received an average of 80% more lawyer contributions than Republicans.[122]

Registration Leads to Confiscation

> The Conventions of a number of the States having, at the time of adopting the Constitution, expressed a desire, in order to prevent misconstruction or abuse of its powers, that further declaratory and restrictive clauses should be added, and as extending

the ground of public confidence in the Government will best insure the beneficent ends of its institution...

Congress shall make no law respecting an establishment of religion, or prohibiting the free exercise thereof; or abridging the freedom of speech, or of the press; or the right of the people peaceably to assemble, and **to petition the government for a redress of grievances**.[123] [Emphasis added]

The 110th Congress's attempt in early 2007 "to provide greater transparency in the legislative process" was a laudable concept, but the Senate proposal went beyond the legislative process to include some social engineering which would have gutted your First Amendment rights.

They wanted to identify and regulate what they called "paid efforts to stimulate grassroots lobbying." Anybody making a "paid attempt to influence the general public " to lobby members of Congress "on behalf of a client" would have to register with the federal government and file regular reports. "Clients" could be any organization you belong to, such as the NRA, Sierra Club, or Joe's Tax Reform Committee (fictional to make a point). Exceptions to this rule would "include any communications by an entity directed to its members, employees, officers, or shareholders." In other words, a large corporation could ask employees to call representatives to vote on favorable legislation, or instigate campaign contribution programs, without requiring registration.

Anybody influencing over 499 "members of the general public" would have to register. A registrant would include anybody who "pays dues or makes a contribution of more than a nominal amount to the entity" or "makes a contribution of more than a nominal amount of time to the entity." No definition was given as to what constitutes "nominal".[124]

The American Civil Liberties Union was quick to point out the smothering effect this legislation would have on the First Amendment:

Section 220, entitled "Disclosure of Paid Efforts to Stimulate Grassroots Lobbying" imposes onerous reporting requirements that will chill constitutionally protected activity. Advocacy organizations large and small would now find their communications to the general public about policy matters redefined as lobbying and therefore subject to registration and quarterly reporting. Failure to register and report could have severe civil and potentially criminal sanctions. Section 220 would apply to even small, state grassroots organizations with no lobbying presence in Washington. When faced with burdensome registration and reporting requirements, some of these organizations may well decide that silence is the best option.[125]

Fortunately, a successful vote removed this section. It is that amendment vote which is the rest of the story.

The examples above appear to be mere preludes to what we might expect in the next Congress: Those voting to retain the anti-First Amendment language garnered

228% more lawyer money (more than double). It is also interesting to note that all 43 votes to retain were from 41 Democrats and the two Vermont senators officially listed as independent but who caucus with the Democrats. Of senators representing non-RTC states, 19 of 20 voted to retain the restrictive language. It is even more interesting that, contrary to popular belief, this vote shows that Democrats will support legislation that benefits corporate interests because of the included exception in this proposed law.

What's more troubling is that while Democrat senators received 73.4% more lawyer contributions than Republicans as of the tort vote in 2005, this differential more than tripled as of this vote. The average lawyer contribution to Democrat senators rose 68.7% from $617,792 in 2005 to $1,042,300 in 2006, while Republican contributions rose 20.1% from an average of $331,108 to $397,615.[126]

What's in it For Them?

Return on investment (ROI) is the term used to calculate the ratio of gain compared to the money spent to attain it.[127] Registration schemes transform law-abiding citizens into criminals, creating more opportunities for litigation. If you spent more than six hours researching an op/ed that gets published, is that "nominal"? By turning a right into a licensable privilege, the government can prosecute you while "nominal" gets defined by lawyers for both sides, all because you published an op/ed resulting in 500+ readers contacting their federal representatives (many of whom are also lawyers). And who determines how many people you "attempt to influence"? Do they go by a newspaper's circulation? The number of unique visitors to the web page? In order to do the latter, this will entail more government surveillance of the internet to keep track of page hits. Once this law was in place, its existence would self-justify the federal government's reducing the threshold to 50 "members of the general public" when it decides there needs to be even "greater transparency in the legislative process." Besides more work for lawyers, this process requires ever-more regulation to identify criteria and monitor them: government pre-conditioning grassroots, First-Amendment activity to justify more government.

As seen with the tobacco litigation, tort cases enable lawyers to transfer vast amounts of wealth, via contingency fees, into their own pockets. This wealth was initially created by production and labor, so tort cases are essentially like draining blood out of the body of the economy. As a result, a massive power shift occurs in favor of the 700,000 or so lawyers in our country, effectively moving them towards becoming an elite class of nobility.

Can you afford the time and resources to properly register yourself as a "paid lobbyist" when you write an article or give a public talk? The proposed legislation would have created an increasingly insurmountable threshold the average citizen must reach in order to keep the channels open so they may "petition the government for a redress of grievances." Unless, of course, you can afford to contribute enough to a powerful lobby in order to influence congressional votes.

Like a Bad Horror Movie...

For those who thought tort reform was a settled issue, it may be so in Congress, but it will remain a bone of contention between municipalities and firearms manufacturers for at least the near future.

A recent federal court ruling enabled continuation of a suit brought by New York City against gun manufacturers. According to the new federal law, litigation may proceed if a "manufacturer or seller of a qualified product knowingly violated a State or Federal statute applicable to the sale or marketing of the product, and the violation was a proximate cause of the harm for which relief is sought."[128] In this case, NYC has a nuisance law which they claim falls into this exception. The federal judge hearing arguments on whether the case could proceed concurred with the city.[129]

This opens a door where any municipality can craft a statute that states if anybody gets shot by a firearm, this is a public nuisance. If the manufacturer continues to sell firearms after enactment of the law, this means the gun maker continued to sell with full knowledge that the state or city considered such sales to be a public nuisance, and therefore the municipality's lawsuit falls under the exception within the national law. What can end up happening is that there will be even more lawsuits with different language to make the suits acceptable under the new law. The dynamics set in motion by all the wealthy lawyers remain in effect, and they may yet see their $780 million (1990-2006) return on investment.[130]

Conclusion

Anti-gun politicians and gun control organizations mistakenly claim that tort reform gives firearms manufacturers special immunity. If criminal misuse of a product becomes the legal standard for suing a manufacturer, then why not initiate lawsuits against auto makers for the car used in a drive-by shooting? Why not sue a sportswear manufacturer for the warm-up suits in vogue with drug gangs who cause so much death and destruction with their turf wars? It seems that the only special privilege trying to be protected here is the ability for trial lawyers to enrich themselves at gun makers' and our expense.

Chapter 5
The Information Machines of Gun Control

For every political goal, there are groups that commit to their desired outcome, regardless of how it may impact society in general. Rather than reporting factual information in an accurate and comprehensive manner, they pick and choose what they put into their publications in order to convince people to support agendas which often end up benefiting an elite few. This has been our political reality since the time of the early republic.

For example, during Washington's second term as president, numerous domestic issues, plus the French Revolution and ongoing tensions with England, all fomented a growing difference of opinion as to their resolution. This resulted in the first manifestation of partisan politics, and the opposing party wasted no time in using the press to promote their agenda, including allegations that Washington was incompetent enough to deserve impeachment.[1]

James Callender worked under Thomas Jefferson's employ to undermine the John Adams presidency by publishing lies and innuendo against the second president. This symbolized the developing power struggle between the Adams's Federalists and the early Republican (now Democrat) party, led by Jefferson, over the direction of the new republic and the use of power by its fledgling national government. When turned down for a postmaster job by now-President Jefferson, Callender swore revenge, switched sides, and began performing the same function against his former employer, to the benefit of the Federalists.[2]

History reveals that using biased reporting to endorse political views lacking factual basis is nothing new. Promoting an ideology, however slanted, brings more supporters into a camp, while allowing an educated reader to reach his own conclusions becomes more fraught with risk as a position or ideology becomes less factually tenable.

It should come as no surprise that reporting today remains biased as power becomes more important than considerations about what is best for the whole population, and the temptation to manipulate truth becomes greater than the average mortal can withstand. As we studied in Chapter 2, this can result in non-beneficial social and political policies. The media becomes a necessary and useful vehicle — often a willing accomplice — in enacting and perpetuating these policies by disseminating misinformation to the public. This allows politicians to put self-serving laws in place.

In this chapter, we will focus on the organizations which use the media for this purpose. John Lott has already documented in *The Bias Against Guns* how the media itself has chosen to participate in slanted coverage of firearms issues. However, the media could not persist in this bias unless they can reference "experts" to support the gun control agenda.

The editorial, *Remember Gun Control*, referenced in the previous chapter is but one example of a more pervasive problem. If a group pushes their agenda in a dishonest manner, would it not seem reasonable to investigate for yourself whether or not their goal can stand on its own merits? (Providing one is even privy to any neutral data on the issue, i.e., if you're alerted to the possible negative slant and can start digging for facts). Even if a group's goal seems desirable, this does not mean it is attainable. Also, should the end always justify the means? Especially when it's been tried before with no proven benefits?

Campaign Finance and Historical Revisionism

> "Historical revisionism"…describes the process that attempts to rewrite history by minimizing, denying or simply ignoring essential facts. Perpetrators of such attempts to distort the historical record often use the term because it allows them to cloak their illegitimate activities with a phrase which has a legitimate meaning.[3]

Chapter 4 examined how campaign contributions from lawyers has a curious correspondence with anti-gun-rights voting in Congress. This section examines how biased media uses narrowly-selected campaign finance data to convince the reader that the "gun lobby" has an undue influence in Congress because of its "overwhelming" campaign spending.

A recent article in *U.S. News & World Report* employs two common myths to explain why pro-gun groups allegedly wield too much political power:

> Saul Cornell of Ohio State's Second Amendment Research Center, says **polls consistently show broad support for gun control**. What gives the gun lobby strength, he says, is that supporters see gun control as a make-or-break issue. With that passion comes money. **Gun-rights groups contributed nearly 14 times as much as gun-control groups** in the 2004 election cycle, according to the Center for Responsive Politics.[4] [Emphasis added]

Professor Cornell chants the oft-repeated mantra: "polls consistently show broad support for gun control." A visit to his Second Amendment Research Center (SARC) web site shows it is a gun control organization. One of their main sponsors is the Joyce Foundation, which has a link on the SARC site.[5] At the Joyce Foundation site, selecting "Gun Violence" on their "Grant List" page displays a roster of Who's Who in gun control: Violence Policy Center, Mayors Fund to Advance New York City, Illinois Council Against Handgun Violence, etc. Joyce Foundation spent $6,650,865 on gun control research in 2005 and 2006.[6] By comparison, the entire gun rights industry contributed a total of $1,291,050 for the two-year 2006 election cycle.[7]

As noted in Chapter 3, opinion polls can be skewed by selecting small numbers of people to survey. Even when phrasing questions in an unbiased manner, sampling error leads to uncertainty over whether the results are an accurate reflection of reality.[8]

According to gun controllers, the reason that election results do not reflect this "broad support for gun control" is not because the majority of Americans believe in the individual right to keep and bear arms, but because the "gun lobby" buys more votes. Biased reporters repeat variations of the companion mantra: "Gun-rights groups contributed nearly 14 times as much as gun-control groups" to campaigns.

Open Secrets, source for the *U.S. News* article, notes that in 2004, gun control groups donated a total of $95,200,[9] while gun rights groups contributed $1,322,174,[10] nearly 14 times as much. So the gun controllers are telling the truth, as far as they choose to go with it. What they don't tell us is how much money was contributed by other organizations and individuals committed to promoting gun control.

First place among gun control contributors was an organization called *John Kerry for President*, which donated $38,563,933 in 2004. *Friends of John Kerry* chipped in another $1,004,000.[11] As noted in Chapter 4, John Kerry has consistently voted for gun control laws.

Emily's List (EL) is ostensibly an organization that supports "electing pro-choice Democratic women to federal, state, and local office."[12] A reference to gun control consists of praise for a candidate supported by EL who won the Missouri Secretary of State election despite being attacked for "her stance on gay marriage and gun control."[13] Another reference is for a male Florida candidate who is "rabidly anti-choice and says the only kind of gun control he favors is 'a steady hand.'"[14] Emily's List donated $3,401,250 in campaign contributions in 2004.[15]

"Friends of Schumer" donated $2,922,504 for Charles Schumer's reelection campaign. Schumer sponsored S. 645, the *Assault Weapons Ban and Law Enforcement Protection Act of 2005*, to reinstate the now-sunset 1994 ban on certain semi-automatic, non-military, firearms.[16]

George Soros's Open Society Institute openly promotes licensing of all U.S. firearms owners and gun registration.[17] Soros donated $23,450,000 to 527 committees in 2004.[18] In addition, the Soros family donated another $531,255 to candidates, Democrat PACs and committees, and 527s in 2004.[19]

Reginald Weaver, current president of The National Education Association, supports more gun control, having praised three top national gun control proponents for their legislative accomplishments:

Thank you Senator Kennedy, Representative McCarthy, and Mrs. [Sarah] Brady. The National Education Association (NEA) commends the sponsors and is proud to offer the support of its 2.4 million members for key provisions of the Children's Gun Violence Prevention Act. [20]

In 2004, the NEA contributed $1,921,597 to Democrats.[21]

At least the *U.S. News* article was honest enough to identify the intent of recent tort reform, while implying it's nothing more than special interest politics:

Meanwhile, with little fanfare, National Rifle Association backers in Congress allowed the assault weapons ban to expire in 2004 and last year shielded gun makers from being sued over crimes committed using their products.[22]

Tens of millions of dollars not on the Brady Campaign ledger were nevertheless wielded to support Brady's goals. In fairness, there are PACs and other organizations which support the right to keep and bear arms, even though this is not their primary mission. The point here is to highlight that as far as campaign finance is concerned, gun control is alive and well. Organizations may not be publicly identified as gun control proponents by the media, but appellations are transient: actions are all that matter.

The Wild West Theory

"Anytime you increase availability of firearms, you see corresponding increases in death and injury," said Thom Mannard, the executive director for the Illinois Coalition Against Handgun Violence.[23]

Increasing the number of weapons actively being handled, if only to be carried around, increases the chance for accidents. That is simple logic. That those weapons will be in places where firearms are not now seen creates more safety concerns.

The odds of having to pull a gun to defend yourself are slim. If pistol-packing residents were constantly using their guns to protect themselves, we'd certainly be hearing more about it from places where a new "Wild West" has broken out.[24]

These quotes are common examples of what anti-gun activists claim when a state legislature considers a right-to-carry law. Since the newspapers that print these claims never challenge their author's veracity or analyze them for statistical validity, independent statistical analysis is necessary to determine if such claims accurately reflect the truth.

One such example is Ohio, which enacted a RTC law in 2004. An Ohio article stated that "crime hasn't dropped noticeably."[25] Examining the time period from 2003-2004, this does indeed seem to be the case, though both the murder rate and rape rate dropped.[26] However, it is dangerous to try to divine a trend by examining two years of data. In the first nine months of the law, 45,497 licenses were issued, but there were no outbreaks of shootouts or vigilante justice, and there might be some protection afforded to women, the counterpoint to findings in Chapter 2 where women were raped more often after civilian firearms were banned.

This article also represents an example of how a gun control organization can make use of the media to promote their agenda. There is a quote by Toby Hoover, executive director of the Ohio Coalition Against Gun Violence, who employs the same facile rationale used in the above two articles to justify continued civilian disarmament:

"If we have 45,000 more cars throughout the state of Ohio, we're going to have more accidents. If we have 45,000 more guns in public, we're going to have more incidents."

What may seem superficially logical is not always born out in reality, and it is necessary to check facts before committing to public policy agendas based only on what "makes sense" on the surface of things.

The first claim in this quote is that more cars equals more accidents. From 1966 to 2004, the motor vehicle traffic fatality rate per 100,000 population dropped from 25.89 to 14.52, a 43.9% decrease, while the number of registered vehicles more than doubled, increasing from less than 96 million to almost 238 million.[27] Between 1988 and 2004, the total number of crashes decreased from 6.9 million to 6.2 million, while the number of registered vehicles increased from 177 million to 230.8 million.[28] As the number of vehicles on the road increased, traffic fatalities and crashes dropped. More cars is not a precursor to more accidents.

As for the assertion that more guns in public will lead to more "incidents," between 1995 and 1996, 10 states enacted right-to-carry laws. From the time the laws went into effect through 2005, the RTC states averaged a 24.0% decrease in their violent crime rate, 31.9% drop in the murder rate, 11.3% drop in rape, 26.5% decrease in robbery, and 24.3% drop in aggravated assault.[29]

There are now 40 states with some liberalized form of right-to-carry, 21 of which passed their laws since 1994.[30] Also, the ATF reports that an average of 4.5 million new firearms are sold each year.[31] Yet we noted in Chapter 2 that the United States has seen a large drop in homicide since 1995. As more guns reach civilian hands and right-to-carry expands, accidental firearm deaths and injuries have decreased, too. It is impossible for a reasonable person to look at the statistical record and conclude that concealed carry laws should be opposed for public safety reasons. More guns in the civilian population have not resulted in "more incidents."

The Ohio article continues:

Ohio is home to about 7.5 million adults old enough to apply for the permit, Hoover said. That only about 45,000 of those applied shows her most Ohioans don't want the law.

"For us, the important part is that it asks a whole society (for something) that only a half percent (of the population) wanted to do," she said. "That in itself is bothersome because the majority of Ohioans don't want to have loaded guns around them all the time."

In all states with right-to-carry, only a small percentage of all residents choose to spend the time and money to obtain a concealed carry permit. For example, since the law's inception in 1995, Texas issued 258,162 concealed carry licenses through

2006, about 1% of the population.[32] As of this writing, Florida has 453,896 valid RTC licenses, about 2% of the total population.[33] Nevertheless, because criminals don't know which person is armed, they are less likely to attack. Citing 2005 FBI crime statistics, we find that the average violent crime rate for RTC states is 394.1 per 100,000 people, while non-RTC states (plus Washington, D.C.) average 498.7 violent crimes per 100,000 people — 26.6% higher than RTC states.[34] With the increased reduction in violent crime, 99% of the population — especially the female portion — benefits from the deterrent effect created by those who are willing to make the investment and take all the physical and legal risks.

Finally, as there are now 35 states with shall-issue RTC laws, two allowing law-abiding citizens to carry without a permit, and three more with fairly administered may-issue laws, Ms. Hoover implies there are an awful lot of states being run by a tyrannical 1-2% of the electorate.[35] As pointed out in Chapter 3, RTC laws take years to pass, with much public deliberation. A reasonable person can only conclude that were there an outcry against such laws by an established majority of the electorate, such laws would never pass. Which brings us to one final but very important point brought out by the Ohio Coalition Against Gun Violence: They have publicly stated their two criteria for the relevance of a subpopulation in determining public policy:

- It is wrong to enact legislation that "asks a whole society for something that only a [small] percent of the population wanted to do."

- Coalition board member Nancy Wellman stated: "This [right-to-carry] law is based on secrecy. That's not what we should be about."[36]

An email message to the Coalition, asking for an estimate of their membership numbers, went unanswered. Brian Patrick, an assistant professor at the University of Toledo, has researched the Coalition, including its membership structure and where it gets its funding. He found that besides relying on secrecy, the Coalition supports a position that only an extremely small percent of the population wants:

The Coalition's primary, perhaps sole, manifestation as an organization seems to be two professional staff members in the basement of a church in downtown Toledo: Toby Hoover, the executive director and a secretary/receptionist. As far as I can tell they have no mass membership whatever. When I asked about membership Toby Hoover answered the question by asking another question: how does one define membership? Apparently they do it by fiat, claiming to speak for an abstract public when in fact no such public may exist.

Regarding funding, they have had sizable support from Joyce Foundation of $200,000. So overall the coalition seems a top-down affair, functioning more or less in the model of missionary or social work, rather than any kind of mass membership, grass-roots citizens group.

One of the things that Hoover does well is function as a press contact. This sort of centralized model is a reliable source for reporters, and thus Hoover often shows up in press accounts. Recently I read a news media piece in which Hoover criticized the Ohio CCW law on its first anniversary because only 45,000 or so people had obtained permits in the first year. This, said Hoover, indicated that the law was bad because such a small portion of the public was thereby represented. However even this 45,000 dwarfs OCAGV, which appears to have no tangible, mass membership at all, even though it claims to speak for millions.[37]

The Joyce Foundation confirms a $200,000 grant to the Ohio Coalition Against Gun Violence for the year 2004 (as well as another $150,000 grant in 2003).[38] On a related page, the Foundation posted a press release entitled *Foundations Should Support Firearms Research.*[39] It cites tragedies such as those we will examine later in this chapter, where guns were used in mass murders. It also makes some curious claims we should discuss now.

The press release comments: "consider the [firearms] deaths that don't make the headlines but add up to a tragic toll of 30,000 each year." Like other gun control organizations, this number includes suicides to inflate the total number of shooting deaths, which we have already discussed as having no reliable correlation to guns. But just as a reminder, between 1982 and 2002, the national suicide rate dropped 16.9%, from 7.15 to 5.94 incidents per 100,000 population,[40] despite the sale of nearly 60 million new firearms, including over 25 million handguns between 1986 and 1999.[41]

The Joyce Foundation press release also discussed how "we lack basic information on violent death generally" and calls for organizations to fund research. Yet a look at their list of grantees, such as the Ohio Coalition, shows they are convinced that strict gun control is the way to go despite their stated lack of information on violent death. This seems contradictory, unless one understands that the Foundation has a bias towards gun control, and while it publicly claims not to know what is best, it believes society is safer without guns, even though no evidence exists to support this assumption. Thus, it does indeed believe it knows what is best for you, even if the outcome ends up being perilous.

Returning to the coverage of the Coalition in the Ohio article, we find one last example of ideological loyalty: Their web site links to an action page that enables people to write Congress regarding the repeal of the Washington D.C. gun ban. They want people to "Send a Message: Keep Our Nation's Capitol Safe."[42]

Their concept of "safe" begs a closer look. In 2005, our nation's capitol experienced a murder rate of 33.5 per 100,000 population, 6 times the national rate, and 7 times the average rate of all RTC states. The D.C. violent crime rate is 2.9 times the national average and 3.5 times the rate of RTC states.[43] This is not a new trend: While D.C. has historically had a higher homicide rate than the national average, it has become more deadly since the 1976 firearm ban. In the 13 years prior to their ban, Washington D.C. had a murder rate 3.6 times the national average. In the 13 years following the ban, this differential rose to 4.3 times the national rate, but in the latest 13 year period, this ratio increased to eight times the national average.[44] After comparing these violent crime rates, one must wonder how D.C. could be any less "safe" if law-abiding citizens had access to personal protection against the violent predators who have already made the city the most dangerous in the country.

Dayton, Ohio – A Dayton man fought back against two suspects who police said were trying to rob him early Friday morning. The incident happened around 1 a.m. at the intersection of Catalpa and Riverview…

Investigators said the victim was walking down the street when, he said, someone came up behind him and pushed him. He said when he turned around, there were two men standing there who demanded his money with a gun.

The victim told police that he pulled out his .40-caliber handgun and fired off close to 10 rounds, striking one of the men. Officers said the men ran off, but were later found at Good Samaritan Hospital.

Authorities said one of the suspects is a 17-year-old who suffered multiple gunshots and remains hospitalized. Officers said they also arrested two 16-year-olds who they said was driving a stolen car.

Police said that all three men face charges of armed robbery. Investigators do not plan to charge the victim for shooting the gun, because police believe the man was acting in self-defense. They said the victim also had a **permit to carry a concealed weapon**.[45]

When Ohio's law allowing residents to carry a concealed weapon went into effect last year, a number of people rushed to get permits so they could legally carry a firearm. The right to do that may have saved a man in Westwood early Wednesday morning. Cincinnati Police say he opened fire on three men who shot him after trying to rob him outside his girlfriend's home…

Pryor obtained his **conceal carry permit** last September. [Girlfriend] Burton says he did so for his own protection.

"He's been robbed before…"

And Burton says after hearing about Charles Pryor's encounter, more people may want to consider a conceal carry permit.

"Maybe they should. Maybe it will save their life. I think it saved his life."[46] [Emphasis added]

Right-to-Carry: Discredited Fantasy?

Gun control organizations like to argue that any research showing the benefits of RTC laws are invalid. In the spring of 2005, the Minnesota state government debated and subsequently enacted the Minnesota Personal Protection Act. An opinion piece by Heather Martens, who calls herself a "writer and researcher," stated:

> One change is the absence of the argument that more guns reduce crime. This argument, the centerpiece of the 2003 campaign, was thoroughly discredited in 2004 by a National Academy of Sciences review of gun research.[47]

Martens was referencing *Firearms and Violence: A Critical Review*, published in 2005 by the National Research Council of the National Academy of Sciences. Two quotes from the book are:

- "It is impossible to draw strong conclusions from the existing literature on the causal impact of these laws."[48]

- "The committee concludes that with the current evidence it is not possible to determine that there is a causal link between the passage of right-to-carry laws and crime rates."[49]

Language is a curious thing, and it is as important to understand what is not being said as it is to read what has been committed to paper. While the authors cannot determine a causal link with "current evidence," it acknowledges that it also cannot draw any "strong conclusions" on the impact of these laws.

In order to "thoroughly discredit" RTC laws, the authors could have stated that:

- They are indeed able to draw a strong conclusion on the causal impact of RTC laws, and

- The committee concludes that with the current literature, they determined there is no beneficial causal link between RTC laws and crime rates.

The National Academy of Sciences group also reviewed research papers critical of right-to-carry, which used statistical models showing that violent crime actually increased in RTC states. For example, citing a paper by Duggan, the NAS report notes: "According to Duggan's estimates, adoption of right-to-carry laws increases the frequencies of rape, robbery, and violent crime as a whole."[50] Yet the NAS does not support such conclusions, either, since it cannot find "a causal link between the passage of right-to-carry laws and crime rates." This means that the authors did not conclude that RTC laws increase crime, which is important because it does not support gun control and does not support what Toby Hoover claimed in Ohio. Therefore, by applying Martens's criterion, the idea that RTC laws create a public danger is also "thoroughly discredited."

According to Martens's standards, the NAS has also "thoroughly discredited" one of the mainstays of the gun control research thesis: the "43 times more likely" claim. In 1986, Kellermann and Reay studied gunshot deaths in King County, Washington. Publishing in the *New England Journal of Medicine,* they concluded: "We noted 43 suicides, criminal homicides, or accidental gunshot deaths involving a gun kept in the home for every case of homicide for self-protection."[51]

This finding is often cited when gun control organizations promote their policies. For example, two representatives of *Ban Handgun Violence,* in their opinion piece supporting San Francisco's proposed 2006 firearms ban, stated:

> The New England Journal of Medicine found that a handgun in the home makes it 43 times more likely that a friend, family member, or acquaintance will be killed than an intruder.[52]

Here is what the National Research Council of the National Academy of Science had to say about Kellermann's and Reay's conclusions:

> Kellermann and Reay find that there were nearly 5 times as many homicides and 37 times as many suicides as perpetrators killed in self-defense. They go on to conclude, "The advisability of keeping a firearm in the home for protection must be questioned."

> Although the facts are in no doubt, the conclusions do not seem to follow. Certainly, effective defensive gun use need not ever lead the perpetrator to be wounded or killed. Rather, to assess the benefits of self-defense, one needs to measure crime and injury averted. The particular outcome of an offender is of little relevance.[53]

The NAS authors actually challenged Kellermann's and Reay's conclusions, saying they were of "little relevance" because there is no simple, numerical correlation between homicide/suicide and defensive shootings of criminal perpetrators. This is a more emphatic conclusion than what they stated about research into RTC laws and their impact on crime rates.

It is also interesting to note that gun control organizations have an inconsistent standard when deciding what research is valid. In a January 2005 radio interview, when Peter Hamm, Communications Director for the Brady Campaign to Prevent Gun Violence, was asked to consider that the firearm-related death rate for minors in Texas, a RTC state, was less than California's, a leader in gun control laws, he called it a "statistical aberration."[54] Therefore, according to Brady criteria the Kellermann paper, which examines only one metropolitan population — less significant in comparison to the two most populous states in the country — is even more of an irrelevant, statistical aberration.

Right-to-Carry: Menace to Society?

Another argument promoted by gun control groups is that concealed-carry licensees are criminals and thugs, and therefore RTC laws endanger society by giving these violent, irresponsible people the legal right to carry firearms. Returning to the Minnesota Personal Protection Act, Martens continues with her opinion piece:

> It's well established in states with longer track records that bad stuff happens with conceal and carry laws. Texas has a much stricter law than the one proposed here, but between 1996 and 2000 there were 3,370 arrests of permit holders for crimes including murder, rape and impersonating a police officer. From May 2000 to August 2001, the state made 1,944 more permit holder arrests – a quick acceleration. Then, surprise! Texas stopped collecting the data.

Martens references the number of arrests compiled by a Violence Policy Center study. Her total number of arrests is 3,370 from years 1996-2000, plus 1,944 for 2000-2001, which equals 5,314, the exact number stated in VPC's *License to Kill IV: More Guns, More Crime*.[55] (Violence Policy Center has a long history of supporting politicians' gun control agendas in Washington, D.C. For example, as of early June, 2005, a search of the VPC web site results in 17 press releases discussing Senator Charles Schumer, five for Senator Barbara Boxer, and 15 for President Bill Clinton.[56])

Taken out of context, this arrest data is disturbing. But one must remember that members of the general population were also getting arrested during this time period. Also, one must remember that in our society, where a person is presumed innocent until proven guilty, arrest does not equal commission of a crime. For example, after a defensive shooting, the RTC licensee might be arrested on suspicion of murder, but subsequent investigation determines it was justifiable homicide because it was done to defend against the commission of a violent felony, such as attempted murder, robbery, or rape. As explained by a member of the Texas Department of Public Safety:

> Texas DPS may not suspend a CHL [Concealed Handgun License] until charges have been formerly filed. So even though an individual is arrested, if they are never indicted for a felony offense or the district/county attorney refuses the case, charges have not been officially filed.[57]

Martens presumes guilt for each permittee who was arrested, counter to an important foundation stone in our legal system:

> One of the most sacred principles in the American criminal justice system, holding that a defendant is innocent until proven guilty. In other words, the prosecution must prove, beyond a reasonable doubt, each element of the crime charged.[58]

Nevertheless, the idea that RTC licensees get arrested is an important argument among the gun control community in their attempt to show that RTC laws are a public danger. So it is vital to put the arrest data into the proper context, which we will do in the next section of this chapter. But first, let us address Martens's "surprise" at being unable to find current arrest data for Texas RTC licensees. The way her editorial is worded, it implies there is a cover-up happening by the Texas government: Perhaps they were forced to "stop collecting the data" by the now-armed tyrannical 1% who have taken the government hostage?

Any researcher could have contacted Texas Department of Public Safety to confirm or refute such an allegation. One such inquiry resulted in this response from an analyst at the Texas DPS Regulatory Licensing Service, which controls the licensing of concealed carry:

> The statistics referenced in [Martens's] article are actually the rates we used to post (which included all convictions) before September 2001, when the law changed. The reason we stopped posting the data referenced in the article is because of HB 2784, and the statistics mentioned in the article are no longer on our website for that same reason. Regarding the conviction rates that we now have the ability to post as a result of HB 2784, it is our intent to post them, but there is a technical issue that is delaying us from figuring the rates for years 2002 and 2003.[59]

The Texas DPS analyst went on to discuss the technical issues involved with upgrading the computer system to reflect changes in law: synchronizing information from the court system, conviction paperwork, and concealed carry information. Then they found errors in their vendor's software being used for part of this process. Because of major upgrades to their computer system, it has taken a while to resolve both programming problems and integrate the new hardware and software systems. While some may want to find fault for this process taking so long, it is hardly a conspiracy of silence aimed at misleading the public.

HB 2784 is an attempt to clarify actual criminal activity among RTC licensees by compiling conviction rates of licensees and comparing them to conviction rates for "all like offenses committed in the state."[60] Also, as noted in the following section, there are some current Texas data available to anyone with an internet connection. As the Minnesota Personal Protection Act was about to be passed, Martens had a deadline and made the call as to what "information" would best swing public opinion and legislative votes against the bill.

Are RTC Licensees Criminals?

Continuing with the "RTC licensees are criminals" gambit, one way to examine this allegation is to look at crime trends from RTC states — arrest and conviction records and RTC license suspension and revocation records — to determine if the legally-armed civilian population perpetrates greater criminal activity, as gun controllers assert.

In a recent article, Brady Campaign's Peter Hamm was quoted as saying:

> There is no reason to pass a law that sends a signal to the most aggressive people in society that they can act more aggressively than they can now.[61]

Mr. Hamm was referring to the "Castle Doctrine" House Bills 5142 and 5143, then being considered in the Michigan House of Representatives. House Bill 5142 would allow the use of "deadly force" without first trying to retreat if a law-abiding gun owner is attacked in their home or on their surrounding land.[62] House Bill 5143 went further by stating that the defender does not have a duty to retreat and is also free from prosecution and civil action if their actions are found to be lawful. Such defense would be allowable in a "dwelling, residence, or occupied vehicle." This bill also mentioned conditions under which the use of deadly force is not acceptable. For instance, in the case of simple trespass, the defender may not use deadly force.[63] The defender is responsible for understanding and following the law or they will suffer terrible consequences, which is simply a continuation of existing law.

As to Mr. Hamm's implication that gun owners are "the most aggressive people," we should at least try to determine if Michigan RTC licensees made the state more violent. After all, Oxford English Dictionary defines aggressive as: "Disposed to attack others."[64] Therefore, there should be some statistical record to show that violent attacks or confrontations increased after Michigan enacted its RTC law in 2001. Instead, what we find is that from 2001 through 2004, rates of four of the five violent crime indices decreased:

- The murder rate dropped 4.5%.

- The rape rate increased 2.8%

- The robbery rate dropped 13.6%.

- The assault rate dropped 13.1%.

- The overall violent crime rate dropped 10%.[65]

There is no indication from this data that those who carry concealed handguns in public are "the most aggressive people". The only question yet to be answered is: Are RTC licensees committing these crimes? After all, it is only a small percentage of the population that gets a license, and it is only a small portion of the population that commits violent crime. Maybe Mr. Hamm is onto something: Are RTC licensees all rapists, enabled by carrying guns in public to commit rape more easily?

Do RTC Licensees Commit More Crimes?

Violence Policy Center considers itself the most effective anti-gun organization in Washington D.C. "Recognizing the VPC's groundbreaking research and unique expertise, VPC staff are frequently quoted by national news media and relied upon by policymakers." They are the self-proclaimed experts in research that leads the fight for civilian disarmament.[66]

When referencing arrest records, gun control supporters prefer to give you an overall total number of arrests only for right-to-carry licensees. For example, Violence Policy Center's *License to Kill IV* tallies the number and categories of Texas licensee arrests, but does not tell you how many total licensees there are in Texas, so you do not know the actual arrest rate among the licensee population. Since state arrest data is not included, the report doesn't compare licensees to the general population in frequency of arrests. How else could one determine whether or not licensees are more "aggressive" and criminal than the rest of us?

In order to place the licensee arrest data into context, it must be compared to the corresponding arrest data for the general population. Since VPC reports the total number of licensee arrests from the inception of the right-to-carry law, we must compare that number to the total number of arrests among the entire Texas population through the same period of 1996 to 2001. Also, we must use the total population over age 21 to enable an "apples-to-apples" comparison between arrest rates for Concealed Handgun License holders (CHLs) and the non-CHL population, as a Texan must be 21 years of age or older to obtain this license.[67]

Violent offenses, as defined by the Texas Office of Court Administration, include: capital murder; murder or voluntary manslaughter; assault or attempted murder; sexual assault of an adult; sexual assault of a child; and robbery.[68] Property offenses include: burglary; theft; auto theft; and arson.[69] Drug offenses include: drug sale or manufacture; and drug possession.[70] The report referenced here does not break out specific categories within each crime index, making it impossible to compare specific crime rates such as murder.

Examining the data, the closest that CHLs came to mirroring the level of crime among the general population is in the category of violent crime, with the general population being over 2.45 times as likely to be arrested as CHLs. However, members of the general population of Texas were arrested for:

- property crime violations over 33 times as often as CHLs, and
- drug violations over 21 times as often as CHLs.

The general population experienced arrest nearly 18 times as often as CHLs when looking at all arrests.[71] Violence Policy Center's own data proves that, based upon arrests, Texas CHLs are far more law-abiding than the rest of the population.

But are Texas statistics the rule or the exception? Comparing arrest rates for two other states — Arizona and Louisiana — where there is readily-available arrest data to make a comparison between concealed carry licensees and the general public. Suspensions are included because they may indicate an arrest, and like any arrest, while it does not imply guilt, it does allow us to more accurately compare bad behavior rates between licensees and the general public.

It is important to remember that not all licensee offenses are crimes against a person (violent crime) or private property (property crime), such as those listed in the FBI crime index. A Texan who is delinquent on his student loan payments may have his CHL revoked.[72] A licensee who is named on a protective order may lose his license as well, even though he may not have committed, nor even be contemplating, an aggressive action against the person requesting the order.[73] In Louisiana, a license may be suspended if the licensee fails to notify the Louisiana Department of Public Safety of an address change within 30 days of moving.[74] A license may also be revoked because the licensee fails to maintain residency in Louisiana, or fails to maintain qualifications.[75]

Like Texas, Arizona and Louisiana have published only total suspensions and revocations from inception of the RTC law to the end of the reporting period. Also like Texas, an annual average for RTC licensees can't be created because the reported totals are not annualized, but arrest totals as a percent of the final population can be compared. The RTC violations represent the total number for an average of nine recording years, while the state arrest rate is available only for the last five years. By extrapolating the number of total arrests using the average annual percent of the adult population arrested for the five years reported, the total number of violations for each population group can be compared, creating an index using the final population, as we did with the Texas comparison. This creates comparable indices for each state. The arrest/violation ratio indicates that the general population gets arrested about 24.4 times as often as RTC licensees.[76]

To estimate the arrest ratio, we must make the assumption that the arrest rate does not change much over time because the percentage of the population arrested each year was fairly consistent, making this a reliable estimate. The arrest percentages are also fairly consistent from year to year in other states.[77]

If we had annual data for RTC licensee violations and could make direct comparisons to FBI arrest data, this would be a more accurate indicator of relative levels of lawfulness. There is one sample of such data from Oklahoma, for the years 2001 through 2004. By comparing the annual number of licensee violations — suspensions plus revocations — to the state's annual arrest data, we find a much higher violation ratio for the general adult population: The general public gets arrested about 45 times as often as RTC licensees get caught violating the law sufficiently to risk losing their concealed carry permit.[78]

In real life, an arrest does not mean the arrestee is guilty of an offense: We must look at conviction rates to get a better idea of the actual level of criminality. The Texas Department of Public Safety published a report for the year 2001, which compared the number of CHL convictions to the number in the general population. In the four main FBI violent crime categories, the general population was convicted nearly three times as often as licensees.[79] Compared to CHLs, the general population:

- was over 2.5 times as likely to be convicted for making terrorist threats,
- was over 3 times as likely to be convicted for simple assault, and
- was convicted of burglary 58 times as often.[80]

Overall, using conviction data as an indicator, the general public committed crime at three times the rate of RTC licensees. If the entire Texas population had been as law-abiding as RTC licensees, the state of Texas would have realized a savings of over $5.1 billion in 2001 from reduced FBI-defined violent crime and burglary alone.[81] To put this another way, the listed FBI crimes cost Texas 1.13% of its Gross State Product (GSP) in 2001. Had the entire population been as law-abiding as CHLs, this cost would have been reduced 59.8% to 0.45% of the GSP.[82] This is another data point demonstrating that right-to-carry licensees are much more law-abiding than the general public.

Final Analysis Of Martens

In 2007, Texas published more comprehensive conviction reports for the years 2002-2005. These reports are helpful in that they already separate out conviction data for those 21 years of age or older.[83]

The non-CHL adult population (age 21 and older) during these reporting years averaged over 10 times more convictions than CHLs. Non-CHLs were over 12 times as likely to be convicted of FBI violent crime — murder, rape, robbery, and aggravated assault — and 49 times more likely to be convicted of burglary. Of all recorded FBI crime categories, the non-CHL population was convicted over 22 times as often. (The FBI tracks two additional property crime categories, larceny/theft and motor vehicle theft, which are not tracked on the DPS conviction reports.)

The year 2005 recorded the lowest ratios of the four reporting years. Even so, using conviction data as an indicator, the non-CHL population committed FBI violent crime nearly 5 times the rate of CHLs, and committed burglary over 32 times as often. Overall, the non-CHL population was convicted over six times as often as CHLs.

Because this type of report is so new, there are only three years' worth of complete data, plus one year (2002) where the adult non-CHL population was estimated using available census data. While the percent reduction (the CHL Effect) of FBI crime categories has trended downwards the last three reporting years — from 98.4% in 2003 to 96.4% in 2004 to 93.1% in 2005 — the limited number of annual data sets makes it difficult to identify a long-term trend. Even so, in 2005 the non-CHL population remained over 8 times as likely to commit an FBI major crime. It should also be noted that the percent reduction for years 2003 and 2004 was higher than 2002 (95.4%), so these percentages may just be fluctuating from year to year.[84]

The total cost to the state of Texas for the five FBI crime categories tracked was about $8.8 billion in 2002, $9.3 billion in 2003, $9.4 billion in 2004, and $9.8 billion in 2005. The four-year total of about $37.3 billion represents about 1.12% of Texas Gross State Product, very consistent with the 2001 data above.[85] If the general population were as law-abiding as CHLs, the corresponding reduction in crime costs would have totaled about $6.8 billion in 2002, $8.3 billion in 2003, $8.9 billion in 2004, and $7.1 billion in 2005. The last two years' total crime cost represents an estimated annual tax rebate of $355 for every Texan man, woman, and child.

Had the general public been as law-abiding as CHLs, the $37.3 billion total cost would have decreased 83.9% to around $6.0 billion, reducing the fiscal bleed to 0.20% of the Texas Gross State Product. These calculations do not include the additional savings the State of Texas would have realized from all the non-FBI categories listed in the DPS reports, as there appear to be no cost estimates available for them.[86]

It should not be surprising that Texas concealed carry licensees are more law-abiding than the general population: They must undergo proper firearms safety training, and they must be certified via two criminal history background checks — FBI and state — that they are sufficiently law-abiding to be entrusted with such responsibility. Also, there are a number of additional requirements to qualify for a CHL. The applicant must:

- Be qualified to purchase a handgun under state and federal regulations.
- Not be charged with or convicted of a felony or class A or B misdemeanor.
- Not be delinquent in child support payments.
- Not be in default on a student loan.
- Not be delinquent on tax payments.
- Not be under a restraining order.
- Not be suffering from a psychiatric disorder or chemical dependency.
- Be capable of "exercising sound judgment with respect to the proper use and storage of a handgun".[87]

As Jerry Patterson, current Land Commissioner of Texas, notes:

Unlawful carry of a firearm is a class A misdemeanor. Is it logical to assume a person inclined to commit a crime with a firearm — such as a felony like capital murder — was even the least bit concerned about an unlawful carry misdemeanor? Is it not bizarre to conclude a violent offense punishable by death was facilitated by the concealed handgun license obtained to avoid a misdemeanor offense punishable by a fine and possibly a few days in jail?[88]

Concealed carry licensees make a considered choice to conduct themselves a certain way in public, and have invested the time, money, and effort to certify that their level of commitment is worthy the public's trust. They voluntarily undergo background checks normally reserved for sensitive jobs or criminal arrests in order to certify that they rank among our most law-abiding citizens prior to receiving their license. These data prove that trust has not been in vain.

Claims by gun control groups, such as Violence Policy Center, that concealed carry is a "License to Kill", or implications that states simply arm violent thugs are inaccurate, and questionable both from a statistical and ethical standpoint. Why do their research papers lack comprehensive data sets which allow comparative analysis? What are the motives driving gun control groups to promote an agenda which cannot be factually supported?

> A fatal shooting at an Albuquerque Wal-Mart last week was the state's first by someone with a concealed-carry gun permit, authorities said.

> Police said Felix Vigil was attacking his ex-wife with a knife near the store's deli counter where she worked when an armed customer intervened and shot him. The woman, Joyce Cordova, was treated for multiple stab wounds and later released from an Albuquerque hospital.

> The armed customer, 72-year-old Due Moore, was interviewed after the shooting last Thursday and released.[89]

Does Joyce Cordova think the elderly man who saved her life was overly aggressive? Or was the man attempting to murder her one of the "most aggressive people" in our society? Gun control groups seem to have a hard time differentiating between the acts of violent criminals and defensive acts of self-preservation or defense of others being violently attacked. As one police officer explains:

> Concealed-carry permit holders act as first responders, as do many ordinary citizens who know CPR, first aid or how to use a fire extinguisher. Their actions are often the difference between life and death. The same holds true for concealed-carry permit holders.

> As police, we simply cannot be everywhere nor would the public want us to be. When most violent criminal acts, including shootings, robberies, rampages and rape, are over within minutes, if not seconds, the response time of police is simply not fast enough. The training individuals will receive to obtain a concealed-weapons permit…will make them qualified first responders. Like those certified in first aid, we won't expect them to perform major surgery. But it will be adequate for stabilizing a bad situation until professionals arrive.[90]

Is There an Intimate-Murder Epidemic?

In *American Roulette*, Violence Policy Center examined murder-suicides in the U.S. because "they almost always involve firearm."[91] Violence Policy Center estimated that there were 1,324 murder-suicide deaths in 2001, including suicides with homicides to show the total death caused by perpetrators.[92] According to VPC, "The pattern to murder-suicide is distressingly simple: a male offender, a female victim, and a gun—but literally anyone can be caught in its wake."[93] VPC states: "The catalytic component in murder-suicide is the use of a firearm,"[94] implying the gun is a necessary and causative factor in domestic violence.

American Roulette is peppered with anecdotes of wives, girlfriends, and children being shot prior to the shooter taking his own life, such as:

MAINE: In February, Harold "Bones" Gray, 68, shot and killed his wife, Christina Gray, 24, and her sister, Vicki Morgan, 19, before turning the gun on himself. The Grays had been married for four years, but were separated and in the process of getting a divorce. Christina Gray had taken out a protection order on her husband in November 2000, an order he was arrested for violating in January 2001. All three were mortally wounded in the parking lot of a convenience store.[95]

At least VPC acknowledges that the murderer in this case had a prior criminal history. (This is an important point examined in greater detail later in this chapter.) VPC also believes "unique factors may drive murder-suicide among the elderly."

If most murder-suicides involve jealousy, a smaller, discrete category exists involving older people and the presence of declining health in either the victim, the offender, or both.[96]

They cite two incidents to support their conclusion:

MICHIGAN: In March, James Leon Russell, 66, called 911 and asked emergency workers to send two body bags to his home. When police arrived, they found Russell and his sister, Joanne, 77, shot to death. A one-page note on the kitchen table stated: "To the cops: I'm tired of living, and my sister Joanne's Alzheimer's disease is deteriorating rapidly. Therefore I'm putting us both out of our misery. Call it euthanasia."

FLORIDA: In June, retired police lieutenant Richard Zachary, 77, shot his wife, Blanche Zachary, 75, as he pushed her in her wheelchair on a sidewalk close to her nursing home. Richard Zachary then shot himself with the 38 caliber revolver which he had carried on duty. The couple had been married for 50 years. Police were not sure if the incident was planned or spontaneous, but friends of the Zachary's [sic] stated that Blanche's health had been deteriorating rapidly after a series of strokes.[97]

As an interesting aside, *American Roulette* cites another incident where law-enforcement officers commit murder-suicide:

NEW YORK: In June, Detective Edwin Patten, 30, shot his girlfriend, Officer Stacie Williamson, 28, four times and then shot himself. Patten used his 9mm service pistol in the shooting, which took place in Williamson's home. The couple, both undercover police officers, had been dating about a year and there were no signs of prior domestic problems.[98]

A more recent incident in California — also confirmed to be murder-suicide — was carried out by an investigator for a district attorney's office, where the officer killed his mother, wife, and three children before turning his service weapon on himself.[99]

Gun control groups generally believe that only government and law-enforcement officials should possess firearms, assuming these people are trained and qualified to use guns in a safe and appropriate manner. Yet VPC states "police may have higher murder-suicide rates."[100]

One source cited in *American Roulette* is a report entitled *Homicide Trends in the United States*, written by the U.S. Department of Justice (DOJ) in 2002. Here are some conclusions from that report:

> The homicide rate doubled from the mid 1960's to the late 1970's. In 1980, it peaked at 10.2 per 100,000 population and subsequently fell off to 7.9 per 100,000 in 1985. It rose again in the late 1980's and early 1990's to another peak in 1991 of 9.8 per 100,000. Since then, the rate has declined sharply, reaching 5.5 per 100,000 by 2000.[101]

> Dramatic increases in both homicide victimization and offending rates were experienced by young males, particularly young black males, in the late 1980's and early 1990's. During the past few years, homicide victimization rates have dropped for all groups.[102]

According to this report, part of what VPC says is true. The DOJ report continues: "Homicides are most often committed with guns, especially handguns."[103] However, the DOJ report also states:

> Gun homicides by adults 25 and older reflect a general downward trend…The sharp increase in homicides in the late 1980's and much of the subsequent decline is attributable to gun violence by juveniles and young adults.[104]

This is a euphemistic way of saying that youth-gang members, interested in protecting lucrative drug businesses, made a major contribution to the homicide rate, not suburban husbands and the elderly. Indeed, the DOJ report says that gun involvement in gang-related homicides increased after 1980, and homicides which occurred during the commission of a felony increased dramatically after 1985, but homicides resulting from arguments — more likely to include domestic conflicts — declined to the lowest levels recorded recently.[105]

There are more conclusions from the DOJ report which conflict with the claims made in *American Roulette*:

- The number of homicides of persons age 65 or older has been decreasing.[106]

- There has been a decline in homicide of intimates, especially male victims.[107]

Another DOJ report notes that the rates of nonfatal intimate partner violence has dropped 49% from 1993-2001, and that between 1993 and 2000, the number of male and female intimate partner murders dropped 37.9% and 21.1%, respectively.[108] These points belie VPC's claim that there is a burgeoning epidemic of domestic gun-involved violence.

Furthermore, the Centers for Disease Control (CDC) confirms that for the period of 1992-2002, not only did the homicide rate decrease across the entire population, but firearms homicide rates decreased at an even faster rate.[109] The CDC also found that firearm-assisted suicide fell at over double the overall suicide rate. While the only positive overall suicide trends cluster in the 40-54 age group, the firearm suicide rates for that age group also dropped.[110] Sadly, the firearm-involved homicide and firearm-assisted suicide rates for the elderly did not drop as fast as the overall rates, giving support to VPC's hypothesis that "unique factors may drive murder-suicide among the elderly," such as failing health and the frustration of diminishing physical faculties. However, the elderly homicide rate trend is only slightly different than the overall rate trend.

Considering that between 1992 and 1999 the ATF recorded an average annual sale of millions of firearms, including nearly 2.4 million handguns, it is impossible to find any statistical support here for any claim that firearms are some sort of causative factor in intimate homicide-suicide.[111] Homicide and suicide rates dropped while civilian firearms ownership increased: Were there a causal link, there should have been a marked rise in firearm homicide and suicide relative to overall rates.

Does Violence Among Intimates Reflect General Violent Crime Rates?

In a special report entitled *Violence Among Family Members and Intimate Partners*, the FBI did its own study of domestic violence for the period of 1996-2001. Some of their findings indicate that domestic violence has a unique set of conditions quite at odds with the types of violent crime studied in their annual *Crime in the United States* reports. For example, *Violence Among Family Members and Intimate Partners* states:

> The Centers for Disease Control and Prevention reported that "nearly two-thirds of women who reported being raped, physically assaulted, or stalked since the age of 18 were victimized by a current or former husband, cohabiting partner, boyfriend, or date."[112]

This indicates that the population group of women in intimate relationships presents some additional, unique dynamics.

Regarding violence against elderly intimates, the FBI study states:

> [N]early a third of the murders of victims 60 years of age or older were committed by a family member. Further, most elder abuse was committed by someone with whom the elderly victim lived. Because most caregivers for the elderly are women, they found that most of the neglect cases were committed by female family members. On the other hand, the most frequent offenders of physical abuse against the elderly were male family members.[113]

The FBI found that firearm use during family violence against the elderly or spouses is nearly equal, but both occurred over 17 times more often than firearm use against children. Separating each group by percent of total incidents, a firearm was used against a spouse in 1.9% of all incidents, a child in 1%, and against an elderly family member in 52.6% of all incidents.[114] This explains in part why the homicide rate for the elderly dropped only slightly less than the overall population's between 1992 and 2002.

Between 1996 and 2001, the FBI found that the percent of homicides as a total of all violent domestic crimes did not rise, nor did overall sexual crime, though the single category of rape itself increased. Aggravated assault, incest, and negligent manslaughter dropped considerably. The largest increases were in robbery and intimidation.[115]

Homicide remained about ¼ of 1% of the total number of violent domestic incidents in both 1996 and 2001, indicating that there is no epidemic in that category. The three least violent categories as rated by the FBI — aggravated assault, simple assault, and intimidation — comprised 88.8% of the total number of incidents in 2001, slightly less than the 89.6% in 1996. Overall, there was not a dramatic change in what percent of the total each category comprised. But this is only part of the story, as this FBI data only shows how much each category comprised of the total number of incidents, not how often each crime occurred or whether those rates of occurrence increased or decreased over time.

By comparing the numbers of incidents to the populations in 1996 and 2001, we can determine the rates per 100,000 population for each violent domestic crime category. Between 1996 and 2001, the total incidence rate for domestic violence increased 186.0%, from 96.1 to 274.8 per 100,000 population. While still comprising only ¼ of 1% of all violent incidents, the domestic homicide rate rose in step with the overall domestic violence rate increase (184.8%), again indicating no special epidemic qualities unique to domestic homicide. The biggest increases were in the categories of rape, robbery, and intimidation, but that comparison is not intended to detract from the fact that domestic violence itself is the epidemic.[116] This conclusion is especially true when comparing domestic violence to the FBI crime categories for the general population. Comparing the rate trends between the two, we find that while these domestic violence rates have increased over 2.5 *times* between the years 1996 to 2001, corresponding FBI violent crime indices have decreased an average of over 20%.[117]

It is very interesting to note that the Justifiable Homicide rate increased 200% faster than the overall domestic violence rate indicating a growing desire by potential victims to defend against intimate attacks.[118]

Another indicator of the uniqueness of domestic violence is in the prevalence of firearms use. In *Weapon Use and Violent Crime*, Department of Justice statistician Craig Perkins notes: "From 1993 through 2001 violent crime declined 54%; weapon violence went down 59%; and firearm violence, 63%."[119] He also notes that while 26% of all the violent crimes committed between 1993 and 2001 involved some sort of weapon, only 10% of all violent crime involved a firearm.[120] In domestic violence situations, firearms were never used in more than 6.5% of all incidents, and that was in 2001. Also, between 1996 and 2001, the rate of firearm usage in domestic violence trended upward 3.2%, again showing how domestic violence is out of synch with overall crime trends.[121]

One of the biggest rate increases was 26.7% increase in the use of motor vehicles as weapons in domestic violence.[122] As with the Consumer Federation of America in Chapter 3, the Violence Policy Center has demurred from promoting additional safety features or government oversight for automobiles. Like the Consumer Federation of America, the VPC declares: "Guns are virtually the only consumer product not regulated for health and safety by a federal agency" and promotes legislation "pending in Congress that would establish comprehensive health and safety regulation of the gun industry" that would "finally end the firearm industry's deadly exemption from regulation."[123] Meanwhile, in Chapter 3 we learned that the firearms accidental death rate is much lower than from automobile accidents. Campaigning for more "health and safety regulation" for a relatively safe and highly-regulated product because of its use in domestic violence, while ignoring another product, is a curious double standard.

From 1996 through 2001, incidents of domestic violence more than tripled while overall violent crime, as well as crimes where the attacker uses a firearm, decreased. The VPC would have us avoid focusing our energy and resources solving the true causes of domestic violence and elder abuse.

An Angelina County grand jury on Tuesday declined to issue a criminal indictment to a Lufkin woman who shot and killed her common-law husband June 7...

The two had a rocky relationship, [District Attorney] Herrington said. The DA's office had handled an earlier case between the two in which Richard had stolen her car, Herrington said.

Whitaker had been in a shelter in September 2004, afraid to go home alone for fear of her husband, Lufkin Police Lt. Greg Denman said earlier. Police worked several domestic violence calls between the two going back to 2002...

Texas law states a person has a right to kill in self-defense if they are threatened by deadly force, and if they try to get away. Whitaker's case met both requirements, Herrington said.[124]

Are Domestic Murderers 'Just Plain Folks'?

Violence Policy Center likes to use fear-based marketing to advance its vision of civilian disarmament. One of the books they promote on their website is entitled *Every Handgun is Aimed at You: The Case for Banning Handguns*, which declares at the beginning of Chapter 1 that handguns are "responsible for an epidemic of death and injury in our nation,"[125] an assumption that available data renders questionable. One conjecture necessary to support VPC's claims and agenda is that all of these tragedies are committed by people who are basically sane and law-abiding, but simply lose control, grab a firearm, and commit murder in a fit of passion. Under the heading of "Most murder-suicides involve an intimate partner," *American Roulette* states:

> [T]his type of murder-suicide typically involves a man between the ages of 18 and 60 years old who develops suspicions of his girlfriend's or wife's infidelity, becomes enraged, murders her, and then commits suicide—usually using a firearm.[126]

American Roulette concludes: "If there had not been easy access to a firearm, these deaths may simply have been injuries, or not have occurred at all." While their claim is at odds with Britain's and Australia's experience of increased violence since their gun bans, as noted in Chapter 2, VPC promotes their thesis of "a male offender, a female victim, and a gun." It merely requires the addition of emotions to become a ready-made tragedy.

In their literature search and review, *The Myth of the Virgin Killer: Law-Abiding Persons Who Kill in a Fit of Rage*, Kates and Polsby discuss the guns-cause-violence thesis. They discovered that people who commit murder are almost always those who lead violent or dysfunctional lives, and who usually have pre-existing criminal records:

> Nearly fifty years of further homicide studies confirm that murderers are almost never ordinary, law-abiding citizens. The great majority are, in fact, extreme aberrants whose life histories are full of violence, psychopathology, crimes (some acquisitive, others completely irrational), substance abuse, and other hazardous behavior and dangerous accidents. The whole corpus of research shows murderers almost always have a long history of involvement in criminal behavior.[127]

Only 15% of Americans in general have a criminal record of any kind. But the overwhelming majority of murderers do. The longest data-set is the murder analyses the Chicago Police Department has published annually from the mid-1960s to date. Those analyses, and various state and national data-sets from the same general period, show upwards of 75% or more of murderers have adult criminal records. Moreover, murderers tend to be career criminals, rather than having just one prior offense. For instance, exclusive of all other offenses they may have had, 80% of Atlanta murder arrestees in 1997 had at least one prior drug offense; fully 70% had 3-5 or more prior drug offenses. Similarly, when the Kennedy School at Harvard studied gun murders occurring in Lowell, MA in 2002, nearly 95 percent of the killers turned out to have been already known to the criminal justice system as gang members or for some other crime; 89 percent had been accused of a prior armed violent crime.[128]

American Roulette includes numerous anecdotes of seemingly innocent, law-abiding people suddenly turning violent, implying that guns were the catalyst for tragedy. Kates and Polsby found otherwise:

> Data reflecting only official crime records greatly under-represent murderers' true histories of prior serious crimes. For instance, such data substantially underestimate the incidence among those who murder relatives or acquaintances of real history of assaultive behavior because their prior victims were less likely to press charges and the police were loathe to interfere in a family matter. A study of police responding to domestic disturbance calls in Kansas City (Missouri) found that 90 percent of all the family homicides were preceded by previous disturbances at the same address, with a median of 5 calls per address. Thus homicide — whether of a stranger or of someone known to the offender — is 'usually part of a pattern of violence, engaged in by people who are known ... as violence prone.'[129]

The Violence Policy Center attempts to convince us that guns in the home are a great danger, since they claim: "Most murder-suicides occur in the home."[130] But it is the type of home that we must examine closely, as it is rarely some type of idyllic suburban setting:

> Likewise, killings between "relatives" cannot be understood as something that occurs in ordinary families. What "relative" denotes in the context of murder is a killing perpetrated by a violent man who has brutalized his mate, children and/or other family members on numerous prior occasions before eventually killing one or more of them. This is typified by the following Nov. 1, 2002 news item: Eric Christopher Kiefer was shot to death by his former wife's current boyfriend after Kiefer broke into to the wife's parents' home and attacked the boyfriend, the parents, and his own daughter with a hatchet. Kiefer was under a restraining order based on his having (in separate incidents): stabbed his former wife; beaten her up; and beaten up the boyfriend. Police had been called to the residence 10 times in the preceding two years to deal with Kiefer's attacks or attempts to break into the home.[131]

Following is another, more recent example, a domestic violence encounter in which the perpetrator became the "victim" because one of his intended targets successfully protected everybody with a firearm. In this case, it was the perpetrator's own son who was the defender, preventing what may have become a mass murder. It is also interesting to note that the perpetrator initiated his attack without the use of a firearm, trusting his superior size and strength, along with his violent demeanor, to carry the day.

FORT WORTH - Casey Morgan didn't plan on killing his father.

He just wanted him to stop.

But Arch Jack Morgan, 43, had been drinking and was angry.

Morgan was mad that he had been arrested outside his brother's Fort Worth home the day before. He was enraged that his brother, fed up with his behavior, had told him that he was no longer welcome at his house.

When his father "barged" into the house and came "toward us pretty quick," Casey picked up his uncle's shotgun and fired once. The grand jury declined to indict, considering it justifiable homicide.

Casey's father had a criminal history dating back to 1981, including felony convictions for robbery and assault.

After an earlier attempt to assault the uncle's girlfriend, the police were called and, after attempting to flee, Morgan was arrested. Since he was only cited for public intoxication and possession of drug paraphernalia, he was released on bond, whereupon he continued his harassment:

> "He was calling in the middle of the night and saying he was coming to lock the house up and he was going to burn the house up with us in it," Casey said.

> When Morgan arrived at the house the next day in a state of fury, Casey was afraid his dad would carry out his threats to kill him, Bradt and Bradt's girlfriend. Morgan was carrying a 40-ounce beer and wearing a black leather glove – one he wore for fighting.

> Inside the cramped living room, Morgan shouted "Your time is up" and then lunged at his brother, witnesses told police.

> Morgan was not brandishing a weapon, but at 6 feet 4 inches, he "didn't need one," Casey said.

> "He was incredibly strong," Casey said. "He's the strongest man I've ever seen."

> At this point, Casey did the only thing he believed would save them all:

> "I shot him for a reason," Casey said. "I didn't make him come in there and try to hurt us and kill us or whatever he was trying to do. I don't feel guilty.

> "I feel bad, but I don't feel guilty."[132]

Here was a criminal with a history of violence, a police record, and an uncontrollable temper, who apparently was released on bail because the criminal justice system was unable to hold him on more serious charges. The system didn't fail so much as prove limited in addressing the situation. Had the teenage boy not had a quick mind and good reflexes — and an available firearm — this story would have turned out worse. As it is, a young man will have to wrestle with reconciling the emotional consequences of shooting his father against the benefit of saving the lives of other family members. Even in the most compelling acts of self-defense, there is no pleasant outcome: There are only better choices.

It is also interesting to note that this case, where a shotgun was used as the defensive tool, is an exception. The majority of self-defense reports involve successful use of a handgun by the defender. Tabulating the five-year period of 2001-2005, the FBI found that of all justifiable homicides by police officers (killing a felon in the line of duty) 98.9% were committed with a firearm, and 85.5% were accomplished with a handgun. Of all justifiable homicide by private citizens (killing a felon during the commission of a felony) 79% were accomplished with a firearm, and 64.5% committed with a handgun. Handguns represent 77.5% of all justifiable homicides involving firearms.[133] The very attributes which make a handgun attractive to a criminal — ease of use, relatively light weight, small, easily concealed, and affordable — also make it a valuable tool for those suddenly in need of defending their lives and the lives of loved ones.

What is the difference between a law-abiding citizen and a criminal? It can be difficult for the average person who lives in a fairly pleasant and secure environment to conceive the drastic difference in the criminal's view of life, because it is so foreign to our experience. Kates and Polsby summarize this conundrum:

> What differentiates criminals and violent psychopaths from ordinary people is not their experiencing hatred or rage, but the ease with which those emotions are prompted and the acts to which they give rise. Killers exhibit an absence of impulse control and a seemingly inexplicable (to ordinary people) propensity to explode into extreme violence over the most trifling matters. On the one hand, ordinary people virtually never kill; on the other hand, the kind of person who murders often does so over things so trivial that we are left aghast not only at the fact of killing but at the inconsequential grievance that engendered it. *The triviality of motive further confirms the extreme deviance of murderers.* However preposterously or insufficiently motivated a killing may seem to ordinary people with ordinary compunctions, it may make perfect sense to a psychopath, sociopath, and/or substance abuser with a life-long record of law breaking and no compunction against extreme violence.[134] (Emphasis added)

What about disarming the general public in order to take guns out of circulation, so that the criminally inclined lose access as well? Kates and Polsby answer with a scholarly version of "if guns are outlawed, only outlaws will have guns:"

> It has long been generally agreed that certain discrete high-risk groups should be denied access to firearms by what we shall call felon-in-possession laws. The difficulty of achieving this goal is that persons who are inclined toward crime may have little compunction about violating laws forbidding them arms, and those laws may be difficult to enforce against them. Had 20th Century Americans not previously understood this, the point would have been made unmistakably clear by the Prohibition experience. As the SATURDAY EVENING POST editorialized in 1925: "If the Federal government cannot prevent the landing and distribution of shiploads of rum, how can it stop the criminal from getting the most easily concealed and vital tool of his trade?"

Eighty subsequent years of trying to enforce narcotics bans have further spotlighted the practical difficulties of enforcing disarmament on either the whole populace or discrete groups therein. Among the major difficulties in a society like ours, whose prisons are overflowing with felons serving sentences for serious criminal acts, available prison space will more likely be devoted to those so convicted than to those convicted of mere mala prohibita like the illegal possession or carrying of a gun. In order to incarcerate murderers and robbers, those convicted of nothing more serious than having or carrying a gun tend to get probation or minimal sentences — even if they have prior felony convictions. However inevitable that is, given the scarcity of our resources, it deprives felon-in-possession laws of their force. The point of these laws is to deter particularly dangerous people from having or carrying a particularly fearsome form of weaponry **before** they have a chance to use it against victims. That point largely disappears if it turns out that the law is only really enforced if they get caught actually using a gun against victims. As the premier study of gun control enforcement concluded over two decades ago: It is very possible that, if gun laws do potentially reduce gun-related crime, the present laws are all that is needed if they are enforced. What good would stronger laws do when the courts have demonstrated that they will not enforce them?[135]

Here is a real-life example of what Kates and Polsby just explained:

SIMI VALLEY, Calif. — A criminal rampage that left four people dead and five hospitalized in a series of murders, pistol whippings and carjackings ended Tuesday when the 38-year-old suspect killed himself inside a Wal-Mart store, authorities said.

The violence started Monday when three people were shot in the front yard of a home in Thousand Oaks. A woman identified as 51-year-old Jan Heyne was pronounced dead at the scene and attorney Steve Mazin, 52, died at a nearby hospital. A third shooting victim, Timothy Heyne, a rock music manager, was hospitalized in critical condition.

Welchel drove a stolen vehicle to a nearby supermarket, and then carjacked a truck at gunpoint and drove it to another house. When a sheriff's deputy arrived, Welchel was shooting at the residents. The deputy, Scott Ramirez, got into a firefight with Welchel and was wounded. Welchel pistol whipped the family at the house, killing the mother and sending their two children to the hospital with head wounds.

"This was an act of unexplained violence. It certainly wasn't the level of force necessary to steal a car, which was his intent," [Sheriff] Brooks said. "It was violence just for violence sake."

Welchel then drove to a Wal-Mart and entered the store. Police surrounded the building and evacuated it. When they entered the store, they found Welchel dead from a self-inflicted gunshot wound. Welchel had a criminal record in Florida, Indiana, and California, and "had a history of committing violent crimes."[136]

One could say the person "just lost it" and this may be valid. But it is also important to remember that he had an extensive criminal history, including prior acts of violence, and it is already illegal for a felon to possess any firearm. The criminal justice system was unable to keep him out of the general population. Law enforcement officers did not catch up to him until he had invaded a Wal-Mart store, terrorized more people, and committed suicide. This is not to find fault with our criminal justice system, but to highlight the fact that people are often left to their own devices when violence erupts, and in many cases proper use of a firearm by the defender halts the very dynamics that often lead to murder-suicide.

What was possibly nothing more than an editorial in 1925 has also been proven true in the United Kingdom, where gun-involved crime has risen dramatically since the gun ban in 1997.[137]

The Violence Policy Center shows only one side of the equation. One can find as many anecdotes as were referenced in *American Roulette* where the intended victim of domestic violence successfully used a handgun to defend herself:

A woman living in Charles County, Md., initially turned to the judicial system to seek protection from an abusive ex-boyfriend. "I have been afraid to come forth and speak out for fear of him doing bodily harm to me and threatening to burn down my home," she said in her petition requesting a protective order. "The last four years have been a living hell. I am contemplating purchasing a handgun for my protection." After twice violating the court order, the man, described as a violent drug addict, broke into the home and began beating her current boyfriend with a metal pipe. This time she was indeed armed with a handgun, which she used to shoot and kill her attacker. Police said she had not been charged with a crime and that they considered her a victim. (Maryland Independent, Charles County, MD, 04/08/05)[138]

The Violence Policy Center would like us to believe that myriad innocent elderly, young people, and women are dying because of the availability of firearms. But the statistical facts from their own sources prove otherwise, showing significant downward trends in the acts of violent crime which the VPC uses to push their agenda of civilian disarmament. FBI crime statistics show a dramatic drop in violent crime among the general population during the period when domestic violence nearly tripled, proving that availability of guns has no relationship to crime, domestic or otherwise.

Rather than focusing on the use of guns in domestic violence, a far more productive area of inquiry would be to determine what special dynamics exist in domestic relationships that make them so increasingly volatile. Understand these factors, and intervention would perhaps be possible before a situation between intimates explodes into domestic violence. A more relevant question the VPC needs to answer first is: If gun control has been such a failure here and abroad, why would it suddenly benefit a statistically-idiosyncratic and unique environment like domestic violence?

Working Hand-in-Glove

A lie can travel halfway around the world while the truth is putting on its shoes.

- Mark Twain (attributed)

A recent article illustrates how gun control organizations work together with politicians to orchestrate campaigns to ban more guns, discussing a new gun in the American market that allegedly is "capable of piercing police body armor". Senator Charles Schumer was quick to introduce legislation to ban the gun, supported by the Brady Campaign to Prevent Gun Violence, which ran tests on the gun:

> When the group tested the gun with the ammunition supplied with it, it readily penetrated a typical police body vest, said the group's president, Michael Barnes. He played a video of that test at the news conference.[139]

The Bureau of Alcohol, Tobacco, and Firearms posted an information page on their web site "in response to numerous questions that ATF has received regarding the capabilities" of this firearm, concluding that the gun is not armor-piercing with the ammunition that is commercially available. ATF also reiterated that armor-piercing ammunition is banned from civilian use.[140] No independent tests were run to verify Brady Campaign's claims about the gun's armor-piercing capabilities, using ammunition that is available to law-abiding gun owners.

Even law enforcement organizations did not agree that the firearm is armor-piercing. The Fraternal Order of Police (FOP), which states it "is the world's largest organization of sworn law enforcement officers, with more than 321,000 members in more than 2,100 lodges,"[141] noted:

> The Brady Campaign United, with the Million Mom March (formerly Handgun Control, Inc.), is organizing media events in which claims about the power of this new handgun may be exaggerated. The International Association of Chiefs of Police (IACP), the National Organization of Black Law Enforcement Executives (NOBLE) and the International Brotherhood of Police Officers (IBPO) recently participated in a press conference about this new weapon.[142]

Regarding armor-piercing capabilities, the FOP notes armor piercing ammunition is "illegal to possess or sell in the United States" and that "the weapon itself is not the determining factor in whether or not a round can pierce body armor." The FOP also acknowledges: "As with any other contraband item, it is possible that there are a limited number of these illegal armor-piercing rounds that were illegally obtained or imported." The gun itself does not pose a special threat to law enforcement. The true threat is once again, criminals who will not be deterred by the police from illegally obtaining banned ammunition. The FOP finishes with the admonition: "Remember–ANY weapon in the hands of a criminal is potentially lethal!"[143]

The Brady Campaign and Disinformation

The Brady Campaign to Prevent Gun Violence has a web page addressing Australian crime since the 1997 gun ban, called *The Truth About Australia*. They open their article with the admonishment: "The National Rifle Association likes to tell tall tales about Australia. The best one is that gun control Down Under is a failure."[144] Brady states:

Between 1987 and 1996, 100 Australians were killed in mass killings of four or more people. Since the new laws went into effect, there has not been a single massacre.[145]

One of the sources they cite in their article, Australia: A Massive Buyback of Low-Risk Guns, found:

Between 1996–97 and 2000–01 there were four mass homicide incidents: two incidents involved four victims (knife and carbon monoxide gas), one incident had five victims (carbon monoxide gas), and another incident fifteen victims (arson/fire).[146]

There seems to be a very elastic definition among gun control organizations as to what comprises a massacre. A Violence Policy Center press release calls the 1989 Stockton, California shooting a "massacre,"[147] where a felon with a criminal history illegally possessed a firearm and killed five school children.[148] Gun Control Australia discusses 32 "gun massacres" where 141 people were killed.[149] This averages out to between 4 and 5 victims per incident. Yet Brady curiously maintains that mass homicide incidents with between four and 15 victims do not qualify as "massacres."

In his book *The Bias Against Guns*, John Lott examined the relationship between gun availability and multiple murders. He concluded:

If right-to-carry laws allow citizens to limit the amount of attacks that still take place, the number of persons harmed should fall relative to the number of shootings… And indeed, that is what we find. The average number of people dying or becoming injured per attack declines by around 50 percent.[150]

Lott also found that both the total number and rate of multiple murders in right-to-carry states are one-third that of restrictive states.[151] In an email interview, he clarified this data by stating:

The simplest numbers showed a 67 percent drop in the number of attacks and about a 79 percent drop in the number of people killed or injured from such attacks. The number of people harmed fell by more than the number of attacks because some attacks that weren't deterred were stopped in progress by people with guns.

One might as easily conclude that the best way to limit multiple murders is not to disarm, but to arm responsible, law-abiding citizens. The Brady Campaign sidesteps statistical reality in order to promote an idyllic fantasy of a peacefully disarmed citizenry. Reality shows that while there have been no mass murders using guns since the Australian gun ban, there have been "massacres" as defined by gun control groups.

Other points in the Brady article concerns homicides involving guns:

- "Homicides committed with firearms have been declining slowly before the Port Arthur Massacre, more sharply since [the ban]" and
- "While the 1996 gun laws did not initiate the decline in firearm homicides, they appear to have accelerated it."[152]

The complete quote from their reference, Australian Crime Facts and Figures 2002, is:

The percentage of homicides committed with a firearm continued its declining trend since 1969. In 2001, 16% of homicides involved firearms. The figure was 18% in 2000.[153]

Nowhere does *Australian Crime Facts and Figures 2002* make any claims about the gun ban affecting homicide rates, and they acknowledge that the decline in firearm homicides is part of a longer-term trend begun over 25 years before the ban. And as noted in Chapter 2, even Australia's top crime statistician, Don Weatherburn, acknowledged the gun ban had no significant impact on the amount of gun crime.

Australia: A Massive Buyback of Low-Risk Guns states:

The total homicide rate has been slowly declining throughout the 1990s. In the five years post-NFA [National Firearms Agreement/gun ban] there has been no pronounced acceleration of that decline."[154]

While it is heartening to see a drop in homicide, keep in mind that since the ban, the Australian murder rate (per 100,000 population) has dropped 15%, while the US murder rate dropped 30%, even though the ATF recorded tens of millions of gun purchases through the 1990s. Also, the use of guns in U.S. homicides has dropped, from 69.9% of all homicides in 1994[155] to 63.4% in 2001.[156] Obviously, if those Australian firearms didn't exist, they could not be used to commit murder. But claiming that banning guns had any effect on the actual firearm murder rate simply does not jibe with statistical reality.

Along with their claims about Australian homicide rates, the Brady Campaign also states:

Australia has seen a decline in the use of firearms in armed robberies. From 1993 to 2001, the proportion of robberies committed with a firearm dropped from 16 to 6 percent.[157]

Brady derives their numbers from the Australian Bureau of Statistics, as does the Australian Institute of Criminology, the publisher of *Australian Crime Facts and Figures 2002*. It is true that in 2001, only 6% of all robberies involved a firearm.[158] However, robbery rates in Australia rose 70% from inception of the gun ban to the end of the reporting period covered in *The Truth About Australia*. During the same time period, the U.S. robbery rate dropped 26.5%, from 201.9 to 148.5 per 100,000 people.[159] Again, Brady's statistical source, *Australian Crime Facts and Figures 2002*, states: "In 2001 the rate for robbery peaked at 136 per 100,000 people—the highest recorded since 1995."[160] As with homicide, if there were no guns, they would not be used in armed robbery. Australian criminals have simply found other methods.

Brady's final point is:

Suicide rates using a firearm show a sharp drop from 1979-98 with rates continuing to drop after 1996 and firearm-related accidental injuries in Australia are also declining.

Their source for this statement, *Australia: A Massive Buyback of Low-Risk Guns*, confirms a decline in the number of suicides by firearm, but also notes an increase in the overall suicide rate,[161] which was reported to be 26.5% higher than the (falling) U.S. rate.[162] This supports the World Health Organization findings discussed in Chapter 3, that firearms availability does not directly influence suicide rates. Nor did *Australia: A Massive Buyback of Low-Risk Guns* credit the gun ban with having any beneficial effect on suicide. They also noted that gun-assisted suicide rates had been dropping since long before the ban:

- "Suicide rates did not fall, though there was a shift toward less use of guns, continuing a very long-term decline."[163]

- "The firearm-related suicide rates had been declining for ten years before the Port Arthur incident."[164]

- "A sharply increasing share of suicides is the result of hanging or suffocation, surely representing different dynamics from instrumentality."[165]

As with violent crime, if there were no guns, there would be no gun-assisted suicide. But since suicide is increasing, the Brady discussion about suicide merely deflects from considering the true causative factors behind killing oneself.

As for the claim that "firearm-related accidental injuries in Australia are also declining," *Australia: A Massive Buyback of Low-Risk Guns* notes that this decline began before the ban, and that the ban has not affected the rate of decline of accidental shootings:

Jenny Mouzos notes that accidental firearm injury rates declined over 1995–99. The number of firearm-related hospitalizations has declined each year between 1994–95 and 1998–99. Over that period, about half each year are classified as accidental. This decline in accidental injury is consistent with diminished stockpile and enhanced safety requirements, but the decline starts well before the NFA implementation and is no sharper following than in the two years before.[166]

Australian sources did not credit the gun ban with any beneficial effect on accidental firearm injury rates. Between 1994 and 2001, the CDC reports that accidental firearms injuries in the U.S. decreased 30%, from 89,744 to 63,012.[167] Therefore, a decline in accidental injury is not related to "diminished stockpile and enhanced safety requirements."

As Dave Kopel writes in *Who Needs Guns*:

It has become a common trick in gun-banning countries to bring all deaths by shooting, including suicide, into a subset of their own and then to claim that "gun deaths" are declining after the passage of legislation. The Australian murder rate has not dropped, and neither has the suicide rate. People continue to kill themselves and one another, but the fact that fewer guns are involved in these deaths is supposedly a great triumph of public policy.[168]

Apparently, the Brady Campaign believes that as long as civilians don't own guns, it is an acceptable price to have more people raped, robbed, and assaulted, as has happened in Australia and the United Kingdom since their gun bans. This attitude hearkens back to feudalism, when everybody's life was cheap, except, of course, those in power who had private standing armies to protect them. Enter Sarah Brady, member of the Washington elite by virtue of her husband, who was press secretary to President Reagan.

The Brady article concludes: "The next time a credulous friend tells you that Australia actually experienced more crime when it got tougher on crime, offer your friend a Fosters and a helping of truth." Here is revealed the true ideology of the gun control organization: civilian disarmament is synonymous with fighting crime, therefore civilian gun ownership is a crime.

Understanding the Brady Campaign Report Card

Brady publishes an annual report card which analyzes a set of gun-law criteria and arrives at a grade from "A" through "F." ("A" being Brady's best grade.) Brady must not be very pleased with the direction of this country, as their national average grade trended from a "C-" in 2001 to a "D+" in 2005. The title of the web page hosting their 2005 edition is entitled *Brady Campaign State Report Cards Show State Legislatures Are Failing to Protect Kids from the Dangers of Illegal Guns*.[169]

States are graded on a set of criteria, ranging from juvenile sale and possession laws to concealed carry laws. In a curious departure from standard operating procedure, Brady created a special criteria for Washington D.C. entitled "Ability of Congress to Repeal DC's gun laws", and assigned D.C. an "F" in this category. Brady ignored two other grading criteria — Juvenile Sale and Safe Guns laws — which would have raised the D.C. grade to an "A." Since D.C. has a complete gun ban, it is impossible for juveniles to buy guns, and any guns still legally owned in D.C. must be rendered inoperable.[170] This special handling of D.C. dropped the grade to a "B" instead of a well-deserved "A" for having the strictest gun control laws in the country.

In 2005, 38 states had right-to-carry laws. The first clue of a possible Brady bias against right-to-carry is that the states of Illinois, Kansas, Nebraska, and Wisconsin got an "A+" for prohibiting all concealed carry.[171] Since Brady Campaign considers each state an equivalent entity in their report, we will follow their lead. By comparing Brady's grading system against each state's violent crime rate, we find that:

- RTC states average a Brady grade of "D," but their average violent crime rate is 395.4 per 100,000 population;

- Non-RTC states (including Washington D.C.) average a grade of "B", but their average violent crime rate is 504.0.[172]

Non-RTC states average 26.6% more violence than RTC states. Of the 38 RTC states, there was only one "A" — Connecticut — five "C's", and 32 states with a grade of "D" or "F". The non-issue states contained three C's", four "B's", six "A's", and no "D" or "F" grades.

Comparing Brady's eight "A-rated" states to their 10 "F-rated" states, we see that Brady's "best" states are 30% more violent than the ones Brady considers the least safe, which all happen to be RTC states. If we remove Connecticut, the lone A-rated RTC state, Brady's "best places to live" become 39.6% more violent.[173]

Even worse for Brady, violent crime trends are not spread equally across all states. Between 2001 and 2005, RTC states (average Brady grade "D") saw an average 2.6% drop in violent crime rates, while non-RTC states (average Brady grade "B") saw a 2.1% decrease. Even when Brady grades synchronize with violent crime trends, it fails to give an accurate picture: Brady dropped the national average grade from "C-" to "D+" in 2005, the same year that the violent crime rate increased 1.3%.[174] This would seem to make sense, as a lower grade is supposed to reflect less safety for citizens. Unfortunately for Brady, most of that increase occurred in non-RTC states, which saw an average increase of 2.8%, while RTC states increased 0.5%. Since 2001, the violent crime differential between RTC and non-RTC states increased from 26.0% to 26.6%, meaning that non-RTC states are becoming relatively more violent compared to RTC states.[175]

These correlations show that the Brady Campaign does not rate states based upon their relative safety, and that their stated concern about "gun violence prevention laws" amounts to nothing more than an unsubstantiated premise that concealed carry laws contribute to violence.

With their penchant for carefully selecting data fragments and partial quotes from studies they reference, it becomes questionable as to whether we should trust organizations like the Violence Policy Center and the Brady Campaign to provide reliable input for public policy-making. For example, ran campaigns to preserve the gun ban in Washington, D.C. VPC's home page announced a new web site that "contains background information on efforts to repeal the District's landmark law" of civilian disarmament as well as "information on the ban's effectiveness."[176] Sarah Brady, chair of the Brady Campaign, is on record as saying: "It would be obscene for Congress to eliminate District of Columbia gun laws."[177]

Examining the FBI violent crime indices for the year 2005, Washington, D.C. had about the same rate of rape as the entire U.S. It gets worse from there, with 2.3 times the rate of aggravated assault, 4.5 times the robbery, and 6 times the homicide rate. Overall, D.C. is 2.9 times as violent as the entire country.[178]

It appears that the "ban's effectiveness" has been to create a decades-long crime wave, persisting even as violent crime rates have fallen during the last 15 years across the nation. As to the allegations of "obscenity," it is clear that the D.C. gun ban had no beneficial effect on crime rates. Considering that RTC laws have not created crime waves in states where they were enacted, it is reasonable to at least experiment by allowing law-abiding residents to own firearms for personal protection. Insisting on maintaining failed policy that results in more citizenry being victimized by thugs seems more in keeping with the definition of "obscenity."

Paul Helmke Continues Brady Tradition

In 2006 Brady Campaign to Prevent Gun Violence introduced their new President, Paul Helmke, in a rebuttal to Florida Governor Bush's statement on the state's decreasing crime rate:

> The truth is that, across the Nation, violent crime, particularly gun crime, has been in sharp decline since the Brady Law went into effect in 1994. Weak gun laws have not made Florida a leader in fighting crime: Arguably, they have helped to make it one of the two most violent states in the Nation.[179]

What Helmke does not say is that the U.S. violent crime rate began dropping two years before passing of the Brady Law. After peaking in 1991, the violent crime rate dropped 5.9% by the end of 1994, the year the Brady Law went into effect.[180] Helmke's implication that the Brady Law helped reduce crime is self-serving and misleading. The National Academy of Science concurs: Their researchers concluded that results are too inconsistent to clearly endorse the Brady Law as a crime-fighting tool.[181]

Helmke ignores Governor Bush's main point: While Florida "weakened" its gun laws to allow concealed carry by law-abiding citizens, violent crime dropped.[182] Florida's violent crime rate reached its peak in 1990, has been falling steadily since 1992, and is at the lowest level since 1977.[183] Between 1987 and 2005, Florida has beaten all five U.S. violent crime indices: overall violent crime by 7.4 percentage points: murder by 23.6; rape by 10.7; robbery by 18.3; and aggravated assault by 0.4 points.[184]

Another Helmke claim is:

According to FBI figures, in 2004 Florida had the second highest violent crime rate of any state in the Nation. Only South Carolina, also with weak gun laws, was more violent.

Gun controllers like to ignore Washington D.C. crime statistics when discussing which state is most violent, even though its population is larger than Wyoming's.[185] Using the FBI report cited by Helmke, our nation's capitol was the most violent jurisdiction in 2004, with a 74.9% higher violent crime rate than second-place South Carolina. Maryland was a close fourth to Florida — just a 1.5% lower violent crime rate — and it also has "strong gun laws" by Brady criteria.[186] Average the two most violent "weak gun law" and the two "strong gun law" jurisdictions, and you get equal average ratings of 2.5. (As noted above in the discussion of their report card, Brady's definition of "weak gun laws" means states with right-to-carry laws.)

The five least violent states — North Dakota, Maine, Vermont, New Hampshire, and South Dakota — all have "weak gun laws" according to Brady criteria.[187] In 2004, RTC states had an average violent crime rate of 388.6, while Brady's "strong gun law" (non-RTC) states rate of 491.2 was 26.4% higher. Brady's favorite states had a 39.1% higher murder rate, a 74.8% higher robbery rate, and 15.1% higher aggravated assault rate. In fairness, it must be noted that RTC states had an 18.9% higher rate of rape.

Another Helmke quote highlights the inconsistent application of their own standards in order to highlight their bias against RTC in the most ideal manner:

Explaining and understanding increases or decreases in crime is always difficult. To argue that putting guns into our communities leads to a reduction in crime makes no sense.

Between 2000 and 2005, the FBI reported that Florida's general population committed FBI violent and property crimes at the rate of 5,155.9 incidents per 100,000 population.[188] The rate of RTC licensees who committed any crime after licensure averaged 101.2 during the same time period. The general population committed FBI crime 72.6 times as often as RTC licensees committed any crime. Using this as an indicator, if Florida's general population were as law-abiding as RTC licensees, the state's crime rate would have decreased over 98%.[189]

This does not prove that RTC reduces crime, but it does show that licensees represent a safer, more responsible population group that requires a much lower expenditure of tax dollars on criminal justice resources. More importantly, it also justifies the right of law-abiding citizens to bear arms in public for self-defense, which is at the core of Governor Bush's statements:

"Law abiding citizens that have guns for protection actually probably are part of the reason we have a lower crime rate."

"The people that commit the majority of the crimes are habitual offenders. They're the ones that commit a crime after crime after crime."[190]

By Helmke's criterion, laid out in the first sentence of his opening quote in this section, to argue that *not* putting guns into our communities leads to a reduction in crime makes no sense, especially in light of the data above.

Helmke at the Helm

It would seem that as mayor, Helmke should have been able to demonstrate his leadership in fighting crime in Fort Wayne, Indiana, considering his posturing as a person who wishes to do so. During Helmke's last five years as mayor (he held the office 1988-2000), the national violent crime rate fell 7.0 percentage points faster, murder fell 12.5 more, and rape fell 12.1 faster, while the aggravated assault rate in Fort Wayne actually rose 15.9%, trailing the national index by 38.4 points. In the five years since Helmke left office, Fort Wayne has beaten the national violent crime index by 11.1 percentage points. He can't blame his failure to rein in crime on the state criminal justice environment. During his last five years as mayor, Indiana realized a 33.5% drop in the violent crime rate, beating the national index by 7.5 points and leaving Fort Wayne 14.5 points behind the state index. In the five years since Helmke left office, Fort Wayne's violent crime index was 11.2% lower than the state's, again showing that state dynamics and policies do not affect the city's ability to fight crime.[191] Given that Helmke had about 8 years to put policies and personnel in place prior to this time period, his management skills as mayor were at odds with both national and state violent crime trends, calling into question his ability to determine what is the best crime-fighting policy direction for our country.

Chapter 4 Redux

MIAMI Employee parking lots have become an unlikely focus in the fight over gun rights.

The nation's largest lawyers group is taking on the biggest gun rights organization over employers' rights to bar workers from leaving guns in their cars while on the job.

The American Bar Association says the issue is workplace violence and how to reduce it.

CLASH OVER GUNS

The ABA, meeting in Miami, is expected to go on record early next week supporting the right of employers "to exclude from the workplace and other private property, persons in possession of firearms or other weapons."

Roughly 1,000 people are killed at work each year, and guns are used in 80 percent of those incidents, the ABA says, citing federal estimates.[192]

Chapter 4 examined the links between lawyer and law firm campaign contributions and anti-gun-rights voting in Congress, so it should come as no surprise that the American Bar Association is on the anti-gun side over the subject of employees leaving firearms in their car when at work. Nor should it be a surprise to find that the ABA plays loose with the numbers they toss around.

"Roughly 1,000 people are killed at work each year" is a vague statement. Employees can be killed at work due to industrial accident or from malicious intent. In 2005 there were 5,702 total workplace deaths, intentional and accidental. Of these, there were 787 total deaths by assaults and violent acts. This still leaves a large rounding error to reach 1,000. But the Bureau of Labor Statistics considered 564 of these to be homicides, which results in an even larger rounding error. Since 439 (77.8%) of these were shooting deaths, the "80%" claim is fairly accurate.[193] Nevertheless, the implication in the above quote is that about 800 people are shot to death at work each year, which is in itself over 80% off.

The following discussion will examine research being cited to support the idea that guns in the workplace present a danger, and shed light on some of the dynamics behind workplace shootings.

Is Brady For or Against Workplace Safety?

In Fall 2005, the Brady Campaign published a report called *Forced Entry: The National Rifle Association's Campaign To Force Business To Accept Guns At Work*. It includes the term "CCW" 17 times by the end of page 1 and contains an appendix entitled CCW License Holders: "Law-Abiding Citizens?"[194] This makes it reasonable to infer that this report is just as much an attempt to condemn right-to-carry as it is an argument against permitting qualified employees to bear arms to or at work.

Citing Bureau of Labor Statistics (BLS) data, Brady implies that workplace violence is at epidemic levels. It notes:

Moreover, the level of gun violence at work remains high. Almost 500 firearm homicides were committed in the workplace in 2003, with almost 90% of these occurring in the private sector. In addition, another three private sector employees are wounded each week by shootings at the workplace.[195]

Referring to the BLS, we see that there were 487 workplace homicides in 2003, with 433, or 89%, occurring in the private sector.[196] Despite rounding errors which make their numbers more sinister, Brady seems to be on track, so we will use their data sources in this discussion.

Bureau of Labor Statistics data shows that the only category with a smaller number of non-fatal incidents is rape, and shootings make up 0.6% of all assaults and violent acts. People are four times more likely to get bitten at work than shot.[197] Brady states:

> Companies have an obligation in most cases to protect employees and customers from foreseeable acts of violence on company property.[198]

Using this criteria, banning teeth would make the workplace four times safer than banning guns, and companies should "have an obligation" to do so. Brady continues with their anti-RTC message:

> Given the uncertain character of and lack of training for CCW licensees, coupled with the pervasive problems of workplace violence, increasing the number of guns on company property increases the chances for gun violence.[199]

From 1992 to 2005, the BLS notes that homicides in the workplace dropped from 1,044 to 564, a 46% decrease. This betters the national decrease of 39.6% in the murder rate during the same time period.[200] In 1992, homicides were the second most common cause of workplace fatalities, trailing highway incidents by only 10%. By 2005, homicides dropped to the fourth most common cause, trailing highway incidents by over 60%. Most interesting is that occurrences of the three other most frequent causes of workplace fatality have increased since 1992, while homicide declined dramatically: highway accidents increased 23.3%, falls 27.8%, and being struck by an object 8.4%.[201] It would seem reasonable that Brady should rename itself to the *Campaign Against Falling* if it were truly concerned over workplace safety.

During this time frame, 21 states enacted shall-issue right-to-carry (RTC) laws, more than doubling the number of RTC states.[202] Also during this time, the national violent crime rate dropped 38.1% and the murder rate decreased 39.6%.[203] According to Brady logic, this should "prove" that RTC will reduce workplace homicides: Guns in public increased while the chance for violence decreased, therefore "increasing the number of guns on company property" should *decrease* the chance of violence.

None of the BLS data identifies whether an incident was part of intentional crime such as robbery, nor does it indicate whether the perpetrator was a RTC licensee, so there is no documented link between RTC and increased workplace violence from Brady's source.

What is very interesting is that when divided by the total number of private and public employees, the workplace homicide rate in 2005 was 0.4 per 100,000 population,[204] compared to the national homicide rate of 5.6 (14 times higher).[205]

Appendix A of *Forced Entry* contains what Brady calls "The Incident File".[206] It lists 41 alleged firearm violations by RTC licensees, committed over the seven-year period of 1996-2002, 30 of which actually involved somebody getting shot. One of the incidents was ruled self-defense:

On July 6, 2001, an unnamed man fatally shot 17-year-old Jacob W. Walton during a road rage altercation in Spokane, WA.[207,208]

Brady includes six incidents that were accidental discharges, leaving 23 incidents with criminal intent. Guy Smith, in his book *Gun Facts*, notes four violent acts and one property crime by gun control advocates during the year 2000: one shooting, two assaults, one theft, and one terrorist threat.[209] The Brady Campaign expects perfection from gun owners, but a search of its web site shows it is curiously quiet regarding these incidents. Anecdotes can be found favoring both sides of this argument, but they prove nothing except Brady's double standard.

The Brady Campaign set out to prove that guns are bad and RTC licensees are worse, but their own data sources do not support their contentions.

Does Biased Research Foster Workplace Danger?

To bolster their hypothetical link between concealed carry and workplace violence, the Brady Campaign references a paper published by researchers from the University of North Carolina:

As a result of the NRA's shall-issue laws, companies that have not taken affirmative steps to keep guns out of the workplace and off company property have faced an increased risk of workplace violence. Indeed, a study published in May 2005 in the American Journal of Public Health concluded:

"[W]orkplaces where guns were specifically permitted were 5 to 7 times more likely to be the site of a worker homicide relative to those where all weapons were prohibited."[210]

Brady cited a paper entitled *Employer Policies Toward Guns and the Risk of Homicide in the Workplace*. The authors, Loomis and Marshall, surveyed companies in North Carolina about policies regarding firearms in the workplace and concluded:

Workplaces where guns were permitted were about 5 times as likely to experience a homicide as those where all weapons were prohibited…The findings suggest that policies allowing guns in the workplace might increase workers' risk of homicide.[211]

The authors introduce their topic by stating their real agenda as an assumption: "We hypothesized that policies allowing guns in the workplace may increase the risk of homicide for workers."[212] In scientific research, a more appropriate hypothesis would have been: "Do policies allowing guns in the workplace have an impact on the risk of homicide?" The authors admit:

This study was limited by the nature of the data available on worker's exposure to guns. We generally did not know how often employees had guns at work, whether worker's guns were used during the fatal events, and whether perpetrators came armed or used the victims' own weapons. The inability to examine worker's or perpetrators' actions limited the ability of the current study to look beyond employers' policies.[213]

Relevant data points are missing. The authors do not know if concealed carry licensees were involved in any of the shootings, or if these licensees had any moderating effect on the attacks. The authors do not know how often or how many employees brought firearms to work, so they do not know if greater presence of firearms at the time of incident had a positive or negative effect on the attack. All the authors can address is the relative restrictiveness of an employer's policy regarding firearms possession on the premises.

Even though they conclude there is a correlation between an employer's liberal firearms policy and shootings, they ignore the causal relationship: Did the employer allow trusted employees to carry on the job because they recognized their business was more at risk for an attack? The authors note that workplaces with security "control measures" such as locked entrances, bright lighting and alarms had the greatest probability of homicide, and also note that high-risk workplaces have the second-highest probability.[214] Curiously, the authors derogate their own findings:

Although we collected data on workplaces' experience with robbery and violent crime, we did not control for it in the models presented here because adjustment for a determinant of exposure generally is not appropriate.[215]

Nor do they answer another relevant question: If firearms in the workplace lead to more shootings, why do we not read reports of incidents occurring in police stations, where virtually everybody is armed?

Anti-rights organizations often cite such research papers to promote their agenda. As noted earlier in this chapter, the National Research Council of the National Academy of Science (NAS) actually challenged Kellermann's and Reay's 1986 paper, saying their conclusions were of "little relevance" because there is no established relationship between homicide/suicide and defense against criminal perpetrators.

Like that paper, this one also highlights the problem of sampling error. Loomis and Marshall based their conclusions on 296 businesses,[216] but the Small Business Administration notes that in 2003 — the latest data available at the time of this writing — there were 166,070 employer businesses in North Carolina alone.[217] Loomis and Marshall based their conclusions on less than 0.2% of all North Carolina businesses: This highlights how fragile such conclusions are when compared to national data sets.

Loomis and Marshall cite other Kellermann research as the basis for their assumption that guns in the workplace increase homicide risk.[218] The NAS panel found Kellermann's conclusions in the Loomis and Marshall reference "are not tenable."[219] Furthermore, they quote Kellermann's own disclaimer: "it is possible that reverse causation accounted for some of the association we observed between gun ownership and homicide."[220] Kellermann acknowledges uncertainty over his own conclusion that guns on the premises cause more homicide.

Loomis and Marshall rely upon discredited research to justify making a biased conclusion at the outset of their study. They then ignore their own findings as inappropriate when those findings conflict with the authors' predetermined outcome. Basing policy upon such a questionable publication invites its own risk.

The Miami Herald's Bias Against Self-Defense

"The advertisement is the most truthful part of a newspaper." — Thomas Jefferson

A series of Miami Herald articles highlight a media attempt to mix selected data with opinion in order to transform reporting into social engineering. The first article begins innocuously enough, describing how a sleeping man was awakened by three men breaking into his residence. He grabbed his pistol and confronted the invaders, telling them to leave. When they attacked him, he shot at them in self-defense, killing one.

Then the author takes a turn we have come to expect from mainstream media. In order the make the criminal into the victim, a biased report is not complete without a Gratuitous Friend Testimonial: "He was a gentleman all around…He had a good spirit. We just can't believe it."[221]

Oxford English Dictionary defines "gentleman" as: "A man who demonstrates his gentle birth by appropriate behavior or moral qualities, e.g. chivalrous conduct, consideration for others, sense of honor, etc.; [generally] a man (of whatever rank) who displays such qualities."[222] Home invasion is neither gentlemanly nor chivalrous.

This article ends with: "The law may be on his side. Florida's new 'Stand Your Ground' [Castle Doctrine] law allows anyone who feels threatened — even if they don't see a gun — to shoot."

The author's choice of words is curious. Under current law regarding the justifiable use of deadly force, the word "feel" does not appear. The word "threaten" appears twice, specifically addressing circumstances where law enforcement officers, not private citizens, may use force in making an arrest. "Feeling threatened" is not considered a valid criteria for the use of lethal force.[223]

In order to turn her article into an editorial without bearing any burden of proof for asserting that Castle Doctrine makes it easier for people to get away with murder, the writer resorts to the phrase "the law may be on his side", fomenting suspicion in the reader's mind that Castle Doctrine "may be" a danger to society. An email request for clarification elicited the following response:

The new law, sir, passed last year in April, removes the so-called "responsibility to run" that made it illegal to shoot if you had a way to escape.

I know of three incidents within the last year when someone shot another person because they felt "threatened" and the state attorneys [sic] office declined to press charges.

The men that broke into Mr. McKinley's town home did not have weapons and he did have a way out of the home. He didn't have to confront them.[224]

Florida statutes from 2004 show that before Castle Doctrine, there was no requirement for a resident to be threatened with a gun to justify using deadly force in their home.[225] Nor did previous jury instructions require proof that a resident tried to first retreat when confronted by persons committing forcible felonies — such as home-invasion robbery — in the defender's home.[226,227] Since legal references included here are accessible online, why was this "Investigative Reporter" from one of the country's largest newspapers unable to give the public the facts, or at least a reasonable description of the law in question?[228]

Her email response also took liberty with reality, as two intruders were still at large and nobody knew if they had weapons. Even if caught without weapons, there was sufficient opportunity to dispose of them prior to capture. The author knew this, as her article stated:

"BSO [Broward Sheriff's Office] used dogs on the ground and a helicopter in the air to search the neighborhood for the two other men for several hours. Late Wednesday, they hadn't been found."[229]

An email request for clarification on this point resulted in journalistic double-speak:

Police also told us off the record they didn't believe that they were carrying weapons but since they didn't know if the suspects had thrown them away they couldn't say for sure on the record that they were unarmed. The victim told police he didn't see a gun.[230]

In this journalist's mind, police are telepathic. Perhaps this is why the media supports civilian disarmament: If the police possess such powers of omnipotence, they should stop all crime before it occurs, similar to the (fictional) movie Minority Report, thereby eliminating the need for self-defense.

Email interviews with two police officers resulted in the response that a resident confronted with three intruders, armed or not, is reasonably justified in using whatever force is necessary to end the threat:

The general guideline is always "reasonableness." This guy was confronted by multiple suspects. If he delays reaction he would be risking his own demise.[231]

Common sense dictates that, as these men entered, uninvited (illegally), under cover of darkness, that their intentions are not good...Unarmed? How many people are killed or injured by bludgeoning or cutting instruments commonly found around the house? How much damage can three men do to one if they decide to beat him with their bare hands?[232]

To summarize, the Herald author used revisionist history to misrepresent a defender's duty to retreat under pre-existing Florida law, made unsubstantiated claims the invaders were unarmed, and transmuted a criminal into a "gentleman" to create a fantasy victim scenario where Castle Doctrine law was "used" to get away with murder.

The reason for so much detail on the above article is because it appears to be part of an orchestrated campaign by the Herald to discredit and repeal Florida's Castle Doctrine law. Another Herald article written around the same time, where security guards at a night club defended themselves against somebody using his car as a weapon, repeated the invalid criteria for using deadly force:

It is not clear if the guards will face charges. Florida's new "Stand Your Ground" law, passed last year, allows someone who feels threatened to shoot in self-defense, even if they don't see a gun.[233]

Being run over by a car isn't a threat? The Centers for Disease Control recorded 51 homicides in 2004 where the perpetrator used a motor vehicle as a weapon.[234]

Around the same time, two more articles appeared in the Herald, using misinformation to motivate people to sign a petition to repeal Castle Doctrine. One begins by citing case histories from before the new law, employing the emotionally satisfying "For the Children" gambit:

Of at least 13 cases of children and teenagers killed by stray bullets since 1993, only one defendant went to prison for life. In some cases, shooters were acquitted after claiming self-defense.[235]

Apparently, the author does not realize she just documented how Castle Doctrine is irrelevant to her discussion: People claimed self-defense before and they will in the future; people can get away with murder when the prosecutor doesn't prove his case beyond a reasonable doubt. Unintentionally, the author proves we cannot rely on the criminal justice system to protect us.

She continued by implying there is blanket immunity in defensive shootings, mixing truth with fiction, again using (is there a trend here?), the word "feel":

Under the new law, when people feel threatened, even if they don't see a gun, they can shoot – whether they're standing on a street corner, in their cars or inside their homes. And if they kill someone, they can't be sued by the victim's family.[236]

Actually, Florida Castle Doctrine law specifies the defender cannot be sued only if the shooting is ruled justified.[237]

The fourth article calls Castle Doctrine "Extreme Self-Defense", promoting its repeal as a way to stop felons from shooting children:

> Still, they go out to get more and more signatures on a petition to support changing the law that *could be used* to defend the two men accused of killing Sherdavia, just 9, shot to death while playing on her porch one Saturday afternoon. [Italics added]

> The Stand Your Ground law, passed last year by state legislators to protect average citizens from reasonable fear, says those feeling threatened have "no duty to retreat and [have] the right to stand his or her ground and meet force with force, including deadly force."

> The law, also passed in 14 other states, has taken root in the harshest urban places where gun play is too often a casual reaction to conflict. And now, it has been twisted into an unintended defense for the criminally minded.[238]

It is interesting to note that two Herald reporters wrote an article weeks earlier documenting that both shooters referred to in this article were arrested.[239] Less than a week later, other publications confirmed that both were charged with multiple felonies:

> Both suspects were charged with 2nd Degree Murder With a Deadly Weapon, Attempted 2nd Degree Murder With a Deadly Weapon and Possession of a Weapon/Firearm by a Convicted Felon.[240]

This hardly sounds like they "used" Castle Doctrine to avoid being charged.

The *Miami Herald* blatantly ignores an even more important point which nullifies their anti-Castle Doctrine campaign. Studying the Florida statute, one finds:

> "A person who uses force as permitted in s. 776.012, s. 776.013, or s. 776.031 is justified in using such force and is immune from criminal prosecution and civil action for the use of such force…"

Section 776.012 permits deadly force "to prevent imminent death or great bodily harm to himself or herself or another or to prevent the imminent commission of a forcible felony." Section 776.013 permits deadly force against a person forcefully entering the defender's "dwelling, residence, or occupied vehicle…" Section 776.031 permits deadly force if the defender "reasonably believes that such force is necessary to prevent the imminent commission of a forcible felony."[241]

Castle Doctrine protects the justified defender only from civil action brought by the attacker or his family. To state otherwise is to imply a state of chaos where, for instance, a drug dealer could legally defend himself against a rival's attack and then use the opportunity to kill non-involved competitors, ex-girlfriends, etc. Castle

Doctrine cannot be "twisted into an unintended defense" by criminals, but this hasn't stopped the Herald staff from saying otherwise.

A more recent homicide investigation brought some curiously conflicting information to light. In this case, a 45-year-old man entered the home of his 65-year-old father and began an argument. As the argument escalated, the father "got a handgun and shot the son once in the torso in the back yard of the home." When interviewed, Sergeant Charles E. Mulligan of the St. Johns County Sheriff's Department stated:

> "According to the law, we have to look into all of the facts in this case ... that state of mind was, what the son was doing there, what his intentions were and what threats, if any, were made during the argument," Mulligan said on Monday.[242]

Comparing repeated assertions by the *Miami Herald* to Sergeant Mulligan's statement about having to "look into all of the facts in this case", there appears to be a disconnect between one newspaper's interpretation of Castle Doctrine and the reality of a current investigation by Florida law enforcement. A phone conversation with Sergeant Mulligan discussed the following questions:

- Does Castle Doctrine restrict law enforcement's ability to perform a complete investigation in order to determine whether a shooting is homicide or self-defense?

- Does claiming to be in fear for your life place you in a special, untouchable category?

Sergeant Mulligan's initial response was "No, absolutely not." He went on to expand upon this by explaining some of the basic processes of a homicide investigation. With the advent of Castle Doctrine in Florida, the only aspect that changed was a duty to retreat. Under the old law, one criterion that needed to be evaluated in order to justify a defensive shooting was: "Should you have run out of your house to avoid confronting them? At what point did you have the right to defend yourself in your own house?"

Sergeant Mulligan said law enforcement's standard operating procedure is to sit down with prosecuting attorneys to review the elements of each case. They look at the same set of objective criteria that they did prior to Castle Doctrine, such as the attacker's frame of mind, relative size and physicality of the attacker to the defender; toxicology reports, witness statements, etc. In other words, there are certain questions which must be satisfactorily answered in order to rule a shooting justified. The only change is that the law has "opened up a little" regarding the requirement to retreat. What never changed is that the shooter still has to explain "why": The criteria that existed before Castle Doctrine still exist today.[243]

Counter to *Miami Herald's* claims, Floridians are not "allowed" any more justification than they previously possessed for shooting another person. Also, a shooter may claim they felt in fear for their life, regardless of whether their state has

Castle Doctrine law or not, but in Florida, here is proof that investigations proceed as they always have, regardless of the shooter's claims.

To write about Castle Doctrine in a manner implying that "feeling threatened" is sufficient justification to shoot somebody is misleading at best, and dangerous disinformation at worst. The *Miami Herald's* use of grieving parents, inaccuracies, and myth to promote a repeal of a law they dislike is a public disservice. Their refusal to distinguish between law-abiding citizens protecting themselves and criminals acting badly reveals a contempt for regular people and a "guilty until proven innocent" attitude towards your right to self-defense.[244]

Does Brady Care More About Criminals than Law-Abiding Victims?

When Castle Doctrine law was being considered in the Texas legislature, it received the typical Brady Campaign treatment. An examination of their tactics is a good study for any state considering the law.

Brady came out against Castle Doctrine because of its impact on criminals:

"The law only changes things for the bad guy," Mr. Ragbourn said. "The good guys already had the law on their side."[245]

It appears Brady is in sync with the *Miami Herald*, in that the anti-gun-rights people all believe Castle Doctrine will place the law on the side of the bad guys. They continue with misleading partial truths in an attempt to convince us this law is unnecessary, when Mr. Ragbourn states: "case law already allows people to defend themselves."[246]

Under current law, citizens *usually* have the "right" to defend themselves, but that does not preclude overly-aggressive prosecution or being robbed a second time via civil suit. After telling a home invader— on probation from a prior offense — to leave, Michael Rainiero shot him once, wounding him. The district attorney ruled it justified self-defense, but the criminal sued Rainiero in civil court for "severe and permanent injuries, relentless pain, and loss of earning capacity."[247]

When a criminal entered their place of business and threatened them with a gun, Eli Crespo and Jerry Vega attacked and disarmed him. The aggressor "pleaded guilty to first-degree robbery and was sentenced to 18 years in prison as a repeat violent felon." That didn't stop him from suing the store and employees, accusing them of "intentionally inflicted emotional distress."[248]

The best-case scenario in the above stories is that the defender pays a large legal bill. Castle Doctrine law would protect defenders from such frivolous law suits, forcing the consequences of such action back upon the criminal:

It is an affirmative defense to a civil action for damages for personal injury or death that the defendant, at the time the cause of action arose, was justified in using force or deadly force...

A defendant who prevails in asserting the affirmative defense…may recover from the plaintiff all court costs, reasonable attorney's fees, earned income that was lost as a result of the suit, and other reasonable expenses.[249]

Revealing his bias, Brady's Ragbourn continues:

All that's changed is there is now an extra defense for somebody who shoots somebody.

The castle doctrine laws are so broad…that they allow people to kill someone and then tell law enforcement they were afraid for their safety at the time.[250]

Not ignoring an opportunity to talk to the press, Brady's Peter Hamm chimes in:

It's not Castle Doctrine. That's in the home and you have a right to defend the home…This is the Kingdom Doctrine and you can kill someone anywhere in public. That's a far cry from the home."[251]

The Texas legislation specifies precise criteria for justifying deadly force, even including specific forcible felonies against which lethal force is allowed:

[W]hen and to the degree the actor reasonably believes the deadly force is immediately necessary:

(A) to protect the actor against the other's use or attempted use of unlawful deadly force; or

(B) to prevent the other's imminent commission of aggravated kidnapping, murder, sexual assault, aggravated sexual assault, robbery, or aggravated robbery.[252]

Furthermore, such force is justified only if the aggressor :

(1) unlawfully entered, or was attempting to enter unlawfully, the actor 's habitation, vehicle, or place of business or employment;

(2) unlawfully removed, or was attempting to remove unlawfully, the actor from the actor's habitation, vehicle, or place of business or employment of the actor; or

(3) was committing or attempting to commit an offense described [above].[253]

Being "afraid for [one's] safety" is a very vague reason for justifying deadly force, and not one that is defined in Texas law.

Hamm states: "you have a right to defend the home." Richard Dixon had no such right. This Navy veteran shot and wounded a "career burglar" with a "14-page rap sheet" who broke into his family's New York City home that he worked seven days a week to pay the mortgage for. Dixon used a handgun he had legally purchased before moving to NYC, and was in the process of registering it as per NYC law. Because the gun was unlicensed, he was charged with a crime.[254]

As noted in Chapter 1, NYC's 1911 Sullivan Act assumes anybody with a handgun is a criminal or intends to commit a crime unless he can prove otherwise. But as with many gun control laws, the unintended consequences here resulted in a hardworking, law-abiding citizen being treated as a criminal just because he used a firearm to protect his family.

Brady gave New York a B+ in their 2005 report card, indicating support for the state's restrictive gun laws.[255] By Brady's standards, it's not about Castle Doctrine: It's about gun confiscation.

Mr. Hamm believes: "[Y]ou can kill someone anywhere in public." This sounds remarkably blood-thirsty for somebody whose organization claims to promote civility. One should understand law-abiding citizens before condemning them.

Criminal firearm murders increased 13.6% between 2001 and 2005, while justifiable homicides (JH) by private citizens using firearms decreased 21.9%, with an overall drop of 13.5% in civilian JH.[256] This seems to be a general trend, as law enforcement JH dropped 9.8% overall and 10.1% where a firearm was employed.[257] Between 2001 and 2005, the number of states with shall-issue concealed carry laws increased from 32 to 38, while civilian JH using a handgun decreased 16.8%, and law enforcement JH with a handgun dropped 6.9%.[258] This indicates responsible use and highlights the psychological difference between criminals and peaceable citizens. Who is focusing on killing here?

For that matter, who is focusing on telling the truth? The following section will put all this Castle Doctrine misinformation into perspective.

California Screaming

LOS ANGELES, January 17, 2007 - Two men arrested in connection with a stray shot that killed a 9-year-old girl in Angelino Heights were released without being charged after authorities determined the bullet that killed the girl was fired in self-defense, it was reported Wednesday.[259]

This case is eerily similar to the one covered by the *Miami Herald* above. It started out sensibly enough, though tragically. On December 22, 2006 the Los Angeles Police Department announced the arrest of "two key suspects [Cesar Zamora and Steven Castanon] connected with the shooting" of a 9-year-old girl, and their bail was set at $500,000 each. At the time, the girl was hospitalized in critical condition.[260]

Less than a month later, the Los Angeles district attorney's office explained why they declined to bring charges against the alleged killers. (The girl died six days after being shot.) It came down to insufficient testimony from the three witnesses, with one witness initially claiming he saw Zamora shoot back at a man who got out of a car and shot first, but on two subsequent interviews claimed he never saw Zamora shoot. The DA continued:

Even if the third witness was willing to admit to his earlier statement to police, he gives a factual scenario that may give rise to a valid claim of self-defense for Zamora and Castanon; thus, it may be that the man who exited the car and attempted to fire at Zamora and Castanon provoked them into responding.[261]

Police were convinced this shooting was "gang-related," but also believed Zamora and Castanon were justified because they were shot at first. Robert Pugsley, criminal law professor at Southwestern Law School in Los Angeles, stated: "A person has a right of self-defense, and third-party damage, as sad as it may be, is considered an unintended consequence." Peter Keane, professor of law at Golden Gate Law School in San Francisco, agreed. Prosecutors and police mentioned that both Zamora and Castanon were previously-convicted criminals when they said: "they could still charge Zamora and Castanon with a lesser crime—such as a weapons or probation violation." There was also indication that the scene of the shooting was a "gathering point for gang associates", and the DA had "taken initial steps to have the residence declared a nuisance property." [262]

Perusing California law on justifiable homicide, one sees why two California law professors reached the same conclusion. California Penal Code states that homicide is justifiable: "When resisting any attempt to murder any person, or to commit a felony, or to do some great bodily injury upon any person." It makes no specification that this force is justified only against the attacker.[263] Thus, two law professors concluded that since the bullet that killed the girl was shot in self-defense against attempted murder, the shooters cannot be prosecuted for murder.

California's gun laws receive strong approbation from the Brady Campaign to Prevent Gun Violence, having received a grade of A- on Brady's latest report card, the highest grade awarded for the 2005.[264]

A second California case also started reasonably enough. On November 11, 2005, the San Diego *Union-Tribune* reported:

LOS ANGELES – The boyfriend of a former Burbank city councilwoman faces a maximum life sentence after pleading guilty to a charge related to his trading two handguns to a gang member in exchange for cocaine, authorities said.[265]

Scott Schaffer pleaded guilty to "using a handgun to further a drug trafficking crime" and faced "at least five years in prison," according to the Burbank Police Department.

However, a February 2007 report noted that the defendant was sentenced to 13 months in prison. He expressed remorse and told the judge he did not know he was trading guns to gang members.[266] Another report noted that this sentence "fell eight months shy of government prosecutors' recommendation of 21 months in prison."

Schaffer's lesser sentence was due, in part, to an outpouring of letters submitted to the court on Schaffer's behalf... One letter in particular, from former Burbank Police Department Lt. Don Brown, described Schaffer in "glowing" terms...

Current members of Burbank PD were "outraged" because Schaffer "supplied guns to a member of the same gang implicated in the shooting death of Officer Matthew Pavelka in November 2003."[267]

Considering the California legislature is a full-time body, reviewing about 2,500 bills each year, it seems reasonable that this loophole in self-defense law could have been addressed.[268] But remember that California is home to the Ninth Circuit Court of Appeals, which found that a felon's possession of a machine gun was not illegal while at the same time concluding the Second Amendment "was not adopted in order to afford rights to individuals with respect to private gun ownership or possession." (At least the latter conclusion gave them reason to uphold his 'felon in possession' conviction.)[269]

So consider this: If you were an anti-gun politician looking for a way to get public support for confiscatory laws, how would you do it? You could:

- Create self-defense law that is intentionally vague, neglecting to include language that specifically justifies defensive use of lethal force only against the attacker.

- Promote a judicial system that is lenient towards felons, declaring that in an enlightened society, these folk need to be understood and appreciated as victims of materialism; disadvantaged socially and economically, etc.

- Condemn incarceration for the same reason.

- Create and strictly enforce gun laws only against heretofore law-abiding citizens, e.g.: require registration (Handgun Safety Certificate[270]), and then classify guns as "assault weapons",[271] clearing a path for government-approved confiscation.

- Declare that your hands are tied and that the only way to get guns out of the hands of felons is to ban guns completely.

If a 9-year-old and a cop get murdered in the process, well...it's for the greater good.

Two states — Florida and Texas — passed laws aimed at reducing the burden of frivolous lawsuits on law-abiding citizens who are forced into the unfortunate position of having to use lethal force to defend against violent crime. The laws were written to circumscribe the use of such force in a manner designed to avoid criminals claiming self-defense to get away with murder. Another state, California, that leads the country in gun control laws and does not intend to pass Castle Doctrine lets killers go free because they are entitled to defend themselves, even if they are already committing a crime by possessing firearms. The Brady Campaign and its willing accomplices in the *Miami Herald* obviously do not support the rights of decent folk.

Blame It on the Gun Lobby

As discussed in Chapter 4, it is a favored gambit to raise the specter of a vague yet powerful "gun lobby" that is operating in the shadows and terrorizing legislators into passing laws which "most people" do not want. As with the Ohio concealed carry story covered earlier in this chapter, media outlets seek out a member of some gun control organization that claims to represent the overwhelming majority of the populace, who then decries the victimization of the people by this dark conspiracy.

A couple of examples of this appeared during the passage of Minnesota's RTC law in the year 2005. An article posted on the web site of a local network TV affiliate summarizes the legislative action as a defeat for gun control groups:

> Gun control advocates in the Senate got an opportunity they were denied two years ago, as they tried but ultimately failed to set stricter limits on who can carry a handgun in public as their fellow lawmakers voted to revive a court-overturned 2003 gun permit law.
>
> "I will not be silenced on this bill and I will not hesitate to point out what a terrible bill it is," said Sen. Wes Skoglund, DFL [Democratic Farmer Labor Party]-Minneapolis, even as a bipartisan group of senators methodically rejected multiple efforts to create more gun-free zones, limits on who can carry guns and deeper background checks on permit applicants.
>
> After hours of debate the Senate voted 44-21 for the handgun bill, a duplicate of the 2003 act that courts struck down because of the flawed method lawmakers used to pass it. At the time, supporters of the bill attached it to an unrelated measure, robbing opponents of the chance to make changes they sought.
>
> Those opponents were able to attach some of those changes to the bill last week in a Senate committee, but found themselves stymied as supporters of the handgun law stripped them right back out during Friday's floor debate, saying they trampled the freedom of gun owners.[272]

What is interesting is that the Minnesota Department of Public Safety has posted guidelines which contradict the article's implication that those who do not want guns on their premises are being victimized. A permit holder is specifically prohibited from carrying on school property. Public colleges and universities, private establishments, and places of employment also have the right of restricting the "carrying of weapons."[273]

Rebecca Thorman, executive director of Citizens for a Safer Minnesota, was quoted: "They're just showing the sway that the gun lobby has over the Legislature." The group's web site has a page that urges citizens to "please express your disappointment with these legislators who ignored their constituents and voted with the gun lobby."[274] Since the Minnesota Personal Protection Act came close to passing in 2001, this gave the alleged gun control "majority" at least two election cycles to place their representatives in legislature.[275] Considering the media's preference for featuring gun control organizations in any article about right-to-carry, and those organizations' position on gun control, had there been some "gun lobby" conspiracy manipulating all those local elections for the last 4+ years, at least one investigative reporter or a Brady/Violence Policy Center press release should have announced some documentation of such clandestine activity. Since nothing remotely like this has ever been reported — or even rumored — we are left with the impression that, like all the RTC laws enacted in other states, Minnesota's was also the result of a lengthy public debate, and thus more closely represents the people's will.

When Gun Banners Tell the Truth

Sometimes, even the most statistically illiterate people can get it right. Unfortunately for the gun control organizations, when they are honest, they contradict everything they stand for. An executive of an Illinois gun control group recently admitted that Chicago's reduction in homicides was due to new policing strategies, not its handgun ban:

> In 2003, there were 620 homicides in Chicago before a dramatic drop in 2004 to 450.

> The number of homicides is set to be even smaller this year, but that's not necessarily attributable to the handgun ban, said Thom Mannard, executive director of the Illinois Council Against Handgun Violence.

> Instead, he said, the decline is due to a better Chicago police strategy of allocating more officers to areas where guns are known to be ubiquitous.[276]

It is interesting to note that good people with guns, in this case police, are the reason for the decline in homicides. Actually, Mr. Mannard merely repeats what law enforcement professionals have been saying all along. Two other big cities with longstanding civilian disarmament laws finally began to see drops in their above-average violent crime rates because of enhanced policing techniques:

> The District [of Columbia] had fewer than 200 homicides last year for the first time in nearly two decades, a steep drop from the deadly bloodshed that was fueled by drugs and gangs in the 1980s and 1990s.

> D.C. Police Chief Charles H. Ramsey said police got results by making more arrests and seizing more guns, rigorously analyzing crime trends and joining other city agencies in focusing on 14 "hot spots." Overall, crime in those areas dropped by 30 percent last year, he said.

> "Aggressively attacking crime has had an impact on the streets," said Ramsey, who became chief in 1998. "We feel good that we were able to drive the numbers down."[277]

[New York] Citywide, serious crime is expected to fall for the 13th straight year in 2004. The homicide tally so far this year — 547 — is down 4.4 percent from last year, and should stay below 600 for the third year in a row, a level comparable to the early 1960s. New York had a record 2,245 killings in 1990.

Officials with the New York Police Department credit their success to a series of crime-fighting initiatives. One involves assigning a roving team of 1,000 officers to make more arrests in so-called "impact zones."[278]

These examples beg the question: If violent crime is addressed via innovative law enforcement practices, why are gun bans continued to be touted as a way to reduce violent crime?

Sometimes gun controllers, in their honesty, reveal an even more sinister side. A recent article discussed the need for police officers to be outfitted with high-powered rifles. As law enforcement agencies noted the increasing use of illegal, fully automatic weapons by criminals who are practicing their shooting skills more, there is a need for police departments to protect their officers and empower them to have sufficient capabilities to successfully deal with violent encounters. This pattern caused great concern for the Violence Policy Center:

"Because the bad guys have assault rifles, law enforcement officers should?" asks Tom Diaz, senior policy analyst for the Violence Policy Center, a Washington, D.C.-based nonprofit organization that advocates gun control.[279]

After explaining that civilians don't need firearms anymore because the police supposedly will protect us, now VPC wants the police to be disarmed relative to the violent predators they are supposedly protecting us from. It's very interesting to note when an agenda is so much more important than anything else, a gun controller reveals how little he values the lives of the law-abiding — including our law enforcement professionals. In Mr. Diaz's world, only the criminals would have access to military-grade weaponry. In this case, by supplying ready outlets for the pronouncements of such "experts," the media unwittingly provides a valuable service to society by showing the rest of us the true nature of the gun-banner.

Conclusion

Gun control organizations find willing partners in the media, which rely on these groups to provide the sound bites that are credited as if they are the final word. These quotes and misinformation then get picked up by the politicians, who refer to the media and gun control groups' verbiage as authoritative, which gives the media more sound bites, and then the cycle repeats itself, with each iteration creating more of an aura of unassailable truth. However, when one begins to examine the methods and data which gun control organizations use to promote their agenda, their entire logic structure, conclusions, and stated goals begin to disintegrate. If they are not acting in the best interests of public safety, what are they *really* trying to accomplish? (To be answered in the next chapter.)

Chapter 6
The United Nations and Global Disarmament

More than 500,000 people have been killed by firearms in Brazil between 1979 and 2003, according to a new report by the United Nations.

The study found that there were more gun-related killings in Brazil than in most war zones.

Guns are the single biggest cause of death among young people in the Latin American nation, the organisation says.

The U.N. has urged lawmakers to approve plans for a referendum in October on whether to ban the sale of firearms.[1]

The United Nations has been promoting world-wide civilian disarmament since the 1990s. Their professed goals are encapsulated in the reference above: Guns kill people, therefore the people should not have access to guns. As noted in Chapter 2, civilian disarmament on a national scale did not succeed, but what if the entire world's civilian population were disarmed? If all guns were restricted from public access, would this halt criminals' international arms trade, eliminating criminal access and reducing crime as well? Most importantly, is it true that civilian firearms are the biggest threat to our global safety and security?

The United Nations and 'Consolidation of Peace'

Beginning in the mid-1990s, the United Nations began to focus on the idea that global disarmament was a way to promote peace. On the face of it, this sounds like a wonderful thing, for who doesn't want peace? Here are some excerpts from a draft resolution entitled *Consolidation of peace through practical disarmament measures*:

"Convinced that a comprehensive and integrated approach towards certain practical disarmament measures…"

"…the readiness of the international community to assist affected States in their efforts to consolidate peace would greatly benefit the effective implementation of practical disarmament measures…"

"…the importance of such practical disarmament measures has received growing attention from the international community in general, and from interested and affected Member States in particular, as well as from the Secretary-General…"[2]

Rebecca Peters is director of the International Action Network on Small Arms, an advocacy group that works with the U.N. to ban civilian firearms. The IANSA declares as part of its program: "New thematic networks built around key issues, such as public health, women and children will increase international expertise and cooperation in joint efforts for change."[3] Ms. Peters career in gun control got its start in Australia, where she was an important contributor to that country's current gun ban.[4] As pointed out in Chapter 2, the rates of rape, robbery, and assault have increased since Australia enacted its ban, and women and children in that country have not realized enhanced safety and security as a result. Is Australia's experience the rule or the exception? More importantly, has the U.N. created, nurtured and furthered a global environment of "consolidated peace"?

U.N. Peacekeeping Experiences

Beginning in 1991, revolution in Sierra Leone resulted in slaughter of unarmed civilians:

> Sweeping into villages, the rebels round up alleged government sympathizers, including women and children, and summarily execute them or lop off arms, legs and other body parts.

> On the other side is the democratically-elected government, which is supported by a large Nigerian military force known as ECOMOG. Unfortunately, ECOMOG was criticized just last week by United Nations Secretary General Kofi Annan for conducting its own barbarisms against those it deemed sympathetic to the rebels.

> And caught in the middle is the civilian population.[5]

The international community "either has been unable or unwilling to broker an accord, and relief agencies, including the Red Cross, have largely left the area because of threats from both sides." The United Nations was accused of "ignoring the brutal killing" in this West African nation "while focusing on the massacres in Yugoslavia's Kosovo province." The Security Council's response was to issue a statement expressing "grave concern" about the situation in Sierra Leone but "made no attempts to intervene in the conflict."[6]

The Rwanda Massacre

Rwanda was a U.N. member during their genocide of 1994. As Professor Rudolph J. Rummel, Professor Emeritus of the University of Hawaii, explains:

> The Western media have greatly misunderstood the 1994 genocide as a tribal meltdown, as ethnic hatred and intolerance run amok. The mental picture is of a Hutu running widely down a street swinging a machete at any Tutsi he can catch. This is a myth. Rather, the genocide was a well-calculated mass murder planned by Hutu government leaders.

> President Habyarimana's government allowed Rwandans virtually no freedom. He created a strict one-party state with the intention of being able to control and quickly mobilize the population. The government divided people into communes, and if a citizen wanted to move in or out of his assigned commune, he had to report to the police.

> This was not an act of massacre by the uneducated, undisciplined masses, ordinary folk easily misled and aroused. As with the Holocaust, when Nazi killing squads were often led and composed of PhDs and other professionals, the claims of the powerful and authoritative easily swayed the well educated to murder. In the Great Genocide, Hutu

lawyers, teachers, professors, medical doctors, journalists, and other professionals, made their contribution to the methodical annihilation of the Tutsi or defiant Hutu.[7]

During the conflict, the U.N. either couldn't or didn't protect refugees, who from all reports were unarmed. The U.N. slowed the process of repatriation of refugees to native Rwanda, preferring to send in "human rights investigators" as a solution to the ongoing problem of violence, of which there was plenty of evidence:

Aid workers and journalists, who yesterday discovered over 5,000 missing refugees coming out of the forests south of Kisangani, came across the scene of a massacre in Biaro camp, 41 kilometres from the town. CNN showed pictures of rotting corpses and people dying in a tented hospital. The refugees claimed they were attacked by soldiers. In an interview, EU Special Envoy Aldo Ajello said he believed the attacks were carried out by "army groups acting alone".

Meanwhile the search was underway for tens of thousands of refugees still missing from Biaro and the two camps at Kasese, further north. An estimated 85,000 have disappeared. This figure represents about a third of all Rwandan refugees still unaccounted for.[8]

Human Rights Watch summarized the entire episode in their paper *Leave None to Tell the Story*: "In the thirteen weeks after April 6, 1994, at least half a million people perished in the Rwandan genocide, perhaps as many as three quarters of the Tutsi population." Corroborating Rummel's conclusions, *Leave None* states: "This genocide resulted from the deliberate choice of a modern elite to foster hatred and fear to keep itself in power." *Leave None* also confirms that the international community failed to take action when it was clear what was about to happen:

Policymakers in France, Belgium, and the United States and at the United Nations all knew of the preparations for massive slaughter and failed to take the steps needed to prevent it.[9]

Leave None tells of how President Juvenal Habyarimana was losing popularity after two decades in power. As the Rwandan Patriotic Front began to attack from Uganda, he and his colleagues embarked on a massive propaganda campaign to regain power:

For three and a half years, this elite worked to redefine the population of Rwanda into "Rwandans," meaning those who backed the president, and the "ibyitso" or "accomplices of the enemy," meaning the Tutsi minority and Hutu opposed to him.[10]

By 1993, the U.N. believed that Rwanda would give the U.N. "a successful peacekeeping operation to offset the failure in Somalia," where U.N. peacekeepers were supposed to:

[M]onitor the cease-fire in Mogadishu, the capital of Somalia, and to provide protection and security for United Nations personnel, equipment and supplies at the seaports and airports in Mogadishu and escort deliveries of humanitarian supplies from there to distribution centers in the city and its immediate environs.[11]

But concerns about the cost of a peacekeeping mission in Rwanda caused not only delays in implementation but also reduced the eventual size of the peacekeeping force.

In 1993, the Habyarimana government was forced to sign a peace accord with the well-armed Rwandan Patriotic Front. Nevertheless since the ruling elite had already succeeded in creating racial division between the Hutu and Tutsi using "attacks, virulent propaganda, and persistent political maneuvering," they prepared an armed force to attack the minority Tutsi:

Soldiers and political leaders distributed firearms to militia and other supporters of Habyarimana in 1993 and early 1994, but Bagosora and others concluded that firearms were too costly to distribute to all participants in the "civilian self-defense" program. They advocated arming most of the young men with such weapons as machetes. Businessmen close to Habyarimana imported large numbers of machetes, enough to arm every third adult Hutu male.

In this case, "militia" was the term for civilians recruited to assist in the planned genocide, who were often led by former military personnel. The Habyarimana assassination on April 6, 1994 provided the perfect excuse for a "planned extermination" by his followers, using ethnic cleansing as an excuse to consolidate power:

The Presidential Guard and other troops commanded by Colonel [Théoneste] Bagosora, backed by militia, murdered Hutu government officials and leaders of the political opposition, creating a vacuum in which Bagosora and his supporters could take control. Soldiers and militia also began systematically slaughtering Tutsi.[12]

When the commander of the U.N. peacekeeping force in Rwanda notified his superiors in New York of the impending massacre, the gravity of these warnings were not passed along. As a result, "the Security Council made only small changes in the rate of troop deployment, measures too limited to affect the development of the situation."[13]

Next, rather than committing peacekeeping forces to stop the atrocities, the U.N. enabled genocide by making the safety of its peacekeeping troops a priority:

But instead of using the peacekeeping troops to stop the genocide, the U.N. sought primarily to protect its soldiers from harm. [UN Commander] Dallaire was ordered to make avoiding risk to soldiers the priority, not saving the lives of Rwandans. To do so, he regrouped his troops, leaving exposed the Rwandans who had sought shelter in certain outposts under U.N. protection. In the most dramatic case—for which responsibility may belong to commanding officers in Belgium as much as to Dallaire— nearly one hundred Belgian peacekeepers abandoned some two thousand unarmed civilians, leaving them defenseless against attacks by militia and military. As the Belgians went out one gate, the assailants came in the other. More than a thousand Rwandans died there or in flight, trying to reach another U.N. post.[14]

During the internal struggles to take command of the country's military, U.N. peacekeepers might have been able to stop further depredations, but they were ordered not to intervene, which allowed Bagosora time to finish consolidating power, resulting in a far more "efficient" implementation of the program of genocide:

> By April 15, it was clear that the U.N. Security Council would not order the peacekeepers to try to stop the violence and might even withdraw them completely. By this date, the organizers of the genocide had also expanded their ranks considerably and were strong enough to remove opponents and impose compliance with the killing campaign.[15]

> By appropriating the well-established hierarchies of the military, administrative and political systems, leaders of the genocide were able to exterminate Tutsi with astonishing speed and thoroughness.[16]

Unprotected by any peacekeeping force, the disarmed victims were left to their own devices, either fleeing, hiding, or participating in an almost predestined tragedy of self-defense:

> Many Tutsi and those Hutu associated with them fought to save their lives. We know of their heroic resistance, usually armed only with sticks and stones...but we have no way of knowing about the countless small encounters where targeted people struggled to defend themselves and their families in their homes, on dusty paths, and in the fields of sorghum.[17]

Others found ways to accommodate their attackers, paying "repeatedly for their safety over a period of weeks, either with money or with sexual services." Their choices were limited to those of serfs or slaves: death resulting from attempted resistance or complete subservience in hopes of purchasing another day of physical survival.

Nor was this a one-sided slaughter. The Rwandan Patriotic Front was participating in its own program of mass murder, massacring "unarmed civilians, many of them women and children, who had assembled for a meeting on their orders."[18] *Leave None* found not only a continued lack of action, but an actual suppression of the truth, by the U.N.:

> The crimes committed by RPF soldiers were so systematic and widespread and took place over so long a period of time that commanding officers must have been aware of them. Even if they did not specifically order these practices, in most cases they did not halt them and punish those responsible.

After some early but limited reports of killings by the RPF, the first substantial charges against RPF forces were made by Robert Gersony, a consultant to the U.N. High Commissioner for Refugees. After interviewing hundreds of Rwandans inside and outside the country in July and August 1994, he concluded that the RPF had engaged in widespread and systematic slaughter of unarmed civilians. In September 1994, the U.N., in agreement with the U.S. and perhaps others, agreed to suppress the report but demanded that the RPF halt the killings. The number of killings declined markedly after September in the face of this international pressure.[19]

Leave None found that lack of international response was a major contributing factor in the duration and size of the Rwandan massacre. Dating back to 1990, "influential donors of international aid" concerned themselves more with the Habyarimana government's stability than political and economic reforms. When the massacres began, despite them being "solidly documented by local and international human rights groups and by a special reporter for the U.N. Commission on Human Rights," nobody "openly challenged Rwandan explanations that the killings were spontaneous and uncontrollable and none used its influence to see that the guilty were brought to justice."[20]

As the result of the U.N. and its member nations denying, delaying, and putting troop safety ahead of accomplishing their mission, Human Rights Watch estimated "at least one half million" Tutsis died between April and July 1994 in the genocide, about 75% of their population. Another 25,000-60,000 were killed by the Rwanda Patriotic Front.[21] Compared to the 500,000 Brazilians estimated to have been killed by guns in 25 years, an equal number of Rwandans were slaughtered, with government sanction, by regular military and their armed cohorts — some armed only with machetes — in just four months. Even when motivated by an opportunity for positive publicity, the U.N. failed to "consolidate the peace."

One Last Story of U.N. Peacekeeping Failure

A more recent genocide occurred in Burundi under similar circumstances, where the Hutu-Tutsi tribal differences that were used to ignite the Rwandan massacre continued to cause regional strife. In August 2004, 159 people were killed in a refugee camp for Congolese Tutsis. The article notes: "The Hutu National Liberation Forces (FNL), the only rebel group still fighting in Burundi, immediately claimed responsibility for the raid."

The DRC [Democratic Republic of Congo] Information Minister Henri Mova Sakanyi, while expressing his government's regret, said he was astonished the refugees protected by the United Nations High Commission for Refugees and the Burundian government "should be savagely murdered with impunity."

"Yet this camp is located close to a Burundian army camp," he said, calling for the U.N. and the Bujumbura government to accept their share of responsibility.

Burundi is slowly emerging from a civil war that began in 1993 and has so far claimed some 300,000 lives. The FNL has consistently refused to join a peace deal which last November formed a power-sharing Hutu-Tutsi government.[22]

Besides the fact that the United Nations peacekeeping missions fail to effectively "consolidate the peace", we also find that in spite of U.N. efforts, far more people have been killed during armed conflict than have been reported killed in Brazil by firearms, contrary to the U.N. allegation that "most war zones" are safer than countries where civilians own firearms.

Brazil Redux

The Brazilian people must have known this already: In 2005 they rejected a government proposal to ban civilian firearms in their country.

But the referendum backfired for proponents. Earlier this year, support for the ban was running as high as 80 percent. But in the weeks before the referendum, both sides were granted free time to present their cases on prime-time TV, and the pro-gun lobby began to grow.

Analysts said the pro-gun lobby benefited from equal time on television in the final weeks of the campaign and that they cannily cashed in on Brazilian skepticism of the police.

"They ask the question: 'Do you feel protected and do you think the government is protecting you?' and the answer is a violent no," said political scientist David Fleischer of the University of Brasilia.[23]

Curiously, only after Brazil's vote on the referendum did reports begin to surface documenting this "Brazilian skepticism of the police." One such report noted that Brazilian police committed numerous "cold-blooded executions" of those considered to be drug-gang members. At times, the police were documented to commit mass murder in a manner more in keeping with the gangsters they reputedly hunted:

The authorities say it is mainly criminals caught in military-style raids on drug gangs but according to a former senior official, new evidence suggests that many of the shootings are cold-blooded executions conducted by the police.

But in the spring of this year events took a sinister turn when, on 31 March, two men entered a bar and started shooting, not once or twice, but again and again. Most of the victims were shot at close range — in the chest and in the head.

In all, 29 people were shot dead, apparently not by members of a criminal drug gang — but by off-duty police officers.

"Around 60% of the bodies of people that were killed by the police had more than six shots," explains Professor Lemgruber.

"Most of them [were shot] in the head and in the back — mostly executions."[24]

Another article reported that in recent years, about 5% of the 20,000+ average annual firearms-related killings mentioned at the beginning of this chapter have been committed by Rio De Janeiro police alone:

> According to human rights organizations and government statistics, police in Rio and its suburbs—home to a population of 11 million—have taken the lives of more than 4,000 people in the past five years. In the first 10 months of this year, more than 900 died at the hands of police.[25]

During the 2007 New Year's tourist season, gang warfare erupted again in Rio De Janeiro:

> RIO DE JANEIRO (Reuters) - Gangs attacked buses and police posts in Rio de Janeiro on Thursday in a wave of violence that killed at least 18 people as the Brazilian city fills up with tourists for New Year celebrations.[26]

Police killed seven "suspected attackers" while losing two of their own. Seven more people were burned to death when their bus was set on fire.[27]

This follows another wave of violence in May 2006 where over 200 people were killed in Sao Paulo after a "powerful prison gang" ordered attacks on "public targets." Police "retaliated in violence that continued into July."[28]

As Brazilian police are armed with military-grade weapons, perhaps it is true, as the U.N. asserts, that Brazil really is a war zone, which explains the unusually high murder rate:

> Rio police are notorious for tough tactics and their retaliation could be harsh. Police kill over a 1,000 suspects per year in Rio, more than in some war zones, and human rights groups accuse police of summary executions.[29]

What is more important to remember is that Brazil had effectively banned firearms ownership among the general population in 2004:

> Only strictly defined groups of people — including police, security officials, target shooters and transport companies — will be able to obtain a gun licence.

> The legal age for owning a gun is being raised from 21 to 25.[30]

However, the two groups doing nearly all of the killing are not affected by gun control: Police are government-sanctioned and criminals don't care what laws are passed. Disarming law-abiding citizens had an insignificant affect in Brazil's level of violence, which gives it "one of the worst murder rates in the world."[31] The Brazilian people knew this, and their vote acknowledged the reality of the situation.

Disarmed and Vulnerable

Gun control activists said on Monday the world was awash in small arms, fuelling violence, and called for global cooperation and stricter limits on the trade.

A human rights report by a consortium of groups highlighted the impact of guns on the lives of women, saying they were often the "silent victims" of the small arms trade.

"Given that they are almost never the buyers, owners or users of small arms, (women) suffer disproportionately from armed violence," said Denise Searle of Amnesty International, one of the groups releasing the report.

"Where guns are available, more women are likely to be killed."[32]

In order to implement their policies on the global stage, gun control activists use the image of increased victimization of women as a core feature of their promotional program. Of course, the fact that women in countries with gun control are suffering increasing rates of rape — while the rape rate is dropping in the U.S., where guns are available — does not prove beyond a reasonable doubt that gun ownership is the key factor in protecting them. So let us give the benefit of the doubt and see how women fared when the United Nations peacekeeping forces controlled war-torn places throughout the world, where civilians were disarmed as part of the U.N. mission to "consolidate the peace."

It is curious that Amnesty International — which in the above quote positions itself as a global protector of women — was also among the first organizations to draw attention to U.N. peacekeeping forces' abuse of women. An article dated May 6, 2004 leads in with:

The presence of peacekeepers in Kosovo is fuelling the sexual exploitation of women and encouraging trafficking, according to Amnesty International.[33]

Amnesty International UK Director Kate Allen noted:

Women and girls as young as 11 are being sold into sexual slavery in Kosovo and international peacekeepers are not only failing to stop it they are actively fuelling this despicable trade by themselves paying for sex from trafficked women.[34]

One interviewee said: "I was forced by the boss to serve international soldiers and police officers." The article goes on to point out that U.N. troops are "immune from prosecution in Kosovo" and that those who were dismissed have "escaped any criminal proceedings in their home countries." Allen noted:

The international community in Kosovo is now adding insult to injury by securing immunity from prosecution for its personnel and apparently hushing up their shameful part in the abuse of trafficked women and girls.[35]

In January 2005, the Associate Press reported that "U.N. peacekeepers in the Congo sexually abused and exploited women and girls, some as young as 13." The United Nations Office of Internal Oversight Services (IOS) released a report that found "Peacekeepers regularly had sex with Congolese women and girls, usually in exchange for food or small sums of money." The U.N. IOS also found that:

- "sexual activities continued even while the investigation was going on"

- the "investigation did not act as a deterrent for some of the troops."

- "On several occasions, the commanders of these contingents either failed to provide the requested information or assistance or actively interfered with the investigation."[36]

In March 2005, a series of articles highlighted the continuing sexual exploitation by U.N. peacekeepers. One article reported that in Haiti, "rape is becoming a common tool of oppression."

Women and young girls are raped because their father or another relative is a member of Lavalas or is targeted (by the political opposition). They are raped as a form of punishment. The victims do not feel they can go to the police for help with their problems because in many areas the people who victimized them are the ones running the show; they are the ones patrolling the streets as if they are police, committing crimes with impunity under the eyes of the UN.

Not only are the U.N. peacekeepers not protecting women, they were also accused of participating in the depredations of women:

United Nations soldiers have also been accused of participating in sexual attacks. Damian Onses-Cardona, spokesperson for the U.N. mission in Haiti, announced this week that they are "very urgently" investigating a case in which Pakistani soldiers were accused of raping a 23-year-old woman at a banana plantation in the northern town of Gonaives.[37]

On the same day, another article reported: "the United Nations' top representative in the Congo, is set to resign in the wake of a sexual misconduct scandal involving U.N. peacekeepers." His resignation was the result of findings that indicated a pattern of long-standing violations that had not been addressed:

U.N. peacekeeping missions, including those in Cambodia, Bosnia and several African countries, have been dogged by sexual abuse scandals since the early 1990s. But few U.N. peacekeepers, who are shielded from prosecution by military agreements, have faced legal action for sex crimes.[38]

Again, there is mention of the issue of peacekeeper immunity to prosecution. The U.N. reportedly was forcing out a high-level bureaucrat to "send a signal that senior U.N. officials will be held accountable for not cracking down on misconduct by U.N. personnel under their watch." It is difficult to understand how an issue like sexual assault can be "cracked down" upon when the perpetrators know they will suffer no consequences. Firing a high-level official thus becomes no more than a publicity stunt to convince the public that "something is being done about it."

Over the next few days, more articles dealt specifically with the situation in the Congo. The first one confirmed the earlier report noted above:

Five years ago, more than 10,000 peacekeepers working for the United Nations came to the Democratic Republic of Congo to help end a six-nation war. But reports of sexual abuse of local women and girls began soon after they arrived from Morocco, South Africa, Australia, India and Europe.

In January, the U.N. Office of Internal Oversight Services released a report claiming peacekeepers regularly had sex with the Congolese women and girls in exchange for food or small sums of money.[39]

The article cited six confirmed cases where under-age girls were raped by U.N. peacekeepers and quoted a number of witnesses to other incidents. One U.N. official said these "issues are relatively new." Considering that armed males have been forcing themselves upon women for millennia as part of a program of conquest, it strains credibility to think that the issue of rape by the only armed force among a disarmed female population is "relatively new."

A second article found:

Militiamen and renegade soldiers have raped and beaten tens of thousands of women and young girls in eastern Congo, and nearly all the crimes have gone unpunished by the country's broken judicial system, an international human rights group said Monday.[40]

The article cited Human Rights Watch and the World Health Organization as two of its sources, and agreed with Amnesty International that U.N. peacekeepers contributed to the problem:

Warring ethnic Hema and Lendu militia continue to terrorize Bunia—kicking down doors in the night and snatching girls in the fields—despite the presence of thousands of U.N. peacekeepers based there.

Peacekeepers in Bunia have also been accused of raping young girls living in the town's sprawling camp for those displaced by fighting, or trading sweets and pocket change for sex.[41]

This issue goes far beyond the incidents themselves, as peacekeepers are also forcing additional children (via unwanted pregnancies) and health issues onto an already stressed economy and health care system. In the Congo alone, there are an "estimated hundreds of mixed-race children abandoned by U.N. workers at the end of their 6-month tours of duty." One victim said: "There is no help from the U.N. They just make women pregnant and leave. They never take care of their kids."

Another victim "contracted the AIDS virus from a peacekeeper, and has since passed it on to her husband and child." The victim's husband said: "I know the United Nations is here to support us, but it's unbelievable for me to see a thing like this. The one that came to support us is the one that took our ladies, who come to take everything." The HIV infections are the result of the fact that "current U.N. policy does not require peacekeepers to be tested for HIV before, during or after their deployments."[42]

Meanwhile, an estimated 24 children were dying each day — a rate of 8,760 per year — in two Congolese refugee camps, where another estimated 4 million died during the five-year intertribal war that ended in 2002, a rate of 800,000 deaths per year, or forty times the annual murders in Brazil.[43] Yet the U.N. "peacekeepers" get to rape, impregnate, and overpopulate a poor country with impunity, and the people are supposed to acquiesce to being disarmed and victimized by those supposedly there to protect them.

In East Timor, Jordanian peacekeepers were involved in "a series of horrific sex crimes involving children living in the war-battered Oecussi enclave." Perhaps the worst part of the episode was that "the U.N. mission in East Timor...did its best to keep the matter hushed up" and that the "U.N. military command at the time was only too happy to oblige."[44]

Another article reported that the U.N. response was to issue a report "on how to hold peacekeepers accountable when they are accused of sexual abuse and other violations in strife-torn parts of the world." Kofi Annan was reported to be "coming down on it hard." Unfortunately, one military officer, with considerable experience supporting U.N. peacekeeping missions in Haiti, Sierra Leone and the Republic of Congo, had a more cautionary note to sound regarding the possibility of enforcing any rules against peacekeeper violations:

> It gets down to accountability and, the U.N. being an international body without sovereignty unto itself ... It can't prosecute acts of heinous crimes of personnel and soldiers given to it by member states. If you [allow the U.N. to prosecute international personnel], then you supersede laws of the international nations ... how much sovereignty does a state want to give up to the United Nations? And the answer is, not much.[45]

One witness was in Sierra Leone as a legal aid worker in the summer of 2003. He reported:

> Sex crimes are only one especially disturbing symptom of a culture of abuse that exists in the United Nations precisely because the United Nations and its staff lack accountability.

> This lack of accountability is the central blemish on today's United Nations, and it lies behind most of the recent headlines. Whether taking advantage of a malnourished

refugee or of a lucrative oil-for-food contract, the temptation is there, the act is easy and the risk of punishment is nil.[46]

He found that "U.N. leaders had simply not expended any effort beyond lip service to carry out [Kofi Annan's expressly ordered] zero tolerance policy." He found "injustices" reached far beyond sexual depredations: Non-governmental organizations (NGOs) embezzled food and funds intended for the relief effort, and brutally enforced rules in a manner more in keeping with tyrants:

Utterly arbitrary judicial systems in the camps subjected refugees to violent physical punishment or months in prison for trivial offenses — all at the whim of officials and in the absence of any sort of hearing.[47]

The legal aid worker also found that the "risk to these staff members is low in U.N. refugee camps, because peacekeepers engaged in criminal acts are immune from local prosecution." Injured parties would have to "travel to the peacekeeper's home country" in order to pursue justice. Considering their economic status, such travel is effectively impossible. In cases where the U.N. worker is from a country with an "unresponsive legal system," even pleading one's case is pointless. The author concludes:

After the 2002 report documented sexual abuse, Annan's steely resolve led to exactly zero criminal prosecutions of U.N. officials for sexual abuse. I expect little difference now that refugee camp conditions have returned to the headlines. As before, Annan has delivered vague statements but prosecuted no one. It appears that the status quo reigns and that those perpetrating all sorts of abuses in refugee camps may continue undisturbed. The United Nations is a vital institution that needs a housecleaning.[48]

In early 2007, news reports surfaced that U.N. peacekeepers were participating in sexual abuse in the Sudan:

NEW YORK — Six Bangladeshi peacekeepers under United Nations command were demoted, dismissed or reprimanded for their roles in a sex-abuse case while on assignment in the Sudan, but U.N. officials are powerless to bring charges or prosecute the soldiers for their alleged crime.

Nonetheless, Jane Holl Lute, assistant secretary-general for peacekeeping operations, thinks the punishment is enough.

"I think it sent a very clear message," Lute told reporters Friday in response to growing questions about the U.N.'s handling of the case.[49]

Unfortunately, the "clear message" being sent is that if one perpetrates rape under the auspices of the United Nations, one can expect disproportionately minor consequences.

Now consider the contrasting experience with women in Liberia. Some were abused, and some were not. The reason for the latter is most instructive. The first report states: "U.N. peacekeepers sexually abused and exploited local women and girls in Liberia." The allegations ranged from "the exchange of goods, money or services for sex to the sexual exploitation of minors." Repeating a now-familiar refrain, the article noted: "Currently, U.N. troops and employees accused of wrongdoing are sent home to be dealt with by their own government but are often never punished."[50]

During the African conflicts, the general rule was that women had to either buy their lives with "sexual services," suffer loss of body parts, or become camp followers and prostitutes in order to survive:

In other African conflicts, like Uganda and Congo, women have participated in rebel movements, but usually in supporting roles. They cook, clean, and often sleep with soldiers — not always by choice.[51]

Counter to the stories of exploitation by both locals and U.N. peacekeepers, many women in Liberia found that by arming themselves and uniting into combat units, they were able to protect their personal sovereignty during that country's civil war:

Black Diamond, 22, says she joined the rebel forces after being gang-raped by the notoriously ill-disciplined and unpaid forces loyal to former President Charles Taylor in the northern Lofa County in 1999.

"There were many reasons, but that was the key one. It made me want to fight the man who caused all that, because if you are a good leader you can't behave like that," she is quoted as saying by Reuters news agency.

Many of Black Diamond's female comrades have similar tales…[52]

Not only are the women able to move about in relative security — considering this is a war zone — they were respected as fighters as well. Most importantly, they had the means to defend the honor of their fighting comrades as well as other female victims:

Liberia's Health Minister Peter Coleman has met many women fighters during the 14 years of warfare and says they are prized by their senior commanders.

"They don't get drunk and they take their mission very seriously," he said.

"I saw a woman shoot another officer because he raped a woman."[53]

It would seem that one possible answer to the problem of exploitation, maiming, and murder of women would be to arm them. It is curious that Amnesty International does not consider this option, preferring to tell women what their choices will be, even though all these well-meaning human rights organizations won't be there to defend the women when the very people assigned to protect them behave like a conquering horde. All these case studies show that rather than being safer when civilians are disarmed, women are far more at risk of not only murder, but being forced to endure what amounts to nothing more than a living death. Most importantly, it points out what a horrible record the U.N. has in protecting women's rights, and how little concern and accountability it displays after perpetrating what amounts to heinous war crimes.

Between lack of protection and pursuit of sexual gratification, the U.N. has done quite the opposite of accomplishing the IANSA's goals of enhancing public health and promoting security for women and children. As far as successful management and police oversight of war zones lethal to women and children, the U.N. has failed miserably and consistently.

How Well Does the United Nations Represent Freedom?

Freedom House comes out each year with a new edition of their research paper entitled *Freedom in the World*, in which they rate each country by its level of political rights and civil liberties, categories which are defined as follows:

> Political rights enable people to participate freely in the political process, including through the right to vote, compete for public office, and elect representatives who have a decisive impact on public policies and are accountable to the electorate. Civil liberties allow for the freedoms of expression and belief, associational and organizational rights, rule of law, and personal autonomy without interference from the state.[34]

Countries are rated on a scale of 1 to 7 for each category, with 1 being the most individual rights. By cross-indexing *Freedom in the World, 2007* with the list of U.N. member states, we find that only 46% percent of U.N. members are considered free countries.[55] Any vote of the U.N. membership on issues affecting personal liberties may easily go in favor of authoritarian policies, simply because those countries might feel it infringes on their sovereign way of doing things.

As late as 2005, the percent of free countries on U.N. Human Rights Commission was even less at 42%,[56] though it improved in 2007 to 51%.[57] It is not surprising that a coalition of organizations including Human Rights Watch and Freedom House issued a press release calling for creation of a permanent "United Nations democracy caucus" to address the need for a "higher number of democratic states as members of the Human Rights Commission." They cited the example of Sudan, on the Commission in 2004, whose government was backing militias which were "systematically destroying whole villages, executing civilians, raping women, and displacing hundreds of thousands of people." Joanna Weschler of Human Rights Watch stated:

> A government that engages in wholesale abuses of its citizens should not be eligible for a seat at the table, especially a country just criticized by the Commission. This is a major credibility test of the regional bloc structure at the U.N. in terms of how it nominates candidates for key U.N. posts.[58]

After the 2005 tsunami, Indonesia — another country not rated "free" — was causing concern for organizations donating money and materials for the rebuilding effort:

Britain hopes to devote some of its reconstruction aid for Indonesia's tsunami-devastated Aceh province to providing systems to prevent corruption, a British junior minister for international development said on Monday.

Watchdog groups regularly rank Indonesia as among the 10 most corrupt countries in the world, and some donors are concerned a substantial part of the billions of dollars in promised aid for Aceh could be diverted from its intended recipients.[59]

According to Leonard Simanjuntak, Deputy Executive Director of Transparency International:

Corruption is rooted in every aspect of society in Indonesia because law enforcement is weak, there is no proper monitoring mechanism, the bureaucratic system nationally and locally is not transparent, and government officials always use their authority and power to gain personal benefits. Besides that, public awareness about the damaging effects of corruption is still low. With these kinds of conditions in Indonesia, the sudden flow of large amount of money, goods and services will increase the risk of misuse of the tsunami aid.[60]

This example shows how governments which hold their populations in less-than-free conditions are also more likely to ignore or minimize the humanitarian needs of their people.

Transparency International (TI) releases an annual report entitled *Corruption Perceptions Index*, which tracks the level of government corruption in countries. TI defines corruption as: "the abuse of public office for private gain."[61] When cross-referencing their corruption ratings of U.N. member nations with those rated in *Freedom in the World*, we find that corruption correlates with reduced political and civil rights. The countries that are most free, with political and civil rights ratings of "1," have an average corruption index of 7.1. (A value of 10 means no corruption.) All countries that Freedom House rates as "free" have an 86.2% better corruption rating than those countries rated "not free" (5.4 to 2.9, respectively).[62]

Of the 159 U.N. member nations that Transparency International rated in their latest report (2007), the overall average corruption index was 4.0, which means that government officials in the average U.N. member nation use their authority and power to gain personal benefits. The corollary of this is that they generally do not seek to benefit the people. Not even the U.N. Security Council seems capable of providing any counterbalancing force: While the 2007 Council is 73% "free," its average corruption index is 4.7, scant reassurance that the Security Council represents the "little people" in the world.[63]

Is There a Link Between Freedom and Prosperity?

The World Bank has a ranking system — called Purchasing Power Parity — to determine the relative wealth of people living in each country, defined as "exchange rates used in international comparisons of standard of living."[64] Eighteen of the World Bank's 20 top rated countries are also rated "free" by Freedom House, 17 which were given the top rating of "1" in both political and civil rights. The exception was Japan, given a "2" for civil rights. By comparison, the bottom 20 in the PPP only contained two countries rated "free" by Freedom House, and both of those rated 2 in both political rights and civil liberties. Likewise, the 35 U.N. countries rated by Freedom House with the exemplary "1" for both political and civil rights had an average rank of 37 by the World Bank, while the lowest 35 countries — 34 rated "Not Free" and 1 rated "Partially Free" by Freedom House — had an average PPP rank of 137.[65] (Includes those countries rated by both organizations.)

For cross-referencing purposes, Heritage Foundation has created an Economic Freedom Index, arrived at by analyzing ten economic variables for each country. Heritage Foundation explains the reason for this report as follows:

> The authors of the Index perceive economic freedom as a positive concept, recognizing that its traditional definition as an absence of government coercion or constraint must also include a sense of liberty as distinct from anarchy. Governments are instituted to create basic protections against the ravages of nature, so that positive economic rights such as property and contract are given social as well as individual defense against the destructive tendencies of others. The definition of economic freedom therefore encompasses all liberties and rights of production, distribution, or consumption of goods and services. The highest form of economic freedom provides an absolute right of property ownership, fully realized freedoms of movement for labor, capital, and goods, and an absolute absence of coercion or constraint of economic liberty beyond the extent necessary for citizens to protect and maintain liberty itself. In other words, individuals are free to work, produce, consume, and invest in any way they please, and that freedom is both protected by the state and unconstrained by the state.[66]

Heritage Foundation rates countries by the following grading scale: Economically "free" countries have an overall score of 80-100; "mostly free" between 70 and 79.9; "moderately free" between 60 and 69.9, "mostly unfree" between 50 and 59.9; and economically "repressed" countries average an overall score of less than 50.[67]

There is a correlation between the World Bank Purchasing Power Parity and Heritage Foundation Economic Freedom Index grading systems for countries ranked by both economic scoring systems: as PPP improves, economic freedom increases.[68] Countries that the World Bank ranks as having the highest standard of living also tend to have more economic freedom.

The top quartile of economically free countries, as rated by Heritage Foundation, have an average of 1.51 in combined political and civil rights, according to the Freedom House rating system, well within the rating of "free." By comparison, the bottom quartile, as graded by Heritage Foundation, were rated an average of 4.86, towards the lower end of "partly free" before it transitions into "not free."[69] There is a link between personal freedom, as represented by political and civil rights, and economic prosperity. Conversely, there also seems to be a link between autocratic, totalitarian government and poverty. As Heritage Foundation explains:

> All government action involves coercion. Some minimal coercion is necessary for the citizens of a community or nation to defend themselves, promote the evolution of civil society, and enjoy the fruits of their labor. This Lockean idea is embodied in the U.S. Constitution. For example, citizens are taxed to provide revenue for the protection of person and property as well as for a common defense. Most political theorists also accept that certain goods—what economists call "public goods"—can be supplied more conveniently by government than through private means. Of particular interest are those economic freedoms that are also public goods, such as the maintenance of a police force to protect property rights, a monetary authority to maintain a sound currency, and an impartial judiciary to enforce contracts among parties.

> When government coercion rises beyond the minimal level, however, it becomes corrosive to freedom—and the first freedom affected is economic freedom. Logically, an expansion of state power requires enforcement and therefore funding, which is extracted from the people. Exactly where that line is crossed is open to reasoned debate.[70]

The purpose of discussing the relationship between freedom and prosperity is to examine the United Nation's ability to resolve humanitarian problems from another angle. As there is a relationship between reduced freedom and increased government corruption, there is also a relationship between corruption levels, personal freedom, and economic freedom: More economic, political, and civil liberty exists in those countries with the least government corruption. For example, when rated by corruption, the third and fourth quartiles — those which are most corrupt countries — also contain all of the countries rated as economically "repressed" by Heritage Foundation, while all of the economically "free" countries lie in the least-corrupt quartile.[71] This trend verifies the quote above: "When government coercion rises beyond the minimal level, however, it becomes corrosive to freedom."

How does this relate to the United Nations and its ability to successfully carry out humanitarian missions such as "consolidating the peace"? Of the 142 United Nations countries that are rated by all three organizations — Freedom House (Freedom Rating), Transparency International (Corruption Index) and Heritage Foundation (Economic Freedom Index) — their average Freedom House rating is

3.20 (Partly Free), their average Corruption Index is 4.15 (more corrupt than not), and their average Economic Freedom Index is 61.5, on the border between "Moderately Free" and "Mostly Unfree." How can the U.N. be a leader in political rights, civil liberties, and economic development for the world's peoples, when its member countries do not exemplify such attributes? How can one expect the U.N. to be free of corruption when its member countries are mostly corrupt? How can the U.N. protect the people of the world when the bulk of its member governments rely on coercion to such an extent that it has become corrosive to people's freedom?

As noted with the Indonesian tsunami relief effort, based upon the average ratings for freedom, corruption, and prosperity, it is hard to conceive of how the United Nations member states are conceptually or philosophically prepared to successfully undertake complex missions that will improve the lives of anyone, anywhere.

Freedom and Genocide

Governments which sponsored or condoned mass homicide — performed on unarmed civilians in their countries — represent some of the worst examples of coercion and corruption in the world. Of nine countries which were U.N. members during some or all of their mass murder events, their average Freedom Index is 5.7, the Corruption Index is 2.5, and the Economic Freedom Index is 47.9, all well-below even U.N. averages.[72] (Portugal was omitted because it was transformed from a dictatorship into a democracy after a genocide, drastically altering its ratings.)

Here is a partial list of countries that, in the 20th century, disarmed the populace and proceeded with government-sponsored mass murder, termed "democide" by Professor Rudy Rummel: People's Republic of China (76.7 million murdered);[73] USSR (61.9 million); and Cambodia (2 million). Other countries listed by Professor Rummel that were U.N. members during democide include: Indonesia, Vietnam, Pakistan, and Yugoslavia, resulting in another 4.9 million murdered by their own governments. Other homicidal countries, prior to founding of the U.N., included Nazi Germany (21 million) and Turkey (1.9 million).[74] These numbers are beyond comprehension, as Professor Rummel explains:

[W]ho can digest a total of 1,000,000 or more murdered. It is near impossible to empathize with the human catastrophe such statistics dimly reflect when we have difficulty getting a feel for numbers greater than six or seven. A murderer tortures and kills three people, and that gets into our gut – three loving, feeling, human beings killed in agony. We can imagine this happening to our family or circle of close friends. But mention 10,000, 100,000, or 1,000,000, and that is beyond imagination and feeling; they are only numbers.[75]

Professor Rummel recently updated his research, concluding that 262 million people were killed by their governments in the 20th Century, and offering us another way to conceive of the inconceivable:

Just to give perspective on this absolutely incredible murder by government, if all these bodies were laid head to toe, with the average height being 5', then they would circle the earth ten times. Also, this democide murdered 6 times more people than died in combat in all the foreign and internal wars of the century. Finally, given popular estimates of the dead in a major nuclear war, this total democide is as though such a war did occur, but with its dead spread over a century.[76]

To highlight the effectiveness of predatory governments acting against an unarmed populace, in 2006 there were 17,034 murders in the United States.[77] At that rate, it would take U.S. criminals 15,381 years — nearly 154 centuries — to attain what governments accomplished legally, according to their sovereign laws, during the 20th century. It would take these same criminals 1,233 years to murder as many people as the Nazis did just between 1933 and 1945.

Is a global organization that is beholden only to its member states' governments — not the people living in those countries — the best way to implement a program of "consolidating the peace?" It's reasonable to question the veracity of U.N. claims about civilian disarmament being of great benefit when U.N. member countries have shown little inclination to acknowledge the basic political and civil rights of their own people. With so many countries as well as the U.N. peacekeeping forces consistently demonstrating irresponsible and predatory behavior — murder, rape, and enslavement — when the balance of armament is in their favor, why afford them greater opportunity?

In light of this, the United Nations' claim that civilian disarmament is the key to reducing civilian violence appears to be so much cover for their true motive: preservation of power.

To classify the deaths from legitimate wars of national liberation (against tyrants, foreign or domestic) as one of the problems caused by small arms, and as a problem that should be eliminated by more stringent international weapons laws, is to say that no tyrant should ever again be overthrown by an armed populace.[78]

Civilian Arms Ownership and Freedom

The Graduate Institute of International Studies in Geneva, Switzerland publishes an annual report entitled *Small Arms Survey*. The 2003-2005 and 2007 editions contain tables estimating the number of firearms per civilian in selected countries. Collating this firearms-per-capita data with the indices on personal freedom, corruption, and economic freedom elicits some very interesting correlations.

It should be noted here that the *Small Arms Survey* can hardly be considered to support civilian firearms ownership. Their home page contained this quote by Kofi Annan, the recently-retired U.N. Secretary-General who oversaw that organization's growing movement towards civilian disarmament among its member countries:

> "The proliferation of small arms, and munitions and explosives has also aggravated the violence associated with terrorism and organized crime. Even in societies not beset by civil war, the easy availability of small arms has in many cases contributed to violence and political instability. These, in turn, have damaged development prospects and imperilled human security in every way." [79]

Sorting countries into quartiles — similar to grading them "A" through "D" — shows that countries with the most firearms per capita have the lowest corruption index and the most personal and economic freedom. The first quartile — countries with the highest rate of civilian firearms ownership — averaged 1.93, or "free" according to Freedom House. These countries were also rated economically at the upper end of "moderately free" (69.79) by Heritage Foundation, and their Corruption Index averaged 7.09 (relatively low corruption). The second and third quartiles averaged "partly free" by Freedom House, relatively corrupt according to Transparency International, and at the lower end of "moderately free" according to the Heritage Foundation, with all values being lower than the first quartile. The fourth quartile's averages were surprising similar to quartiles two and three.

What is most interesting is the similarity of the grades among the three lower quartiles. For example, their Corruption Indexes averaged between 4.31 and 4.75 and their Economic Freedom indexes average between 62.57 and 63.59. Combined into one group, countries in quartiles 2-4 all indicated a higher level of autocratic and economically destructive behavior demonstrated by government agents, their composite Freedom House rating was "partly free" and there was less economic freedom. Countries in quartile 1 had a 360.0% higher civilian firearms ownership rate, experienced a 32.2% better Freedom Index, a 58.6% better Corruption Index, and a 10.7% better Economic Index.[80] Separating out the top 11 countries, in terms of civilian firearms ownership — roughly the top 20% — highlights this distinction even more clearly. The top countries had a 366.2% higher civilian firearms ownership rate, averaged a 93.3% better Freedom Index, a 61.2% better Corruption Index, and an 12.8% higher Economic Index.[81] Once again, the correlation between corruption and freedom is validated, with the added correlation that more firearms per capita correlates with increased personal freedom and decreased government corruption.

Even for world's 26 freest countries — those earning a "1" in both political and civil rights — the positive correlation remains consistent when comparing firearms ownership to the other indices. When sorted by Corruption Index, the top half (less corrupt) has a 42.3% better Corruption Index, an 8.3% better Economic Index and a 20.1% higher rate of civilian firearms ownership. When sorted by Economic Index, the top half has a 25.3% better Corruption Index, a 15.5% better Economic Index, and a 57.2% higher rate of civilian firearms ownership. When sorted by PPP, the top half has a 41.7% better Corruption Index, a 10.4% better Economic Index, and a 146.1% higher rate of civilian firearms ownership. Even among the most free countries in the world, firearms ownership consistently correlates with less-corrupt government and more economic freedom.[82]

These findings contradict Annan's claim that "availability of small arms" has "damaged development prospects and imperilled human security in every way." It is most interesting that while the authors of the *Small Arms Survey* promote Annan's "peace through disarmament" campaign, they also admit that there is no correlation between civilian gun ownership and violence:

> The connection between gun availability and violence is one of the most controversial topics of gun policy debate. It is widely accepted that "'[g]un cultures" do not automatically translate into armed conflict'...Many of the examples explored in this chapter illustrate a strong connection between ownership levels and depravity. Others show that weapons proliferation does not always lead to social chaos.[83]

Considering the material covered so far in this chapter, it calls into question the true motive for banning civilian firearms: Will this result in true peace, or the "peace" of enslavement? Conversely, why would the average U.N. member nation give a tool of freedom to the people it coerces and oppresses for the benefit of the few?

On the other hand, if a corrupt, coercive government is overthrown, and a more democratic government installed, more lives may be saved than lost during a war for freedom. Creating an environment where people achieve more freedom and economic security reduces the potential for future mass murder through government-sponsored genocide or corruption-induced famine and disease.

Small Arms Proliferation Is Condoned by International Law

> The U.N. recommends that weapons not be sold to dictatorships, countries at war, or countries that will re-export them. But Brazil exported arms to Iraq while it was ruled by Saddam Hussein (1979-2003) as well as to Angola during the civil war there. It also continues to sell weapons to Paraguay, which subsequently make their way back into Brazil illegally, said Rangel Bandeira. [coordinator of the Viva Rio Disarmament Project]

> Exporting as many arms as possible is "faulty pragmatism", argued Rangel, considering the "boomerang effect" through which exported guns later fall into the hands of criminals in Brazil. Despite the progress made in terms of legislation, this has still not translated into effective control of both domestic and foreign sales of weapons.

Brazilian-made pistols used by the Colombian guerrilla forces have been found in Brazil itself, while research by Viva Rio reveals that many of the guns seized from drug traffickers in Rio de Janeiro had been exported to Paraguay.[84]

At the beginning of this chapter is an article stating "guns are the single biggest cause of death among young people" in Brazil, and as a solution, the United Nations urged Brazil to consider banning the sale of civilian firearms. Now we find that Brazil, by contravening a U.N. recommendation, has actually brought its own consequences down upon itself. The above quote shows once again that criminals do not care about laws, U.N. regulations or the "consolidation of peace," but seek to carry out their own agendas with no regard to the consequences for others. More importantly, it shows that national governments, in cahoots with arms manufacturers within their country, conspire to enlarge their bottom line at the expense of the people.

The United Nations, in spite of all the evidence, still insists that civilian disarmament is the way to peace. Giving the benefit of the doubt, perhaps Brazil is the only country involved in this game of seeking short-term financial gain through arms sales, while subjecting their own people to increased risk as those "crows" come home to roost.

Russia has a lucrative arms industry through its government-owned exporting firm Rosoboronexport. Russia is still recovering from the economic contraction that followed the fall of the Soviet Union, having just reached 90% of its 1991 Gross Domestic Product level.[85] One article noted:

Russia's arms exports last year totaled US$5.8 billion, achieving a post-Soviet sales record, [head of Rosoboronexport] Chemezov said, adding that Rosoboronexport accounted for about 90 percent of the sales.[86]

Arms sales accounted for over 5% of the country's revenues in 2004.[87] Considering an economic recovery that is over a decade old now, this income is no doubt a greatly appreciated boon. Russia says it will not cooperate with the United States regarding arms sales, and declared that what it is doing is legal according to international law:

Chemezov said that his company was strictly observing international law while selling weapons abroad, but warned that it wouldn't obey U.S. recommendations.

"If the United States makes its own decisions, it has no effect on us: we proceed from international law," he said at a news conference.

One such issue between the U.S. and Russia centers around a recent sale to Venezuela:

The Bush administration has lodged a formal protest with Russia for agreeing to provide the government of Venezuelan President Hugo Chavez more than 100,000 AK-47 rifles that U.S. officials believe could be used to aid left-wing uprisings in Latin America.[88]

Venezuelan President Hugo Chavez has reportedly been "working behind the scenes to prop up left-wing revolutionary movements in the region while retrenching from democratic principles at home." He has been a "vocal supporter of Cuban dictator Fidel Castro and other revolutionaries, and has encouraged the Iraqi insurgency." There is also concern that older military arms replaced by this purchase will be given to rebel movements. Bernardo Alvarez, Venezuela's ambassador to the U.S., disagreed with this assessment, saying that Venezuela is buying the rifles only for "defensive purposes."

While this article says the arms purchase may be for up to 300,000 rifles, another article says that Venezuela's armed forces number about 100,000. Apparently, the other 200,000 rifles will be used in part to arm "popular defense units" of between ten and 500 persons each, to be used in poor neighborhoods and factories. Since there is no evidence of war against Venezuela, it is hard to determine who needs defending at this time.[89]

Considering that this arms deal is worth over $500 million, about 10% of last year's arms-sales income, this one sale is very beneficial for Russia's economy.[90]

This is not the only controversial arms deal involving Russia. Despite protests from Israel and the United States over them falling into the hands of terrorists, Russia decided to go ahead and sell anti-aircraft missiles to Syria.[91]

Russia made another deal to sell launch-rocket systems to India "for no less than 36 multiple-launch rocket systems for a sum of no less than $450 million."[92] These weapons are designed for ground forces. Since India has been involved in a low-level dispute with Pakistan over Kashmir, one can wonder how these weapons might be deployed, possibly causing more instability in the region. Since it is often young men, and now young women as well, who fight the wars that older men ignite with their posturing and rhetoric, this type of arms sale may end up being more lethal to young people than guns in Brazil.

Russia also has a growing business with Yemen:

Russia's weapon exports to Yemen are expected to exceed $100 million this year, the Itar-Tass news agency quoted the general director of Rosoboronexport arms exports company, Sergei Chemezov, as saying.

Russia's weapon exports to Yemen are expected to grow in the near future, the official said on Monday. Yemen currently imports Russian helicopters, infantry fighting vehicles, ammunition and small arms, Chemezov said. Yemen is interested in purchasing new military aircraft and vehicles, as well as air defense systems, he said.

The delivery of Russian military equipment to Yemen began in 2000 when Russia supplied the country with 31 modern T-80 tanks. In 2001 Moscow and Sanaa signed a contract for the delivery of MiG-29 fighter planes. The first batch was delivered to Yemen in 2002.[93]

This same article goes on to describe Russia's growing international arms business, which is no doubt assisting their long-term economic recovery:

In 2004, Russia's total arms exports are expected to be "no lower than in 2003", Mikhail Borovik, a department head with Rosoboronexport, told reporters in June. In 2003, weapons and military equipment exports increased 21.4 percent on the year in monetary terms to $5.1 billion, which was a record for Russia.

It is interesting to note that in spite of severe restrictions on civilian handgun ownership, Russia has the second highest suicide rate,[94] the second highest number of murders,[95] and the fifth highest murder rate per capita in the world.[96]

As far as keeping non-military arms out of the country, Russia has a major challenge due to its level of organized crime, which is believed to control much of Russia's economy. One of the biggest "mafia groups" in Russia "specializes in drugs and gun smuggling."[97] Official Russian estimates say the number of organized crime groups in the country grew more than tenfold in just five years, from 785 at the end of the Soviet era to 8,000 in 1996. "The government in Moscow estimates the Russian mafia controls 40% of private business and 60% of state-owned companies." As far as affecting the murder rate, in spite of gun control, "Russia sees around 10,000 fatal shootings a year, 600 of which are contract killings."[98] Obviously, gun smuggling is quite lucrative a business. As Kates notes:

Today, though handguns remain virtually unavailable to ordinary Russian citizens, homicide rates remain high, being committed by those criminals in Russia, Latvia, Lithuania, etc., who seem to have no difficulty acquiring both Russian and foreign-made handguns and suitable ammunition.[99]

Rather than supporting the U.N. plan to reduce the international small arms business, Russia has recently called upon the United Nations to protect its "intellectual property" of the AK-47 design:

Russia plans to call in the support of the United Nations in its battle to regain leadership of the small arms market, a Foreign Ministry official said Wednesday.

In a move to tackle unlicensed manufacturing of arms including its best selling Kalashnikov assault rifle, Russia wants to have its intellectual property rights on small arms recognized under a U.N. initiative against illicit trade in small weapons.[100]

This is about profit, as Russia knows the AK-47 design is very popular, and they want to use international regulation to stifle competition. As the above article notes, while Russia has been selling about $60 million in small arms each year, this year their $50 million deal with Venezuela shows the market potential is expanding, and they want to insure that this very lucrative addition to their gross national product is protected under United Nations regulations as "intellectual property."

Not to be left out of the profitable trade, the European Union recently moved to lift an arms embargo with China:

> France is spearheading efforts to lift the Chinese arms embargo, gaining backing last year from previous holdouts Britain and Germany. France says the arms embargo is out of tune with the times because it groups the world's most populous nation and fastest-growing major economy with countries including Myanmar and Zimbabwe that also face EU weapons-sales curbs.

> China's arms purchases have tripled in four years, according to the London-based International Institute for Strategic Studies.[101]

The United States asked the EU to not lift the embargo until China made progress on human rights, but was rebuffed. There are still 2,000 people in prison there who were arrested during the Tiananmen uprising. There is similar sentiment among the people of Europe:

> In a reflection of European public opinion, the European Parliament passed a non-binding resolution in November calling for the curbs to remain in place until China "has taken concrete steps toward improving the human-rights situation in that country."

The European Union passed a largely symbolic resolution agreeing to keep the embargo in place, while the member governments are looking at the more practical matter of cash flow.

China has made scant progress on human rights. A recent article reported that "words deemed taboo by the communist authorities — such as 'democracy,' 'freedom' and 'human rights'" that appear on web pages in China receive a message: "Prohibited language in text, please delete." Web sites which conflict with the Chinese government's politics or policies are blocked by the authorities:

> A search on Google for such topics as Taiwan or Tibetan independence, the banned group Falun Gong, the Dalai Lama or the China Democracy Party inevitably leads to a "site cannot be found" message.[102]

Amnesty International notes:

> China is the only major arms exporting power that has not entered into any multilateral agreement which sets out criteria, including respect for human rights, to guide arms export licensing decisions. Many of the companies involved in the arms trade were established under the control of China's People's Liberation Army (PLA) and the police state agency. The flow of arms is often to countries where there are real risks that the arms are used to commit serious abuses.

For example, China has continued to allow military equipment to be sent to Sudan despite well-documented and widespread killings, rapes and abductions by government armed forces and allied military groups in Darfur. In Nepal, China has supplied small arms and light weapons to the armed forces, which have been responsible for much of the killings and torture, often of civilians, in the internal armed conflict. Lethal force has also been used on pro-democracy protests in Nepal, resulting in torture, arbitrary arrests, unwarranted injuries and even deaths. In South Africa, guns seized from armed criminals have frequently been of Chinese origin.[103]

China certainly has some interesting trading partners. Sudan gets a "7" from Freedom House, the worst grade possible. Sudan's corruption index is 2.0: only four countries have a lower grade. Nepal is rated 5.5, or partly free, by Freedom House, and its corruption index is 2.5. With an economic freedom index of 3.53, Nepal is considered by Heritage House to be mostly unfree.

Amnesty International also notes how companies in the European Union, contrary to the EU's resolution, assisted China in developing a new military attack helicopter. Canada also provided parts for the helicopter, despite the fact that:

Canada, the European states, Russia and the USA have agreed to the 1993 Organisation, for Security and Corporation of Europe (OSCE) Principles Governing Conventional Arms which include a commitment to "avoid the transfer of arms which would be likely to be used for the violation or suppression of human rights and fundamental freedoms.". The principles cover conventional arms and related technology. These states are also parties to the Wassenaar Arrangement on Export Controls for Conventional Arms and Dual-Use Goods and Technologies.[104]

It is interesting to note that of the four United Nations countries that call themselves a "People's Republic" (like China) or "Democratic People's Republic," Freedom House rates them all "Not Free," their average Corruption Index is 2.63 (very corrupt), and their average Economic Freedom Index is 35.4 (Repressed).

Rather than seeking to limit the proliferation of arms, the U.N. supports it, as long as it is done by governments or under U.N. auspices. Iran has also been busy in the international arms market, with the blessing and participation of the United Nations:

Still, suspect material is reaching Iran in connection with an aid program created in 1996 by the U.N. drugs office, which also provides training, vehicles and other help to fight what is generally acknowledged as a serious drug problem.[105]

Iran is quietly building a stockpile of thousands of high-tech small arms and other military equipment — from armor-piercing snipers' rifles to night-vision goggles — through legal weapons deals and a U.N. anti-drug program, according to an internal U.N. document, arms dealers and Western diplomats.

Iran purchased tanks and missiles from Belarus and China, helicopters and artillery from Russia, and sniper rifles from Austria. It appears that France and Britain have placed profits before their own security concerns, as both countries sold Iran night vision equipment, despite a senior U.N. official stating:

The U.S. and Britain and France had questions as to what the intention and purpose of the proposal is. One of the worries — is it only drugs they are worried about or something they could use to track other things?

This is a valid question because Iran wanted to develop a spy satellite system to help with their fight against the drug trade, but security concerns put that plan on hold:

A draft proposal obtained by AP, to create a regional satellite network that would survey Afghanistan, Iran and Iraq is on hold, with Iran shifting it to the U.N. office on drugs and crime after opposition stalled it in the U.N. office on space affairs, also based in Vienna.

This surveillance system would have been powerful enough to track activities in Iraq and Afghanistan, and with concerns about Iran's support of terrorists, this could have put coalition and security personnel — and even neighboring governments — at risk.

The United States is not innocent in all this profit-making with a sanctioned country:

WASHINGTON — The U.S. military has sold forbidden equipment at least a half-dozen times to middlemen for countries — including Iran and China — who exploited security flaws in the Defense Department's surplus auctions. The sales include fighter jet parts and missile components.[106]

When the Pentagon retires military equipment, including fighter jets and helicopters, it auctions them off through its "Defense Reutilization and Marketing Service." Buyers have been able to resell this equipment to whomever they please. Some examples:

Arif Ali Durrani, a Pakistani, was convicted last year in California in the illegal export of weapons components to the United Arab Emirates, Malaysia and Belgium in 2004 and 2005 and sentenced to just over 12 years in prison. Customs investigators say the items included Chinook helicopter engine parts for Iran that he bought from a U.S. company that acquired them from a Pentagon surplus sale, and that those parts made it to Iran via Malaysia. Durrani is appealing his conviction.

An accomplice, former Naval intelligence officer George Budenz, pleaded guilty and was sentenced in July to a year in prison. Durrani's prison term is his second; he was convicted in 1987 of illegally exporting U.S. missile parts to Iran.

State Metal Industries, a Camden, New Jersey, company convicted in June of violating export laws over a shipment of AIM-7 Sparrow missile guidance parts it bought from Pentagon surplus in 2003 and sold to an entity partly owned by the Chinese government. The company pleaded guilty to an export violation, was fined $250,000 (euro193,185) and placed on probation for three years. Customs and Border Protection inspectors seized the parts — nearly 200 pieces of the guidance system for the Sparrow missile system — while inspecting cargo at a New Jersey port.

A California company, All Ports, shipped hundreds of containers of U.S. military technology to China between 1994 and 1999, much of it acquired in Pentagon surplus sales, court documents show. Customs agents discovered the sales in May 1999 when All Ports tried to ship to China components for guided missiles, bombs, the B-1 bomber and underwater mines. The company and its owners were convicted in 2000; an appeals court upheld the conviction in 2002.[107]

The General Accounting Office sent undercover agents to make illegal purchases, finding such activity surprisingly easy to accomplish:

The GAO, the investigative arm of Congress, found it alarmingly easy to acquire sensitive surplus. Last year, its agents bought $1.1 million (euro850,000) worth — including rocket launchers, body armor and surveillance antennas — by driving onto a base and posing as defense contractors.

"They helped us load our van," Kutz said. Investigators used a fake identity to access a surplus Web site operated by a Pentagon contractor and bought still more, including a dozen microcircuits used on F-14 fighters.

The undercover buyers received phone calls from the Defense Department asking why they had no Social Security number or credit history, but they deflected the questions by presenting a phony utility bill and claiming to be an identity theft victim.[108]

Russia recently concluded a deal with Iran to sell them surface to air missiles.[109] In early 2007, the $700 million deal was concluded, whereby Iran took ownership of 29 "sophisticated" surface-to-air missile defense systems.[110] This comes at a time when Iran is forging ahead with their nuclear power program, and Iran's president has called for the removal of Israel from the Middle East, previously stating that Israel be "wiped off the map."[111]

The most interesting confirmation of the points being made here comes from a most unlikely source. The most recent U.N. meeting to discuss new international regulation of the small arms trade occurred in July 2006. The meeting ended in a "total meltdown," reaching no agreement on how to proceed. According to leading international gun advocate IANSA, the culprits were the very countries written about above, who seek to protect their sovereign right to buy and sell any arms they please:

But Rebecca Peters of the London-based International Action Network on Small Arms accused governments of letting a few states "hold them all hostage and to derail any plans which might have brought any improvements in this global crisis."

IANSA identified the main players blocking agreement as Cuba, India, Iran, Pakistan and Russia. Other gun control activists named China, Egypt and Venezuela as well.[112]

The End of Allies

There can be no greater error to expect, or calculate upon real favors from Nation to Nation. 'Tis an illusion which experience must cure, which a just pride ought to discard.
– George Washington[113]

Even Israel has come into conflict with its long-term ally the United States. The U.S. did not want Israel to sell attack drones to China, for fear it will "tilt the balance of power and make it more difficult to defend Taiwan, which Beijing deems a renegade province." Israel countered that "Washington should also cut back on weapons transfers to Arab countries such as Saudi Arabia and Egypt." Israel also leveled the accusation that this is simply a U.S. manipulation of the arms market covered with high-sounding words:

Some Israeli officials believe U.S. attempts to limit Israeli arms sales stemmed from a desire to ensure U.S. defense contractors competing with Israeli firms won lucrative international contracts.[114]

Such criteria did not stop Israel from protesting a planned U.S. arms sale:

WASHINGTON, April 4 — A major arms-sale package that the Bush administration is planning to offer Saudi Arabia and other Persian Gulf allies to deter Iran has been delayed because of objections from Israel, which says that the advanced weaponry would erode its military advantage over its regional rivals, according to senior United States officials.[115]

This is part of a long-term Israeli resistance to U.S. arms sales to neighboring countries:

Israeli officials and their allies in Washington, led by the American Israel Public Affairs Committee, have long opposed American arms sales to Saudi Arabia and Arab states.[116]

Apparently, when it comes to profit in the international arms market, there are no friends and allies. George Washington's observation that nations always act out of self-interest remains true today.

As long as countries declare a need for more armament for "defense" or to enhance their political or economic standing in various regions of the world, there will be internationally sanctioned dealers — ready to help their country's bottom line — and illicit "business organizations" ready to supply the demand. The U.N. knows this, and sometimes even assists the process. As with the lack of accountability with peacekeepers' sex crimes, countries hide behind their sovereignty when asked to reduce the international arms trade, even when their short-term profit-seeking puts their own people at risk. But when it comes to your sovereignty in terms of your ability to live life and pursue economic freedom — or to protect your family from harm — there is no consideration. It is curious that governments will not grant you the same right to arms they demand for themselves. Rather, you are being blamed for failed government policy that is supported by the United Nations, which behaves like nothing more than an arms-industry lobbyist and market-protection organization for its member states.

Chapter 7
By Their Own Words

Previous chapters examined gun control from a more defensive posture: were the claims of gun-ban proponents supported by available data? Now we will go a step further and determine exactly what gun control organizations prove with the data-sets and criteria they use to support their agenda of civilian disarmament.

Associated Press Blames NRA for Violent Crime

A June 2006 Associate Press article noted that the preliminary FBI crime report for 2005 indicated a rise in violent crime. Quoting a college criminal justice professor, the article claimed the increase was due to government's waning support of law enforcement. Even more interesting was their attempt to link this with the National Rifle Association's increased political power:

> Criminal justice experts said the statistics reflect U.S. complacency in fighting crime, a product of dramatic declines in the 1990s and the abandonment of effective programs that emphasized prevention, putting more police officers on the street and controlling the spread of guns.

> "We see that budgets for policing are being slashed and the federal government has gotten out of that business," said James Alan Fox, a criminal justice professor at Northeastern University in Boston. "Funding for prevention at the federal level and many localities are down and the (National Rifle Association) has renewed strength."[1]

The AP article implied that the Bush administration has done nothing to control crime, reinforcing its message that the President caters to the NRA rather than fulfilling his obligations to the American People:

> Violent crimes peaked at 1.9 million in 1992 and fell steadily through the end of that decade. The number has been relatively stable for the past six years.[2]

However, the FBI reports that the annual number of violent crimes dropped 10.9% during its last six reporting years, while the rate per 100,000 population dropped 18%. More to the innuendo, the number of violent crimes dropped 4.1% during the first four years of the Bush administration, while the rate dropped 8.1%.[3] (Latest final FBI data available as of the date of this AP article.)

Professor Fox's personal web site links to his Bureau of Justice Statistics page at the U.S. Department of Justice.[4] Using Fox's own statistical compilation on justifiable homicide (JH), we find that law enforcement is rarely present to stop an attack on a citizen, but that most law enforcement officers' (LEO) JH are due to criminal attacks on LEO, justifying self-defense. Between 1976 and 2004, only 2.0% of LEO JH occurred during a criminal attack on a citizen, while 50.7% occurred during an attack on a LEO. Fox's data also shows that 27.6% of citizen JH was self-defense, but 60.9% came while disrupting crime, including defense of others at risk of forcible felonies, compared to 23.2% LEO JH disrupting crimes in progress.[5]

Fox's own data supports concealed carry: Using justifiable homicide as an indicator, citizens were far more likely than police to be present to stop violent crimes in progress. Keep in mind that most defensive shootings are not fatal. Kleck and Gertz found that of all defensive gun uses, 8.3% wounded or killed the criminal attacker, and only 15.6% actually fired the gun.[6] This means that many more crimes were averted by an armed citizen that did not result in JH. The only way to change that fact is for government to put "more officers on the street" and disarm you in order to "control the spread of guns."

Fox's implication that the NRA supports anti-LEO policies runs counter to NRA history. The NRA established a law enforcement training program in 1960, and has continuously upgraded it to provide a variety of trainings for law enforcement officers. Furthermore, law enforcement professionals, including police chiefs and FBI agents, have either run the program or had significant influence on its development, and its mission is to enhance officers' safety:

> Our ultimate goal is the saving of lives and prevention of injuries through the safe, effective, and timely use of the law enforcement firearm. This is done by providing the law enforcement firearm instructor with the knowledge, skills, and abilities necessary to teach their students how to "WIN A LETHAL ENCOUNTER!"[7]

Kayne Robinson, elected NRA's president in 2003, retired as Assistant Chief of Police in Des Moines, Iowa and was past President of the Iowa Association of Chiefs of Police.[8] NRA supports President Bush's Project Safe Neighborhoods, a program aimed at putting armed, violent criminals in federal prison where parole is not an option.[9] John Sigler, the current NRA president, joined the Dover (Delaware) Police Department after retiring from the Navy:

> After serving in the U.S. Navy, where he was assigned to ballistic submarines, he joined the Dover Police Department, where he served as a patrol officer, detective, firearms instructor and captain of the Dover Police Pistol Team. He also at various times oversaw training, planning, administration and the detective unit...

> He retired from the Dover Police Department in 1991 with the rank of captain.[10]

In the first three years of the Bush administration, prosecution of federal gun law violators increased 67%.[11] A recent study of the effectiveness of this program estimated that because of the longer prison sentences in federal court, numerous crimes were not committed — in Kansas alone — by habitual offenders because they were removed from society by longer sentences.[12]

As noted in Chapter 5, Kellermann and Reay studied gunshot deaths in a single county in Washington state and concluded: "We noted 43 suicides, criminal homicides, or accidental gunshot deaths involving a gun kept in the home for every case of homicide for self-protection."[13]

Ever since Kellermann laid out the template, gun controllers have used this flawed logic process to "prove" that guns are a dangerous liability in the hands of civilians. As noted in Chapter 5, the National Academy of Science concluded that selecting an iota of data and extrapolating it over a vastly larger population group results in conclusions of "little relevance" to reality. If Kellermann's perception was accurate, the NRA would have long since ceased to exist: its firearms-owning members would all be dead or in prison!

Violence Policy Center Proves Pro-Gun Means Less Crime

Violence Policy Center examined part of the 2003 fatal injury data from the Centers for Disease Control, and concluded that the ten most deadly states for "per capita gun death" were "pro-gun." VPC Executive Director Josh Sugarmann concluded: "All of these states pride themselves on being 'pro-gun'—but the numbers show that guns kill."[14]

The problem is that it is impossible to tell much from VPC's isolated data, in this case one column of data from a complex chart that includes both intentional and accidental fatal injuries of all causes, not just firearms. This is the moving keyhole effect: if you point it at only the data you want to see, you can prove anything.

A phone call to VPC asking them to define their criteria of "pro-gun" went unreturned. Lacking a clear explanation of what they construe to be "pro-gun," one known criterion applying to VPC's "top 10" states is that they all have shall-issue, right-to-carry (RTC) laws.

As with the Brady reports, VPC excludes the District of Columbia, obviously not "pro-gun" by VPC criteria due to their ban on all functioning civilian firearms.[15] Washington, D.C. would appear first on this list. This omission immediately skews results in favor of VPC's desired outcome.

Using the CDC data referenced by VPC, it is apparent that in 2003, RTC states had a 23% higher average fatal injury rate for all intents and causes than non-RTC states. Further examination shows that RTC states had 32.6% higher overall rates of suicide and 33.7% more fatal accidents, accounting for 85.8% of all fatal injuries. This indicates more complex dynamics than simple civilian firearm inventory or usage. Also, we don't know if legally purchased firearms were used in these incidents, nor if the people involved were in legal possession of the firearms.[16]

Here is where it gets interesting: While homicides account for 10.8% of all fatal injuries, firearms homicides account for 39.6% of all fatal firearm injuries.[17] This indicates the importance of intent when considering firearms lethality. When it comes to violent crime and homicide rates, non-RTC states are more dangerous, whether citing FBI or CDC data. In 2003, non-RTC states averaged 26.3% more violent crime and 35.3% more homicide. Even if we select data according to VPC criteria, and compare only the 10 RTC and non-RTC states with the highest total firearm injury rates, RTC states are safer. The "Top Ten" non-RTC states averaged 17.2% higher violent crime rates and 22.9% higher homicide rates, according to the FBI. The CDC data shows that non-RTC states average 12.4% higher rates of gun homicide.[18] When it comes to criminals with guns, RTC states are the safer places for the law-abiding: even firearms homicide rates are lower in RTC states.

VPC's argument is that more guns equals more fatal firearm injuries. VPC's Executive Director links higher "gun death" to the "pro-gun" states, stating that the reason these states have more "gun death" is because "guns kill," thereby inferring that more guns cause more fatal injuries. By promulgating the theory that guns are a causative factor, VPC proves by its own logic that more guns means less violent crime.

People living in certain states seem to be more suicidal, and may be more accident-prone, drink too often, or need safety training. These are complex social issues beyond simple availability of firearms. When it comes to malicious intent, the "non-pro-gun" states have higher rates of overall violence and homicide, whether the killer uses a firearm or not.

In their rush to demonize guns, Violence Policy Center stumbled into a trap of their own devising. They used a data set that, when considered in its more complete version in conjunction with VPC criteria, shows that more guns means less violent crime.

Brady's Concealed Truth

The Brady Campaign to Prevent Gun Violence web site contains a report entitled *Concealed Truth: Concealed Weapons Laws and Trends in Violent Crime in the United States*. Even though it was published in 1999, it is available online, so they still consider it a relevant and accurate portrayal of concealed carry laws.

Since Brady does not include any data sets or references in this report, we do not know how they arrived at their conclusions, but it is possible to rebuild their crime data set from the source they reference, as they mention: "According to the Federal Bureau of Investigation's Uniform Crime Reports..."

There are nine references to the year 1998 in their text, but the included table is entitled "The Percentage and Number of States with Increases in Crime between 1992 & 1997." For this paper, 1998 will be the consistent ending year. Brady claims:

Between 1992 and 1998, over a quarter (27%, 3/11) of the states that were "shall issue" during this entire time period experienced an increase in the violent crime rate, as well as in the robbery rate. This compares to increases in violent crime over the same 6 year time period in just 18% (4/22) of states with strict carry laws. Only 18% (4/22) of states with strict carry laws experienced an increase in robberies.[19]

The included table claims that 27% of shall-issue states saw robbery rates increase.[20]

In 1991, there were 17 states with shall-issue right-to-carry (RTC) laws. Brady claims there were 11, but without their data set, it is impossible to determine how they erred. Between 1992 and 1998 another 14 states enacted RTC, so they cannot be included in this comparison. This leaves 20 states — 19 states plus Washington D.C., which was also included in the Brady study — without RTC during this time period.[21]

Contrary to Brady's claim above, three of 17 RTC states saw increases in their overall violent crime rates (17.6%) but 4 of the 20 non-RTC states did as well (20.0%). Three RTC states saw increases in their robbery rates (17.6%) but five non-RTC states (25%) did, too. Brady's miscalculations erode the report's reliability: Their percentages are nearly the exact opposite of the truth.

Brady is mostly correct in their comparison of trends between the two groups. Between 1992 and 1998, non-RTC states beat RTC states in four of five violent crime trends: overall violent crime decreased 4.6 percentage points more in non-RTC states; murder, 13.6; rape, 2.5; and robbery, 13.1. RTC states led in aggravated assault by 0.9 points.

However, this only shows part of the picture. By comparing both groups' trends to the national average, non-RTC states remained the more dangerous places to live. Between 1992 and 1998, both groups of states crept slightly closer to the national average violent crime rate, RTC from below and non-RTC from the high side. RTC states saw modest "increases" in murder, rape and robbery relative to the national averages, while non-RTC states' rates dropped as a percent of the national rates. But when expressed as percent of the national rate, RTC states remained far safer. By 1998, RTC states averaged 71.9% of the national murder rate, 90.7% for rape, and 66% for robbery. Non-RTC states averaged 113.8% of the national murder rate, 97.9% for rape, and 130.7% for robbery.

Both RTC and non-RTC states improved slightly in aggravated assault, relative to the national rate, but RTC states ended up 32.1% below the national average rate while non-RTC states remained 15.8% above. Overall, RTC states maintained a 31% lower average violent crime rate than the entire country, while non-RTC states remained 18.7% higher. RTC states maintained lower-than-average rates for all five violent crime indices, while non-RTC states remained higher-than-average in all categories except rape, which was only 2.1% below the national average.[22] Describing this as a failure for concealed carry laws is at best a Pyrrhic victory for Brady.

Looking at actual violent crime rates (incidents per 100,000 population) exposes another part of the picture ignored by Brady Campaign. Non-RTC states' average violent crime rate was 751.6 in 1992, compared to RTC states' 412.1. By 1998, non-RTC states saw a 22.5% decrease while RTC states saw "only" a 17.9% decrease. But when it comes to violent crime levels, non-RTC states unfortunately remained "above average." Furthermore, when compared to RTC states, Brady's non-RTC states maintained significantly higher violent crime rates in all categories: at the end of the study period, non-RTC states maintained a 72.1% higher violent crime rate, 58.4% higher murder rate, 7.9% higher rape rate, 98.1% higher robbery rate (nearly double!), and 70.4% higher aggravated assault rate.[23]

It is most curious that in Chapter 5, Brady made much of the fact that Florida had a relatively high violent crime rate as a reason to derogate its RTC law, but conveniently ignored the fact that Florida realized a more rapid decline in violent crime rates since enacting RTC, compared to U.S. trends. Now, Brady focuses on the fact that non-RTC states — their ideal — saw faster decreases in violent crime, conveniently ignoring their inordinately high rates. It appears Brady constantly shifts its criteria in search of a datum that validates its agenda.

The Brady Campaign makes three vital points in *Concealed Truth*:

- They mention the word "concealed" 23 times in their report, either in conjunction with "carry", "weapons", or "handgun." Therefore, Brady considers RTC laws a causative factor in violent crime rates.

- They identify the time period of 1992-1998 as valid for showing the link between RTC laws and violent crime rates.

- They insist that a state's concealed carry law is of primary importance in affecting its violent crime rate.

A fourth criteria requires deeper study:

Perhaps most compelling is the fact that robbery has declined twice as quickly in states with strict licensing or that do not allow concealed carrying at all than in states with lax CCW systems. If carrying concealed weapons reduces crime, it would be expected that the greatest effects would be seen on crimes that most often occur between strangers in public places, such as robbery.[24]

Brady over-dramatizes a bit, as the non-RTC states' average percent of decline in the robbery rate was 59.6% greater, not double (100%) that of RTC states (35.2% versus 22.0%, respectively). But they state their criteria clearly in this passage: If RTC is beneficial, then the greatest effect should be seen in crimes where the victim and perpetrator are strangers.

The Bureau of Justice Statistics has data available for the years 1996 through 2005, estimating the number of attacks by strangers and non-strangers for the three violent crime categories of rape, robbery, and aggravated assault. Averaging these years, 72.7% of all robberies were perpetrated by strangers, in keeping with Brady's claim. Strangers also perpetrated 54.4% of all aggravated assaults. This is not much different than the averages for 1996-1998: 71.4% for robbery and 53.5% for aggravated assault, if it is important to include data only in the Brady time period.[25]

Aggravated assault should be included in this discussion, according to Brady's criteria: "If carrying concealed weapons reduces crime, it would be expected that the greatest effects would be seen on crimes that *most often* occur between strangers in public places..." [Italics added]

As noted above, non-RTC states did not see any special advantage over RTC states in aggravated assault rate trends. Brady selected only the data that was useful to their agenda, ignoring that which was not.

Also, Brady did not address the 14 states which enacted RTC during Brady's study period. Brady gives great credence to robbery rate trends to "prove" that there is a negative causal relationship between RTC and violent crime trends. This is a very important criteria to remember when examining states excluded from their study. In 1992, these states looked more like non-RTC states: Their average violent crime rate was 636.5, closer to the non-RTC states' average of 751.6 than the RTC states' 412.1. Separating violent crime trends into two periods, before and after RTC enactment, produces two trend periods for each state. These states averaged a negligible decrease in violent crime (-0.1%) before RTC enactment. From RTC enactment through 1998, this index decreased far more dramatically (-14.4%). This "RTC Effect" is noticeable for all crime categories except rape: -10.9% before RTC, but rape still decreased another 7.4% after RTC.[26] The most significant indicators, according to Brady, are the two crime categories perpetrated most often upon strangers: Robbery rates declined 2.4% before RTC but 18.4% after; aggravated assault rates *increased* 2% before RTC, but declined 13.5% after.

Seven states saw *increases* in their violent crime rates from 1992 through RTC enactment, while all 14 states saw a decrease afterwards. This RTC effect carries across all violent crime categories except rape: before RTC, five states saw a rise in the murder rate, but only two saw increases afterwards; seven states experienced more robbery before but one afterwards; seven states saw more aggravated assault before but only one afterwards; one state saw an increase in rape before and one after.[27]

These dramatic before/after trend patterns lend credence to the idea that more guns in the hands of law-abiding citizens reduces violent crime and demolish Brady's contention that concealed carry laws contribute to crime.

Brady Campaign believes the time period of 1992-1998 tells us what we need to know about concealed carry and its impact on violent crime. Their data set and criteria prove that more guns means less crime.

Conclusion

Anti-gun-rights organizations have a long and consistent history of parsing data sets in order to find "proof" that guns in the hands of the law-abiding either present a danger to society or do not provide for the general defense. Also with great consistency, their own data sources and data sets, if taken in toto, show just the opposite from what anti-rights groups intend.

Gun control or gun rights: Which argument is based upon fear, and which is fact?

Chapter 8
"Call the Police"

(Author's note: The following discussion is not intended in any way to impugn the law enforcement officers who put their lives on the line to help defend against anarchy on the street. As the following discussion will show, any indication that our law enforcement programs are less than exemplary most likely results from failed government initiatives and/or mismanagement.)

WASHINGTON — Violent crime continued to increase in the first six months of [2006], highlighted by a growing trend of teenagers shooting robbery victims even if they surrender their valuables.

That was the message from Wednesday's National Violent Crime Summit, at which 170 police chiefs, mayors and other government officials compared local crime statistics that they have not yet shared with the FBI...

Robbers, especially juveniles, are more likely than ever to shoot victims, even when they do not resist. **"There's almost a different code on the street, that it's not a robbery unless you shoot somebody,"** said Thomas Streicher, police chief in Cincinnati.[1] [Emphasis added]

A 76-year-old Eastside jewelry store owner opened fired on two suspected robbers Wednesday morning, killing one and trapping the second upstairs until police arrived.

Indianapolis police say Roscoe Parmley shot and killed Corey Artry, 18, at Rosco Jewelry, 5416 E. Washington St.

Police captured Artry's brother, Nicholas Artry, 20, in a second-floor room. He was arrested on preliminary charges of robbery and felony murder. The murder charge arises from the allegation that he was involved in a crime that led to a death.

Dozens of officers were on the scene minutes after the shooting was reported at 10:56 a.m., but Indianapolis Police Department Chief Michael Spears said **officers could do little to prevent this kind of "brazen" attack**. [Emphasis added]

"Two apparently able-bodied young men decided they would try to victimize an honest store owner," Spears said. "Now we have one man dead and another who is probably going to spend a significant amount of his life in prison."[2]

Three robbery suspects tried to hit a jewelry store Wednesday night, but the victim turned the tables on them. The owner of the jewelry store opened fire hitting one suspect. Two are still on the run...

Just after 7 p.m., the suspects, two men and one woman, tricked the owners to let them into the secured store by posing as customers. Once inside they pulled out at least one gun and demanded jewelry.

Both owners were forced to the ground but one of them was able to get a gun...

This is the third incident in the last month where either a shop owner or clerk has shot a robbery suspect.

"You have the right to protect yourself and your family. And I'm sure people are tired of being robbed and I don't blame them," [Las Vegas] Metro Sgt. Hunt continued.[3] [Emphasis added]

Some valley store owners say they are tired of being victimized and now they're fighting back. For the third time in a month, a store clerk shot an armed robber. The suspect in this recent case was killed.

An employee shot and injured an armed intruder at a smoke shop near Washington and Lamb last month. Two weeks later, the owners of a jewelry store at Charleston and Mohave wrestled the gun away from a would-be robber and shot and killed him during the scuffle.

On Sunday morning, North Las Vegas Police say a convenience store clerk threatened at gunpoint pulled out his own gun and shot the armed suspect killing him.

"This has been more common here recently that our store owners are not laying down to be victims, they're taking steps to protect themselves and other patrons in the store," said Sean Walker, North Las Vegas Police Department.

Restaurant manager Mina Reyes says her sandwich shop on South Rainbow has been hit twice by armed masked gunman despite the store's obvious security surveillance system.

"I don't feel safe here, especially at night because it is so dark in this area," said Reyes.

She says she's had one employee quit after being held up and says its [sic] difficult to hire people once they hear the restaurant has been robbed twice. Police understand how tempting it is for shop owners and managers to arm themselves but they have serious reservations about it.

"Defending yourself with a weapon is not for everyone. If you choose to do it, we advise you to take a weapons course, practice, and remember, you have to be willing to use it," Walker said.

Police say as a general rule, the safer option is to give an armed assailant what they want because nothing is more valuable than your life.[4]

The above articles present a spectrum of media interpretations regarding self-defense. The first article notes how big-city police acknowledge a trend in which armed robbers are becoming more likely to shoot their victims even after receiving the property they demand. The second article law enforcement's admission that they could not have prevented a robbery in which two young men attacked a 76-year-old store owner. The third notes how law enforcement is aware that people are "tired of being robbed" and are defending themselves instead. The fourth article echoes the third, with the addition of an editorial by the author, who contradicts what "170 police chiefs, mayors and other government officials" stated in the first article.

Is it reasonable for us to demand that a robbery victim, staring down the barrel of a gun, stop and consider: "Does he just want the money, or is he going to use that thing?" Also, in all the defensive shooting articles studied on the Internet in the last three years, less than 10% reported the defender being wounded, and none reported the defender being killed when resisting with a firearm. This finding reflects the research examined in Chapter 3, showing that those who resisted with a firearm were less likely to be injured than those who did nothing or resisted by physically fighting.

The main concern here is: If you decide to take a passive approach and let the perpetrator have his way, can you rely on the government to provide the justice demanded for the crime committed?

Did COPS Help?

A 2003 article by *Washington Monthly* editor Benjamin Wallace-Wells praised the Clinton Administration for his community policing initiative:

> The [community policing] movement took hold in some cities in the early 1990s, with dramatic, well-publicized drops in crime in Boston, New York, and San Diego. But the idea went national in 1994, when President Clinton convinced a supportive Democratic Congress to pass the Community Oriented Policing Services (COPS) bill, which promised federal grants to help local departments put 100,000 new cops on the street. By 2000, COPS had helped departments hire about 70,000 new officers (upping local police strength by 12 percent nationally), and required that all of the new cops be out on street beats. In those six years, violent crime declined by 46 percent nationally, the most sustained, dramatic decline in the last hundred years.[5]

Next, Wallace-Wells derogated President Bush for greatly reducing COPS funding, complaining that police departments couldn't cover the funding shortfall because of a "lousy economy." These are curious allegations, as the U.S. Gross Domestic Product increased every year from 2002-2005.[6] At the time of this article, the unemployment rate was near the historical average of 5.6% for the years 1948-2005 and about to drop below it.[7,8]

Wallace-Wells further contradicted himself in that he knew COPS was originally authorized for six years, yet complained that the current president somehow betrayed law enforcement by cutting funding. Finally, he ignored the impact of a new anti-crime program, Project Safe Neighborhoods.[9]

Wallace-Wells also needed to review actual crime statistics. The FBI reports that the violent crime rate dropped 29% between 1994 and 2000, making his "46%" over 50% higher than reality.[10]

Perhaps most importantly, he also miscalculated the effect COPS had on law enforcement officer (LEO) staffing levels. To begin with, his recap of the Clinton administration is flawed, according to Clinton's own staff. Roth and Ryan of the National Institute of Justice (part of Janet Reno's Department of Justice) evaluated the COPS program in 2000. They summarized the goals of COPS grants:

Title I authorized the expenditure of approximately $9 billion over 6 years for use in three primary approaches to achieving the goals. The first approach was to award 3-year grants to law enforcement agencies for hiring police officers to engage in community policing activities. The second was to award grants for acquiring technology, hiring civilians, and, initially, paying officer overtime—all with the intent of increasing existing officers' productivity and redeploying their freed-up time to community policing. The third was to award grants to agencies for innovative programs with special purposes, such as reducing youth gun violence and domestic violence.[11]

Hiring grants were supposed to "prime the pump" and motivate local police departments to find ways to permanently fund these positions:

The hiring grants were limited to 75 percent of each hired officer's salary and fringe benefits, normally up to a "3-year cap" of $75,000...Normally, grantees were required to match the awards with at least 25 percent of the program costs, to submit acceptable strategies for implementing community policing in their jurisdictions, and to retain the COPS-funded officer positions using local funds after the 3-year grants expired.[12]

COPS was not intended by the Clinton administration to be a permanent solution for increasing LEO staffing levels.

Over a year before this report, on May 12, 1999, the Clinton administration declared COPS a success:

At a ceremony that day, the White House announced that the goal of funding 100,000 police officers had been reached. We estimate that by then, the COPS Office and its predecessors had awarded $4.27 billion in hiring grants.[13]

However, the NIJ study took issue with how the administration calculated "100,000 police officers" and reported that COPS would not result in permanent staffing increases anywhere close to that number.

By May 1999, the COPS Office had awarded agencies approximately 60,900 officers through hiring grants. Under the best case scenario, we project that these awards will produce a peak effect of 57,200 officers by the year 2001, and that after post-grant attrition, the permanent effect of the grants will stabilize at 55,400 officers by 2003. The minimum retention scenario, in contrast, suggests the net impact of these awards will peak at 48,900 officers in 2000 but then decline to a permanent level of 39,000 officers by 2003.[14]

By 2000 there was an estimated 93,058 more full-time LEOs than in 1994, according to the FBI. Since FBI reports cover only about 94% of the population, staffing data could be extrapolated, assuming identical LEO density among the remaining 6% of the population. This would increase the 2000 staffing level to an estimated 97,805 more full-time LEOs than in 1994, which is fairly close to "the goal of funding 100,000 police officers." However, one more factor must be considered in order to determine if COPS, by itself, caused this increase.

Had staffing levels remained constant at the 1994 rate of 230 LEO per 100,000 population—in other words, had budgets grown to reflect only population growth—by 2000 there would have been about 646,297 officers nationwide, 49,359 less than actual. This difference could be called the "COPS Effect", and it approximates the NIJ study's "minimum retention scenario" of "48,900 officers in 2000." Reality is 40% different than Wallace-Wells' estimate that "COPS had helped departments hire about 70,000 new officers."

The year 1999 saw the peak of the COPS Effect, resulting in about 60,269 more LEOs than if staffing rates remained at the 1994 level. This calculation is close to the NIJ estimate of "approximately 60,900 [additional] officers through hiring grants."

By 2003, the COPS influence resulted in only about 36,395 additional LEOs, within 10% of the NIJ's predicted "minimum retention scenario" of a "decline to a permanent level of 39,000 officers by 2003." This decreasing trend supports the idea that as the COPS program ended its proposed six-year duration, loss of federal funding resulted in fewer LEO positions. It also indicates that local police departments did not uphold their side of the agreement: "to retain the COPS-funded officer positions using local funds after the 3-year grants expired."[15]

Between 1994 and 2005, sworn full-time officers increased 5% in terms of LEOs per 100,000 population. Between 1995 and 2005—giving a year for COPS to get under way—while the nation's violent crime rate dropped 31.5%, the rate of violent offenses cleared by police (per 1,000 officers) dropped 31.9%, meaning that clearance rates were dropping slightly faster than the crime rate. Breaking this out further shows some interesting trends. Between 1995 and 2000 (Clinton administration) the violent crime rate dropped 26%, but the clearance rate per 1,000 LEO dropped 33.8%. Clearance rates dropped in all four violent crime categories at faster rates than the drop in their corresponding crime rates. The murder rate dropped 32.6%, but the clearance rate for murders dropped 39.9%. The rape rate declined 13.6%, but its clearance rate dropped 21.3%. The robbery rate dropped 34.4%, but the clearance rate declined 43.1%. The aggravated assault rate dropped 22.5%, but its clearance rate decreased 29.7%.

Between 2001 and 2005—giving a year for the Bush administration to take over the Justice Department—the violent crime rate dropped 7% while the overall violent crime clearance rate increased 14.4%. Clearance rates increased across all four violent crime categories, while crime rates dropped in all categories except murder. The murder rate rose slightly at 0.2%, while the clearance rate for murders rose 14.4%. The rape rate declined 0.5%, but its clearance rate increased 18.4%. The robbery rate dropped 5.2%, but the clearance rate increased 13.7%. The aggravated assault rate dropped 8.6%, but its clearance rate rose 14.3%.[16]

These data show that law enforcement became less efficient during the Clinton administration and became more efficient during the Bush administration.

A research paper from the Police Executive Research Forum corroborates these Clinton era clearance calculations. Based upon a survey of urban police departments, Sidrow found that a certain number of respondents noted a decrease in homicide clearance rates regardless of whether their homicide rates were increasing, decreasing, or constant.[17]

During the COPS program, the hiring of civilian staff showed the biggest growth. From 1994 to 2005, civilian personnel increased 17.5% (civilian staff per 100,000 population), over three times the 5% growth rate for LEOs. Again, there is an interesting trend revealed when breaking this out by administration. During the Clinton years of 1994-2000, civilian staffing rates increased 13.9% while LEO rates increased 7.6%. For the Bush years of 2001-2005, civilian staffing rates increased 1.5% while LEO rates dropped 1.9%. Obviously, hiring more dispatchers and implementing better command and control technology may help officers stop crimes in progress and resolve cases. Perhaps the intention was that more support staff enabled LEOs to perform more effectively on the street. If the measure of efficiency is clearing cases, then the increased civilian staffing didn't help until after the year 2000, again contrary to Wallace-Wells' allegations.[18]

President Bush approved over $360 million in COPS funding for 2005.[19] Wallace-Wells is correct for once: This is less than the average annual amount under the original COPS program. Nevertheless, it continues the program five years beyond its original plan.

While law enforcement became more efficient in closing cases during the Bush administration, other research calls the original COPS program into question.

Eisler and Johnson reported that COPS money intended for hiring LEOs was "misspent:"

But now, with the largest buildup of local law enforcement in U.S. history winding down, a less flattering view of the COPS program is emerging: Federal audits of just 3% of all COPS grants have alleged that $277 million was misspent. Tens of thousands of jobs funded by the grants were never filled, or weren't filled for long, auditors found.[20]

They cite one example where COPS grant money was misused to pay normal operating expenses:

Puerto Rico's San Juan Police Department seemed to win big under COPS. Starting in 1994, when the force had about 450 people, it got $39 million to hire 813 officers.

But an audit by Justice's inspector general in November 2003 found that San Juan had fallen hundreds of officers short of its hiring commitments under the grants. The audit questioned $7.1 million in grant spending, and suggested that San Juan used much of it to pay expenses that should have been covered by the local police budget.[21]

Citing government oversight and independent research studies, Eisler and Johnson report a large discrepancy between the announced hiring levels and reality, corroborating NIJ and calculated staffing numbers discussed earlier:

Officially, the Justice Department says the COPS program "funded" 118,000 new police positions across the USA. But a review of Justice programs last year by the White House Office of Management and Budget said that COPS had put "fewer than 90,000" officers on the street. A University of Pennsylvania study in 2002 found that the number probably would wind up closer to 82,000 — or 30% fewer cops than Justice's estimate.[22]

It turns out that the San Juan case highlights the creative accounting techniques for calculating the purported "100,000 police officers:"

The San Juan case reflects the calculus the Justice Department has used to claim that COPS is responsible for 118,000 new officers. The grants have indeed "funded" that many jobs, but scores of agencies failed to hire all the officers they were supposed to. According to federal audits and police staffing data obtained by USA TODAY from the 20 largest recipients of COPS grants, thousands of hires funded by COPS never materialized.[23]

Eisler and Johnson cite additional studies concluding COPS failed. It is interesting to note that the one study that praised COPS was done by the same government department that controlled the program from the outset:

Meanwhile, few crime analysts say that COPS grants were significant in reducing crime. Analysts such as Stanford University's Joseph McNamara say that a much bigger factor has been the strong economy, which has kept many young people employed and away from crime.

Of three studies on the issue, only one — which was funded by the Justice Department — found that the police hiring program was chiefly responsible for drops in violent crime rates among big cities. The General Accounting Office, Congress' research arm, dismissed that study as "inconclusive."

The link between COPS grants and lower crime rates has been further obscured by the experience of cities such as Oklahoma City, which did not participate in the police hiring program — and yet saw crime rates drop by as much as those in cities that got grants.[24]

Richardson and Kosa note that Oklahoma City uses a comprehensive case management system to maintain a homicide clearance rate of 90%.[25] This is over 25% higher than the national rate for the same reporting year.[26]

Wallace-Wells' own words contradict his claims, as the quote from his article at the beginning of this section notes three cities which found out how to best combat crime before COPS began. Even an Associated Press article, which infers that Bush policies are responsible for the 2005 rise in violent crime, supports the idea that other factors besides COPS funding affects crime, citing three big-city exceptions:

Murders rose 4.8 percent, meaning there were more than 16,900 victims in 2005. That would be the most since 1998 and the largest percentage increase in 15 years.

Murders jumped from 272 to 334 in Houston, a 23 percent spike; from 330 to 377 in Philadelphia, a 14 percent rise; and from 131 to 144 in Las Vegas, a 10 percent increase.

Despite the national numbers, Detroit, Los Angeles and New York were among several large cities that saw the number of murders drop...

Criminal justice experts said the statistics reflect U.S. complacency in fighting crime, a product of dramatic declines in the 1990s and the abandonment of effective programs that emphasized prevention, putting more police officers on the street and controlling the spread of guns. [27]

Another article cites how New York City uses creative policing strategies in high-crime areas:

Officials with the New York Police Department credit their success to a series of crime-fighting initiatives. One involves assigning a roving team of 1,000 officers to make more arrests in so-called "impact zones." [28]

This indicates that there are enough LEOs to get the job done in high-crime big cities, when there is the will to do so.

Among all the errors in his article, it is easy to miss one outcome of Wallace-Wells' promotion of a new federal policy where local law enforcement is entitled to federal salaries, rather than allowing municipalities to use home rule to allocate their own tax dollars: This effectively moves us towards a federal police system. Of course, with such an organization, an anti-liberty president will have an easier time coordinating a national pogrom of civilian disarmament. This destroys the boundary that the Posse Comitatus Act is supposed to keep between locally-controlled law enforcement and federal troops:

It generally prohibits Federal military personnel and units of the United States National Guard under Federal authority from acting in a law enforcement capacity within the United States, except where expressly authorized by the Constitution or Congress. The Posse Comitatus Act and the Insurrection Act substantially limit the powers of the Federal government to use the military for law enforcement. [29]

How Efficient is the Criminal Justice System?

In Chapter 1, we noted that the Supreme Court consistently rules that police have no obligation to protect specific members of the general public, citing Castle Rock v. Gonzales as an example.

Another Supreme Court case, Deshaney v. Winebago, is interesting because it covers government agencies other than law enforcement. This shows that all government services appear to enjoy this blanket immunity from prosecution for failing to protect specific individuals. In this case, social service employees failed to protect a child after multiple notices that the boy was beaten by his father:

> Petitioner is a child who was subjected to a series of beatings by his father, with whom he lived. Respondents, a county department of social services and several of its social workers, received complaints that petitioner was being abused by his father and took various steps to protect him; they did not, however, act to remove petitioner from his father's custody. Petitioner's father finally beat him so severely that he suffered permanent brain damage and was rendered profoundly retarded. Petitioner and his mother sued respondents under 42 U.S.C. 1983, alleging that respondents had deprived petitioner of his liberty interest in bodily integrity, in violation of his rights under the substantive component of the Fourteenth Amendment's Due Process Clause, by failing to intervene to protect him against his father's violence. The District Court granted summary judgment for respondents, and the Court of Appeals affirmed.

The Supreme Court concluded that despite knowledge that the child was in danger:

> (a) A State's failure to protect an individual against private violence generally does not constitute a violation of the Due Process Clause, because the Clause imposes no duty on the State to provide members of the general public with adequate protective services.

> (b) There is no merit to petitioner's contention that the State's knowledge of his danger and expressions of willingness to protect him against that danger established a "special relationship" giving rise to an affirmative constitutional duty to protect.[30]

The reason this is brought up again is to place the following discussion into context: When it comes to fighting crime, the criminal justice system can only do so much.

Just as the highest court in the land recognizes that government agencies have no legal obligation to protect you and your family, the criminal justice system also has no obligation to lock up violent criminals.

A 2004 U.S. Department of Justice survey (the latest data available) estimates that rape victims only report 35.8% of all incidents to police.[31] This is because women who are raped often feel shame or self-blame, or believe that there is nothing the police can do. Since 67% of rapes are committed by somebody she knows, victims often fear that after having been brutally assaulted, it could easily happen again if they tried to prosecute the offender.[32] This means that for every 1,000 rapes committed, 358 are reported to police.

In 2004, the FBI reported that 41.8% of all reported rapes were cleared by police, meaning that the suspect was arrested and charged, the suspect died before arrest, or the victim refused to cooperate after the suspect was arrested.[33] This means that for every 1,000 rapes committed, only 150 were referred for prosecution.

To get an idea of how the court system processes these arrests, we will continue with data compiled by the DOJ, using as an indicator 2004 violent sexual offenses referred to U.S. attorneys for prosecution in U.S. district courts. Of these, prosecuting attorneys declined to prosecute 52.4% of the cases.[34] Reasons for declining cases include weak evidence and lack of resources.[35] Some cases were referred to other authorities for prosecution, such as state-level prosecution.[36] So for the 150 cleared by police and referred to federal prosecutors, 71 cases would be prosecuted in district courts by U.S. attorneys (eliminating referred cases from this calculation). Of all violent sexual offense cases completed, 89.7% of them resulted in conviction.[37] This means that only about 64 of the original 1,000 violent sex crime incidents result in conviction. But only 94.2% of the convictions resulted in sentences of incarceration, meaning that of the 1,000 rapes, only 60 resulted in prison time. The median prison sentence was 97 months, meaning that half of those convicted were sentenced to less than eight years.[38]

For the time period of 1994-2004, after calculating the total percent of cases accepted by federal prosecutors, and the percentages of cases convicted and sent to prison, for every 1,000 rapes, 171 rapists are referred for adjudication and 60 are sent to prison. Looking at it from the criminal's viewpoint, this means that a rapist has a 17% chance of being arrested and only a 6% chance of going to prison for his crime.

(Note: The above discussion assumes that each rapist gets arrested after the first crime: a condition where the criminal justice system operates most efficiently.)

The incarceration rates for the three other violent crime categories are somewhat better. Between 1994 and 2004, for every 1,000 reported incidents, 284 murderers, 122 robbers, and 132 aggravated assault perpetrators received prison sentences.[39]

How Does State-Level Data Compare?

The Department of Justice publishes a biennial publication, *Felony Defendants in Large Urban Counties*. Currently, reports are available through 2002. From this, we can derive an indicator on the efficiency of state court systems. As noted in the 1994 edition, these counties cover over one-third of the U.S. population, and account for over one-half of the violent crime in the United States:

In 1994, the 75 largest counties accounted for 36% of the U.S. population. According to the FBI's Uniform Crime Reports program for 1994, these jurisdictions accounted for 52% of all reported serious violent crimes in the United States, including 63% of all robberies. They accounted for 43% of all reported serious property crimes.

According to the BJS National Judicial Reporting Program, about half of all felony convictions in 1994 occurred in the 75 largest counties.[40]

There is one datum missing in these state-level reports that makes them inconsistent with the federal-level ones: There is no count of the exact number of arrestees whose cases were accepted or declined for prosecution. A request for this information resulted in the following response from the Bureau of Justice Statistics:

> The State Court Processing Statistics (SCPS) data collection series, which we use to produce Felony Defendants in Large Urban Counties, does not contain information on the number of felony cases accepted for prosecution. Unlike the Compendium, the Felony Defendants report does not contain prosecution information at that level of detail. You can use the Felony Defendants report to examine the percentage of felony arrests that resulted in a conviction or dismissal. In this way, the Felony Defendants report can serve as a rough indictor of how many felony arrests actually make it through the prosecution acceptance process to conviction.[41]

Using the recommended BJS formula, one can derive the number of defendants convicted, not convicted, or subjected to "other outcomes" (diversion programs and deferred adjudication) to attain an estimated number of defendants accepted by state court systems. Subtracting this number from the number of arrests will result in an estimate of arrestees who were declined for prosecution.

The purpose here is to see if the results from the DOJ's study of federal criminal justice data are reflected in state-level data. For the time period of 1994-2002, after calculating the total percent of cases accepted by state prosecutors, and the percentages of cases convicted and sent to prison: for every 1,000 murders, 161 defendants were incarcerated; for every 1,000 rapes, 43 were incarcerated; for every 1,000 robberies, 47 were incarcerated; for every 1,000 aggravated assaults, 66 were incarcerated. These calculations are all lower than the federal-level data, though it must be reiterated that, as BJS notes, this is a "rough indicator."[42]

It must also be reiterated that this discussion is not intended to find fault with the criminal justice system. Many factors outside the control of prosecutors come into play to affect the final outcome: E.g. insufficient evidence to warrant investing public resources for a prosecution, or victims unwilling to be witnesses or who retract their accusations. The main point here is that those who choose not to resist because they believe the criminal justice system will come to their rescue stand a very good chance of being disappointed.

Clinton/Reno Versus Bush/Ashcroft

Returning to the earlier allegation that President Bush is somehow softer on crime than Clinton, examining incarceration rates and sentence lengths brings some interesting trends to light.

During the Clinton/Reno years of 1994-2000, in terms of incarceration trends, Clinton/Reno trailed Bush/Ashcroft in three of four categories. Incarceration rates between 1994 and 2000 decreased 1.5% annually for murder while increasing 3.1% for robbery and 1.1% for assault. Between 2001 and 2004, incarceration rates increased 2.1% annually for murder, 3.3% for robbery, and 13.2% for assault. The one exception to this trend, incarceration rates for rape increased 9.4% annually between 1994-2000 compared to a 3.3% annual increase between 2001 and 2004.

In terms of incarcerations per 1,000 incidents, Clinton/Reno again trailed in three categories. Between 1994 and 2000, there was an estimated average of 333 incarcerations for every 1,000 homicides, compared to an average of 257 between 2001 and 2004. There were 55 incarcerations for every 1,000 rapes during the 1994-2000 period, compared to 66 for 2001-2004. Robbery incarceration averages showed a similar trend: 119 to 130 for the periods of 1994-2000 and 2001-2004, respectively. Assault trends were similar as well: 126 to 150, for the periods of 1994-2000 and 2001-2004, respectively.[43]

Sentencing trends show an even more interesting — and consistent — trend. During the Clinton/Reno years, median sentence lengths fell across the board. In terms of months sentenced to prison, murder sentences dropped an average of 8.8% annually and assault sentences dropped 4.2%. Robbery sentences remained even and rape sentences increased 12.1% annually. During the Bush/Ashcroft years, sentence lengths increased in all categories: murder sentences increased 10.1% (annual increases for all categories); rape increased 44.2%; robbery sentences increased 26.4%; and assault increased 3.3%.

For all the media rhetoric about COPS and Clinton's get-tough-on-crime mythology, the criminal justice system was generally more efficient and more effective after Clinton left the White House.

The federal 'assault weapons' ban, one of the most sweeping gun control laws ever passed by Congress, was championed by Bill Clinton. While gun ownership for law-abiding citizens was restricted by this onerous law, criminal prosecution of gun laws, and sentencing for violations, actually dropped. The Syracuse Transactional Records Access Clearinghouse, or TRAC, shows that during the Reno Department of Justice, Bureau of Alcohol, Tobacco, and Firearms (ATF) referrals for prosecution dropped by almost half from 1992 to 1998. The Bush administration had no problem referring federal firearms law-breakers for prosecution: In the first three years of the Ashcroft DOJ, ATF referrals increased 67%.[44] Also during the

Clinton administration, the median prison sentence for ATF cases remained flat while the median prison sentence for other agencies rose.[45]

More interesting is the list of Clinton's pardons. Out of 141 pardons, 15 were involved with the cocaine trade and four were firearms related, including one arms dealer.[46] This is a curious fact. Who is more likely to use a firearm in a felony: a cocaine dealer or a law-abiding citizen?

Conclusion

Bush detractors wish to use revisionist history to distract us from Clinton's history of anti-liberty legislation, poor law enforcement and criminal behavior, and instead direct attention towards recent imagined slights done to police departments.

In reality, another multi-billion dollar Clinton program promised to make us safer, but research doesn't verify this claim. (This finding is consistent with Clinton gun control policies.) Our tax dollars were wasted. Law enforcement clearance rates dropped during the Clinton Administration, perhaps reflecting Clinton's inability to prosecute criminals who violated federal gun laws. Nevertheless, violent crime decreased during this time period, in spite of Clinton's much-vaunted COPS, showing that factors besides federal legislation impacted violent crime.

Wrapping It Up

Gun control proponents praise the National Academy of Sciences for apparently derogating research by John Lott, conveniently ignoring that the NAS reserves even greater negation for one of the gun banners' sacred cows: "a handgun in the home makes it 43 times more likely that a friend, family member, or acquaintance will be killed than an intruder." Nor do gun controllers like to acknowledge that their vaunted authority, the NAS, found that gun control legislation, such as the Brady Law, showed no positive affect in fighting crime. Gun control politicians justify passing laws which prohibit gun ownership only for law-abiding citizens by claiming that 8 children a day are killed by firearms, but examination of data from the Federal Bureau of Investigation and the Centers for Disease Control prove that less than one child is killed by firearms every day. CDC data also proves that nearly all of these are murders and suicides, which could just as easily be done by other means. The CDC also shows that accidental firearm injury and death rates have been dropping precipitously over the last 20+ years. Gun controllers claim that the United States is the most dangerous country in the world because of private gun ownership, but data from the United Nations and other international sources show that homicide and suicide rates are completely unrelated to rates of civilian firearms ownership, and that the United States is neither the most violent nor the most homicidal country in the world. Gun controllers claim that Australia and Britain are on the right track by severely limiting gun ownership or completely banning it, yet crime data from those countries proves that violent crime, especially rape, has risen in both countries since enactment of draconian gun control laws, and crime involving guns has risen in the UK.

If further gun control is necessary for the public good, it should first be proven that civilian gun ownership is a public hazard. Drawing from numerous sources from around the world and across time, the case for gun control has not been proven beyond a reasonable doubt. Inconsistencies and outright manipulation of partial data sets by gun control organizations undercuts the veracity of their claims that civilian disarmament is beneficial. History demonstrates time after tragic time that disarmed civilian populations were not protected by their armed government officials, but were instead preyed upon by those who ostensibly were supposed to protect them. Conversely, those same population groups became empowered to protect their personal liberty when they gained access to firearms. Gun control has not worked for the people gun control organizations claim to care about; it *has* worked for governments seeking more power.

Civilian disarmament has had its "day in court" and it has failed. The idea that further civilian disarmament will somehow magically alter such consistent outcomes is ludicrous at best; at worst, it is part of an intentional program by corrupt national governments to ensure wealth and power for a few elites.

Appendix A – Tables

Table 2.1 – Percent responding "Yes" to Violent Crime Victimization in 1992 Survey

Country	Robbery[1]	Sexual Assault on Women[2]	Assault With Force[3]
Australia	1.1	1.9	2.8
United Kingdom	.9	.3	1.1
United States	1.7	1.5	2.2

Table 2.2 – Percent responding "Yes" in 1992 and 2000 to Violent Crime Victimization

Country	1992*	2000[4]	Percent Change
Australia	5.8	4.1	-29.3%
United Kingdom	2.3	3.6	+56.5%
United States	5.4	1.9	-66.7%

* Violent crimes of robbery, sexual assault, and assault with force from the 1992 survey are combined into one index.

Table 2.3 – Violent Crime Rates 1995 and 2005 (per 100,000 pop.)

Crime	Country	1995	2006	Change (%)
Homicide	Australia	2.0[5]	1.5[6]	-21.8
	United Kingdom	1.3[7]	1.3[8]	-1.7
	United States[9]	8.2	5.7	-30.6
Rape/Sexual Assault	Australia	72.5	88.0	+21.4
	United Kingdom	37.7	66.5	+76.5
	United States	37.1	31.7	-16.8
Robbery	Australia	80.6	83.5	+3.6
	United Kingdom	117.1	162.1	+38.1
	United States	220.9	140.7	-32.4
Assault*	Australia	562.8	825.6	+46.7
	United Kingdom	259.2[10]	309.6	+19.4
	United States	418.3	291.1	-31.3

* Due to incomplete police records on assault in the UK; trend is for 1998 to 2005.

Table 2.4 – Violent Crime Rates 1995 and 2003 (per 100,000 pop.) Adjusted for Assumed Effect of NCRS

Crime	Country	1995	2003	Change (%)
Homicide	United Kingdom[11]	1.3	1.8	+36.3
	United States	8.2	5.7	-30.5
Rape/Sexual Assault	United Kingdom	37.7	46.8	+24.2
	United States	37.1	32.1	-13.5
Robbery	United Kingdom	117.4	139.6	+18.9
	United States	220.9	142.2	-35.6
Assault	United Kingdom*	259.2	302.6	+16.7
	United States	418.3	295.0	-29.5

* Due to incomplete police records on assault in the UK; trend is for 1998-2003.

Table 2.5 – Substitution Effect in United Kingdom*
(Rates per 100,000 population)

Category	1998[12]	2005[13]	% Change
Property Crime	7,364.3	6,928.8	-5.9
Violent Crime	1,036.6	1,967.6	+89.8

* Some crime categories were not recorded prior to 1998.

Table 2.6 – Substitution Effect in Australia
(Rates per 100,000 population)

Category	1995[14]	2005[15]	% Change
Property Crime	5,548.8	3,931.7	-29.1
Violent Crime	717.9	986.5	+37.4

Table 2.7 – Substitution Effect in United States[16]
(Rates per 100,000 population)

Category	1995	1998	2005	% Change 1995-2005	% Change 1998-2005
Property Crime	4,590.5	4,052.5	3,429.8	-25.3	-15.4
Violent Crime	684.5	567.6	469.2	-31.5	-17.3

Table 3.1: Unintentional Deaths, Selected Categories[17]

Category	1994 Total	1994 Rate (per 100k)	2004 Total	2004 Rate (per 100k)	% Change in Rate
Poison	8,994	3.42	20,950	7.13	+108.7
Drowning	3,942	1.50	3,308	1.13	-24.8
Motor Vehicle	42,524	16.16	44,933	15.30	-5.3
Suffocation	4,143	1.57	5,891	2.01	+27.4
Firearms	1,356	0.52	649	0.22	-57.1

Table 3.2: U.S. Injury-Related Deaths–2003[18]

Injury

All	167,184
Unintentional	112,012
Homicide	17,357
Legal intervention	372
Suicide	32,439
Undetermined intent	4,976

Firearm

All	29,569
Unintentional	649
Homicide	11,624
Legal intervention	311
Suicide	16,750
Undetermined intent	235

Motor Vehicle

All	45,113
Unintentional	44,933
Homicide	51
Legal intervention	N/A
Suicide	108
Undetermined intent	21

Table 3.3: Suicide Rates (per 100,000 population)[19]

	1995	*1999/2000*	*Change*
AUS	12.0	12.5	4.2%
UK	7.4	7.5	1.4%
USA	11.9	10.4	-12.6%

Table 3.4: Other Intentional Causes of Death–2004[20]

Cut/Pierce	2,079
Drown	56
Fire/Burn	143
Poison	103
Suffocation	664

Table 3.5: Unintentional Death and Injury Rate Trends, Motor Vehicle and Firearms (per 100,000 population)

	1979 Death Rate	2004 Death Rate	% Change	1993 Injury Rate	2004 Injury Rate	% Change
Firearm	.89[21]	.22[22]	-75.3	40.5[23]	5.64[24]	-86.1
Motor Vehicle[25]	22.70	14.52	-36.0	1,222	950	-22.3

Table 3.6: CDC Non-Fatal Injuries–2004[26]

Overall

All	29,654,475
Unintentional	27,436,649
Assault	1,718,894
Legal intervention	73,282
Self-harm	425,650

Firearm

All	64,389
Unintentional	16,555
Assault	43,592
Legal intervention	890
Self-harm	3,352

Motor Vehicle

All	3,008,202
Unintentional	3,000,866
Assault	4,724
Legal intervention	950
Self-harm	1,662

Table 3.7: Crime Victimization 2002/3

	Assault	*Robbery*
Number of Victims	1,045,610	554,310
with injury[27]	338,930	213,250
Pct w/Injury	32	38
Kleck, Gertz Injury %	57,509	30,487
Reduction	281,421	182,763
Annual Reduction	140,711	91,382
Cost per injury[28]	24,000	19,000
Cost, no injury	2,000	2,000
Cost adjustment	22,000	17,000
Annual Savings*	$3,095,642,000	$1,553,494,000
2002 $ Conversion[29]	1.2407	
2003 $ Conversion	1.2641	
Average	1.2524	
Adj. Annual Savings	$3,876,982,041	$1,945,595,886

* Initial savings amount based upon 1993 dollars. Final amount is calculated using conversion factors to adjust for inflation.

Table 3.8: DWI vs. Firearms Deaths, 2004

	DWI Deaths	*Firearm Deaths*
Number of Victims	16,694[30]	9,326
Cost per injury[31]	3,180,000	2,940,000
Annual Savings*	53,086,047,984	27,418,440,000
2004 $ Conversion[32]	1.3052	
Adj. Annual Savings	$69,289,047,984	$35,786,547,888

* Initial savings amount based upon 1993 dollars. Final amount is calculated using conversion factors to adjust for inflation.

Table 3.9: Rape Reduction 2002/3

Number of Victims	223,290
Reduction	211,456
Annual Reduction	105,728
Cost per injury	$87,000
Annual Savings*	$9,198,336,000
2002 $ Conversion	1.2407
2003 $ Conversion	1.2641
Average	1.2524

Adj. Annual Savings	$11,519,996,006

* Initial savings amount based upon 1993 dollars. Final amount is calculated using conversion factors to adjust for inflation.

Table 4.1: Firearms Manufacturers by Size, 2002[33]

Units	<100	100-999	1,000-9,999	10,000-100,000	>100,000	Totals
Pistol	29	9	15	15	1	69
Rifle	121	38	21	11	5	196
Shotgun	23	7	6	3	3	42
Totals	173	54	42	29	9	307

Table 4.2: Firearms Deaths for Children-2003[34]

	Boxer	Puberty
Age Range	0-19	0-14
Homicide	1,822	235
Legal Intervention	22	2
Suicide	810	74
Unintentional	151	56
Undetermined	44	13
Total all intents	2,849	380
Deaths Per Day	7.9	1.1

Table 4.3: Leading Causes of Injury Deaths, 2003, Age 0-14[35]

Category	Total
Unintentional Motor Vehicle	2,154
Unintentional Suffocation	859
Unintentional Drowning	782
Unintentional Fire/Burn	272
Homicide, firearm	235

Table 4.4: Unintentional Death of Children Under 15, Selected Categories

	1990[36]		2004[37]		
Category	Total	Rate (per 100k)	Total	Rate (per 100k)	% Change in Rate
Drowning	1,148	2.12	761	1.25	-41.0
Firearms	236	0.44	63	0.10	-77.3
Motor Vehicle	3,182	5.88	2,431	4.00	-32.0
Poison	113	0.21	86	0.14	-33.3
Suffocation	677	1.25	963	1.58	+26.4

Table 5.1: Do More Cars Result in More Fatalities?[38]

	1966	2004	Trend
Registered Vehicles	95,703,000	237,961,000	+148.6%
Licensed Drivers	100,998,000	198,889,000	+96.9%
Traffic Fatalities	50,894	42,636	-16.2%

Do More Cars Result in More Crashes?[39]

	1988*	2004	Trend
Registered Vehicles	95,703,000	237,961,000	+34.1%
Total Crashes	6,887,000	6,181,000	-10.3%

* Total crash data not available until 1988.

Table 5.2: DC/U.S. Homicide Ratio Violent Crime Rates DC 1960-2005[40]

	United States				Washington, D.C.					
	Violent crime	*Annual Percent Change*	*Murder*	*Percent Change*	*Violent crime*	*Percent Change*	*Ratio to US*	*Murder*	*Annual Percent Change*	*Ratio to US*
					(Rates per 100,000 Inhabitants)					
Year:										
1960	160.9		5.1		553.7		3.4	10.6		2.1
1961	158.1	-1.7	4.8	-5.9	587.9	6.2	3.7	11.5	8.5	2.4
1962	162.3	2.7	4.6	-4.2	605.9	3.1	3.7	11.6	0.9	2.5
1963	168.2	3.6	4.6	0.0	594.0	-2.0	3.5	11.9	2.6	2.6
1964	190.6	13.3	4.9	6.5	632.7	6.5	3.3	16.3	37.0	3.3
1965	200.2	5.0	5.1	4.1	722.8	14.2	3.6	18.4	12.9	3.6
1966	220.0	9.9	5.6	9.8	885.5	22.5	4.0	17.5	-4.9	3.1
1967	253.2	15.1	6.2	10.7	1143.6	29.1	4.5	22.0	25.7	3.5
1968	298.4	17.9	6.9	11.3	1505.6	31.7	5.0	24.1	9.5	3.5
1969	328.7	10.2	7.3	5.8	2135.1	41.8	6.5	36.0	49.4	4.9
1970	363.5	10.6	7.9	8.2	2226.8	4.3	6.1	29.2	-18.9	3.7
1971	396.0	8.9	8.6	8.9	2170.6	-2.5	5.5	37.1	27.1	4.3
1972	401.0	1.3	9.0	4.7	1685.4	-22.4	4.2	32.8	-11.6	3.6
1973	417.4	4.1	9.4	4.4	1558.4	-7.5	3.7	35.9	9.5	3.8
1974	461.1	10.5	9.8	4.3	1603.7	2.9	3.5	38.3	6.7	3.9
1975	487.8	5.8	9.6	-2.0	1774.3	10.6	3.6	32.8	-14.4	3.4
1976	467.8	-4.1	8.8	-8.3	1481.3	-16.5	3.2	26.8	-18.3	3.0
1977	475.9	1.7	8.8	0.0	1426.5	-3.7	3.0	27.8	3.7	3.2
1978	497.8	4.6	9.0	2.3	1411.7	-1.0	2.8	28.0	0.7	3.1
1979	548.9	10.3	9.7	7.8	1608.7	14.0	2.9	27.4	-2.1	2.8
1980	596.6	8.7	10.2	5.2	2010.6	25.0	3.4	31.5	15.0	3.1
1981	594.3	-0.4	9.8	-3.9	2274.8	13.1	3.8	35.1	11.4	3.6
1982	571.1	-3.9	9.1	-7.1	2123.1	-6.7	3.7	30.7	-12.5	3.4
1983	537.7	-5.8	8.3	-8.8	1915.4	-9.8	3.6	29.4	-4.2	3.5
1984	539.9	0.4	7.9	-4.8	1721.5	-10.1	3.2	28.1	-4.4	3.6
1985	558.1	3.4	8.0	1.3	1624.8	-5.6	2.9	23.5	-16.4	2.9
1986	620.1	11.1	8.6	7.5	1505.3	-7.4	2.4	31.0	31.9	3.6
1987	612.5	-1.2	8.3	-3.5	1610.3	7.0	2.6	36.2	16.8	4.4

Table 5.2, Continued: DC/U.S. Homicide Ratio Violent Crime Rates DC 1960-2005[41]

	United States				Washington, D.C.					
	Violent crime	Annual Percent Change	Murder	Percent Change	Violent crime	Percent Change	Ratio to US	Murder	Annual Percent Change	Ratio to US
1988	640.6	4.6	8.5	2.4	1921.6	19.3	3.0	59.5	64.4	7.0
1989	666.9	4.1	8.7	2.4	2141.9	11.5	3.2	71.9	20.8	8.3
1990	729.6	9.4	9.4	8.0	2458.2	14.8	3.4	77.8	8.2	8.3
1991	758.2	3.9	9.8	4.3	2453.3	-0.2	3.2	80.6	3.6	8.2
1992	757.7	-0.1	9.3	-5.1	2832.8	15.5	3.7	75.2	-6.7	8.1
1993	747.1	-1.4	9.5	2.2	2921.8	3.1	3.9	78.5	4.4	8.3
1994	713.6	-4.5	9.0	-5.3	2662.6	-8.9	3.7	70.0	-10.8	7.8
1995	684.5	-4.1	8.2	-8.9	2661.4	0.0	3.9	65.0	-7.1	7.9
1996	636.6	-7.0	7.4	-9.8	2469.8	-7.2	3.9	73.1	12.5	9.9
1997	611.0	-4.0	6.8	-8.1	2024.2	-18.0	3.3	56.9	-22.2	8.4
1998	567.6	-7.1	6.3	-7.4	1718.5	-15.1	3.0	49.7	-12.7	7.9
1999	523.0	-7.9	5.7	-9.5	1627.7	-5.3	3.1	46.4	-6.6	8.1
2000	506.5	-3.2	5.5	-3.5	1507.9	-7.4	3.0	41.8	-9.9	7.6
2001	504.5	-0.4	5.6	1.8	1736.7	15.2	3.4	40.6	-2.9	7.3
2002	494.4	-2.0	5.6	0.0	1632.9	-6.0	3.3	46.2	13.8	8.3
2003	475.8	-3.8	5.7	1.8	1608.1	-1.5	3.4	44.2	-4.3	7.8
2004	463.2	-2.2	5.5	-3.5	1371.2	-14.7	2.9	35.8	-19.0	6.5
2005	469.0	1.3	5.6	2.4	1380.0	6.4	2.9	33.5	-1.1	6.0
13-Year Averages										
1963-76	332.4		7.4		1437.1		4.3	27.1		3.6
1977-90	585.0	76.0	8.9	19.9	1,839.6	28.0	3.1	38.4	41.9	4.3
1991-2004	603.1	3.1	7.1	-19.6	2,087.8	13.5	3.4	57.4	49.5	8.0

Table 5.3: Michigan Violent Crime Rates Since RTC Law

	Murder	Rape	Robbery	Assault	Violence
2001[42]	6.7	52.7	129.5	365.8	544.7
2004[43]	6.4	54.2	111.9	317.7	490.2
% Change	-4.5	2.8	-13.6	-13.1	-10.0

Table 5.4: Texas Arrest Comparison 1996-08/2001

	CHL Licensees		General Public		
Arrest Type	Arrests[44]	Percent of CHLs*	Arrests[45]	Percent of Adult Pop.	Ratio
Violent Crime	1,189	0.55	188,560	1.33	2.45
Property Crime	330	0.15	709,003	5.01	33.13
Drug Crime	404	0.19	570,994	4.04	21.79
All Arrests	5,314	2.44	6,159,629	43.56	17.87
Total Population		218,010[46]		21,325,018[47]	

*Concealed Handgun License

Table 5.5: Extrapolated Violation Ratio of General Population to RTC Licensees

	Adult Population			RTC Licensees			
State	Arrests[48]	Population	Percent	Sus/Rev	Licensees	Percent	Ratio
Arizona[49]	2,549,103	5,593,717	45.6	1,395	67,689	2.1	21.7
Louisiana[50]	2,015,692	3,144,321	62.6	449	19,920	2.3	27.0

Appendix A – Tables

Table 5.6: Arrest Trends - Selected States

State/Year	Arrests	Adult Population	Per 100k	Pct Diff From Avg.
Arizona				
2000[51]	271,233	4,648,179	5,835.3	2.0%
2001[52]	284,696	5,016,343	5,675.4	-0.8%
2002[53]	298,631	5,164,982	5,781.8	1.1%
2003[54]	305,252	5,365,487	5,689.2	-0.5%
2004[55]	315,007	5,593,717	5,631.4	-1.5%
Average	294,964	5,157,742	5,718.9	
Florida				
2000	881,709	15,689,964	5,619.6	-1.1%
2001	922,333	16,377,083	5,631.9	-0.9%
2002	912,998	16,589,355	5,503.5	-3.2%
2003	974,805	17,012,655	5,729.9	0.8%
2004	1,028,856	17,390,278	5,916.3	4.1%
Average	944,140	16,611,867	5,683.5	
Louisiana				
2000	182,120	3,082,240	5,908.7	-12.4%
2001	220,687	3,202,673	6,890.7	2.2%
2002	216,444	3,185,679	6,794.3	0.8%
2003	219,924	3,281,940	6,701.0	-0.6%
2004	232,707	3,144,321	7,400.9	9.8%
Average	214,376	3,179,371	6,742.7	
Michigan				
2000	308,491	8,432,749	3,658.2	-0.3%
2001	304,577	8,315,523	3,662.8	-0.1%
2002	371,037	9,625,166	3,854.9	5.1%
2003	353,346	9,724,692	3,633.5	-0.9%
2004	331,479	9,403,375	3,525.1	-3.9%
Average	333,786	9,100,301	3,667.9	

Table 5.6, cont'd: Arrest Trends - Selected States

	Arrests	*Population*	*Per 100k*	*Pct Diff From Average*
North Carolina				
2000	419,589	6,394,723	6,561.5	0.1%
2001	499,642	7,477,980	6,681.5	1.9%
2002	447,259	6,907,574	6,474.9	-1.2%
2003	432,569	6,614,261	6,539.9	-0.2%
2004	393,819	6,056,872	6,502.0	-0.8%
Average	438,576	6,690,282	6,555.4	
Oklahoma				
2000	164,613	3,450,654	4,770.5	0.9%
2001	154,382	3,257,436	4,739.4	0.3%
2002	161,363	3,424,485	4,712.0	-0.3%
2003	166,495	3,511,532	4,741.4	0.3%
2004	158,957	3,406,862	4,665.8	-1.3%
Average	161,162	3,410,194	4,725.9	
Texas				
2000	1,041,179	19,991,434	5,208.1	5.7%
2001	1,013,175	20,738,511	4,885.5	-0.9%
2002	1,036,323	21,447,682	4,831.9	-1.9%
2003	982,963	20,875,272	4,708.7	-4.4%
2004	1,116,524	22,272,789	5,013.0	1.7%
Average	1,038,033	21,065,138	4,929.4	
Utah				
2000	92,080	1,553,493	5,927.3	3.8%
2001	94,473	1,730,721	5,458.6	-4.4%
2002	121,200	2,201,721	5,504.8	-3.6%
2003	98,509	1,690,633	5,826.8	2.1%
2004	90,811	1,532,299	5,926.5	3.8%
Average	99,415	1,741,773	5,728.8	

Appendix A – Tables

Table 5.7: Violation Ratio of Oklahoma General Population to RTC Licensees

	Adult Population			RTC Licensees			
Year	Arrests	Population56	Percent	Sus/Rev	Licensees	Percent	Ratio
2001	154,382[57]	2,587,876	5.97	27[58]	15,081[59]	0.18	33.3
2002	161,363[60]	2,608,135	6.19	49[61]	23,853[62]	0.21	30.1
2003	166,495[63]	2,635,814	6.32	55[64]	32,032[65]	0.17	36.8
2004	158,957[66]	2,663,683	5.97	37[67]	49,614[68]	0.07	80.0

Table 5.8: Texas 2001 Conviction Rates[69]

Violent Crime

Category	CHL Licensees*		Non-CHL Public		Non:CHL Ratio	Crime Reduction	Percent Reduction	Cost Savings[70]
	Convictions	Percent of CHLs	Convictions	Percent of Pop.				
Homicide	1	0.0005	157	0.0011	2.42	782	41.3	$2,816,806,329
Rape/Sexual Assault	9	0.0041	1,359	0.0096	2.33	4,660	57.0	496,906,534
Robbery	0	0.0000	1,360	0.0096	N/A*	35,348	100.0	346,587,140
Aggravated Assault	17	0.0078	2,259	0.0160	2.05	39,574	51.2	1,164,058,454
Total Violent Crime	27	0.0124	5,135	0.0363	2.93	80,364	48.6	$4,824,358,456

Property Crime

Burglary	1	0.0005	5,675	0.0401	87.5	202,026	98.9	$346,677,266
Populations		218,010[71]	14,139,842[72]				Total Savings:	$5,171,035,722
Total Convictions	180	0.0826	35,070	0.2480	3.00			

* Divide-by-zero error, as no CHLs convicted of this crime.

Table 5.9: Texas CHL Convictions vs. General Population (FBI Crime Only)

	CHL Licensees			Non-CHL Population Over 21		
Year	Convictions	Pop.	Rate (per 100K)	Convictions	Pop.[73]	Rate (per 100K).
2002[74]	13	224,172[75]	5.80	9,339	14,463,249	64.57
2003[76]	8	239,863[77]	3.34	10,453	14,735,247	70.94
2004[78]	13	239,940[79]	5.42	10,945	15,035,475	72.79
2005[80]	34	248,874[81]	13.66	10,201	15,319,721	66.57
Average	17	238,212	7.17	10,235	14,888,423	68.74

Table 5.10: Annual Conviction Non-CHL:CHL Ratios[82]

Year	FBI Violence	Burglary (FBI)	Total FBI	All Convictions	Non-FBI Convictions
2002	11.13	27.67	15.73	11.52	10.17
2003	21.27	100.00*	41.34	13.69	10.18
2004	13.44	87.07	23.25	10.25	7.93
2005	4.87	32.21	8.38	6.45	5.79
Average	12.68	48.98	22.18	10.48	8.52

* CHLs had no burglary convictions in 2003. A value of 100 was assigned in order to remove a divide-by-zero error and calculate a reasonable average ratio.

Table 5.11: Cost Per Crime Incident

	Murder	Rape	Robbery	Aggravated Assault	Burglary
In 1993 dollars[83]	$2,940,000	$87,000	$8,000	$24,000	$1,400
2002 Cost[84]	3,660,249	108,313	9,960	29,880	1,743
2003 Cost	3,743,668	110,782	10,187	30,561	1,783
2004 Cost	3,843,363	113,732	10,458	31,374	1,830
2005 Cost	3,973,578	117,585	10,812	32,437	1,892

Table 5.12: Cost/Savings If Non-CHL Population As Law Abiding as Licensees[85]

	FBI Crimes	Total Crime Cost	CHL "Effect"	CHL "Savings"
		2002		
Homicide	1,302	4,765,644,198	868	3,176,639,687
Rape	8,508	921,527,004	6,628	717,912,039
Robbery	37,580	374,296,800	36,947	367,993,203
Aggravated Assault	78,628	2,349,404,640	73,682	2,201,617,624
Burglary	212,602	370,565,286	204,918	357,171,264
2002 Totals:		$8,781,437,928		$6,821,333,888
		2003		
Homicide	1,418	5,308,521,224	1,224	4,580,591,082
Rape	8,012	887,585,384	7,365	815,934,815
Robbery	37,018	377,102,366	36,489	371,717,399
Aggravated Assault	75,753	2,315,087,433	71,671	2,190,332,794
Burglary	219,785	391,876,655	219,785	391,876,655
2003 Totals:		$9,280,173,062		$8,350,452,745
		2004		
Homicide	1,364	5,242,347,132	1,364	5,242,347,132
Rape	8,388	953,984,016	7,091	806,439,902
Robbery	35,817	374,574,186	35,307	369,239,613
Aggravated Assault	75,985	2,383,953,390	68,034	2,134,490,303
Burglary	220,118	402,815,940	217,590	398,189,502
2004 Totals:		$9,357,674,664		$8,950,706,452
		2005		
Homicide	1,407	5,590,824,246	941	3,737,236,168
Rape	8,511	1,000,765,935	4,149	487,832,706
Robbery	35,790	386,961,480	33,527	362,493,219
Aggravated Assault	75,383	2,445,198,371	65,681	2,130,497,448
Burglary	219,828	415,914,576	213,004	403,003,788
2005 Totals:		$9,839,664,608		$7,121,063,328
Four-Year Totals:		$37,258,950,262		$31,243,556,413

Table 5.13: CDC Homicide Rate Comparison[86]

	Overall			Firearm		
Age Group	1992 Rate	2002 Rate	Trend	1992 Rate	2002 Rate	Trend
0-4	3.87	3.71	-4.1%	0.41	0.30	-27.7%
5-9	0.79	0.70	-11.5%	0.30	0.28	-9.3%
10-14	2.41	1.02	-57.4%	1.90	0.71	-62.5%
15-19	18.99	9.30	-51.0%	16.55	7.70	-53.5%
20-24	24.28	16.37	-32.6%	20.05	13.53	-32.5%
25-29	18.82	13.30	-29.3%	14.08	10.68	-24.2%
30-34	15.01	9.49	-36.8%	10.44	6.95	-33.4%
35-39	11.99	7.95	-33.7%	7.93	5.21	-34.4%
40-44	9.75	6.56	-32.7%	6.23	3.95	-36.5%
45-49	7.89	5.43	-31.2%	4.87	2.84	-41.6%
50-54	6.48	4.05	-37.5%	3.77	2.24	-40.6%
55-59	4.97	3.49	-29.7%	2.97	1.76	-40.8%
60-64	4.39	2.74	-37.5%	2.38	1.26	-47.0%
65-69	3.78	2.39	-36.8%	1.60	0.96	-40.0%
70-74	3.66	2.20	-39.8%	1.27	0.79	-37.7%
75-79	3.59	2.27	-36.7%	1.28	0.97	-24.4%
80-84	4.12	2.39	-41.9%	1.18	0.81	-31.3%
85+	4.04	2.08	-48.6%	0.87	0.42	-52.5%
Broader Age Groups						
0-14	2.38	1.78	-25.1%	0.86	0.43	-49.4%
15-24	21.78	12.83	-41.1%	18.39	10.61	-42.3%
25-44	13.99	9.15	-34.6%	9.74	6.52	-33.1%
45-64	6.15	4.14	-32.7%	3.64	2.15	-40.9%
65+	3.78	2.28	-39.7%	1.32	0.83	-37.4%
Total	9.80	6.12	-37.5%	6.82	4.11	-39.7%

Table 5.14: CDC Suicide Rate Comparison[87]

Age Group	Overall 1992 Rate	Overall 2002 Rate	Overall Trend	Firearm 1992 Rate	Firearm 2002 Rate	Firearm Trend
0-4	0.00	0.00	N/A	0.00	0.00	N/A
5-9	0.05	0.02	-63.1%	0.02	0.00	-100.0%
10-14	1.67	1.23	-26.0%	0.94	0.41	-56.8%
15-19	10.71	7.44	-30.6%	7.25	3.65	-49.7%
20-24	14.83	12.28	-17.2%	9.50	6.62	-30.3%
25-29	13.97	12.82	-8.2%	7.99	6.44	-19.5%
30-34	14.71	12.60	-14.3%	7.64	5.68	-25.7%
35-39	15.00	14.40	-3.9%	7.67	6.65	-13.3%
40-44	15.07	16.17	+7.3%	7.74	7.44	-3.9%
45-49	14.60	16.33	+11.8%	8.18	7.77	-5.0%
50-54	14.56	15.11	+3.8%	8.48	7.91	-6.7%
55-59	14.65	14.60	-0.3%	9.37	8.65	-7.7%
60-64	14.93	12.35	-17.3%	9.30	8.10	-12.9%
65-69	15.56	12.49	-19.7%	10.79	8.83	-18.2%
70-74	17.47	14.54	-16.8%	12.80	10.68	-16.6%
75-79	21.67	16.56	-23.6%	15.06	12.35	-18.0%
80-84	24.57	19.36	-21.2%	16.34	14.35	-12.2%
85+	21.54	18.07	-16.1%	12.79	12.03	-5.9%
Broader Age Groups						
0-14	0.56	0.44	-22.1%	0.31	0.14	-54.4%
15-24	12.88	9.86	-23.5%	8.43	5.13	-39.1%
25-44	14.68	14.09	-4.1%	7.76	6.58	-15.2%
45-64	14.67	14.90	+1.6%	8.75	8.06	-7.9%
65+	19.04	15.58	-18.2%	13.08	11.25	-14.0%
Total	11.88	10.99	-7.5%	7.08	5.94	-16.1%

Table 5.15: Incidents with a Domestic Violent Crime - Percent Trend[88]

	1996	2001	Trend
Murder/Non-negligent Manslaughter	0.23%	0.23%	-0.41%
Negligent Manslaughter	0.03%	0.02%	-33.05%
Justifiable Homicide	0.01%	0.01%	4.73%
Forcible Rape	1.93%	2.07%	6.85%
Forcible Sodomy	0.52%	0.49%	-6.46%
Sexual Assault with an Object	0.29%	0.28%	-4.61%
Forcible Fondling	2.30%	2.27%	-1.19%
Incest	0.08%	0.06%	-23.27%
Statutory Rape	0.37%	0.36%	-4.10%
Total Rape and Sexual Assault*	5.49%	5.51%	0.46%
Robbery	4.63%	5.46%	17.99%
Aggravated Assault	19.26%	14.54%	-24.51%
Simple Assault	56.52%	57.97%	2.56%
Intimidation	13.84%	16.26%	17.53%

*Forcible Rape plus Forcible Sodomy, Sexual Assault with an Object, Forcible Fondling, Incest, and Statutory Rape

Table 5.16: Number of Incidents with a Domestic Violent Crime - Rate Trend[89]

	1996	Rate	2001	Rate	Trend
Murder/Non-negligent Manslaughter	594	0.2	1,820	0.6	184.82%
Negligent Manslaughter	67	0.0	138	0.0	91.47%
Justifiable Homicide	18	0.0	58	0.0	199.53%
Forcible Rape	4,929	1.9	16,204	5.7	205.60%
Forcible Sodomy	1,327	0.5	3,819	1.3	167.53%
Sexual Assault with an Object	737	0.3	2,163	0.8	172.82%
Forcible Fondling	5,854	2.2	17,796	6.2	182.59%
Incest	194	0.1	458	0.2	119.46%
Statutory Rape	951	0.4	2,806	1.0	174.28%
Total Rape and Sexual Assault	13,992	5.3	43,246	15.2	187.31%
Robbery	11,805	4.5	42,855	15.0	237.46%
Aggravated Assault	49,083	18.5	114,002	40.0	115.91%
Simple Assault	144,060	54.3	454,558	159.3	193.32%
Intimidation	35,263	13.3	127,512	44.7	236.14%
Totals:	254,882	96.1	784,189	274.8	186.00%
Populations	265,228,572		285,317,559		

Table 5.17: Comparison Between Domestic and FBI Crime

Domestic Violence	1996	2001	Trend
Murder/Non-negligent Manslaughter	0.2	0.6	184.82%
Total Rape and Sexual Assault*	5.3	15.2	187.31%
Robbery	4.5	15.0	237.46%
Aggravated Assault	18.5	40.0	115.91%
Total Domestic Violence Index	28.5	70.8	148.70%
FBI Violent Crime[90]			
Murder/Non-negligent Manslaughter	7.4	5.6	-24.32%
Rape	36.3	31.8	-12.40%
Robbery	201.9	148.5	-26.45%
Aggravated Assault	391.0	318.6	-18.52%
Total FBI Violent Crime Index	636.6	504.5	-20.75%

Table 5.18: Justifiable Homicide by Weapon, 2001-2005

By Law Enforcement[91]

Year	Total	Total Firearms	Pct of Total	Handguns	Pct of Firearms	Pct of Total
2001	378	375	99.2	318	84.8	84.1
2002	341	338	99.1	296	87.6	86.8
2003	373	366	98.1	318	86.9	85.3
2004	367	364	99.2	310	85.2	84.5
2005	341	337	98.8	296	87.8	86.8
Average			98.9		86.5	85.5

By Private Citizen[92]

Year	Total	Total Firearms	Pct of Total	Handguns	Pct of Firearms	Pct of Total
2001	222	183	82.4	143	78.1	64.4
2002	233	189	81.1	158	83.6	67.8
2003	247	203	82.2	163	80.3	66.0
2004	222	166	74.8	138	83.1	62.2
2005	192	143	74.5	119	83.2	62.0
Average			79.0		81.7	64.5

Total

Year	Total	Total Firearms	Pct of Total	Handguns	Pct of Firearms	Pct of Total
2001	600	558	93.0	461	82.6	76.8
2002	574	527	91.8	454	86.1	79.1
2003	620	569	91.8	481	84.5	77.6
2004	589	530	90.0	445	84.5	76.1
2005	533	480	90.1	415	86.5	77.9
Average			91.3		84.9	77.5

Table 5.19: Comparison Between Brady Grades and Concealed Carry Laws

State Legislation	Average Grade[93]	Average Violent Crime Rate[94]
Shall Issue	D	394.0
Restricted/Non-Issue	B	498.7

Table 5.20: "A" vs. "F" States, Violent Crime[95]

"A" States	Rate	"F" States	Rate
California	526.0	Alabama*	432.6
Connecticut*	272.6	Alaska	632.3
District of Columbia	1,380.0	Florida	708.9
Hawaii	255.5	Idaho	256.8
Illinois	552.2	Kentucky	266.8
Maryland	704.3	Louisiana	596.6
Massachusetts	460.8	Mississippi	279.6
New Jersey	355.3	Montana	281.8
		New Mexico	646.3
		Wyoming	230.3
Average	563.3	Average	433.2

*Considered fairly administered discretionary-issue for concealed carry. All other "F" states shall-issue, all other "A" states non-RTC.

Table 5.21: Brady Report Card Trends

	2001[96]	2004[97]	2005[98]	Five-Year Trend	One-Year Trend
National Grade Average	1.59	1.52	1.48	-7.4%	-3.0%
	C-	C-	D+		
Average Crime Rate	443.5	416.3	420.7	-5.1%	1.1%
CCW States	404.4	393.2	394.0	-2.6%	0.2%
non-CCW States	509.4	477.4	498.7	-2.1%	4.5%
Percent Difference	26.0%	21.4%	26.6%		

Table 5.22: Violent Crime, DC vs. U.S. - 2005

	National[99]	DC[100]	Ratio
Murder	5.6	33.5	6.0
Rape	31.8	28.5	0.9
Robbery	140.8	635.7	4.5
Aggravated Assault	290.8	682.2	2.3
Total	469.0	1,380.0	2.9

Table 5.23: Violent Crime Trends, U.S. and Florida, 1987-2005

Year	Violence	Murder	Rape	Robbery	Aggravated. Assault
		United States[101]			
1987	612.5	8.3	37.6	213.7	352.9
2005	469.0	5.6	31.8	140.8	290.8
% Change	-23.4	-32.5	-15.4	-34.1	-17.6
		Florida			
1987[102]	1,024.4	11.4	50.2	356.6	606.3
2005[103]	708.9	5.0	37.1	169.6	497.2
% Change	-30.8	-56.1	-26.1	-52.4	-18.0
Rate Difference	+7.4	+23.6	+10.7	+18.3	+0.4

Table 5.24: Crime Rates, General Population vs. CCW Licensees 2000-2005

Year	CCW Licensees	Crime After Licensure	Rate	Pct. Of Gen. Pop. Rate, FBI Crime
2000[104]	252,887	243	96.1	1.7
2001[105]	275,340	157	57.0	1.0
2002[106]	309,826	119	38.4	0.7
2003[107]	328,929	602	183.0	3.5
2004[108]	340,288	524	154.0	3.1
2005[109]	362,085	266	73.5	1.6
Average		334	101.2	2.0

General Population – FBI Crimes

Year	Total Population	Total FBI Crimes	Rate	Gen. Pop.:CCW Ratio
2000[110]	15,982,378	910,154	5,694.7	58.0
2001[111]	16,396,515	913,230	5,569.7	97.7
2002[112]	16,713,146	905,957	5,420.6	141.1
2003[113]	17,019,068	881,976	5,185.3	28.3
2004[114]	17,397,161	850,895	4,891.0	31.8
2005[115]	17,789,864	838,955	4,715.9	64.2
Average		878,203	5,155.9	70.2

Table 5.25: Violent Crime Trends 1995-2000 and 2000-2005 (In Percent)

Time Period	Violence	Murder	Rape	Robbery	Aggravated Assault
		United States[116]			
1995-2000	-26.0	-32.6	-13.6	-34.4	-22.5
2000-2005	-7.4	+1.7	-1.1	-2.9	-10.1
		Indiana			
1995[117]-2000[118]	-33.5	-27.9	-13.0	-23.6	-39.4
2000-2005[119]	-7.3	-2.0	+2.3	+5.1	-14.8
		Fort Wayne			
1995[120]-2000[121]	-19.0	-20.1	-1.5	-35.0	+15.9
2000-2005[122]	-18.5	+14.1	-14.8	-18.5	-22.0

Table 5.26: Four Most Frequent Causes of Workplace Mortality, 1992-2005[123]

Year	Highway Incidents	Falls	Struck by Object	Homicides
1992	1,158	600	557	1,044
2005	1,428	767	604	564
Trend	23.3%	27.8%	8.4%	(46.0%)

Table 6.1: Freedom vs. Corruption*

Country Rated	Number of Countries	Freedom House Rating[124]	Corruption Index[125]
[Most Free]	36	1	7.1
Free	70	1–2.5	5.4
Partly Free	49	3–5	3.0
Not Free	40	5.5–7	2.9

* Spreadsheet available, but too large and complex to include here.

Table 6.2: PPP vs. Economic Freedom Index*

PPP Quartile[126]	PPP	EFI[127]
1	27.56	72.48
2	82.43	61.80
3	136.83	58.26
4	185.49	53.24

* Includes only countries rated by both organizations. Spreadsheet available, but too large and complex to include here.

Table 6.3: Corruption vs. Economic and Personal Freedom

Corruption Index	PPP	Economic Freedom Index	Freedom House Rating
7.47	33.83	73.06	1.74
3.97	90.51	62.73	2.61
2.82	145.42	57.31	3.60
2.27	162.11	52.69	4.89

* Includes only countries rated by all organizations. Spreadsheet available, but too large and complex to include here.

Table 6.4: Genocides in UN Member Countries[128]

Year covered: 2006

Country	PR	CL	AVE	Rating	Transparency International CPI	PPP	EI
Cambodia	6	5	5.5	NF	2.1	152	56.5
China	7	6	6.5	NF	3.3	102	54.0
Indonesia	2	3	2.5	F	2.4	143	55.1
Korea (North)	7	7	7.0	NF	N/A	N/A	3.0
Pakistan	6	5	5.5	NF	2.2	161	58.2
Russian Federation	6	5	5.5	NF	2.5	78	54.0
Rwanda	6	5	5.5	NF	2.5	187	52.1
Sudan	7	7	7.0	NF	2.0	171	N/A
Vietnam	7	5	6.0	NF	2.6	150	50.0
Averages			5.7	NF	2.5	143	47.9

Table 6.5: Freedom Indices vs. Firearms Ownership*

Quartile	Freedom[129]	Corruption[130]	Economic Freedom[131]	Firearms per Capita[132]
1	1.93	7.09	69.79	0.388
2	2.80	4.35	63.59	0.145
3	2.53	4.75	62.57	0.081
4	2.32	4.31	63.03	0.024

* The final data set contained 59 countries because they were included in the freedom, corruption, and economic indexes. Spreadsheet available, but too large and complex to include here.

Table 6.6: Freedom Indices vs. Firearms Ownership, Top 11 Vs. Remainder[133]

Group	Freedom	Corruption	Economic Freedom	Firearms per Capita
Top 11	1.36	7.44	71.37	0.448
Bottom 48	2.64	4.61	63.26	0.096

Table 6.7: Most-Free Countries, Freedom Indices vs. Firearms Ownership, Sorted by Index[134]

Group	Corruption	Economic Freedom	Firearms per Capita
		Sort by Corruption Index	
Top Half	8.99	77.17	0.257
Bottom Half	6.32	71.25	0.214
% Diff.	42.30	8.31	20.10
		Sort by Economic Index	
Top Half	8.51	79.39	0.275
Bottom Half	6.79	68.73	0.175
% Diff.	25.30	15.52	57.24
		Sort by PPP	
Top Half	8.65	76.46	0.317
Bottom Half	6.11	69.27	0.129
% Diff.	41.67	10.38	146.06

Table 7.1: 2003 CDC Fatal Injury Data – Average Rates per 100,000 Population[135]

	All Intents		Suicide		Unintentional		Homicide	
	All Causes	Firearms	All Causes	Firearms	All Causes	Firearms	All Causes	Firearms
Non-RTC	52.74	8.89	8.99	3.58	33.04	0.14	6.94	4.98
RTC*	64.85	12.11	13.33	7.93	44.19	0.39	5.42	3.52
% Diff. RTC	+23.0	+36.2	+32.6	+54.9	+33.7	+172.7	-21.8	-29.3

*Iowa and Ohio were officially RTC states in 2004, but their RTC laws were well on the way to enactment in 2003, so these two states are considered "pro-gun."

Table 7.2: Selected 2003 Crime Rates

| | All States - FBI | | Top 10 "Pro-Gun" and not "Pro-Gun" | | | |
| | | | FBI Data[136] | | CDC Data[137] | |
	Violence	Homicide	Violence	Homicide	Homicide	Gun Homicide
Non-RTC	531.8	7.5	588.2	9.1	8.4	6.1
RTC	392.2	4.9	486.8	7.1	8.1	5.3
% Diff. RTC	-26.3	-35.3	-17.2	-22.9	-3.2	-12.4

Table 7.3: Percent of U.S. Rate, 1992[138] and 1998[139]

Year	Violence	Murder	Rape	Robbery	Aggravated Assault
		RTC States			
1992	67.9	65.4	89.6	60.1	69.4
1998	69.0	71.9	90.7	66.0	67.9
		Non-RTC States			
1992	123.9	123.7	99.6	143.1	117.0
1998	118.7	113.8	97.9	130.7	115.8

Table 7.4: Rate Trends, 1992[140]-1998[141]

Year	Violence	Murder	Rape	Robbery	Aggravated Assault
		RTC States			
1992	412.1	5.5	38.1	111.4	257.2
1998	338.4	4.6	31.5	86.8	215.4
Percent Change	-17.9	-16.6	-17.3	-22.0	-16.2
		Non-RTC States			
1992	751.6	10.3	42.4	265.3	433.5
1998	582.2	7.2	34.0	172.0	367.1
Percent Change	-22.5	-30.2	-19.8	-35.2	-15.3
Pct of RTC Rates	+72.1	+58.4	+7.9	+98.1	+70.4

Table 7.5: Before/After RTC Enactment Percent of Rate Trends, 1992[142]-1998[143]

Year	Violence	Murder	Rape	Robbery	Aggravated Assault
1992-RTC	-0.1	-1.1	-10.9	-2.4	+2.0
States with Increase	7	5	1	7	7
RTC-1998	-14.4	-18.9	-7.4	-18.4	-13.5
States with Increase	0	2	1	1	1

Table 8.1: Staffing Changes, 1994-2005

Year	Population Covered	LEO	LEO/ 100k Population	Total Population	Estimated Total LEO
2005[144]	279,200,617	673,146	241	296,410,404	714,638
2004[145]	278,433,063	675,734	243	293,655,404	712,677
2003[146]	274,104,414	663,796	242	290,809,777	704,251
2002[147]	271,240,537	665,555	245	287,973,924	706,614
2001[148]	268,055,247	659,104	246	285,317,559	701,549
2000[149]	264,813,489	654,601	247	281,421,906	695,656
1999[150]	253,242,000	637,551	252	272,690,813	686,514
1998[151]	259,549,000	641,208	247	270,248,003	667,640
1997[152]	251,315,000	618,127	246	267,783,607	658,633
1996[153]	248,724,000	595,170	239	265,228,572	634,664
1995[154]	245,846,000	586,756	239	262,803,276	627,228
1994[155]	244,517,000	561,543	230	260,327,021	597,851

Table 8.2: Assuming No Change In 1994 Staffing Rate

	Calculated Total LEO	Actual Increase Since 1994	"COPS Effect"
2005	680,718	116,787	33,920
2004	674,391	114,826	38,286
2003	667,856	106,400	36,395
2002	661,344	108,763	45,270
2001	655,243	103,698	46,306
2000	646,297	97,805	49,359
1999	626,245	88,663	60,269
1998	620,635	69,789	47,005
1997	614,976	60,782	43,657
1996	609,108	36,813	25,556
1995	603,538	29,377	23,690

Table 8.3: Offenses Cleared

Year	Homicide	Rape	Robbery	Assault
2005[156]	14,430	82,118	353,050	747,491
2004[157]	13,662	80,939	329,578	728,554
2003[158]	13,373	76,714	328,951	707,142
2002[159]	13,561	80,515	343,023	747,354
2001[160]	11,982	67,907	304,077	640,168
2000[161]	12,291	72,453	319,078	728,101
1999[162]	12,266	72,809	330,601	748,704
1998[163]	13,134	71,040	350,937	743,277
1997[164]	14,759	78,975	411,137	838,771
1996[165]	15,487	73,349	429,368	775,204
1995[166]	18,324	82,538	502,352	928,489
Trends				
1995-2005	-21.3%	-0.5%	-29.7%	-19.5%
1995-2000	-32.9%	-12.2%	-36.5%	-21.6%
2001-2005	20.4%	20.9%	16.1%	16.8%

Table 8.4: Clearance Rate per 1,000 LEO

Year	LEO Population*	Violence	Homicide	Rape	Robbery	Assault
2005	673,146	1,778.3	21.4	122.0	524.5	1,110.4
2004	675,734	1,705.9	20.2	119.8	487.7	1,078.2
2003	663,796	1,696.6	20.1	115.6	495.6	1,065.3
2002	665,555	1,779.6	20.4	121.0	515.4	1,122.9
2001	659,104	1,553.8	18.2	103.0	461.3	971.3
2000	654,601	1,729.2	18.8	110.7	487.4	1,112.3
1999	637,551	1,826.3	19.2	114.2	518.5	1,174.3
1998	641,208	1,837.8	20.5	110.8	547.3	1,159.2
1997	618,127	2,173.7	23.9	127.8	665.1	1,357.0
1996	595,170	2,173.2	26.0	123.2	721.4	1,302.5
1995	586,756	2,610.5	31.2	140.7	856.2	1,582.4
Average	642,795	1,896.8	21.8	119.0	571.0	1,185.1
Trends						
1995-2005		-31.9%	-31.4%	-13.3%	-38.7%	-29.8%
1995-2000		-33.8%	-39.9%	-21.3%	-43.1%	-29.7%
2001-2005		14.4%	17.9%	18.4%	13.7%	14.3%

* Refer to Table 8.1 for LEO population references.

Table 8.5: Violent Crime Rates for Selected Years[167]

Year	Violence	Homicide	Rape	Robbery	Assault
2005	469.2	5.6	31.7	140.7	291.1
2001	504.5	5.6	31.8	148.5	318.6
2000	506.5	5.5	32.0	145.0	324.0
1995	684.5	8.2	37.1	220.9	418.3
Trends					
1995-2005	-31.5%	-31.5%	-14.6%	-36.3%	-30.4%
1995-2000	-26.0%	-32.6%	-13.6%	-34.4%	-22.5%
2001-2005	-7.0%	0.2%	-0.5%	-5.2%	-8.6%

Table 8.6: Law Enforcement New Hires, 1994-2005[168]

Year	Pop Covered	LEO	Per 100k Pop	Civilians	Per 100k Pop
2005	279,200,617	673,146	241	295,924	106
2004	278,433,063	675,734	243	294,854	106
2003	274,104,414	663,796	242	285,146	104
2002	271,240,537	665,555	245	291,947	108
2001	268,055,247	659,104	246	279,926	104
2000	264,813,489	654,601	247	271,982	103
1999	253,242,000	637,551	252	261,567	103
1998	259,549,000	641,208	247	253,327	98
1997	251,315,000	618,127	246	240,405	96
1996	248,724,000	595,170	239	234,668	94
1995	245,846,000	586,756	239	226,780	92
1994	244,517,000	561,543	230	220,567	90
		Trends (Percent)			
1994-2005		19.9	5.0	34.2	17.5
1994-2000		16.6	7.6	23.3	13.9
2001-2005		2.1	-1.9	5.7	1.5

Table 8.7: Federal Incarceration Rate Trends (Percent)[169]

Time Period	Murder	Rape	Robbery	Aggravated Assault
1994-2000	-1.5	+9.4	+3.1	+1.1
2001-2004	+2.1	+3.3	+3.3	+13.2

Table 8.8: Federal Incarceration Averages per 1,000 Incidents[170]

Time Period	Murder	Rape	Robbery	Aggravated Assault
1994-2000	333	55	119	126
2001-2004	257	66	130	150

Endnotes

Chapter 1

1 John Winthrop, Wikipedia. http://en.wikipedia.org/wiki/John_Winthrop

2 "A Model of Christian Charity" by John Winthrop, 1630, Collections of the Massachusetts Historical Society (Boston, 1838), 3rd series 7:31-48, Hanover College Department of History. http://history.hanover.edu/texts/winthmod.html

3 The New Shorter Oxford English Dictionary, Thumb Index Edition, 1993 Edition, Clarendon Press, page 2301.

4 Manifest Destiny, Wikipedia. http://en.wikipedia.org/wiki/Manifest_Destiny

5 Records of the Governor and Company of the Massachusetts Bay in New England, Volume I, 1628-1641, April 17, 1629, edited by Nathaniel B. Shurtleff, M.D. http://www.claytoncramer.com/primary/militia/RecMassBay1-392.jpg

6 Ibid, May 17, 1637. http://www.claytoncramer.com/primary/militia/RecMassBay1-196.jpg

7 The Public Records of the Colony of Connecticut 1636-1776, Volume 1, page 1, April 26, 1636, University of Connecticut, Copyright 2000, 2001.
http://www.colonialct.uconn.edu/ViewPageByPageNew.cfm?v=1&p=1&c=4

8 Ibid, page 96 December 18, 1642.
http://www.colonialct.uconn.edu/ViewPageBySequentialID.cfm?v=1&p=96&c=4&StartVolume=1&StartPage=1

9 Ibid, page 129, October 25, 1644.
http://www.colonialct.uconn.edu/ViewPageBySequentialID.cfm?v=1&p=129&c=4&StartVolume=1&StartPage=1

10 Ibid, page 130, October 25, 1644.
http://www.colonialct.uconn.edu/ViewPageBySequentialID.cfm?v=1&p=130&c=4&StartVolume=1&StartPage=1

11 Ibid, page 138, April 9, 1646.
http://www.colonialct.uconn.edu/ViewPageByPageNew.cfm?v=1&p=138&c=4

12 Ibid page 197, September 18, 1649.
http://www.colonialct.uconn.edu/ViewPageByPageNew.cfm?v=1&p=197&c=4

13 Wampanoag History, Lee Sultzman. http://www.tolatsga.org/wampa.html

14 Colin Powell with Joesph E. Persico, My American Journey, Random House, copyright 1995, pages 276-277.

15 Clayton Cramer, Race-Specific and Religion-Specific Gun Control Statutes, Primary Historical Sources, downloaded May 18, 2007. http://www.claytoncramer.com/primary.html#RaceGunControlStatutes

16 Laws of Virginia, January 1839-1840.
http://www.claytoncramer.com/primary/militia/Hening1-226227.jpg

17 Laws of Virginia, Section XIV, May 1723. http://www.claytoncramer.com/primary/militia/Hening4-130131.jpg

18 Ibid, Section XV.

19 Maryland Archives, 1715 Statute. http://www.claytoncramer.com/primary/militia/ArchMd75-268.jpg

20 The Statutes at Large of Pennsylvania from 1682 to 1801, Volume 11, 1700 to 1712, Section V, Busch, 1896.
http://www.claytoncramer.com/primary/other/PA1700ActForTrialOfNegroes.pdf

21 Joseph J. Ellis, His Excellency: George Washington, Alfred A. Knopf, 2004, page 84.

22 The Militia Act of 1792, Passed May 8, 1792, Article I.

23 Clayton E. Cramer, Racist Roots of Gun Control, University of Kansas Journal of Law and Public Policy, Winter 1995.
http://www.lizmichael.com/racistro.htm

24 Stephen P. Halbrook, The Jurisprudence of the Second and Fourteenth Amendments, page 15. Originally published as 4 George Mason Univ. Law Review 1-69 (1981). http://www.constitution.org/2ll/2ndschol/44halj.pdf

25 Steve Goldman, The Southhampton Slave Revolt, History Buff.
http://www.historybuff.com/library/refslave.html

26 Clayton E. Cramer, Racist Roots of Gun Control.

27 State v. Huntly, 25 N.C. (3 Ired.) 418 (1843)
http://www-2.cs.cmu.edu/afs/cs/user/wbardwel/public/nfalist/state_v_huntly.txt

28 State v. Newsom, 5 Ired. (N.C.) 250 (1844) http://www-2.cs.cmu.edu/afs/cs.cmu.edu/user/wbardwel/public/nfalist/state_v_newsom.txt

29 Ibid.

30 Ibid.

31 Clayton E. Cramer, Racist Roots of Gun Control.

32 Mississippi Black Codes, Penal Code, Section 1, November 1865.
http://www.nv.cc.va.us/home/nvsageh/Hist122/Part1/MissBlCode.htm.

33 Ibid.

34 Constitutional Rights Foundation, Bill of Right [sic] in Action, Spring 1999 (15:2)
http://www.crf-usa.org/bria/bria15_2.html#black

35 Stephen P. Halbrook, The Jurisprudence of the Second and Fourteenth Amendments, page 17.

[36] The African American Journey: Reconstruction, The World Book.
http://www2.worldbook.com/wc/popup?path=features/aajourney_new&page=html/aa_3_reconstruction.shtml&direct=
yes

[37] NAACP Proposed Strategic Priorities and Goals, 2002-2006, April 21, 2001, page 15.
http://www.naacp.org/inc/pdf/priorities.pdf

[38] Clayton E. Cramer, *Racist Roots of Gun Control.*

[39] Barry Schweid, *Rice says gun rights are as important as right to free speech and religion,* Associated Press, Sign On San Diego, May 11, 2005. http://www.signonsandiego.com/news/nation/20050511-1803-rice-guns.html

[40] Professor Ronald Hutton, *The Masquerading Monarch,* BBC History, January 4, 2004, page 1.
http://www.bbc.co.uk/history/state/monarchs_leaders/charlesii_masq_01.shtml

[41] Professor Ronald Hutton, *The Masquerading Monarch,* page 3.
http://www.bbc.co.uk/history/state/monarchs_leaders/charlesii_masq_03.shtml

[42] Ibid.

[43] Joyce Lee Malcolm, *Guns and Violence: The English Experience,* Harvard University Press, copyright 2002, page 52.

[44] James A. Swan, *Countryside Uprising,* ESPN Outdoors.
http://espn.go.com/outdoors/general/columns/swan_james/1554110.html

[45] T. Markus Funk, *Gun Control and Economic Discrimination: The Melting-Point Case-in-Point,* originally published as 85 Journal Of Criminal Law & Criminology, 764-806 (1995). Archived at
http://web.archive.org/web/20011101114812/http://www.2ndlawlib.org/journals/economic.html

[46] Darling v. Warden, 154 App. Div. 413, 139 N.Y.S. 277 (1913)
http://www.guncite.com/court/state/139nys277.html

[47] DESHANEY v. WINNEBAGO CTY. SOC. SERVS. DEPT., 489 U.S. 189 (1989)
http://caselaw.lp.findlaw.com/scripts/getcase.pl?court=US&vol=489&invol=189
Warren et al v. District of Columbia, 444 A.2d 1 (D.C.App. 1981)
http://www.healylaw.com/cases/warren2.htm
Riss v. City of New York, 22 N.Y.2d 579 (1968)
http://www.healylaw.com/cases/riss.htm
John D. Brophy, *Public Safety: Fact or Fiction?* August 14, 2003.
http://famguardian.org/Subjects/Crime/Articles/PublicSafetyFactOrFiction.htm

[48] Gina Holland, *Cops Can't Be Sued for Restraining Orders,* Associated Press, Las Vegas Sun, June 27, 2005.
http://www.lasvegassun.com/sunbin/stories/bw-scotus/2005/jun/27/062708395.html

[49] Town of Castle Rock, Colorado, Petitioner v. Jessica Gonzales, No. 04-278, United States Supreme Court, page 8.
http://www.usdoj.gov/osg/briefs/2004/3mer/1ami/2004-0278.mer.ami.pdf

[50] Chronology of 1942 San Francisco War Events, Internment of San Francisco Japanese, San Francisco Museum.
http://www.sfmuseum.org/war/42.html

[51] Enemy Alien Curfew Friday, The San Francisco News, March 24, 1942.
http://www.sfmuseum.org/hist8/intern1.html

[52] Japanese American Internment, Civil Rights and History, United States Department of Justice.
http://www.usdoj.gov/kidspage/crt/redress.htm

[53] Daniel Polsby and Don Kates, *Of Holocausts and Gun Control,* Washington University Law Quarterly, Volume 75, Number 3, Fall 1997. Cite as 75 Wash. U. L.Q. 1237.
http://law.wustl.edu/WULQ/75-3/753-4.html ·

[54] Kristallnacht, Jewish Virtual Library. http://www.jewishvirtuallibrary.org/jsource/Holocaust/kristallnacht.html

[55] Regulations Against Jews' Possession of Weapons, November 11, 1938.
http://vikingphoenix.com/politics/nwl_1573_1938.htm

[56] Daniel Polsby and Don Kates, *Of Holocausts and Gun Control..*

[57] Stephen P. Halbrook, *The Jurisprudence of the Second and Fourteenth Amendments,* page 50.

Chapter 2

[1] Reuter and Mouzos, *Australia: A Massive Buyback of Low-Risk Guns,* 2002, page 125.
http://www.puaf.umd.edu/faculty/papers/reuter/gun%20chapter.pdf

[2] Joyce Lee Malcolm, *Guns and Violence: The English Experience,* page 205.

[3] Reuter and Mouzos, *Australia: A Massive Buyback of Low-Risk Guns,* page 129.

[4] Ibid, page 122.

[5] Van Dijk and Mayhew, *Crime Victimisation in the Industrialised World: Key Findings of the 1989 and 1992 International Crime Surveys,* The Hague: Ministry of Justice, Department of Crime Prevention, 1993, page 3.
http://www.unicri.it/icvs/publications/index_pub.htm

6 Van Kesteren, Mayhew and Nieuwbeerta, *Criminal Victimisation in Seventeen Industrialised Countries: Key-findings from the 2000 international Crime Victims Survey*, The Hague: Ministry of Justice, Department of Crime Prevention, 2000, pages 2-3. Downloaded from http://www.unicri.it/icvs/publications/index_pub.htm

7 See Table 2.1, Appendix A.

8 See Table 2.1, Appendix A.

9 See Table 2.2, Appendix A.

10 See Table 2.2 Appendix A.

11 *Australian Crime: Facts and Figures 2003*, Australian Institute of Criminology, December, 2003, page 18. http://www.aic.gov.au/publications/facts/2003/facts_and_figures_2003.pdf

12 Ibid, page 19.

13 *Australian Crime: Facts and Figures 2005*, page 7, Australian Institute of Criminology, December, 2003. http://www.aic.gov.au/publications/facts/2003/facts_and_figures_2003.pdf

14 *Australian Crime: Facts and Figures 2003*, Australian Institute of Criminology, December, 2003, page 19.

15 Ibid, page 31.

16 *Crime in England and Wales 2002/2003*, British Home Office, July 2003, page 12. http://www.homeoffice.gov.uk/rds/pdfs2/hosb703.pdf

17 Ibid, page 12.

18 Shannan M. Catalano, *National Crime Victimization Survey 2004*, Bureau of Justice Statistics, U.S. Department of Justice, September 2005, page 10. http://www.ojp.usdoj.gov/bjs/pub/pdf/cv04.pdf

19 FBI Uniform Crime Reporting Handbook, revised 2004, page 10. http://www.fbi.gov/ucr/handbook/ucrhandbook04.pdf

20 See Table 2.3, Appendix A.

21 FBI, Table 1 - Crime in the United States by Volume and Rate per 100,000 Inhabitants, 1987–2006. http://www.fbi.gov/ucr/cius2006/data/table_01.html

22 Peace Movement Aotearoa home page. http://www.converge.org.nz/pma/index.htm

23 *Sharp Drop in Gun Crime Follows Tough Australian Firearm Laws*, Peace Movement Aotearoa, February, 2000. http://www.converge.org.nz/pma/gunaus.htm

24 *Australian Crime: Facts and Figures 2003*, homicide on page 25 and robbery on page 34. http://www.aic.gov.au/publications/facts/2003/facts_and_figures_2003.pdf

25 Stop Violence Against Women, Stories: Rebecca Peters, Amnesty International. http://web.amnesty.org/actforwomen/Rebecca_Peters-eng

26 *Australian Crime: Facts and Figures 2002*, page 47, Australian Institute of Criminology, November, 2002. http://www.aic.gov.au/publications/facts/2002/facts_and_figures_2002.pdf

27 *Australian Crime: Facts and Figures 2003*, page 31.

28 See Table 2.3, Appendix A.

29 Robert Wainright, *Gun laws fall short in war on crime*, Sydney Morning Herald, October 29, 2005. http://www.smh.com.au/news/national/gun-laws-fall-short-in-war-on-crime/2005/10/28/1130400366681.html

30 Ibid.

31 Associated Press, Police: Wheelchair-bound NYC woman shoots mugger, *Staten Island Advance*, September 8, 2006. http://www.silive.com/newsflash/metro/index.ssf?/base/news-20/115776237854020.xml&storylist=simetro

32 Buyback guns in hands of outlaws, *Sydney Morning Herald*, February 10, 2007. http://www.smh.com.au/news/national/buyback-guns-in-the-hands-of-outlaws/2007/02/09/1170524303919.html

33 *Crime in England and Wales 2002/2003*, page 2.

34 Ibid, page 4.

35 Ibid, page 6.

36 Ibid, Table 3.04, pages 40-44.

37 Ibid, page 37.

38 Ibid, page 34.

39 Ibid, page 34.

40 See Table 2.4 Appendix A.

41 *Crime in England and Wales 2002/2003*, page 10.

42 Ibid, page 41.

43 *Population Estimates: Aging*, Office for National Statistics. http://www.statistics.gov.uk/cci/nugget.asp?ID=949

44 *Population in custody: by type of custody and sex*, Research Development Statistics, Home Office. http://www.homeoffice.gov.uk/rds/pdfs04/prisnov04.xls

45 *Crime in England and Wales 2002/2003*, page 113.

46 *Violent crime figures rise by 12%*, BBC, July 22, 2004. http://news.bbc.co.uk/1/hi/uk/3914289.stm

[47] *Violent offences top million mark*, BBC, July 21, 2005. http://news.bbc.co.uk/1/hi/uk_politics/4700575.stm

[48] Muggings and violent attacks up by more than 10%, Richard Ford, *Times Online*, January 27, 2006. http://www.timesonline.co.uk/article/0,,2-2011705,00.html

[49] Ibid.

[50] Sean O'Neill, Armed and dangerous, the boys aged 12 recruited by street gangs, *Times Online*, October 6, 2006. http://www.timesonline.co.uk/article/0,,29389-2390854,00.html

[51] Violent crime and robbery on rise, BBC, January 26, 2006. http://news.bbc.co.uk/2/hi/uk_news/politics/4648042.stm

[52] *Crime in England and Wales 2002/2003*, page 127.

[53] Ibid, page 130.

[54] Nick Allen, *U.K. School Kids Strap on Stat-Proof Vests as Knife Crime Soars*, Bloomberg.com, March 22, 2007. http://www.bloomberg.com/apps/news?pid=email_en&refer=home&sid=a_gP7Pj2387g

[55] Richard Ford and Philip Webster, Weapons sell for just £50 as suspects and victims grow ever younger, *Times Online*, August 24, 2007. http://timesonline.co.uk/tol/news/uk/crime/article2317307.ece

[56] Ibid.

[57] Universal Currency Converter, XE.com. http://www.xe.com/ucc/convert.cgi

[58] Richard Ford and Philip Webster, Weapons sell for just £50 as suspects and victims grow ever younger, *Times Online*, August 24, 2007.

[59] Ibid.

[60] Catherine Mayer, Britain's Mean Streets, *Time*, March 26, 2008.
Page 1: http://www.time.com/time/magazine/article/0,9171,1725547,00.html
Page 2: http://www.time.com/time/magazine/article/0,9171,1725547-2,00.html
Page 3: http://www.time.com/time/magazine/article/0,9171,1725547-3,00.html
Page 4: http://www.time.com/time/magazine/article/0,9171,1725547-4,00.html

[61] John R. Lott, Jr., *The Bias Against Guns: Why Almost Everything You're Heard About Gun Control Is Wrong*, Regnery Publishing, 2003, page 11.

[62] See Table 2.5, Appendix A.

[63] See Table 2.6, Appendix A.

[64] See Table 2.7, Appendix A.

[65] *Firearms Commerce in the United States 2001/2002*. Bureau of Alcohol, Tobacco, and Firearms. http://www.atf.gov/pub/fire-explo_pub/firearmscommerce/firearmscommerce.pdf

[66] *Double jeopardy law ushered out*, BBC News, April 3, 2005. http://news.bbc.co.uk/1/hi/uk/4406129.stm

[67] Criminal Justice Act 2003, 2003 Chapter 44: Amendments of Police and Criminal Evidence Act 1984, Chapter 2, paragraph 116. http://www.hmso.gov.uk/acts/acts2003/20030044.htm

[68] Nicholas Kralev, *Scotland Yard on a Recruiting Binge*, The Washington Times, June 7, 2002. http://www.nicholaskralev.com/WT-scotland-yard.html

[69] Ibid.

[70] Rowena Johns, *Double Jeopardy Briefing Paper 16/2003*, Parliament of New South Wales. http://www.parliament.nsw.gov.au/prod/parlment/publications.nsf/0/89C20D04902F4102CA256ECF00098187

[71] Council for Civil Liberties, *Double Jeopardy*, University of New South Wales. http://www.nswccl.org.au/unswccl/issues/double%20jeopardy.php

[72] Model Criminal Code Officers Committee, *Double Jeopardy: MCCOC Report - March 2004*, Attorney-General's Department, Australian Government. http://www.ag.gov.au/agd/WWW/agdHome.nsf/Page/Publications_Publications_2003_Model_Criminal_Code_Report_-_Double_Jeopardy

[73] Ibid.

[74] Eugene Volokh and David Newman, *In Defense of the Slippery Slope*, Legal Affairs, March/April 2003, page 22. http://www1.law.ucla.edu/~volokh/slipperymag.pdf

[75] Don B. Kates, retired professor of constitutional and criminal law and author, in an email interview May 9, 2005.

[76] *Farmer guilty of murdering burglar*, BBC News, April, 20, 2000. http://news.bbc.co.uk/1/hi/uk/717511.stm

[77] Audrey Gillan, *Life for farmer who shot burglar*, The Guardian, April 20, 2000. http://www.guardian.co.uk/martin/article/0,2763,214334,00.html

[78] *79-Year-Old Shoots Two Intruders, Police Say*, News 5 Channel Cincinnati, July 9, 2005. http://www.channelcincinnati.com/news/4702890/detail.html#

[79] Violent crime on the increase, *The Daily Mail*, January 26, 2006. http://www.dailymail.co.uk/pages/live/articles/news/news.html?in_article_id=375164&in_page_id=1770

[80] Police force has 'no time for small crime,' *The Daily Mail*, March 22, 2006. http://www.dailymail.co.uk/pages/live/articles/news/news.html?in_article_id=380646&in_page_id=1770

81 'Let burglars off with caution', police told, *The Daily Mail*, April 3, 2006.
http://www.dailymail.co.uk/pages/live/articles/news/news.html?in_article_id=381799&in_page_id=1770
82 Kristy Walker and James Chapman, Convicts handed keys to the cell, *Daily Mail*, March 26, 2007.
http://www.dailymail.co.uk/pages/live/articles/news/news.html?in_article_id=444586&in_page_id=1770&ct=5
83 Guns becoming 'a fashion accessory', *BBC News*, February 15, 2007.
http://news.bbc.co.uk/1/hi/england/london/6365187.stm
84 Guns becoming 'a fashion accessory', *BBC News*, February 15, 2007.
85 Violent crime and robbery on rise, *BBC News*, January 26, 2006. http://news.bbc.co.uk/1/hi/uk_politics/4648042.stm
86 Ibid.

Chapter 3

1 Consumer Federation of America: About CFA. http://www.consumerfed.org/backpage/about.html
2 Consumer Federation of America, *Buyer Beware: Defective Firearms and America's Unregulated Gun Industry*, February 2005, page 4. http://www.consumerfed.org/buyerbeware_report.pdf
3 Ibid, pages 4-5.
4 Buyer Beware, page 5.
5 See Table 3.1, Appendix A.
6 Consumer Federation of America: Product Safety. http://www.consumerfed.org/backpage/psafety.cfm
Consumer Federation of America: Child Safety. http://www.consumerfed.org/backpage/csafety.cfm
7 Buyer Beware, page 5.
8 See Table 3.2, Appendix A.
9 See Table 3.3, Appendix A.
10 Martin L. Fackler, *Firearms in America: The Facts*, News Max, December 25, 2000.
http://www.newsmax.com/archives/articles/2000/12/23/225251.shtml
11 See Table 3.4, Appendix A.
12 WISQARS Leading Causes of Death Reports, 1999 – 2004, National Center for Injury Prevention and Control, Centers for Disease Control. http://webappa.cdc.gov/sasweb/ncipc/leadcaus10.html
13 WISQARS Fatal Injuries: Mortality Reports, National Center for Injury Prevention and Control, Centers for Disease Control. http://webappa.cdc.gov/sasweb/ncipc/mortrate.html
14 Regulate Guns Home Page. http://www.regulateguns.org/
15 National Highway Traffic Safety Administration, Traffic Safety Facts 2004: A Compilation of Motor Vehicle Crash Data from the Fatality Analysis Reporting System and the General Estimates System, Table 2, page 15. http://www-nrd.nhtsa.dot.gov/pdf/nrd-30/NCSA/TSFAnn/TSF2004.pdf
16 See Table 3.5, Appendix A.
17 Report Unsafe Automobiles, Tires, Trucks and Motorcycles, Consumer Product Safety Commission web site. http://www.cpsc.gov/tires.html"
18 Consumer Federation of America: Auto Safety. http://www.consumerfed.org/backpage/asafety.cfm
19 Consumer Federation of America: Guns. http://www.consumerfed.org/backpage/guns.cfm
20 Rajesh Subramanian, *Motor Vehicle Traffic Crashes as a Leading Cause of Death in the United States, 2003*, National Highway Traffic Safety Administration, March 2006, page 2. http://www-nrd.nhtsa.dot.gov/pdf/nrd-30/NCSA/RNotes/2006/810568.pdf
21 Ibid, page 1.
22 Traffic Safety Facts 2004, Table 23, page 44.
23 Ibid, Table 53, page 86.
24 Ibid, Table 60, page 92.
25 FBI, *Uniform Crime Reports 2004*, Table 2.12, Murder Circumstances by Weapon. http://www.fbi.gov/ucr/cius_04/documents/CIUS_2004_Section2.pdf
26 See Table 3.6, Appendix A.
27 *Ford Recalls Fire-Prone Trucks*, Consumer Affairs News, January 27, 2005.
http://www.consumeraffairs.com/news04/2005/ford_f150_recall.html
28 *Houston Lawyers Sue Ford Over F-150 Fires*, Consumer Affairs News, January 31, 2005.
http://www.consumeraffairs.com/news04/2005/flaming_fords_suit.html
29 *Ford Focus Recall*, Consumer Affairs News, February 7, 2005.
http://www.consumeraffairs.com/recalls04/2005/ford_focus.html
30 *GM Recalls Chevrolet, Oldsmobile, Pontiac Minivans*, Consumer Affairs News, December 23, 2004.
http://www.consumeraffairs.com/recalls04/gm_minivans.html

31 Associated Press, *GM recalls 155,465 pickups, vans and SUVs for brake problem*, Auto Insider, February 10, 2005. http://www.detnews.com/2005/autoinsider/0502/10/01-86233.htm
32 *Mitsubishi Recalls SUVs, Chrysler Recalls Pacificas*, Consumer Affairs News, March 4, 2005. http://www.consumeraffairs.com/recalls04/2005/mitsubishi-chrysler.html
33 Statement of Chairman Hal Stratton Regarding the CPSC v. Daisy Manufacturing Co., Docket No. 02-02, Consumer Product Safety Commission settlement against Daisy Manufacturing, pages 4-5. http://www.cpsc.gov/CPSCPUB/PREREL/prhtml04/04033stratton.pdf
34 Statement of the Honorable Mary Sheila Gall on Proposed Consent Agreement and Order Submitted by Daisy, Consumer Product Safety Commission, November 14, 2003, pages 2-3. http://www.cpsc.gov/CPSCPUB/PREREL/prhtml04/04033gall.pdf
35 Statement of Chairman Hal Stratton Regarding the CPSC v. Daisy Manufacturing Co., Docket No. 02-02, Consumer Product Safety Commission settlement against Daisy Manufacturing, page 5.
36 National Rifle Association, *NRA Gun Safety Rules*. http://www.nrahq.org/education/guide.asp
37 National Rifle Association, *Education & Training*. http://www.nrahq.org/education/index.asp
38 ASTM Mission Statement. http://www.astm.org/cgi-bin/SoftCart.exe/NEWS/Mission2.html?L+mystore+jrps1141+1111869970
39 About ASTM International, Overview. http://www.astm.org/cgi-bin/SoftCart.exe/ABOUT/aboutASTM.html?L+mystore+jrps1141+1111869923
40 Statement of Chairman Hal Stratton Regarding the CPSC v. Daisy Manufacturing Co., Consumer Product Safety Commission settlement against Daisy Manufacturing, page 2.
41 Stratton, page 3.
42 Gall, page 1.
43 Stratton, page 4.
44 Consumer Federation of America, *Dangerously Flawed Firearms That Could be Recalled Under The Firearms Safety and Consumer Protection Act*. http://www.consumerfed.org/Firearms.pdf
45 Buyer Beware, page 5.
46 Statement of Michael D. Gulledge, Director, Evaluation and Inspections Division, U.S. Department of Justice Office of the Inspector General, before the House Committee on Government Reform Subcommittee on National Security, Emerging Threats and International Relations, August 2, 2004. http://www.usdoj.gov/oig/testimony/0408/index.htm
47 Phone and email conversation with firearms retailer, March 24, 2005.
48 Phone conversation with Inge Jones, Procurement and Licensing Manager, Heckler-Koch USA, on March 24, 2005; Phone conversation with US firearms manufacturer, March 24, 2005.
49 Phone conversation with Public Information Officer at BATF Washington Field Office, March 24, 2005.
50 Motor Vehicle Safety, Title 49, National Highway Traffic Safety Administration, U.S. Department of Transportation, November 2000, Section 30166: Inspections, investigations, and records, Subsection a.
51 Buyer Beware, pages 4-5.
52 Technical Publications, Sporting Arms and Manufacturers' Institute. http://www.saami.org/
53 Ibid.
54 Ibid.
55 Ibid.
56 2004 ANSI Compliance Form, January, 2004, page 2. http://public.ansi.org/ansionline/Documents/Standards%20Activities/American%20National%20Standards/Procedures,%20Guides,%20and%20Forms/2004%20Compliance%20Form/comply2004.doc
57 Ibid.
58 NIOSH eNews, New ANSI Standard on motor vehicle fleet safety, National Institute for Occupational Safety And Health. April 12, 2006. http://www.cdc.gov/niosh/enews/enewsV3N12.html#n
59 Bureau of Labor Statistics, *National Census of Fatal Occupational Injuries in 2005*, United States Department of Labor, August 10, 2006, page 2. http://www.bls.gov/news.release/pdf/cfoi.pdf
60 Association of Firearms & Tool Mark Examiners Home Page. http://www.afte.org/index_forum.php
61 Association of Firearms & Tool Mark Examiners History. http://www.afte.org/AssociationInfo/a_history.htm
62 Association of Firearms & Tool Mark Examiners Bylaws. http://www.afte.org/AssociationInfo/a_bylaws.htm
63 Association of Firearms & Tool Mark Examiners Code of Ethics. http://www.afte.org/AssociationInfo/a_codeofethics.htm
64 Michael Rand, *Guns and Crime: Handgun Victimization, Firearm Self-Defense, and Firearm Theft, NCJ-147003*, Bureau of Justice Statistics, U.S. Department of Justice, April 1994. http://www.ojp.usdoj.gov/bjs/pub/ascii/hvfsdaft.txt
65 Gary Kleck and Marc Gertz, *Armed Resistance to Crime: The Prevalence and Nature of Self-Defense with a Gun*, Journal of Criminal Law and Criminology, vol. 86, issue 1, 1995, page 175. http://www.saf.org/LawReviews/KleckAndGertz1.htm
66 Ibid.

67 Ibid, page 176.

68 Ibid, Table 2, page 184.

69 Ibid, Hart and Mauser surveys, Table 1, page 182-3.

70 Ibid, Table 3, page 185.

71 Ibid, pages 180-181.

72 Shannan M. Catalano, *National Crime Victimization Survey 2003*, Bureau of Justice Statistics, U.S. Department of Justice, September 2004, Table 2, page 3. http://www.ojp.usdoj.gov/bjs/pub/pdf/cv03.pdf

73 Miller, Cohen, Wiersema, *Victim Costs and Consequences: A New Look*, National Institute of Justice Research Report, US Department of Justice, January, 1996, page 1. http://www.ncjrs.org/pdffiles/victcost.pdf

74 Ibid.

75 See Table 3.7 Appendix A.

76 Miller, Cohen, Wiersema, Victim Costs and Consequences: A New Look, page 6.

77 See Table 3.8, Appendix A.

78 Countries of the World, Gross National Product Distribution – 2005. http://www.studentsoftheworld.info/infopays/rank/PNB2.html

79 Determinants of Completing Rape and Assault, Lizotte, Journal of Quantitative Criminology, Vol. 2, No. 3, 1986, page 213.

80 Ibid, page 214.

81 Kleck and Sayles, *Rape and Resistance*, Social Problems, Vol. 37, No. 2, May 1990, page 154.

82 Ibid, page 157.

83 Furby, Fischhoff, and Morgan, *Judged Effectiveness of Common Rape Prevention and Self-Defense Strategies*, Journal of Interpersonal Violence, Vol. 4, No. 1, March 1989, page 59.

84 Ibid, page 57.

85 Ibid, pages 50-51.

86 Ibid, page 52.

87 Cross-referencing Victim Costs Victim Costs and Consequences: A New Look (Table 2, page 9) with National Crime Victimization Survey 2003, (Table 2, page 3). See also Table 3.9 in Appendix A.

88 U.S. Department of State, Bureau of Diplomatic Security, *Sexual Assault: Reducing the Risk and Coping with an Attack*, August 1994, page 8.

89 Quinsey and Upfold, *Rape Completion and victim injury as a function of female resistance strategy*, Canadian Journal of Behavioral Science, Vol. 17(1), 1985, page 46.

90 Kleck and Sayles, *Rape and Resistance*, page 157.

91 Ibid.

92 Ibid, pages 157-8.

93 Martin L. Fackler, MD, *Firearms in America: The Facts*, December 25, 2000.

94 Tom Smith, *1999 National Gun Policy Survey of the National Opinion Research Center: Research Findings*, National Opinion Research Center, April, 2000, pages 1-2. http://www.consumerfed.org/survey99.pdf

95 NRA-ILA, *Right-To-Carry 2007*, January 16, 2007. http://www.nraila.org/issues/FactSheets/Read.aspx?ID=18

96 NRA-ILA, *What is the Gun Lobby?* January 23, 2001. http://www.nraila.org/Issues/FactSheets/Read.aspx?ID=20

97 *CONSUMERS STRONGLY SUPPORT RENEWING AND STRENGTHENING THE FEDERAL ASSAULT WEAPONS BAN*, Consumer Federation of America Survey, pages 1-2. http://www.consumerfed.org/ASSAULTWEAPONSURVEY2004.pdf

98 National Rifle Association-Political Victory Fund, *Victory Report: Election 2004, December 6, 2004*. http://www.nrapvf.org/news/article.aspx?id=154

99 U.S. Senate Roll Call Votes 108th Congress - 2nd Session, vote number 24, March 2, 2004. http://www.senate.gov/legislative/LIS/roll_call_lists/roll_call_vote_cfm.cfm?congress=108&session=2&vote=00024

100 Bradbury, Nielson, Jr., Marshall, *WHETHER THE SECOND AMENDMENT SECURES AN INDIVIDUAL RIGHT*, US Department of Justice Memorandum, August 24, 2004. http://www.usdoj.gov/olc/secondamendment2.htm

Chapter 4

1 See Table 4.1 in Appendix A.

2 History of the Springfield Armory 1777-1968, US National Park Service. http://www.nps.gov/spar/history.html

3 Springfield Armory, Past, Present and Future. http://www.springfield-armory.com/sitefeat-abtus.shtml

4 Colt History Society. http://www.archeryinfo.info/HistColt.html

5 Smith & Wesson – An All American Company. http://home.smith-wesson.com/pages/company/history

6 The New Shorter Oxford English Dictionary, Thumb Index Edition, 1993 Edition, Clarendon Press, page 2275.

[7] Ibid, page 2315.

[8] Agenda, The Democratic Party. http://www.democrats.org/agenda.html#civilrights

[9] Civil Rights, The Democratic Party. http://www.democrats.org/a/national/civil_rights/

[10] Kopel, Gallant, and Eisen, *Her Own Bodyguard: Gun-packing First Lady*, Independence Institute, January 24, 2002. http://www.nationalreview.com/kopel/kopel012402.shtml

[11] Letter from President John F. Kennedy to the NRA, March 20, 1961. http://www.nracentral.com/jfk-nra-life-membership.php

[12] Who Were the Minutemen? Andrew Ronemus, US History. http://www.ushistory.org/brandywine/special/art01.htm

[13] Lawyers/Law Firms: Long-Term Contribution Trends, Center for Responsive Politics. http://www.opensecrets.org/industries/indus.asp?Ind=K01

[14] Lawyers/Law Firms: Top 20 Senators 2004, Center for Responsive Politics. http://www.opensecrets.org/industries/recips.asp?Ind=K01&cycle=2004&recipdetail=S&Mem=Y&sortorder=U

[15] Lawyers/Law Firms: Top 20 Members of the House 2004, Center for Responsive Politics. http://www.opensecrets.org/industries/recips.asp?Ind=K01&cycle=2004&recipdetail=H&Mem=Y&sortorder=U

[16] Lawyers/Law Firms: Top 20 Senate Candidates 2004, Center for Responsive Politics. http://www.opensecrets.org/industries/recips.asp?Ind=K01&cycle=2004&recipdetail=S&Mem=N&sortorder=U

[17] Lawyers/Law Firms: Top 20 House Candidates 2004, Center for Responsive Politics. http://www.opensecrets.org/industries/recips.asp?Ind=K01&cycle=2004&recipdetail=H&Mem=N&sortorder=U

[18] Lawyers/Law Firms: Long-Term Contribution Trends, Center for Responsive Politics. http://www.opensecrets.org/industries/indus.asp?Ind=K01

[19] Lawyers/Law Firms: Top Contributors to Federal Candidates and Parties 2004, Center for Responsive Politics. http://www.opensecrets.org/industries/contrib.asp?Ind=K01&Cycle=2004

[20] Gun Rights: Long-Term Contributions Trends, Center for Responsive Politics. http://www.opensecrets.org/industries/indus.asp?ind=Q13

[21] Gun Rights: Top Contributors to Federal Candidates and Parties, Center for Responsive Politics. http://www.opensecrets.org/industries/contrib.asp?Ind=Q13&Cycle=2004

[22] Gun Violence Victims Urge Congress to Err on the Side of Life, Reject Legal Protection for Gun Sellers, Brady Press Release, April 5, 2005. http://www.bradycampaign.org/press/release.php?release=636

[23] Tough on terror, weak on guns, Mark Benjamin, Salon.com, March 28, 2005. http://www.salon.com/news/feature/2005/03/28/guns/index_np.html

[24] Dan Morales and Marc Murr Have Some Explaining to Do to All Texans, John R. Butler, Houston Chronicle, May 7, 1999. http://www.texansforreasonablelegalfees.com/explaining.asp

[25] The Great Tobacco Robbery: Lawyers Grab Billions, Robert Levy, Cato Institute, March 6, 1999. http://www.cato.org/dailys/03-06-99.html

[26] Lawyers/Law Firms: Long-Term Contribution Trends, Center for Responsive Politics. http://www.opensecrets.org/industries/indus.asp?Ind=K01

[27] Money Matters: State's share of tobacco settlement will go into general fund, Chris Schreiber, Nurse Week, July 1, 1999. http://www.nurseweek.com/features/99-7/settle.html

[28] Fiscal 2002-03 appropriations from tobacco-settlement receipts, Texas Department of State Health Services. http://www.dshs.state.tx.us/tobacco/pdf/settlement.pdf

[29] The New Shorter Oxford English Dictionary, Thumb Index Edition, 1993 Edition, Clarendon Press, page 3229.

[30] Financial Information, Philip Morris, USA. http://www.philipmorrisusa.com/en/about_us/financial_information.asp

[31] Investors Overview, Altria. http://www.altria.com/investors/02_00_investorsOver.asp

[32] Consolidated Balance Sheet, 2002 Annual Report, Altria, page 25. http://www.altria.com/AnnualReport2002/AR2002_07_03_0100.asp

[33] R.J. Reynolds Tobacco Company Fact Book. http://www.rjrt.com/company/profileFactBook.aspx

[34] Heat Seal Lidding, RJR Packaging – Products. http://www.rjrpackaging.com/

[35] The Law Encyclopedia: Case Law. http://www.thelawencyclopedia.com/term/case_law

[36] U.S. Chamber of Commerce Letter to Congress, R. Bruce Josten, July 22, 2005. http://www.hsshf.org/share/PLCAA/072205_b.pdf

[37] Letter to Full House, John Engler, National Association of Manufacturers, October 17, 2005. http://www.nam.org/s_nam/bin.asp?TrackID=&SID=1&DID=235464&CID=202203&VID=2

[38] Charles Schumer on Gun Control, On the Issues. http://www.issues2000.org/Domestic/Charles_Schumer_Gun_Control.htm

[39] Lawyers/Law Firms: Top 20 Senate Candidates 2004, Center for Responsive Politics.

[40] Charles E. Schumer (D-NY), Top Industries. http://www.opensecrets.org/politicians/indus.asp?CID=N00001093&cycle=2006

[41] Lawyers/Law Firms: Top 20 Senate Candidates 2004, Center for Responsive Politics.

[42] 2002 Race: Massachusetts Senate, Top Industries, Center for Responsive Politics. http://www.opensecrets.org/races/indus.asp?ID=MAS2&cycle=2002&special=N

[43] John Kerry on Gun Control, On the Issues. http://www.issues2000.org/2004/John_Kerry_Gun_Control.htm

[44] National Instant Criminal Background Check System Program Summary, Department of Justice. http://www.fbi.gov/hq/cjisd/nics.htm

[45] Fully-Automatic Firearms, NRA-ILA Fact Sheet. http://www.nraila.org/Issues/FactSheets/Read.aspx?ID=130

[46] Yemen's weapon culture, Richard Engel, BBC, January 22, 2002. http://news.bbc.co.uk/1/hi/world/middle_east/1775938.stm

[47] A Tamil Tiger Primer on International Arms Bazaar, Raymond Bonner, New York Times Service, International Herald Tribune, March 10, 1998. http://www.lankaweb.com/news/items/180398-1.html

[48] Lawyers/Law Firms: Top 20 Senate Candidates 2004, Center for Responsive Politics.

[49] Barbara Boxer on Gun Control, On the Issues. http://www.issues2000.org/Domestic/Barbara_Boxer_Gun_Control.htm

[50] Senate Amendment to S. 1805. http://thomas.loc.gov/cgi-bin/bdquery/D?d108:4:./temp/~bd9ktm::

[51] Lawyers/Law Firms: Top 20 Senate Candidates 2004, Center for Responsive Politics.

[52] Hillary Clinton (D-NY), Top Industries. http://www.opensecrets.org/politicians/indus.asp?CID=N00000019&cycle=2006

[53] Hillary Clinton on Gun Control, On the Issues. http://www.issues2000.org/Domestic/Hillary_Clinton_Gun_Control.htm

[54] U.S. Senate Roll Call Votes 108th Congress - 2nd Session, Vote on S. 1805. http://www.senate.gov/legislative/LIS/roll_call_lists/roll_call_vote_cfm.cfm?congress=108&session=2&vote=00030

[55] Amendments for S.1805. http://thomas.loc.gov/cgi-bin/bdquery/L?d108:./temp/~bdadh3t:1|1-21|(Amendments_For_S.1805)&./temp/~bddfk1

[56] Office of the Sergeant at Arms and Doorkeeper, US Senate website. http://www.senate.gov/reference/office/sergeant_at_arms.htm

[57] Kids Corner, U.S. Senator Barbara Boxer Official Website. http://boxer.senate.gov/kids/about.cfm

[58] Senate Demands 'Safety' Locks on All Handguns, News Max, February 26, 2004. http://www.newsmax.com/archives/articles/2004/2/26/133417.shtml

[59] Murder Victims by Age, by Weapon, 2003, FBI. http://www.fbi.gov/ucr/cius_03/xl/03tbl2-10.xls

[60] WISQARS Fatal Injuries: Mortality Reports, National Center for Injury Prevention and Control, Centers for Disease Control. http://webappa.cdc.gov/sasweb/ncipc/mortrate.html

[61] 5-4 Supreme Court Abolishes Juvenile Executions, Charles Lane, Washington Post, March 2, 2005. http://www.washingtonpost.com/wp-dyn/articles/A62584-2005Mar1.html

[62] WISQARS Fatal Injuries: Mortality Reports, National Center for Injury Prevention and Control, Centers for Disease Control.

[63] The New Shorter Oxford English Dictionary, Thumb Index Edition, 1993 Edition, page 386.

[64] Ibid, page 2404.

[65] Google search: definitions on puberty. http://www.google.com/search?hl=en&lr=&ie=UTF-8&oi=defmore&q=define:puberty

[66] See Table 4.2 in Appendix A.

[67] Firearms and Violence: A Critical Review, Charles F. Wellford, John V. Pepper, Carol V. Petrie, et al, Committee on Law and Justice, National Research Council, National Academy of Sciences, Copyright 2005, page 219.

[68] First Reports Evaluating the Effectiveness of Strategies for Preventing Violence: Firearms Laws, Findings from the Task Force on Community Preventive Services, Centers for Disease Control, October 3, 2003. http://www.cdc.gov/mmwr/preview/mmwrhtml/rr5214a2.htm

[69] The Bias Against Guns, John R. Lott, Jr., Regnery Publishing, 2003, pages 146-7.

[70] Ibid, pages 147-148.

[71] Mortality: Self-Harm, Nationmaster.com, compiled January 2004. http://www.nationmaster.com/graph-T/mor_sel_har_cap

[72] Cross-Sectional Study of the Relationship Between Levels of Gun Ownership and Violent Deaths, Greenwood, March 2000, page 2. http://www.wfsa.net/adobe_documents/Cross_Sectional_Study.PDF

[73] Ibid.

[74] Murder Circumstances by Weapon, 2003, FBI. http://www.fbi.gov/ucr/cius_03/xl/03tbl2-12.xls

[75] Murder Circumstances by Relationship, 2003, FBI. http://www.fbi.gov/ucr/cius_03/xl/03tbl2-11.xls

[76] See Table 4.3, Appendix A.

[77] Vehicular manslaughter, Dictionary, Law.com.
http://dictionary.law.com/default2.asp?selected=2212&bold=%7C%7C%7C%7C%7C

[78] Child Welfare Information Gateway, Child maltreatment 2004: Summary of Key Findings, U.S. Department of Health and Human Services, page 3. http://www.childwelfare.gov/pubs/factsheets/canstats.pdf

[79] National Center for Injury Prevention and Control, WISQARS Fatal Injuries: Mortality Reports 1999-2004, Centers for Disease Control. http://webappa.cdc.gov/sasweb/ncipc/mortrate10_sy.html

[80] Child Welfare Information Gateway, Child maltreatment 2004: Summary of Key Findings, U.S. Department of Health and Human Services, page 3.

[81] Safety Programs: Eddie Eagle, National Rifle Association. http://www.nrahq.org/safety/eddie/

[82] See Table 4.4 in Appendix A.

[83] National Center for Injury Prevention and Control, WISQARS Fatal Injuries: Mortality Reports, Centers for Disease Control. http://webappa.cdc.gov/sasweb/ncipc/mortrate.html

[84] Commerce in Firearms in the United States, Bureau of Alcohol, Tobacco, & Firearms, February, 2000, page 1. http://www.atf.gov/pub/fire-explo_pub/020400report.pdf

[85] The Bias Against Guns, John R. Lott, Jr., Regnery Publishing, 2003, page 143.

[86] National Center for Injury Prevention and Control, WISQARS Fatal Injuries: Mortality Reports, Centers for Disease Control.

[87] Mary Ann Cavazos, Police: Intruder was in prison several times, *Corpus Christi Caller-Times*, October 11, 2006. http://www.caller.com/ccct/local_news/article/0,1641,CCCT_811_5058140,00.html

[88] Barbara Ramirez, Ruling: Boy, 14, acted in defense, *Corpus Christi Caller-Times*, October 13, 2006. http://www1.caller.com/ccct/local_news/article/0,1641,CCCT_811_5063627,00.html

[89] Remember Gun Control? Los Angeles Times Editorial, April 11, 2005. http://www.latimes.com/news/opinion/editorials/la-ed-guns11apr11.story

[90] Protect the Rights of Gun Violence Victims, Form Letter to Congressional Representatives, Brady Campaign to Prevent Gun Violence.
https://secure2.convio.net/mmm/site/Advocacy?JServSessionIdr010=r9oarymrj1.app24a&page=UserAction&cmd=display&id=537

[91] Gun Violence Victims Urge Congress to Err on the Side of Life,
Reject Legal Protection for Gun Sellers, Brady Press Release, April 5, 2005.
http://www.bradycampaign.org/press/release.php?release=636

[92] Protection of Lawful Commerce in Arms Act, Senate Bill 397, 109th Congress, 1st Session, February 17, 2005. http://thomas.loc.gov/cgi-bin/query/query

[93] The Legal Action Project, Brady Campaign to Prevent Gun Violence. http://www.gunlawsuits.org/features/

[94] Statement of Michael Barnes on Senate Action to Deny Justice to Gun Violence Victims, U.S. Newswire, July 29, 2005. http://releases.usnewswire.com/GetRelease.asp?id=51147

[95] Biography of Michael Barnes, Brady Campaign to Prevent Handgun Violence.
http://www.bradycampaign.org/press/?page=mbbio

[96] Lawyers/Law Firms: Top Contributors to Federal Candidates and Parties, Open Secrets.org, Center for Responsive Politics. http://www.opensecrets.org/industries/contrib.asp?Ind=K01&Cycle=2004

[97] Special Projects, Washington Lawyers' Committee for Civil Rights and Urban Affairs.
http://www.washlaw.org/projects/special_projects/default.htm

[98] Compiled from campaign contribution records available at Open Secrets, the website of the Center for Responsive Politics, large spreadsheet compiled using data available as of Roll Call date. Spreadsheet available upon request.

[99] U.S. Senate Roll Call Votes 109th Congress – 1st Session, Vote Number 219, July 29, 2005.
http://www.senate.gov/legislative/LIS/roll_call_lists/roll_call_vote_cfm.cfm?congress=109&session=1&vote=00219

[100] Occupational Outlook Handbook: Lawyers, Bureau of Labor Statistics, U.S. Department of Labor. http://stats.bls.gov/oco/ocos053.htm

[101] Lawyers/Law Firms: Long-Term Contributions, Open Secrets.org, Center for Responsive Politics. http://www.opensecrets.org/industries/indus.asp?Ind=K01

[102] Gun Rights: Top Contributors to Federal Candidates and Parties, 2002 Election Cycle, Open Secrets.org, Center for Responsive Politics. http://www.opensecrets.org/industries/contrib.asp?Ind=Q13&Cycle=2002

[103] A Brief History of the NRA, National Rifle Association Headquarters. http://www.nrahq.org/history.asp

[104] Ibid.

[105] Gun Rights: Top Contributors to Federal Candidates and Parties, 2004 Election Cycle, Open Secrets.org, Center for Responsive Politics. http://www.opensecrets.org/industries/contrib.asp?Ind=Q13&Cycle=2004

[106] Lawyers/Law Firms: Top Contributors to Federal Candidates and Parties, Open Secrets.org, Center for Responsive Politics. http://www.opensecrets.org/industries/contrib.asp?Ind=K01&Cycle=2004

[107] About Us, Baron & Budd. http://www.baronandbudd.com/ABOUT_HOME.html

[108] Infant 10th fatality in farmers Market Crash, CNN, July 17, 2003.
http://www.cnn.com/2003/US/West/07/17/farmers.market.crash/
[109] Lawsuits filed in Santa Monica farmers market crash that killed 10, Associated Press, San Francisco Chronicle, July 13, 2004. http://sfgate.com/cgi-bin/article.cgi?f=/news/archive/2004/07/13/national2157EDT0765.DTL
[110] Testimony of Lawrence G. Keane, Senior Vice President & General Counsel
National Shooting Sports Foundation, Inc., House Subcommittee on Commercial and Administrative Law, March 15, 2005. http://judiciary.house.gov/HearingTestimony.aspx?ID=257
[111] Ibid.
[112] Compiled from campaign contribution records available at Open Secrets, the website of the Center for Responsive Politics, large spreadsheet compiled using data available as of Roll Call date. Spreadsheet available upon request.
[113] Mark Dayton: Senate bows shamefully to powerful gun lobby, StarTribune, August 2, 2005.
http://www.startribune.com/stories/1519/5537795.html
[114] Top Industries 2000 Race: Minnesota Senate, Center for Responsive Politics.
http://www.opensecrets.org/races/indus.asp?ID=MNS2&cycle=2000&special=N
[115] Mark Dayton: Senate bows shamefully to powerful gun lobby, StarTribune, August 2, 2005.
[116] *Lawyers/Law Firms: Long-Term Contribution Trends*, Center for Responsive Politics.
http://www.opensecrets.org/industries/indus.asp?Ind=K01
[117] *Gun Rights: Long-Term Contribution Trends*, Center for Responsive Politics.
http://www.opensecrets.org/industries/indus.asp?cycle=2006&ind=Q13
[118] *Lawyers/Law Firms: Long-Term Contribution Trends*, Center for Responsive Politics.
[119] Compiled from campaign contribution records available at Open Secrets, the website of the Center for Responsive Politics. Counts Kansas and Nebraska as RTC states for shall-issue laws passed legislature during 2006. Spreadsheet available upon request.
[120] *Lawyers/Law Firms: Long-Term Contribution Trends*, Center for Responsive Politics.
http://www.opensecrets.org/industries/indus.asp?Ind=K01
[121] *Gun Rights: Long-Term Contribution Trends*, Center for Responsive Politics.
http://www.opensecrets.org/industries/indus.asp?cycle=2006&ind=Q13
[122] Compiled from campaign contribution records available at Open Secrets, the website of the Center for Responsive Politics. Counts Kansas and Nebraska as RTC states for shall-issue laws passed legislature during 2006. Spreadsheet available upon request.
[123] Preamble (first paragraph) and First Amendment, The Bill of Rights, U.S. Department of State, downloaded January 20, 2007. http://usinfo.state.gov/usa/infousa/facts/funddocs/billeng.htm
[124] Senate Bill 1, Section 220–Disclosure of Paid Efforts to Stimulate Grassroots Lobbying, Thomas (Library of Congress), downloaded January 20, 2007.
[125] ACLU Letter to the Senate Urging Support of the Bennett Amendment to Senate Bill 1, American Civil Liberties Union, January 17, 2007. http://www.aclu.org/freespeech/gen/28036leg20070117.html
[126] Compiled from campaign contribution records available at Open Secrets, the website of the Center for Responsive Politics, cross-referenced with Bennett-McConnell Amdt No. 20, U.S. Senate Roll Call Votes 110th Congress - 1st Session, January 18, 2007, 08:21 PM.
http://www.senate.gov/legislative/LIS/roll_call_lists/roll_call_vote_cfm.cfm?congress=110&session=1&vote=00017
Spreadsheet available upon request.
[127] Return on Investment – ROI, Investopedia. http://www.investopedia.com/terms/r/returnoninvestment.asp
[128] Protection of Lawful Commerce in Arms Act, Senate Bill 397, 109th Congress, 1st Session, February 17, 2005, Section 4, Paragraph 5, A, iii.
[129] NYC Wins Bid to Sue Gun Manufacturers Over Marketing, Tom Perrotta, New York Law Journal, December 5, 2005. http://www.law.com/jsp/article.jsp?id=1133517916932&rss=newswire
[130] *Lawyers/Law Firms: Long-Term Contribution Trends*, Center for Responsive Politics.

Chapter 5

[1] Joseph J. Ellis, *His Excellency: George Washington*, Alfred A. Knopf, 2004, pages 221-230.
[2] Joseph J. Ellis, *American Sphinx: The Character of Thomas Jefferson*, Alfred A. Knopf, 1997, pages 218-9.
[3] Wikipedia, *Historical revisionism (negationism)*, last modified October 21, 2007.
http://en.wikipedia.org/wiki/Historical_revisionism_%28negationism%29
[4] Will Sullivan, Packing heat on the hill, *U.S. News & World Report*, July 9, 2006.
http://www.usnews.com/usnews/news/articles/060709/17guns.htm
[5] Second Amendment Research Center, *About Us*. http://www.secondamendmentcenter.org/about_us.asp
[6] Joyce Foundation, Grant List. http://www.joycefdn.org/GrantList/Default.aspx

[7] Open Secrets, *Gun Rights: Long-Term Contributions*, The Center for Responsive Politics. http://www.opensecrets.org/industries/indus.asp?Ind=Q13

[8] Wikipedia, *Opinion Poll: Potential for innacuracy*, last modified July 10, 2006. http://en.wikipedia.org/wiki/Opinion_poll

[9] Open Secrets, *Gun Control: Long-Term Contributions*, The Center for Responsive Politics. http://www.opensecrets.org/industries/indus.asp?cycle=2006&ind=Q12

[10] Open Secrets, *Gun Rights: Long-Term Contributions*, The Center for Responsive Politics.

[11] Open Secrets, *Ideology/Single-issue: Top Contributors to Federal Candidates and Parties*, The Center for Responsive Politics. http://www.opensecrets.org/industries/contrib.asp?Ind=Q&Cycle=2004

[12] Emily's List, About–*Who We Are*, Copyright 2006. http://www.emilyslist.org/about/

[13] Emily's List, *Victory Highlights*, Copyright 2006. http://www.emilyslist.org/do/pop/victoryhighlights.html

[14] Emily's List, *Insider News: Week of December 15, 2003*, Copyright 2006. http://www.emilyslist.org/happening/insider-news/20031215.html

[15] Open Secrets, *Ideology/Single-issue: Top Contributors to Federal Candidates and Parties*, The Center for Responsive Politics.

[16] The Library of Congress, *S. 645, the Assault Weapons Ban and Law Enforcement Protection Act of 2005*, March 16, 2005. http://thomas.loc.gov/cgi-bin/query/D?c109:2:./temp/~c109lPzLXs::

[17] Open Society Institute, *Gun Control in the United States*, April 2000, page 12. http://www.soros.org/initiatives/justice/articles_publications/publications/gun_report_20000401/GunReport.pdf

[18] Open Secrets, *Top Individual Contributors to 527 Committees, 2004 Election Cycle*, The Center for Responsive Politics. http://www.opensecrets.org/527s/527indivs.asp?cycle=2004

[19] Open Secrets, *Donor Lookup, 2004: Soros*, The Center for Responsive Politics. http://www.opensecrets.org/indivs/search.asp?NumOfThou=0&txtName=soros&txtState=%28all+states%29&txtZip=&txtEmploy=&txtCand=&txt2004=Y&Order=N

[20] National Education Association, *Statement of Reginald Weaver, Vice President National Education Association On the Introduction of the Children's Gun Violence Prevention Act of 1998*, June, 17, 1998. http://www.aft.org/presscenter/speeches-columns/wws/1999/0799.htm

[21] Open Secrets, *National Education Assn*, The Center for Responsive Politics. http://www.opensecrets.org/orgs/summary.asp?ID=D000000064&Name=National+Education+Assn

[22] Will Sullivan, Packing heat on the hill, *U.S. News & World Report*, July 9, 2006.

[23] Karina Gonzalez, *Bill would make carrying concealed firearm legal in Illinois*, Quad-Cities Online, The Dispatch, March 29, 2005. http://qconline.com/archives/qco/sections.cgi?press=display&id=236106

[24] *Combs should keep her gun bill holstered*, Editorial, Lincoln Journal Star, May 17, 2005. http://www.journalstar.com/articles/2005/05/17/editorial_main/doc42892e5003610526040357.txt

[25] Daniel Prazer, *Ohio handgun law has had little effect*, Gannett News Service, Telegraph-Forum, April 4, 2005. http://www.bucyrustelegraphforum.com/apps/pbcs.dll/article?AID=/20050404/NEWS01/504040301/1002

[26] FBI Crime in the United States, 2004, Table 4: Crime in the United States by Region, Geographic Division, and State, 2003-2004, page 78. http://www.fbi.gov/ucr/cius_04/documents/CIUS2004.pdf

[27] Traffic Safety Facts 2004: A Compilation of Motor Vehicle Crash Data from the Fatality Analysis Reporting System and the General Estimates System, National Highway Traffic Safety Administration, Table 2, page 15. http://www-nrd.nhtsa.dot.gov/pdf/nrd-30/NCSA/TSF Ann/TSF2004.pdf

[28] See Table 5.1, Appendix A.

[29] FBI Uniform Crime Reports. http://www.fbi.gov/ucr/ucr.htm Selected data from 1995, 1996, and 2004.

[30] Institute for Legislative Action, *Right-to-Carry 2007*, National Rifle Association, January 16, 2007. http://www.nraila.org//Issues/FactSheets/Read.aspx?ID=18

[31] *Commerce in Firearms in the United States*, Bureau of Alcohol, Tobacco, & Firearms, February, 2000, page 1. http://www.atf.gov/pub/fire-explo_pub/020400report.pdf

[32] *Active License Holders and Certified Instructors, Period: As of 12/31/2006*, Texas Department of Public Safety. http://www.txdps.state.tx.us/administration/crime_records/chl/PDF/ActLicAndInstr/ActiveLicandInstr2006.pdf cross-referenced with Table 5 - Crime in the United States by State, 2006, FBI. http://www.fbi.gov/ucr/cius2006/data/table_05.html

[33] Concealed Weapon/Firearm Summary Report October 1, 1987 – February 28, 2007, Florida Department of Agriculture and Consumer Services, Division of Licensing. http://licgweb.doacs.state.fl.us/stats/cw_monthly.html cross-referenced with Table 5 - Crime in the United States by State, 2006, FBI

[34] Tabulated from FBI, Table 4: by Region, Geographic Division, and State, 2005–2006. http://www.fbi.gov/ucr/cius2006/data/documents/06tbl04.xls

[35] Institute for Legislative Action, *Right-to-Carry 2007*, National Rifle Association, January 16, 2007.

[36] Robin Erb, *Both sides want Ohio to tweak its gun law*, Toledo Blade, April 4, 2005. http://toledoblade.com/apps/pbcs.dll/article?AID=/20050404/NEWS08/504040326

37 Email from Brian Patrick, Assistant Professor, Communication, University of Toledo, received 5/27/05.

38 Joyce Foundation Gun Violence Grants. http://www.joycefdn.org/GrantList/Default.aspx

39 *Foundations Should Support Firearms Research*, Joyce Foundation Press Release, April 12, 2005.
http://www.joycefdn.org/programs/gunviolence/gunviolencemain-fs.html

40 WISQARS Fatal Injuries: Mortality Reports, National Center for Injury Prevention and Control, Centers for Disease Control. http://webappa.cdc.gov/sasweb/ncipc/mortrate.html

41 *Firearms Commerce in the United States 2001/2002*, Bureau of Alcohol, Tobacco, and Firearms.
http://www.atf.gov/pub/fire-explo_pub/firearmscommerce/firearmscommerce.pdf

42 Take Action! Send a Message: Keep Our Nation's Capitol Safe. Urges Congress to not repeal the DC gun ban.
http://action.csgv.org//action/index.asp?step=2&item=21846

43 Tabulated from Table 4: Crime in the United States by Region, Geographic Division, and State, 2005-2006.
http://www.fbi.gov/ucr/cius2006/data/documents/06tbl04.xls

44 See Table 5.2, Appendix A.

45 *Dayton Man Fights Back During Robbery Attempt*, WHIO TV, June 3, 2005.
http://www.whiotv.com/news/4565662/detail.html

46 Larry Davis, *Robbery Victim Shot, Shoots Suspect*, WKRC Local 12, Cincinnati, Ohio.
http://www.wkrc.com/mediacenter/?videoId=4684

47 Heather Martens, *Gun-permit proposal's back, packing few facts*, May 4, 2005.
http://www.startribune.com/stories/1519/5383773.html

48 Charles F. Wellford, John V. Pepper, Carol V. Petrie, et al, *Firearms and Violence: A Critical Review*, page 121.

49 Ibid, page 150.

50 Ibid, page 129.

51 Arthur L. Kellerman and Donald T. Reay, *Protection or Peril?: An Analysis of Firearm-Related Deaths in the Home*, 314 New Eng. J. Med. 1557-60 1986, page 1560.

52 Bill Barnes and Burke Strunsky, *NRA out of S.F.*, San Francisco Bay Guardian.
http://www.sfbg.com/39/15/x_oped.html

53 Charles F. Wellford, John V. Pepper, Carol V. Petrie, et al, *Firearms and Violence: A Critical Review*, page 118.

54 Peter Hamm Interview by Cam Edwards, NRA News, January 14, 2005.

55 *License to Kill IV: More Guns, More Crime*, Violence Policy Center, June 2002, page 10.
http://www.vpc.org/graphics/ltk4.pdf

56 Go to www.vpc.org and type keywords into the search function.

57 Email from Systems Analyst, Regulatory Licensing Service, Texas Department of Public Safety, June 7, 2005 at 10:03 AM. (512) 424-2968 office, (512) 424-5599 facsimile.

58 Presumption of innocence, Nolo Press. http://www.nolo.com/definition.cfm/Term/CB98B8AB-560A-4C98-845C8EBD61E795E80/alpha/P/

59 Email from Systems Analyst, Regulatory Licensing Service, May 2005. (512) 424-2968 office, (512) 424-5599 facsimile.

60 Texas H.B. 2784, Enrolled Version. http://www.capitol.state.tx.us/cgi-bin/tlo/textframe.cmd?LEG=77&SESS=R&CHAMBER=H&BILLTYPE=B&BILLSUFFIX=02784&VERSION=5&TYPE=B

61 Alicia Smith, *"Castle Doctrine" bill would expand gun owners' rights*, WWMT News 3, October 25, 2005.
http://wwmt.com/engine.pl?station=wwmt&id=20564&template=breakout_local.html

62 Michigan House Bill 5142, September 7, 2005. http://www.legislature.mi.gov/documents/2005-2006/billintroduced/house/pdf/2005-HIB-5142.pdf

63 Michigan House Bill 5143, September 7, 2005. http://www.legislature.mi.gov/documents/2005-2006/billintroduced/house/pdf/2005-HIB-5143.pdf

64 The New Shorter Oxford English Dictionary, Thumb Index Edition, 1993 Edition, Clarendon Press, page 41.

65 See Table 5.3, Appendix A.

66 About the Violence Policy Center http://www.vpc.org/aboutvpc.htm

67 *Texas Concealed Handgun Laws and Selected Statutes, 2005-2006*, Texas Department of Public Safety, January, 2006, page 3.
http://www.txdps.state.tx.us/ftp/forms/ls-16.pdf

68 *Total Adult Convictions and Deferred Adjudications for All Felony Offenses, Fiscal Years 1988 – 2002*, Criminal Justice Policy Council, January 15, 2003, page 3. http://www.cjpc.state.tx.us/stattabs/courtconvictions/02Courtconvictions_U.pdf

69 Ibid, page 4.

70 Ibid, page 5.

71 See Table 5.4, Appendix A.

72 *Basis for Revocation or Suspension of Texas Concealed Handgun Licenses*, Crime Records Service, Concealed Handgun Licensing Section, Texas Department of Public Safety, May 19, 2000.

73 Ibid.

74 Office of State Police, *Annual Legislative Report, Concealed Handgun Permit Unit 2004-2005*, Louisiana Department of Public Safety, page 10. http://www.lsp.org/pdf/channualreport.pdf

75 Ibid, page 13.

76 See Table 5.5, Appendix A.

77 See Table 5.6, Appendix A.

78 See Table 5.7, Appendix A.

79 See Table 5.8, Appendix A.

80 *2001 Conviction Rates of Concealed Handgun License Holders*, Regulatory Licensing Service, Concealed Handgun Licensing Bureau, Texas Department of Public Safety.
http://www.txdps.state.tx.us/administration/crime_records/chl/convrates.htm

81 See Table 5.8, Appendix A.

82 Derived from Carole Keeton Strayhorn, *Texas Gross State Product Detail: Calendar Years 1990-2029, Billions of Chained 1996 Dollars*, Texas Comptroller's Office, Fall 2004 Forecast. http://www.window.state.tx.us/ecodata/fcst04fall/2gspreal_cal.xls

83 *Conviction Rates for Concealed Handgun License Holders, Reporting Period: 01/01/2003 – 12/31/2003*, Texas Department of Public Safety, February 15, 2007, page 4.
http://www.txdps.state.tx.us/administration/crime_records/chl/ConvictionRatesReport2003.pdf

84 See Tables 5.9 and 5.10, Appendix A.

85 Carol Keeton Strayhorn, Comptroller, Texas Gross State Product Detail, Calendar Years 1990-2029, downloaded April 3, 2007. http://www.window.state.tx.us/ecodata/fcst04fall/2gspreal_cal.xls

86 See Tables 5.11 and 5.12, Appendix A.

87 *Texas Concealed Handgun Laws and Selected Statutes, 2005-2006*, Texas Department of Public Safety, January, 2006, pages 3-5.

88 Email received from Jerry Patterson, Texas Land Commissioner, May 12, 2007, 6:04 PM.

89 Associated Press, *Wal-Mart shooting was first under concealed carry permit*, Free New Mexican, August 30, 2005.
http://www.freenewmexican.com/news/31883.html

90 Adrian Alan, *Concealed carry provides protection*, Opinion & Editorial, Badger Herald, December 9, 2005.
http://badgerherald.com/oped/2005/12/09/concealed_carry_prov.php

91 *American Roulette*, Violence Policy Center, 2002, page 2.
http://www.vpc.org/graphics/amroul.pdf

92 Ibid, page 3.

93 Ibid, page 10.

94 Ibid, page 10.

95 Ibid, page 7.

96 Ibid, page 9.

97 Ibid, page 9.

98 Ibid, page 8.

99 *Sheriff: Deaths at ranch were murder-suicide*, Court TV, May 17, 2005. http://courttv.com/news/2005/0511/sheriff_ap.html

100 *American Roulette*, Violence Policy Center, page 8.

101 James Alan Fox and Marianne W. Zawitz, *Homicide Trends in the United States*, U.S. Department of Justice, Bureau of Justice Statistics, November 2002, page 8.
http://www.ojp.usdoj.gov/bjs/pub/pdf/htius.pdf

102 Ibid, page 66.

103 Ibid, page 141.

104 Ibid, page 141.

105 Ibid, pages 134-135.

106 Ibid, page 89.

107 Ibid, page 98.

108 Rennison, *Intimate Partner Violence 1993-2001*, Bureau of Justice Statistics, U.S. Department of Justice, February, 2003.
http://www.ojp.usdoj.gov/bjs/pub/pdf/ipv01.pdf

109 See Table 5.13, Appendix A.

110 See Table 5.14, Appendix A.

111 *Firearms Commerce in the United States 2001/2002*. Bureau of Alcohol, Tobacco, and Firearms.
http://www.atf.gov/pub/fire-explo_pub/firearmscommerce/firearmscommerce.pdf

112 FBI, *Violence Among Family Members and Intimate Partners*, Section V, Crime in the United States – 2003, page 339.
http://www.fbi.gov/ucr/cius_03/pdf/03sec5.pdf

113 Ibid, page 340.

114 Ibid, Table 5.8: Use of Weapons Within Family Violence Incidents by Family Relationship, page 345.

115 See Table 5.15, Appendix A.

116 See Table 5.16, Appendix A.

117 See Table 5.17, Appendix A.

118 Ibid.

119 Craig Perkins, *Weapon Use and Violent Crime: National Crime Victimization Survey 1993-2001*, Bureau of Justice Statistics, United States Department of Justice, September 2003, page 1. http://www.ojp.usdoj.gov/bjs/pub/pdf/wuvc01.pdf

120 Ibid, page 2.

121 Derived from *Violence Among Family Members and Intimate Partners*, Table 5.7, page 345.

122 Derived from *Violence Among Family Members and Intimate Partners*, Table 5.7, page 345.

123 *American Roulette*, Violence Policy Center, page 10.

124 Ashley Cook, *Grand jury no-bills woman in shooting*, Lufkin Daily News, June 30, 2005. http://www.lufkindailynews.com/news/content/news/stories/2005/06/30/20050630LDNgrand_jury.html

125 Josh Sugarman, *Every Handgun is Aimed at You: The Case for Banning Handguns*, copyright 2001 by Violence Policy Center, page 1.

126 *American Roulette*, Violence Policy Center, page 6.

127 Don B. Kates and Daniel D. Polsby, *The Myth of the "Virgin Killer": Law-Abiding Persons Who Kill in a Fit of Rage*, copyright 2002, page 14. (This paper was presented at a symposium held under the auspices of the Royal Armouries in the Tower of London, May, 2003.

128 Ibid, pages 16-17.

129 Ibid, pages 20-21.

130 *American Roulette*, Violence Policy Center, page 7.

131 Ibid, pages 30-31.

132 Deanna Boyd, *Teen not indicted for killing his father*, Fort Worth Star-Telegram, June 8, 2005. http://www.dfw.com/mld/dfw/11842797.htm

133 See Table 5.18, Appendix A.

134 Don B. Kates and Daniel D. Polsby, *The Myth of the "Virgin Killer": Law-Abiding Persons Who Kill in a Fit of Rage*, pages 37-38.

135 Ibid, pages 4-7.

136 Associated Press, *Gunman Kills Self After Deadly Rampage*, Fox News, May 31, 2005. http://www.foxnews.com/story/0,2933,158229,00.html

137 *Handgun crime soars despite Dunblane Ban*, UK Telegraph , January 11, 2001. http://portal.telegraph.co.uk/news/main.jhtml;$sessionid$2YYLRCAAAAVMNQFIQMFCFFWAVCBQYIV0?xml=/news/2001/01/11/ngun11.xml
Gun crimes soaring despite ban brought in following Dublane, UK Telegraph, July 15, 2001. http://www.telegraph.co.uk/news/main.jhtml?xml=/news/2001/07/15/ngun15.xml

138 The Armed Citizen, NRA Publications. http://www.nrapublications.org/armed%20citizen/Index.asp

139 Ken Fireman, *Armor-piercing gun targeted*, Newsday, March 4, 2005. http://www.newsday.com/news/nationworld/nation/ny-usgun044164683mar04,0,7946076.story?coll=ny-nationalnews-headlines

140 FN 5.7 (Fabrique Nationale) pistol is a semiautomatic pistol in 5.7 X 28 mm caliber, Firearms Technology Branch, Bureau of Alcohol, Tobacco, and Firearms, January 20, 2005. http://www.atf.gov/firearms/firearmstech/fabriquen.htm

141 Home page, Grand Lodge of the Fraternal Order of Police. http://www.grandlodgefop.org/

142 *Accurate Information About a New Type of Handgun*, Grand Lodge of the Fraternal Order of Police. http://www.grandlodgefop.org/newsinfo/FNhandgun.html

143 Ibid.

144 *The Truth About Australia*, Brady Campaign, http://www.bradycampaign.org/facts/factsheets/?page=aust

145 Ibid.

146 Reuter and Mouzos, *Australia: A Massive Buyback of Low-Risk Guns*, page 134.

147 *New Study Shows Florida's "Model" Concealed Carry Law Puts Guns Into the Hands of Criminals*, Violence Policy Center, November, 1, 1995. http://www.vpc.org/press/9511ccw.htm

148 School Massacre Definition, Other primary and elementary school killings, Wikipedia. http://en.wikipedia.org/wiki/School_massacre

149 *Gun Massacres*, Gun Control Australia. http://www.guncontrol.org.au/index.php?article=8

150 John R. Lott, Jr., *The Bias Against Guns*, page 123.

151 Ibid, page 107.

152 *The Truth About Australia*, Brady Campaign.

153 *Australian Crime Facts and Figures 2002*.

154 Reuter and Mouzos, *Australia: A Massive Buyback of Low-Risk Guns*, page 134.

Endnotes 239

155 Derived using Crime in the United States - 1995, FBI Uniform Crime Reports. http://www.fbi.gov/ucr/Cius_97/95CRIME/95crime2.pdf 1994 total murders, page 13 and number homicides using a firearm, page 274.

156 Murder Circumstances by Weapon, 2001, FBI. http://www.fbi.gov/ucr/cius_01/xl/01tbl2-13.xls

157 *The Truth About Australia*, Brady Campaign.

158 *Australian Crime Facts and Figures 2002*, page 24.

159 FBI Crime in the United States by Volume and Rate, 1984-2003. http://www.fbi.gov/ucr/cius_03/xl/03tbl01.xls

160 *Australian Crime Facts and Figures 2002*, page 7.

161 Reuter and Mouzos, *Australia: A Massive Buyback of Low-Risk Guns*, Figure 4-3, page 137.

162 Ibid, page 129.

163 Ibid, page 121.

164 Ibid, page 128.

165 Ibid, page 136.

166 Ibid, page 136.

167 1994 data from: Fatal Firearm-Related Injuries – United States, 1993-1997, Centers for Disease Control, November 189, 1999, Table 1. http://www.cdc.gov/mmwr/preview/mmwrhtml/mm4845a1.htm

2001 data from: WISQARS Nonfatal Injury Reports, Centers for Disease Control, National Center for Injury Prevention and Control. http://webappa.cdc.gov/sasweb/ncipc/nfirates2001.html

168 David Kopel, *Who Needs Guns? Lessons from Down Under*, Copyright 2003, Chronicles Magazine. http://www.chroniclesmagazine.org/Chronicles/October2003/1003Kopel.html

169 Brady Campaign State Report Cards Show State Legislatures Are Failing to Protect Kids from the Dangers of Illegal Guns, The Brady Campaign to Prevent Gun Violence, April 2006. http://www.bradycampaign.org/facts/reportcards/2005/ (Use drop-down list to select each state's 2005 grade.)

170 Firearms Control Regulations Act of 1975, Wikipedia, April 5, 2007. http://en.wikipedia.org/wiki/Firearms_Control_Regulations_Act_of_1975

171 Brady Campaign State Report Cards Show State Legislatures Are Failing to Protect Kids from the Dangers of Illegal Guns, The Brady Campaign to Prevent Gun Violence, April 2006. http://www.bradycampaign.org/facts/reportcards/2005/ (Use drop-down list to select each state's 2005 grade.)

172 See Table 5.19, Appendix A.

173 See Table 5.20, Appendix A.

174 Table 1 – Crime in the United States by Volume and Rate per 100,000 Inhabitants, 1986-2005., Federal Bureau of Investigation. http://www.fbi.gov/ucr/05cius/data/documents/05tbl01.xls

175 See Table 5.21, Appendix A.

176 Violence Policy Center home page, downloaded July 5, 2005. http://www.vpc.org/

177 Statement of Sarah Brady on Legislation Introduced Today by Senators Allen and Hutchison, Brady Campaign to Prevent Gun Violence, May 19, 2005. http://www.bradycampaign.org/press/release.php?release=647

178 See Table 5.22, Appendix A.

179 Brady Campaign, *Statement of Paul Helmke on Remarks by Florida Governor Jeb Bush*, July 12, 2006. http://www.bradycampaign.org/media/?pagename=release&release=765

180 FBI, *Crime in the United States, 2004*, Table 1: Crime in the United States by Volume and Rate per 100,000 Inhabitants, 1985-2004, page 72. http://www.fbi.gov/ucr/cius_04/documents/CIUS2004.pdf

181 Charles F. Wellford, John V. Pepper, Carol V. Petrie, et al, *Firearms and Violence: A Critical Review*, Committee on Law and Justice, National Research Council, National Academy of Sciences, Copyright 2005, pages 93-95.

182 Brent Kallestad, Bush: Florida crime rate down to lowest level since '71, *Palm Beach Post*, July 11, 2006. http://www.palmbeachpost.com/state/content/gen/ap/FL_Florida_Crime.html

183 The Disaster Center, *Florida Crime Rates 1960-2005*. http://www.disastercenter.com/crime/flcrime.htm

184 See Table 5.23, Appendix A.

185 Table 5 - Crime in the United States by State, 2005, Federal Bureau of Investigation. http://www.fbi.gov/ucr/05cius/data/documents/05tbl05.xls

186 FBI, *Crime in the United States, 2004*, Table 5: Crime in the United States by State, 2004, pages 86-96.

187 Cross-reference FBI, *Crime in the United States, 2004*, Table 5: Crime in the United States by State, 2004, pages 86-96 with NRA-ILA, *Right-To-Carry 2005*, March 17, 2005. http://www.nraila.org/issues/FactSheets/Read.aspx?ID=18

188 Compiled from arrest data in the FBI's *Crime in the United States* for each year. Reports can be referenced from http://www.fbi.gov/ucr/ucr.htm#cius .

189 See Table 5.24, Appendix A.

190 Brent Kallestad, Bush: Florida crime rate down to lowest level since '71, *Palm Beach Post*, July 11, 2006.

191 See Table 5.25, Appendix A.

192 Mark Sherman (Associated Press), *Lawyers, gun rights groups square off*, Canton Rep, February 10, 2007.
http://www.cantonrep.com/index.php?ID=335373&Category=23

193 Bureau of Labor Statistics, National Census of Fatal Occupational Injuries in 2005, United States Department of Labor,
August 10, 2006, page 7. http://www.bls.gov/news.release/pdf/cfoi.pdf

194 Legal Action Project, *Forced Entry: The National Rifle Association's Campaign To Force Business To Accept Guns At Work*, Brady
Campaign to Prevent Gun Violence, November 2005. http://www.bradycampaign.com/xshare/pdf/forced-entry-
report.pdf

195 *Forced Entry*, page 1.

196 Bureau of Labor Statistics, *Table A-2: Fatal occupational injuries resulting from transportation incidents and homicides, All United
States, 2003*, U.S. Department of Labor, page 1. http://stats.bls.gov/iif/oshwc/cfoi/cftb0188.pdf

197 Bureau of Labor Statistics, Table R31: Number of nonfatal occupational injuries and illnesses involving days away from
work by event or exposure leading to injury or illness and selected natures of injury or illness, 2002, U.S. Department of
Labor, page 13. http://stats.bls.gov/iif/oshwc/osh/case/ostb1298.pdf

198 *Forced Entry*, page 1.
http://www.bradycampaign.com/xshare/pdf/forced-entry-report.pdf

199 *Forced Entry*, page 1.
http://www.bradycampaign.com/xshare/pdf/forced-entry-report.pdf

200 Table 1 – Crime in the United States by Volume and Rate per 100,000 Inhabitants, 1986-2005, Federal Bureau of
Investigation. http://www.fbi.gov/ucr/05cius/data/documents/05tbl01.xls

201 See Table 5.26, Appendix A.

202 Institute for Legislative Action, *Right-to-Carry 2007*, National Rifle Association, January 16, 2007.
http://www.nraila.org/Issues/FactSheets/Read.aspx?ID=18

203 Table 1 – Crime in the United States by Volume and Rate per 100,000 Inhabitants, 1986 – 2005.
http://www.fbi.gov/ucr/05cius/data/documents/05tbl01.xls

204 Divide the numbers from Bureau of Labor Statistics, National Census of Fatal Occupational Injuries in 2005, United
States Department of Labor, August 10, 2006, page 7. http://www.bls.gov/news.release/pdf/cfoi.pdf
by the Total Non-farm employees for December 2005 in Bureau of Labor Statistics, Comparison of All Employees, not
seasonally adjusted, ftp://ftp.bls.gov/pub/suppl/empsit.compaeu.txt

205 Table 1 – Crime in the United States by Volume and Rate per 100,000 Inhabitants, 1986 – 2005.

206 *Forced Entry*, page 15-18.

207 *Forced Entry*, page 15.

208 Concealed carry permit holder shooting ruled self-defense, Keep and Bear Arms, September 4&5, 2001.
http://www.keepandbeararms.com/information/XcIBViewItem.asp?ID=2446

209 Guy Smith, *Gun Facts, Version 4.1*, Copyright 2006, page 71. http://www.gunfacts.info/

210 Legal Action Project, *Forced Entry: The National Rifle Association's Campaign To Force Business To Accept Guns At Work*, Brady
Campaign to Prevent Gun Violence, November 2005, page 1. http://www.bradycampaign.com/xshare/pdf/forced-entry-
report.pdf

211 Dana Loomis, PhD, Stephen W. Marshall, PhD, and Myduc L. Ta, MPH, *Employer Policies Toward Guns and the Risk of
Homicide in the Workplace*, American Journal of Public Health, Vol. 95, No. 5, May 2005, abstract, page 830.

212 Ibid.

213 Ibid, page 831.

214 Ibid.

215 Ibid.

216 Dana Loomis, PhD, Stephen W. Marshall, PhD, and Myduc L. Ta, MPH, *Employer Policies Toward Guns and the Risk of
Homicide in the Workplace*, American Journal of Public Health, Vol. 95, No. 5, May 2005, page 830.

217 Office of Advocacy, *Small Business Profile: North Carolina*, Small Business Administration, 2006, page 2.
http://www.sba.gov/advo/research/profiles/06nc.pdf

218 Dana Loomis, PhD, Stephen W. Marshall, PhD, and Myduc L. Ta, MPH, *Employer Policies Toward Guns and the Risk of
Homicide in the Workplace*, American Journal of Public Health, Vol. 95, No. 5, May 2005, page 832. See their notes 3 and 4.

219 Charles F. Wellford, John V. Pepper, Carol V. Petrie, et al, *Firearms and Violence: A Critical Review*, National Academy of
Science, copyright 2004, page 118.

220 Charles F. Wellford, John V. Pepper, Carol V. Petrie, et al, *Firearms and Violence: A Critical Review*, National Academy of
Science, copyright 2004, page 119.

221 Wanda J. DeMarzo and Jennifer Mooney Piedra, Man awakens, kills intruder, *Miami Herald*, September 21, 2006.
http://www.miami.com/mld/miamiherald/news/local/states/florida/counties/broward_county/15568514.htm

222 The New Shorter Oxford English Dictionary, Thumb Index Edition, 1993 Edition, Clarendon Press, page 1077.

223 The 2006 Florida Statutes, Title XLVI, Chapter 776: Justifiable Use of Force.
http://www.flsenate.gov/statutes/index.cfm?App_mode=Display_Statute&URL=Ch0776/ch0776.htm
224 Email received from Wanda DeMarzo Thursday 9/21/2006 3:55 PM.
225 The 2004 Florida Statutes, Title XLVI, Section 776: Justifiable Use of Force.
http://www.flsenate.gov/statutes/index.cfm?App_mode=Display_Statute&URL=Ch0776/ch0776.htm
226 Proposed revisions to Instruction 3.6(f) – Justifiable Use of Deadly Force, and Instruction 3.6(g) – Justifiable Use of Non-Deadly Force, Florida Supreme Court, May, 2005, page 4.
http://www.floridasupremecourt.org/clerk/comments/2005/05-1621_PublicationNotice.pdf#xml=http://www.floridasupremecourt.org/SCRIPTS/texis.exe/webinator/search/pdfhi.txt?query=JUSTIFIABLE+USE+OF+DEADLY+FORCE+2004&pr=SupremeCourt&prox=page&rorder=500&rprox=500&rdfreq=500&rwfreq=500&rlead=500&sufs=0&order=r&cq=&id=4342846423
227 The 2006 Florida Statutes, Title XLVI, Chapter 776: Justifiable Use of Force.
228 Burrelles Luce, *Top 100 Daily Newspapers in the U.S. by Circulation, 2006*, Copyright 2006.
http://www.burrellesluce.com/top100/2006_Top_100List.pdf
229 Wanda J. DeMarzo and Jennifer Mooney Piedra, Man awakens, kills intruder, *Miami Herald*, September 21, 2006.
230 DeMarzo Email Sunday 9/24/2006 6:17 PM.
231 LEO email sent Monday, September 25, 2006 5:08 AM.
232 LEO email sent Monday, September 25, 2006 5:50 PM.
233 David Ovalle, Dispute at strip club ends in death, *Miami Herald*, October 2, 2006.
http://www.centredaily.com/mld/centredaily/news/nation/15659616.htm
234 WISQARS Fatal Injuries: Mortality Reports, National Center for Injury Prevention and Control, Centers for Disease Control. http://webappa.cdc.gov/sasweb/ncipc/mortrate.html
235 Nicole White and Susannah A. Nesmith , Victims' families want law changes, *Miami Herald*, August 27, 2006.
http://www.miami.com/mld/miamiherald/15371573.htm
236 Ibid.
237 The 2006 Florida Statutes, Title XLVI, Chapter 776: Justifiable Use of Force.
238 Audra D.S. Burch, After little girl's death, parents strive to change state law, *Miami Herald*, October 27, 2006.
http://www.miami.com/mld/miamiherald/news/15859573.htm
239 David Ovalle and Audra D.S. Burch, Joy, pain in 2nd arrest, *Miami Herald*, July 21, 2006.
http://www.miami.com/mld/miamiherald/news/local/15089140.htm?source=rss&channel=miamiherald_local
240 Nefertiti Jáquez, *Man Charged in Death of Sherdaria Jenkins in Court*, CBS4 News, July 27, 2006.
http://cbs4.com/topstories/local_story_207213753.html Also see: *Two Charged With Second-Degree Murder in Child's Death*, NBC 6, July 26, 2006. http://www.nbc6.net/news/9582533/detail.html?rss=ami&psp=news
241 The 2006 Florida Statutes, Title XLVI, Chapter 776: Justifiable Use of Force.
242 *Authorities To Decide If Father Will Be Charged In Son's Fatal Shooting*, WJXT, July 16, 2007.
http://www.news4jax.com/news/13688824/detail.html
243 Phone conversation on July 17, 2007 with Sgt. Charles E. Mulligan, St. Johns County Sheriff's Office, 4015 Lewis Speedway, St., Augustine, FL 32084, T: 904-824-8304.
244 Note: Special thanks to John Frazer and legal staff at NRA HQ, and to Marion Hammer, Executive Director, Unified Sportsmen of Florida for helping assemble the legal analysis.
245 Brandon Formby, Bill to seek 'castle doctrine' crime protection, *The Dallas Morning News*, October 13, 2006.
http://www.dallasnews.com/sharedcontent/dws/news/localnews/stories/DN-castle_13wes.ART0.North.Edition1.3e193c8.html
246 Ibid.
247 Accused Burglar Sues Homeowner Who Shot Him, *Yahoo! News*, September 28, 2006.
http://news.yahoo.com/s/wisn/20060928/lo_wisn/9950016
248 Associated Press, Foiled burglar sues for emotional distress, *Star Tribune*, June 10, 2006.
http://www.startribune.com/484/story/485319.html
249 H.B. 284 A BILL TO BE ENTITLED AN ACT relating to the use of force or deadly force in defense of a person, Texas Legislature, section 4, page 4. http://www.capitol.state.tx.us/tlodocs/80R/billtext/pdf/HB00284I.pdf
250 Brandon Formby, Bill to seek 'castle doctrine' crime protection, *The Dallas Morning News*, October 13, 2006.
251 Jim Vertuno, Bills filed in Austin to shoot first, retreat later in self-defense, *Houston Chronicle*, February 12, 2007.
http://www.chron.com/disp/story.mpl/headline/metro/4547130.html
252 H.B. 284 A BILL TO BE ENTITLED AN ACT relating to the use of force or deadly force in defense of a person, Texas Legislature, Section 2, pages 1-2. http://www.capitol.state.tx.us/tlodocs/80R/billtext/pdf/HB00284I.pdf
253 Ibid, section 3, pages 2-3.
254 Patrice O'Shaughnessy, Hero dad under the gun, *New York Daily News*, January 19, 2003.
http://www.nydailynews.com/front/story/52803p-49473c.html

242   Endnotes

255 *Brady Campaign State Report Cards Show State Legislatures Are Failing to Protect Kids from the Dangers of Illegal Guns*, The Brady Campaign to Prevent Gun Violence, April 2006. http://www.bradycampaign.org/bradyreport/2006/april/reportcards/ (Use drop-down list to select each state's 2005 grade.)

256 Expanded Homicide Data Table 7: Murder Victims by Weapon, 2001-2005, Federal Bureau of Investigation. http://www.fbi.gov/ucr/05cius/offenses/expanded_information/data/shrtable_07.html Expanded Homicide Data Table 14: Justifiable Homicide by Weapon, Private Citizen, 2001-2005, Federal Bureau of Investigation. http://www.fbi.gov/ucr/05cius/offenses/expanded_information/data/shrtable_14.html

257 Expanded Homicide Data Table 13: Justifiable Homicide by Weapon, Law Enforcement, 2001-2005, Federal Bureau of Investigation. http://www.fbi.gov/ucr/05cius/offenses/expanded_information/data/shrtable_13.html

258 Right-to-Carry 2007, National Rifle Association Institute for Legislative Action. http://www.nraila.org/Issues/FactSheets/Read.aspx?ID=18
Expanded Homicide Data Table 13: Justifiable Homicide by Weapon, Law Enforcement, 2001-2005, Federal Bureau of Investigation.
Expanded Homicide Data Table 14: Justifiable Homicide by Weapon, Private Citizen, 2001-2005, Federal Bureau of Investigation.

259 *Two Men Arrested in Fatal Shooting Released*, ABC-7, January 17, 2007. http://abclocal.go.com/kabc/story?section=local&id=4945904

260 *Two Arrested in Shooting of 9 Year Old*, Los Angeles Police Department, December 22, 2006. http://www.lapdonline.org/newsroom/news_view/34244

261 *DA Explains Release Of Suspects In Girl's Shooting Death*, NBC-4, January 17, 2007. http://www.nbc4.tv/news/10777764/detail.html?rss=la&psp=news

262 Richard Winton and Tami Abdollah, 2 men freed in L.A. girl's killing, *Los Angeles Times*, January 17, 2007. http://www.latimes.com/wireless/avantgo/la-me-selfdefense17jan17,0,520022.story

263 California Penal Code, Title 8—Of Crimes Against the Person, Chapter 1–Homicide, Penal Code 187-199, Official California Legislative Information. http://www.leginfo.ca.gov/cgi-bin/displaycode?section=pen&group=00001-01000&file=187-199

264 *Brady Campaign State Report Cards Show State Legislatures Are Failing to Protect Kids from the Dangers of Illegal Guns*, The Brady Campaign to Prevent Gun Violence, April 2006. http://www.bradycampaign.org/bradyreport/2006/april/reportcards/ (Use drop-down list to select each state's 2005 grade.)

265 Associated Press, Boyfriend of ex-Burbank councilwoman pleads guilty to gun charge, *San Diego Union-Tribune*, November 11, 2005. http://www.signonsandiego.com/news/state/20051111-0414-ca-councilwomansboyfriend.html

266 *53-Year-Old Scott Schaffer Expressed Remorse*, KFWB News 980, February 13, 2007. http://kfwb.com/pages/233520.php?contentType=4&contentId=325089

267 Chris Wiebe, Businessman is sentenced, *Glendale News Press*, February 13, 2007. http://www.glendalenewspress.com/articles/2007/02/14/publicsafety/gnp-schaffer13.txt

268 About Legislative Government, California State Government Guide, League of Women Voters of California, August 22, 2005. http://www.smartvoter.org/gtg/ca/state/overview/legislative.html

269 United States v. Stewart, No. 02-10318, November 13, 2003, page 16078. http://caselaw.lp.findlaw.com/data2/circs/9th/0210318p.pdf

270 Handgun Safety Certificate Program, Office of the Attorney General, State of California. http://ag.ca.gov/firearms/hscinfo.php

271 2007 Dangerous Weapons Control Law, Office of the Attorney General, State of California. http://caag.state.ca.us/firearms/dwcl/12275.htm

272 Patrick Condon, *Conceal and Carry Law Passed by Senate*, Associated Press, KARE 11, May 13, 2005. http://www.kare11.com/news/news_article.aspx?storyid=97011

273 *Permit to Carry a Pistol in Minnesota: Frequently Asked Questions*, Minnesota Department of Public Safety. http://www.dps.state.mn.us/bca/CJIS/Documents/CarryPermit/FAQs.html#Can%20I%20prohibit%20firearms%20in%20my%20private%20residence

274 Repeal Conceal page, Citizens for a Safer Minnesota. http://www.endgunviolence.com/index.asp?Type=B_BASIC&SEC={B1D169BE-CAC1-4A2C-ACEF-16AAA6240903}

275 Firearms Carry Laws, Minnesota Legislative Reference Library, June 2005. http://www.leg.state.mn.us/lrl/issues/firearmcarry.asp

276 Tim Harper, *Arms curbs shot down around U.S.*, Toronto Star, December 9, 2005. http://www.thestar.com/NASApp/cs/ContentServer?pagename=thestar/Render&c=Article&cid=1134082212355&call_pageid=968332188774

277 Del Quentin Wilber and Jamie Stockwell, *Killings In D.C. Fewest Since '86*, Washington Post, January 1, 2005. http://www.washingtonpost.com/wp-dyn/articles/A39858-2004Dec31.html

278 *Murder rate decline no comfort to mother of three slain sons*, CNN.com Law Center, December 23, 2004. http://www.cnn.com/2004/LAW/12/23/murder.one.mother.ap/
279 Wanda J. DeMarzo, *Bad guys still have firepower edge on some cops*, Miami Herald, The State South Carolina, December 19, 2005. http://www.thestate.com/mld/thestate/news/nation/13442565.htm

Chapter 6

1 Steve Kingstone, *U.N. highlights Brazil gun crisis*, BBC News, June 27, 2005. http://news.bbc.co.uk/2/hi/americas/4628813.stm
2 *Consolidation of peace through practical disarmament measures, General and Complete Disarmament*, United Nations, October 31, 1997. http://www.smallarmssurvey.org/source_documents/UN°o20Documents/General°o20Assembly/First°o20Committee°o20Draft°o20Resolutions/A_C.1_52_L.18.pdf
3 IANSA About Web Page. http://www.iansa.org/about.htm
4 Rebecca Peters, *Australia: National Uniform Gun Laws*, Trauma Foundation at San Francisco General Hospital, July, 1, 1997. http://www.tf.org/tf/violence/firearms/other/austr2.shtml
5 Stephanie Kriner and Doug Rekenthaler, *Despite Freetown Victory, Sierra Leone's Humanitarian Crisis Worsens*, Disaster Relief, October 8, 2004. http://www.disasterrelief.org/Disasters/990210SierraLeone/
6 Ibid.
7 Rudy Rummel, *Freedom Virtually Ends Genocide and Mass Murder*. http://www.hawaii.edu/powerkills/WF.CHAP6.HTM
8 *Emergency Update No. 160 on the Great Lakes*, United Nations Department of Humanitarian Affairs Integrated Regional Information Network for the Great Lakes, April 29, 1997. http://www.africa.upenn.edu/Hornet/irin160.html
9 Human Rights Watch, *Leave None to Tell the Story: Genocide in Rwanda, Introduction*, updated April 1, 2004. http://www.hrw.org/reports/1999/rwanda/Geno1-3-01.htm#TopOfPage
10 Human Rights Watch, *Leave None to Tell the Story: Genocide in Rwanda: The Strategy of Ethnic Division*. http://www.hrw.org/reports/1999/rwanda/Geno1-3-02.htm#TopOfPage
11 United Nations Operation in Somalia, Department of Public Information, United Nations, March 21, 1997. http://www.un.org/Depts/DPKO/Missions/unosomi.htm
12 Human Rights Watch, *Leave None to Tell the Story: Genocide in Rwanda: The Attack*.
13 Human Rights Watch, *Leave None to Tell the Story: Genocide in Rwanda: International Responsibility*.
14 Human Rights Watch, *Leave None to Tell the Story: Genocide in Rwanda: Military Action and Inaction*.
15 Human Rights Watch, *Leave None to Tell the Story: Genocide in Rwanda: Recruiting for Genocide*.
16 Human Rights Watch, *Leave None to Tell the Story: Genocide in Rwanda: The Structure*.
17 Human Rights Watch, *Leave None to Tell the Story: Genocide in Rwanda: Survival Tactics*.
18 Human Rights Watch, *Leave None to Tell the Story: Genocide in Rwanda: Rwandan Patriotic Front*. http://www.hrw.org/reports/1999/rwanda/Geno1-3-03.htm#TopOfPage
19 Ibid.
20 Human Rights Watch, *Leave None to Tell the Story: Genocide in Rwanda: Tolerating Discrimination and Violence*. http://www.hrw.org/reports/1999/rwanda/Geno1-3-05.htm#TopOfPage
21 Human Rights Watch, *Leave None to Tell the Story: Genocide in Rwanda: Military Action and Inaction*. http://www.hrw.org/reports/1999/rwanda/Geno1-3-04.htm#TopOfPage
22 Esdras Ndikumana, 160 People Killed In Attack On Burundi Refugee Camp, *Turkish Press*, August 14, 2004. http://www.turkishpress.com/turkishpress/news.asp?ID=24547
23 Peter Muello, Brazilians Block Gun Ban, *Fox News*, October 23, 2005. http://www.foxnews.com/story/0,2933,173154,00.html
24 Angus Stickler, Brazil's police 'execute thousands', *BBC News*, November 23, 2005. http://news.bbc.co.uk/2/hi/americas/4463010.stm
25 John Otis, Deaths mount in Rio's war on crime, *Houston Chronicle*, December 4, 2005. http://www.chron.com/disp/story.mpl/front/3501469.html
26 Rodrigo Gaier and Andrei Khalip, *Ware of gang attacks in Rio kills 18 people*, Reuters, December 28, 2006, Page 1. http://today.reuters.com/news/articlenews.aspx?type=worldNews&storyID=2006-12-28T194011Z_01_N28151481_RTRUKOC_0_US-BRAZIL-CRIME-ATTACKS.xml&pageNumber=1&imageid=&cap=&sz=13&WTModLoc=NewsArt-C1-ArticlePage1
27 Ibid.
28 Ibid, page 2. http://today.reuters.com/news/articlenews.aspx?type=worldNews&storyID=2006-12-28T194011Z_01_N28151481_RTRUKOC_0_US-BRAZIL-CRIME-ATTACKS.xml&pageNumber=1&imageid=&cap=&sz=13&WTModLoc=NewsArt-C1-ArticlePage1

29 Ibid, page 3. http://today.reuters.com/news/articlenews.aspx?type=worldNews&storyID=2006-12-28T194011Z_01_N28151481_RTRUKOC_0_US-BRAZIL-CRIME-ATTACKS.xml&pageNumber=2&imageid=&cap=&sz=13&WTModLoc=NewsArt-C1-ArticlePage2

30 Brazil gun law comes into force, *BBC*, July 2, 2004. http://news.bbc.co.uk/2/hi/americas/3862173.stm

31 Ibid.

32 Andrew Quinn, *Activists call for global gun control measures*, Reuters, March 7, 2005. http://www.alertnet.org/thenews/newsdesk/L07716206.htm

33 Kosovo U.N. troops 'fuel sex trade', *BBC News*, May 6, 2004. http://news.bbc.co.uk/2/hi/europe/3686173.stm

34 Ibid.

35 Ibid.

36 Associated Press, Report Confirms U.N. Congo Sex Abuse, *Fox News*, January 7, 2005. http://www.foxnews.com/story/0,2933,143711,00.html

37 Lyn Duff, Haitian soldiers, police accused of mass rape, *SF Bayview*, March, 2, 2005. http://www.sfbayview.com/030205/accused030205.shtml

38 Colum Lynch, U.N. Envoy to Resign in Wake of Sex Scandal, *Washington Post*, March 2, 2005. http://www.washingtonpost.com/wp-dyn/articles/A64482-2005Mar1.html

39 Crisis in the Congo: Sex Charges Roil U.N., *Fox News*, March 3, 2005. http://www.foxnews.com/story/0,2933,149334,00.html

40 Associated Press, Rights Group: Thousands Raped in Congo, *Fox News*, March 7, 2005. http://www.foxnews.com/story/0,2933,149599,00.html

41 Ibid.

42 U.N. Workers Leave Kids, HIV Behind, *Fox News*, March 5, 2005. http://www.foxnews.com/story/0,2933,149522,00.html

43 Associate Press, *U.N.: 20 Kids Die Daily in Congo Camps*, *Fox News*, March 25, 2005. http://www.foxnews.com/story/0,2933,151533,00.html

44 Mark Dodd, Hushed rape of Timor, *The Australian*, March 26, 2005. http://www.theaustralian.news.com.au/common/story_page/0,5744,12655192%5E2703,00.html

45 Liza Porteus, U.N. Grapples With Peacekeeping Abuse, *Fox News*, March 18, 2005. http://www.foxnews.com/story/0,2933,150798,00.html

46 Peter Dennis, The U.N., Preying on the Weak, *Washington Post*, April 12, 2005. http://www.washingtonpost.com/wp-dyn/articles/A45304-2005Apr11.html

47 Ibid.

48 Ibid.

49 Liza Porteus and Jonathan Wachtel , U.N. Peacekeepers Accused in Sudan Sex-Abuse Case Get Reprimand, *Fox News*, January 5, 2007. http://www.foxnews.com/story/0,2933,241960,00.html

50 Associated Press, Probe: U.N. Peacekeepers Sexually Abused Liberian Women, Girls, *Fox News*, April 29, 2005. http://www.foxnews.com/story/0,2933,155084,00.html

51 Nicole Itano, The sisters-in-arms of Liberia's war, *Christian Science Monitor*, August 26, 2003. http://www.csmonitor.com/2003/0826/p07s01-woaf.html

52 Liberia's Women Killers, *BBC*, August 26, 2003. http://news.bbc.co.uk/2/hi/africa/3181529.stm

53 Ibid.

54 *Freedom in the World 2004: Survey Methodology*, Freedom House. http://www.freedomhouse.org/research/freeworld/2004/methodology.htm

55 List of U.N. Member States: http://www.un.org/Overview/unmember.html cross-referenced with *Freedom in the World 2007*, Freedom House. http://www.freedomhouse.org/template.cfm?page=363&year=2007

56 Commission on Human Rights 2005, United Nations. http://www.unhchr.ch/html/menu2/2/chrmem.htm cross-referenced with *Freedom in the World 2007*, Freedom House. http://www.freedomhouse.org/research/freeworld/2005/table2005.pdf

57 Commission on Human Rights 2007, United Nations, cross-referenced with *Freedom in the World 2007*, Freedom House.

58 *More Democracies Needed On U.N. Rights Body*, Freedom House, May 3, 2004. http://www.freedomhouse.org/media/pressrel/050304.htm

59 *Britain plans anti-corruption tsunami aid for Aceh*, Reuters, June 13, 2005. http://www.alertnet.org/thenews/newsdesk/JAK237862.htm

60 Interview with Leonard Simanjuntak, Deputy Executive Director, Transparency International. http://www.transparency.org/in_focus_archive/tsunami/interview_indonesia.html

61 Transparency International, Frequently Asked Questions. http://www.transparency.org/policy_research/surveys_indices/cpi/2007/faq#general1

62 See Table 6.1, Appendix A.

[63] UN Security Council Membership in 2006. http://www.un.org/sc/members.asp cross-referenced with *Corruption Perceptions Index, 2006*, Transparency International, February 3, 2007.
http://www.transparency.org/policy_research/surveys_indices/cpi/2006

[64] Purchasing Power Parity, Wikipedia. http://en.wikipedia.org/wiki/Purchasing_power_parity

[65] *GNI per capita 2006, Atlas method and PPP*, World Bank, July 1, 2007.
http://siteresources.worldbank.org/DATASTATISTICS/Resources/GNIPC.pdf cross-referenced with Freedom in the World 2007.

[66] Tim Kane, Ph.D, Kim R. Holmes, PhD, Mary Anastasia O'Grady et al, *2007 Index of Economic Freedom*, Heritage Foundation, Copyright 2007, page 38. http://www.heritage.org/research/features/index/downloads/Index2007.pdf

[67] Ibid, page 3.

[68] See Table 6.2, Appendix A.

[69] *2007 Index of Economic Freedom*, Heritage Foundation cross-referenced with *Freedom in the World 2007*. Spreadsheet available, but too large and complex to include here.

[70] Tim Kane, Ph.D, Kim R. Holmes, PhD, Mary Anastasia O'Grady et al, *2007 Index of Economic Freedom*, Heritage House, Copyright 2007, page 38.

[71] See Table 6.3, Appendix A.

[72] See Table 6.4, Appendix A.

[73] Rudy Rummel, *20th Century Democide*. http://www.hawaii.edu/powerkills/20TH.HTM

[74] Rudy Rummel, *20th Century Democide*, cross-referenced with Gun Facts, Version 4.0, page 78, copyright Guy Smith, 2004. Go to http://www.gunfacts.info/ and select the format you prefer.

[75] Rudy Rummel, Docudramas. http://www.hawaii.edu/powerkills/DOCUDRAMAS.HTM

[76] Email dated December 11, 2005 from Professor Rummel, updating web page total with recent research of Chinese government-caused famine of 1958-1962.

[77] FBI,Table 1 - Crime in the United States by Volume and Rate per 100,000 Inhabitants, 1987–2006.
http://www.fbi.gov/ucr/cius2006/data/table_01.html

[78] David B. Kopel, Paul Gallant, and Joanne D. Eisen, *GLOBAL DEATHS FROM FIREARMS: SEARCHING FOR PLAUSIBLE ESTIMATES*, page 126. First published in Texas Review of Law & Politics, Volume 8, pages 113-141.
http://www.davekopel.com/2A/Foreign/Global-Deaths-from-Firearms.pdf

[79] Kofi Annan, Statement of the Security Council, Sept. 24, 1999, U.N. Press Release SG/SM/7145, SC/6733.

[80] See Table 6.5.

[81] See Table 6.6.

[82] See Table 6.7.

[83] Graduate Institute of International Studies, *Small Arms Survey 2007: Guns and the City*, Chapter 2-Completing the Count: Civilian Firearms, page 40.
http://www.smallarmssurvey.org/files/sas/publications/year_b_pdf/2007/CH2%20Stockpiles.pdf.

[84] Mario Osava, DISARMAMENT: Fighting the Global Scourge of Small Arms and Light Weapons, *Inter Press Service News Agency*, April 27, 2005. http://www.ipsnews.net/africa/interna.asp?idnews=28475

[85] Michael S. Bernstam and Alvin Rabushka, *China vs. Russia: Wealth Creation vs. Poverty Reduction*, The Russian Economy, 2005. http://www.russianeconomy.org/comments/042505.pdf

[86] *Russia Defies U.S. Pressure on International Arms Sales*, Mosnews.com, February 10, 2005.
http://www.mosnews.com/news/2005/02/10/armstrade.shtml

[87] The World Factbook – Russia, Central Intelligence Agency, United States, last updated July 14, 2005.
http://www.cia.gov/cia/publications/factbook/geos/rs.html

[88] Rowan Scarborough, *Russian arms sale to Chavez irks U.S.*, *Washington Times*, February 10, 2005.
http://washingtontimes.com/national/20050210-123420-3113r.htm

[89] *With help from Russian Arms Chavez takes Venezuelan defense to grass root level*, India Daily, February 8, 2005.
http://www.indiadaily.com/editorial/1550.asp

[90] *Venezuela to Get Russian-Made Weapons*, Global Security, February 24, 2005.
http://www.globalsecurity.org/military/library/news/2005/02/mil-050214-rianovosti02.htm

[91] *Russia Tells Israel It Will Sell Anti-Aircraft Missiles to Syria*, Mosnews.com, February 16, 2005.
http://www.mosnews.com/news/2005/02/16/missilessyria.shtml

[92] *Russia to Sell India Multiple-Launch Rocket Systems Worth $450M — Source*, Mosnews.com, February 3, 2005.
http://www.mosnews.com/money/2005/02/03/indiaarms.shtml

[93] *Russian Arms Exports to Yemen to Exceed $100M in 2004 — Official*, Mosnews.com, November 23, 2004.
http://www.mosnews.com/money/2004/11/23/yemenarms.shtml

[94] Mortality: Self-Harm, Nationmaster.com, compiled January 2004.
http://www.nationmaster.com/graph-T/mor_sel_har_cap

[95] Murder, Nationmaster.com, compiled 2000. http://www.nationmaster.com/graph-T/cri_mur&int=-1

[96] Murders per capita, Nationmaster.com, compiled 1998-2000. http://www.nationmaster.com/graph-T/cri_mur_cap&int=-1

[97] So who are the Russian mafia? *BBC News*, April 1, 1998.
http://news.bbc.co.uk/1/hi/special_report/1998/03/98/russian_mafia/70485.stm

[98] The rise and rise of the Russian mafia, *BBC News*, November 21, 1998.
http://news.bbc.co.uk/1/hi/special_report/1998/03/98/russian_mafia/70095.stm

[99] Don B. Kates, *Gun Laws Around the World: How Do They Work?* First published in The American Guardian, 1997.
http://www.nraila.org/Issues/Articles/Read.aspx?ID=72

[100] Lyuba Pronina, Russia Defends Rights to Arms, *Moscow Times*, August 4, 2005.
http://www.moscowtimes.ru/stories/2005/08/04/041.html

[101] James G. Neuger, *EU to End Embargo on China Arms Sales, Rebuffing Rice (Update1)*, Bloomberg.com, February 9, 2005.
http://www.bloomberg.com/apps/news?pid=10000085&sid=ajEqJ1B9ecWE&refer=europe

[102] Associated Press, Chinese Ban 'Freedom,' 'Democracy' on Web, *Fox News*, June 14, 2005.
http://www.foxnews.com/story/0,2933,159487,00.html

[103] People's Republic of China: Sustaining conflict and human rights abuses,
the flow of arms accelerates, Amnesty International, June 12, 2006.
http://web.amnesty.org/library/index/engasa170302006

[104] Ibid.

[105] Associated Press, AP: Iran Amassing Military Equipment, *Fox News*, March 25, 2005.
http://www.foxnews.com/story/0,2933,151558,00.html

[106] Associate Press, Iran, China Seek Military Equipment From Pentagon Surplus Auctions, *Fox News*, January 16, 2007.
http://www.foxnews.com/story/0,2933,243858,00.html

[107] Ibid.

[108] Ibid.

[109] Reuters, *Iran buys Russian surface to air missiles: paper*, December 2, 2005.
http://today.reuters.com/news/newsarticle.aspx?type=worldNews&storyid=2005-12-02T075544Z_01_KRA228500_RTRUKOC_0_US-RUSSIA-IRAN-ARMS.xml&rpc=22

[110] Associated Press, *Reports: Russia Fulfills Iran Missile Deal*, Access North Georgia, January 23, 2007.
http://hosted.ap.org/dynamic/stories/R/RUSSIA_ARMS?SITE=7219&SECTION=HOME&TEMPLATE=DEFAULT&CTIME=2007-01-23-01-40-36

[111] Iran's president says move Israel, *BBC News*, December 8, 2005. http://news.bbc.co.uk/2/hi/middle_east/4510922.stm

[112] Irwin Arieff, UN *small arms conference ends in "total meltdown"*, Reuters, July 7, 2006.
http://today.reuters.com/news/newsarticle.aspx?type=topNews&storyid=2006-07-08T012534Z_01_N07247158_RTRUKOC_0_US-ARMS-UN.xml&src=rss&rpc=81&rpc=81 and
http://today.reuters.com/news/newsarticle.aspx?type=topNews&storyID=2006-07-08T012534Z_01_N07247158_RTRUKOC_0_US-ARMS-UN.xml&pageNumber=1&imageid=&cap=&sz=13&WTModLoc=NewsArt-C1-ArticlePage1

[113] Joseph J. Ellis, *His Excellency: George Washington*, page 235.

[114] Megan Goldin, Israel tries to defuse arms sale dispute with U.S., Reuters, *Washington Post*, June 14, 2005.
http://www.washingtonpost.com/wp-dyn/content/article/2005/06/14/AR2005061400236_pf.html

[115] David S. Cloud and Helene Cooper, Israel's Protests Are Said to Stall Gulf Arms Sale, *New York Times*, April 5, 2007.
http://www.nytimes.com/2007/04/05/world/middleeast/05weapons.html?ei=5065&en=9cdce962bc943746&ex=1176436800&partner=MYWAY&pagewanted=print

[116] Ibid.

Chapter 7

[1] Associated Press, Violent Crime On the Rise for First Time in 5 Years, FBI Reports, *Fox News*, June 12, 2006.
http://www.foxnews.com/story/0,2933,199096,00.html

[2] Associated Press, Violent Crime On the Rise for First Time in 5 Years, FBI Reports, *Fox News*, June 12, 2006.

[3] Derived from Federal Bureau of Investigation, *Crime in the United States – 2004, Uniform Crime Reports*, Table 1 – Crime in the United States by Volume and Rate per 100,000 Inhabitants, 1985-2004, page 72.

[4] James Alan Fox and Marianne W. Zawitz, *Homicide trends in the United States*, Bureau of Justice Statistics, U.S. Department of Justice, last revised on September 28, 2004. http://www.ojp.usdoj.gov/bjs/homicide/homtrnd.htm

[5] James Alan Fox and Marianne W. Zawitz, *Homicide trends in the United States: Trends in justifiable homicide by justification reason*, Bureau of Justice Statistics, U.S. Department of Justice, last revised on September 28, 2004.
http://www.ojp.usdoj.gov/bjs/homicide/tables/justifyreasontab.htm

[6] Gary Kleck and Marc Gertz, Armed Resistance to Crime: The Prevalence and Nature of Self-Defense with a Gun, *Journal of Criminal Law and Criminology*, vol. 86, issue 1, 1995, Table 3, page 185.
http://www.saf.org/LawReviews/KleckAndGertz1.htm
[7] NRA Law Enforcement Activities Division, National Rifle Association. http://www.nrahq.org/law/index.asp
[8] Kayne Robinson Bio, NRA Leaders. http://www.nraleaders.com/kayne-robinson.html
[9] *President George W. Bush speaks on the Record*, National Rifle Association.
http://www.nraila.org/Issues/Articles/Read.aspx?ID=147
[10] Lee Williams, *Ex-Dover police captain poised to lead NRA*, Delaware Online, April 30, 2007.
http://www.delawareonline.com/apps/pbcs.dll/article?AID=/20070430/NEWS/704300374/1006/NEWS
[11] See *Gun Control: Only the Truth Will Set You Free*. http://www.chronwatch.com/content/contentDisplay.asp?aid=21413
[12] Ron Sylvester, 1,635 crimes that didn't happen, *The Wichita Eagle*, May 25, 2006.
http://www.kansas.com/mld/kansas/14662023.htm
[13] Protection or Peril?: An Analysis of Firearm-Related Deaths in the Home, Arthur L. Kellermann and Donald T. Reay, 314 New Eng. J. Med. 1557-60 1986, page 1560.
[14] "Pro-Gun" States Lead Nation in Per Capita Firearm Death Rates New Violence Policy Center Analysis Reveals, Violence Policy Center. http://www.vpc.org/press/0602rank.htm
[15] States Ranked by Firearms Death Rate, 2003, Violence Policy Center. http://www.vpc.org/fadeathchart.htm
[16] See Table 7.1, Appendix A.
[17] WISQARS Injury Mortality Reports, 1999-2003. National Center for Injury Prevention and Control, Centers for Disease Control.
[18] See Table 7.2, Appendix A.
[19] *Concealed Truth: Concealed Weapons Laws and Trends in Violent Crime in the United States*, Brady Campaign to Prevent Gun Violence, October 22, 1999. http://www.bradycampaign.org/facts/research/?page=conctruth&menu=gvr
[20] Ibid, Table "The Percentage and Number of States with Increases in Crime between 1992 & 1997."
[21] Compiled from NRA-ILA, *Right-To-Carry 2007*, January 16, 2007.
http://www.nraila.org/issues/FactSheets/Read.aspx?ID=18 Email request for Excel spreadsheet.
[22] See Table 7.3, Appendix A.
[23] See Table 7.4, Appendix A.
[24] *Concealed Truth: Concealed Weapons Laws and Trends in Violent Crime in the United States*, Brady Campaign to Prevent Gun Violence, October 22, 1999.
[25] Bureau of Justice Statistics, Table 66 - Personal crimes of violence, 1996-2004, Percent of incidents, by victim-offender relationship, type of crime and weapons use, U.S. Department of Justice.
http://www.ojp.usdoj.gov/bjs/pub/pdf/cvus66.pdf and Bureau of Justice Statistics, Table 66 - Personal crimes of violence, 2005, Percent of incidents, by victim-offender relationship, type of crime and weapons use, U.S. Department of Justice. http://www.ojp.usdoj.gov/bjs/pub/pdf/cvus/current/cv0566.pdf
[26] See Table 7.5, Appendix A.
[27] Ibid.

Chapter 8

[1] Richard Willing, Violent crime on the rise, summit participants say, *USA Today*, August 31, 2006.
http://www.usatoday.com/news/nation/2006-08-30-violent-crimes_x.htm
[2] Vic Ryckaert, Store owner kills robbery suspect, *The Indianapolis Star*, September 28, 2006.
http://www.indystar.com/apps/pbcs.dll/article?AID=/20060928/LOCAL/609280469/-1/ZONES04
[3] Adrian Arambulo, *Jewelry Store Owner Shoots Robbery Suspect*, Las Vegas Now, January 25, 2007. http://www.klas-tv.com/Global/story.asp?S=5989943
[4] *Store Clerk Shoots and Kills Robbery Suspect*, Las Vegas Now, July 9, 2007. http://www.klas-tv.com/Global/story.asp?S=6760618
[5] Benjamin Wallace-Wells, Bush's War on Cops, *Washington Monthly*, September 2003.
http://www.washingtonmonthly.com/features/2003/0309.wallace-wells.html
[6] Bureau of Economic Analysis, News Release, U.S. Department of Commerce, July 28, 2006, page 10.
http://www.bea.gov/bea/newsrelarchive/2006/gdp206a.pdf
[7] Bureau of Labor Statistics, *Employment status, sex, and age*, United States Department of Labor.
http://www.bls.gov/webapps/legacy/cpsatab1.htm Select *Unemployment rate* under the *Total* section and click on the *Retrieve data* button at the bottom of the page. By October, the rate equaled the historical average; by December it dropped below the historical average.
[8] Bureau of Labor Statistics, *Annual average unemployment rate, civilian labor force 16 years and over (percent)*, United States Department of Labor, June 23, 2006. http://www.bls.gov/cps/prev_yrs.htm

9 Project Safe Neighborhoods, Executive Summary. http://www.psn.gov/about/execsumm.html

10 FBI Crime in the United States, 2004, Table 1: Crime in the United States by Volume and Rate per 100,000 Inhabitants, 1985-2004, page 72. http://www.fbi.gov/ucr/cius_04/documents/CIUS2004.pdf

11 Jeffrey A. Roth, Joseph F. Ryan, et al, *National Evaluation of the COPS Program–Title I of the 1994 Crime Act*, National Institute of Justice, August 2000, page 1. http://www.urban.org/pdfs/COPS_fullreport.pdf

12 Ibid.

13 Ibid, page 9.

14 Ibid, pages 16-17

15 See Tables 8.1 and 8.2 in Appendix A.

16 See Tables 8.4 through 8.5 in Appendix A.

17 Christina L. Sidrow, *Automated Information Systems for Homicide Investigation: A Survey of Urban Police Departments*, Police Executive Research Forum, 1999, page 4.
http://www.policeforum.org/upload/Auto%20IS%20for%20Homicide%20Investigation_576683258_12292005161157.pdf

18 See Table 8.6 in Appendix A.

19 U.S Department of Justice, *COPS Grants Awarded in FY 2005*, September 30, 2005, page 2.
http://www.cops.usdoj.gov/mime/open.pdf?Item=1611

20 Peter Eisler and Kevin Johnson, 10 years and $10B later, COPS drawing scrutiny, *USA Today*, April 10, 2005.
http://www.usatoday.com/news/washington/2005-04-10-cops-cover_x.htm

21 Ibid.

22 Ibid.

23 Ibid.

24 Ibid.

25 Deborah A. Richardson and Rachel Kosa, *An Examination of Homicide Clearance Rates: Foundation for the Development of a Homicide Clearance Model*, Police Executive Research Forum, 2001, pages 12-13.
http://www.policeforum.org/upload/Homicide%20Clearance%20Rates%20-%20Model_576683258_1229200516132.pdf

26 Federal Bureau of Investigation, *Crime in the United States – 2001*, Section II Crime Index Offenses Reported, page 220.
http://www.fbi.gov/ucr/cius_01/crime2.pdf

27 Associated Press, Violent Crime On the Rise for First Time in 5 Years, FBI Reports, *Fox News*, June 12, 2006.
http://www.foxnews.com/story/0,2933,199096,00.html

28 Associated Press, Murder rate decline no comfort to mother of three slain sons, *CNN*, December 23, 2004.
http://www.cnn.com/2004/LAW/12/23/murder.one.mother.ap/

29 Wikipedia, *Posse Commitatus Act*, August 13, 2006. http://en.wikipedia.org/wiki/Posse_Comitatus_Act

30 DESHANEY v. WINNEBAGO CTY. SOC. SERVS. DEPT., 489 U.S. 189 (1989)
http://caselaw.lp.findlaw.com/scripts/getcase.pl?court=US&vol=489&invol=189

31 Shannan M. Catalano, *Criminal Victimization, 2004*, Bureau of Justice Statistics,
U.S. Department of Justice, September 2005, page 10.
http://www.ojp.usdoj.gov/bjs/pub/pdf/cv04.pdf

32 Ibid, page 9.

33 Federal Bureau of Investigation, *Crime in the United States, 2004*, page 264.
http://www.fbi.gov/ucr/cius_04/documents/CIUS2004.pdf

34 Steven K. Smith and Mark Motivans et al, *Compendium of Federal Justice Statistics, 2004*, Bureau of Justice Statistics, U.S. Department of Justice, December 2006, Table 2.2, page 32 and Table 2.5, page 35.
http://www.ojp.usdoj.gov/bjs/pub/pdf/cfjs04.pdf

35 Ibid, page 27.

36 Ibid, pages 29 and 35.

37 Ibid, Table 4.2, page 62 and Table 4.4, page 64.

38 Ibid, Table 5.2, page 74.

39 Murder, rape, robbery and assault data compiled from DOJ's *Compendium of Federal Justice Statistics* for years 1994-2004, tables 2.2, 2.5, 4.2, and 5.2, DOJ's *Criminal Victimization* for years 2000-2004 (percent of incidents reported to police) and FBI's *Crime in the United States* for years 1994-2004, table 25 (percent of cases cleared). Spreadsheet data too large to include in this form, but please email request for Excel workbook.

40 Brian A. Reaves, *Felony Defendants in Large Urban Counties, 1994*, Bureau of Justice Statistics, U.S. Department of Justice, January 1998, page 1. http://www.ojp.usdoj.gov/bjs/pub/pdf/fdluc94.pdf

41 Email from Thomas Cohen, Bureau of Justice Statistics, received July 13, 2007.

42 Murder, rape, robbery and assault data compiled from DOJ's *Felony Defendants in Large Urban Counties* for years 1994, 1996, 1998, 2000 and 2002 tables 1, 23 and 30, DOJ's *Criminal Victimization* for years 2000,2 (percent of incidents reported to police) and FBI's *Crime in the United States* for years 1994, 1996, 1998, 2000 and 2002, table 25 (percent of cases cleared).

Spreadsheet data would not fit into book form, but please email request for Excel workbook. BJS reports available at http://www.ojp.usdoj.gov/bjs/cases.htm.
[43] See Tables 8.7 and 8.8 in Appendix A.
[44] ATF Referrals for Criminal Prosecution: 1985-2002, Syracuse Transactional Records Access Clearinghouse, 2003. http://trac.syr.edu/tracatf/trends/current/atfref.html
[45] Median Prison Sentences for Those Convicted By Investigative Agency, Syracuse Transactional Records Access Clearinghouse, 2003. http://trac.syr.edu/tracatf/trends/current/agenmedtime.html
Median Prison Sentences Received on ATF Referrals, Syracuse Transactional Records Access Clearinghouse, 2003. http://trac.syr.edu/tracatf/trends/current/agenmedtimeG.html
[46] Clinton Pardons http://www.usdoj.gov/opa/pardonchartlst.htm

Appendix A

[1] Van Dijk and Mayhew, Crime Victimisation in the Industrialised World: Key Findings of the 1989 and 1992 International Crime Surveys, page 24.
[2] Ibid, page 28.
[3] Ibid, page 32.
[4] Van Kesteren, Mayhew and Nieuwbeerta, Criminal Victimisation in Seventeen Industrialised Countries: Key-findings from the 2000 international Crime Victims Survey, page 33.
[5] To arrive at 1995 rates per 100,000 population, reference the 1995 crime incidents on page 5 of *Australian Crime Facts and Figures 2002*, and Australian 1995 population numbers found at: *Year Book Australia 2002*, Australian Bureau of Statistics. http://www.abs.gov.au/Ausstats/abs"o40.nsf/94713ad445ff1425ca25682000192af2/0db74c39eee3a02fca256b350010b402!OpenDocument
[6] Brian Pink, Recorded Crime - Victims, 2006, Australian Bureau of Statistics, June 6, 2007, pages 8-9.
http://www.ausstats.abs.gov.au/ausstats/subscriber.nsf/0/E9E9A8A4336E01D1CA2572F10017BA43/$File/45100_2006.pdf Murder and robbery data page 11, sexual assault and assault rates totaled from state and territory data pages 17-24. To determine rates, population data derived from: Population by Age and Sex, Australia, 2006.
http://www.abs.gov.au/AUSSTATS/abs@.nsf/Latestproducts/3235.0Main"o20Features32006?opendocument&tabname=Summary&prodno=3235.0&issue=2006&num=&view=
[7] To arrive at UK 1995 rates per 100,000 population, reference the 1995 crime incidents on pages 40-41 of *Crime in England and Wales 2002/2003* and UK 1995 population numbers found at: Interim revised population estimates: *United Kingdom 1992-2000*, United Kingdom National Statistics Online.
http://www.statistics.gov.uk/STATBASE/Expodata/Spreadsheets/D7080.xls
[8] Crime in England and Wales 2005/2006, Table 2.04 – Recorded crime by offence 1996 to 2005/06 and percentage change between 2004/05 and 2005/06, pages 26-30. http://www.homeoffice.gov.uk/rds/pdfs06/hosb1206.pdf
To arrive at 2005 rates per 100,000 population, cross-reference *Population Estimates*, UK National Statistics. http://www.statistics.gov.uk/CCI/nugget.asp?ID=6
[9] Table 1 - Crime in the United States by Volume and Rate per 100,000 Inhabitants, 1987–2006 .
http://www.fbi.gov/ucr/cius2006/data/table_01.html
[10] To arrive at 1998 rates per 100,000 population, reference the 1998 assault incidents on page 40 of Crime in England and Wales 2002/2003. British Home Office, July 2003, Table 3.04, http://www.homeoffice.gov.uk/rds/pdfs2/hosb703.pdf and UK 1998 population numbers found at: Interim revised population estimates: United Kingdom 1992-2000, United Kingdom National Statistics Online.
[11] To arrive at 2003 rates per 100,000 population, reference the 2002/3 crime incidents on pages 40-41 of Crime in England and Wales 2002/2003 and *Population Estimates*, UK National Statistics. http://www.statistics.gov.uk/CCI/nugget.asp?ID=6
[12] To arrive at 1998 rates per 100,000 population, reference the violent crime totals in *Crime in England and Wales 2002/2003*, page 41 and property crime totals on page 43, and UK 1998 population numbers found at: Interim revised population estimates: United Kingdom 1992-2000, United Kingdom National Statistics.
http://www.statistics.gov.uk/STATBASE/Expodata/Spreadsheets/D7080.xls
[13] To arrive at 2005 rates per 100,000 population, reference the violent crime totals in *Crime in England and Wales 2004/2005*, page 128 and property crime totals on page 130, and UK 2005 population numbers found at: *Population Estimates*, Office for National Statistics. http://www.statistics.gov.uk/cci/nugget.asp?id=6
[14] To arrive at 1995 rates per 100,000 population, reference the 1995 violent crime incidents on page 5 and property crime incidents on page 6 of Australian Crime Facts and Figures 2002 and Australian 1995 population numbers found at: Year Book Australia 2002, Australian Bureau of Statistics.
http://www.abs.gov.au/Ausstats/abs"o40.nsf/94713ad445ff1425ca25682000192af2/0db74c39eee3a02fca256b350010b402!OpenDocument

15 To arrive at 2005 rates per 100,000 population, reference Dennis Trewin, Recorded Crime - Victims, 2005, Australian Bureau of Statistics, May 25, 2006, page 11, http://www.ausstats.abs.gov.au/ausstats/subscriber.nsf/0/A05E3DBEC1109735CA257178001B69FC/SFile/45100_2005. pdf and reference Dennis Trewin, 2004-2005 Regional Population Growth, Australian Bureau of Statistics, February 23, 2006, page 11. http://www.ausstats.abs.gov.au/ausstats/subscriber.nsf/0/50A9687C793C52E4CA25711D000DF7C9/SFile/32180_2004-05.pdf

16 FBI Crime in the United States by Volume and Rate, 1984-2005 http://www.fbi.gov/ucr/05cius/data/documents/05tbl01.xls

17 WISQARS Fatal Injuries: Mortality Reports, National Center for Injury Prevention and Control, Centers for Disease Control. http://webappa.cdc.gov/sasweb/ncipc/mortrate.html

18 WISQARS Fatal Injuries: Mortality Reports, National Center for Injury Prevention and Control, Centers for Disease Control. http://webappa.cdc.gov/sasweb/ncipc/mortrate.html

19 Suicide rates for United Kingdom 1950-1999, World Health Organization, 2004. http://www.who.int/mental_health/media/en/373.pdf
Suicide rates for United States 1950-2000, World Health Organization, 2004. http://www.who.int/mental_health/media/en/374.pdf
Suicide rates for Australia 1950-2001, World Health Organization, 2004. http://www.who.int/mental_health/media/en/281.pdf

20 WISQARS Injury Mortality Reports, 1999-2004, National Center for Injury Prevention and Control, Violence-Related Injury Deaths.

21 Table HIST001. Deaths for 113 selected causes by 10-year age groups, race and sex: United States, 1979-98, Centers for Disease Control, November 8, 2001, page 685. http://www.cdc.gov/nchs/data/statab/hist001.pdf cross-referenced with: Infoplease 1979. http://www.infoplease.com/year/1979.html

22 WISQARS Injury Mortality Reports, 1999 – 2004, National Center for Injury Prevention and Control, Centers for Disease Control. http://webappa.cdc.gov/sasweb/ncipc/mortrate10_sy.html

23 Nonfatal and Fatal Firearm-Related Injuries – United States, 1993-1997, Centers for Disease Control, November 189, 1999, Table 1. http://www.cdc.gov/mmwr/preview/mmwrhtml/mm4845a1.htm

24 Unintentional Firearm Gunshot Nonfatal Injuries and Rates, WISQARS Nonfatal Injury Reports, Centers for Disease Control, National Center for Injury Prevention and Control. http://webappa.cdc.gov/sasweb/ncipc/nfirates.html

25 Traffic Safety Facts 2004: A Compilation of Motor Vehicle Crash Data from the Fatality Analysis Reporting System and the General Estimates System, National Highway Traffic Safety Administration, Table 2, page 15. http://www-nrd.nhtsa.dot.gov/pdf/nrd-30/NCSA/TSFAnn/TSF2004.pdf

26 WISQARS Nonfatal Injury Reports, Centers for Disease Control, National Center for Injury Prevention and Control. http://webappa.cdc.gov/sasweb/ncipc/nfirates.html

27 Shannan M. Catalano, National Crime Victimization Survey 2003, Bureau of Justice Statistics, U.S. Department of Justice, September 2004, Table 2, page 3. http://www.ojp.usdoj.gov/bjs/pub/pdf/cv03.pdf

28 Miller, Cohen, Wiersema, Victim Costs and Consequences: A New Look, National Institute of Justice Research Report, US Department of Justice, January, 1996, Table 2: Losses Per Criminal Victimization, page 9. http://www.ncjrs.org/pdffiles/victcost.pdf

29 Inflation Calculator. http://inflationdata.com/Inflation/Inflation_Rate/InflationCalculator.asp

30 National Highway Traffic Safety Administration, Traffic Safety Facts 2004: A Compilation of Motor Vehicle Crash Data from the Fatality Analysis Reporting System and the General Estimates System, Table 60, page 92. http://www-nrd.nhtsa.dot.gov/pdf/nrd-30/NCSA/TSFAnn/TSF2004.pdf

31 Miller, Cohen, Wiersema, Victim Costs and Consequences: A New Look, National Institute of Justice Research Report, US Department of Justice, January, 1996, Table 2: Losses Per Criminal Victimization, page 9.

32 Inflation Calculator, UnflationData.com. http://inflationdata.com/Inflation/Inflation_Rate/InflationCalculator.asp

33 Annual Firearms Manufacturing and Export Report, Year 2002, Bureau of Alcohol, Tobacco, Firearms, and Explosives, January 8, 2004, received from Frank Briganti, National Shooting Sports Foundation.

34 National Center for Injury Prevention and Control, WISQARS Fatal Injuries: Mortality Reports 1999-2004, Centers for Disease Control. http://webappa.cdc.gov/sasweb/ncipc/mortrate10_sy.html

35 National Center for Injury Prevention and Control, WISQARS Leading Causes of Death Reports, 1999-2004, Centers for Disease Control. http://webappa.cdc.gov/sasweb/ncipc/leadcaus10.html

36 National Center for Injury Prevention and Control, WISQARS Injury Mortality Reports, 1981-1998, Centers for Disease Control.. http://webappa.cdc.gov/sasweb/ncipc/mortrate9.html

37 National Center for Injury Prevention and Control, WISQARS Injury Mortality Reports, 1999-2004, Centers for Disease Control. http://webappa.cdc.gov/sasweb/ncipc/mortrate10_sy.html

[38] Traffic Safety Facts 2004: A Compilation of Motor Vehicle Crash Data from the Fatality Analysis Reporting System and the General Estimates System, National Highway Traffic Safety Administration, Table 2, page 15.

[39] Traffic Safety Facts 2004: A Compilation of Motor Vehicle Crash Data from the Fatality Analysis Reporting System and the General Estimates System, National Highway Traffic Safety Administration, Table 1, page 14.

[40] District of Columbia Crime Rates 1960-2000, The Disaster Center. http://www.disastercenter.com/crime/dccrime.htm United States Crime Rates 1960-2000, The Disaster Center.
http://www.disastercenter.com/crime/uscrime.htm
FBI, Table 4: Crime in the United States by Region, Geographical Division, and State, 2005-2006.
http://www.fbi.gov/ucr/cius2006/data/documents/06tbl04.xls

[41] District of Columbia Crime Rates 1960-2000, The Disaster Center. http://www.disastercenter.com/crime/dccrime.htm United States Crime Rates 1960-2000, The Disaster Center.
http://www.disastercenter.com/crime/uscrime.htm
Table 5: Crime in the United States by State, 2004, FBI Crime in the States, 2004, page 87.
http://www.fbi.gov/ucr/cius_04/documents/CIUS2004.pdf

[42] Table 5: Index of Crime by State, 2001, FBI Crime in the States, 2001, page 80. http://www.fbi.gov/ucr/01cius.htm

[43] Table 5: Crime in the United States by State, 2004, FBI Crime in the States, 2004, page 90.

[44] License to Kill IV: More Guns, More Crime, Violence Policy Center, pages 7-10.

[45] *Arrests in Texas, 1990-2001*, Criminal Justice Policy Council, August 22, 2002 page 12.
http://www.cjpc.state.tx.us/stattabs/arrests/00Arrestsection_U.pdf

[46] Email from Systems Analyst, Regulatory Licensing Service, Texas Department of Public Safety, June 6, 2005.

[47] Population calculated for Texans age 21 and older, using Table ST-EST2002-ASRO-02-48 - State Characteristic Estimates, U.S. Census Bureau, Release Date: September 18, 2003.
http://www.census.gov/popest/archives/2000s/vintage_2002/ST-EST2002/ST-EST2002-ASRO-02-48.xls

[48] Annual Arrest Rates compiled from FBI statistics for years 1995-2004: http://www.fbi.gov/ucr/ucr.htm#cius

[49] Arizona totals are for 1994 through June 2004. FBI arrest statistics extrapolated using the average arrest rate in the general population for 1999-2004 of 5.8% multiplied by state population totals for 1994-1998.

[50] Louisiana totals are for November 1996 through February 2005. FBI arrest statistics extrapolated using the average arrest rate in the general population for 1999-2003 of 6.6% multiplied by state population totals for 1994-1998. Arrest numbers for 2005 not included.

[51] Arrests by State, 2000, FBI. http://www.fbi.gov/ucr/cius_00/xl/rtbl69_00.xls (Same references for all states.)

[52] Arrests by State, 2001, FBI. http://www.fbi.gov/ucr/cius_01/xl/01tbl69.xls

[53] Arrests by State, 2002, FBI. http://www.fbi.gov/ucr/cius_02/xl/02tbl69.xls

[54] Arrests by State, 2003, FBI. http://www.fbi.gov/ucr/cius_03/xl/03tbl69.xls

[55] Arrests by State, Crime in the United States, 2004, FBI, pages 338-345.

[56] Table 2: Annual Estimates of the Population by Sex and Age for Oklahoma: April 1, 2000 to July 1, 2004 (SC-EST2004-02-40). Source: Population Division, U.S. Census Bureau, Release Date: March 2005.
http://www.census.gov/popest/states/asrh/tables/SC-EST2004-02/SC-EST2004-02-40.xls

[57] Arrests by State, 2001, FBI. http://www.fbi.gov/ucr/cius_01/xl/01tbl69.xls

[58] Compiled from: OK CCW Licenses Suspended 2001-2002.
http://www.osbi.state.ok.us/PublicServices/SDA/Suspended.htm plus:
OK CCW Licenses Revoked 2001-2002. http://www.osbi.state.ok.us/PublicServices/SDA/Revoked.htm

[59] Oklahoma Self-Defense Act Statistics, 2001, Oklahoma State Bureau of Investigation.
http://www.osbi.state.ok.us/PublicServices/SDA/Statistics.htm

[60] Arrests by State, 2002, FBI. http://www.fbi.gov/ucr/cius_02/xl/02tbl69.xls

[61] 2001 Oklahoma totals plus: Licenses Approved in 2002, Annual Report, Oklahoma Self-Defense Act 2002, Oklahoma State Bureau of Investigation. http://www.osbi.state.ok.us/PublicServices/SDA/SDA2002Report.pdf

[62] Ibid.

[63] Arrests by State, 2003, FBI. http://www.fbi.gov/ucr/cius_03/xl/03tbl69.xls

[64] *Licenses Revoked and Suspended in 2003*, Annual Report, Oklahoma Self-Defense Act 2003, Oklahoma State Bureau of Investigation, pages 13-15. http://www.osbi.state.ok.us/PublicServices/SDA/SDA2003Report.pdf

[65] 2002 Oklahoma totals plus: Licenses Approved in 2003, Annual Report, Oklahoma Self-Defense Act 2003, Oklahoma State Bureau of Investigation, page 2.

[66] Arrests by State, Crime in the United States, 2004, FBI, pages 338-345.

[67] *Licenses Revoked and Suspended in 2004*, Annual Report, Oklahoma Self-Defense Act 2004, Oklahoma State Bureau of Investigation, pages 13-14. http://www.osbi.state.ok.us/PublicServices/SDA/SDA2004Report.pdf

[68] 2003 Oklahoma totals plus: Licenses Approved in 2004, Annual Report, Oklahoma Self-Defense Act 2004, Oklahoma State Bureau of Investigation, page 2.

69 *2001 Conviction Rates of Concealed Handgun License Holders*, Regulatory Licensing Service, Concealed Handgun Licensing Bureau, Texas Department of Public Safety.
http://www.txdps.state.tx.us/administration/crime_records/chl/convrates.htm
70 Miller, Cohen, Wiersema, Victim Costs and Consequences: A New Look, table 2, page 9. Recalculated to 2001 dollars (1993 dollars used in estimates) using: Bureau of Labor Statistics Inflation Calculator. http://data.bls.gov/cgi-bin/cpicalc.pl
71 Email from Systems Analyst, Regulatory Licensing Service, Texas Department of Public Safety, June 6, 2005.
72 Population calculated for Texans age 21 and older, using Table ST-EST2002-ASRO-02-48 - State Characteristic Estimates, U.S. Census Bureau, Release Date: September 18, 2003.
http://www.census.gov/popest/archives/2000s/vintage_2002/ST-EST2002/ST-EST2002-ASRO-02-48.xls
73 Texas Population Estimates Program, Texas State Data Center and Office of the State Demographer. For years 2003-2005, select appropriate data set from http://txsdc.utsa.edu/tpepp/txpopest.php
2002 non-CHL population estimated from available data: Table 2. Texas Population Estimates by Age and Sex: April 1, 2000 to July 1, 2002, U. S. Census Bureau, September 18, 2003.
http://www.census.gov/popest/archives/2000s/vintage_2002/ST-EST2002/ST-EST2002-ASRO-02-48.xls Request Excel spreadsheet to see formulas used in calculation.
74 Conviction Rates for Concealed Handgun License Holders, Reporting Period: 01/01/2002 – 12/31/2002, Texas Department of Public Safety, February 15, 2007.
http://www.txdps.state.tx.us/administration/crime_records/chl/ConvictionRatesReport2002.pdf
75 Active License Holders and Certified Instructors as of 12/31/2002, Texas Department of Public Safety, downloaded March 28, 2007.
http://www.txdps.state.tx.us/administration/crime_records/chl/PDF/ActLicAndInstr/ActiveLicandInstr2002.pdf
76 Conviction Rates for Concealed Handgun License Holders, Reporting Period: 01/01/2003 – 12/31/2003, Texas Department of Public Safety, February 15, 2007.
77 *Active License Holders and Certified Instructors as of 12/31/2003*, Texas Department of Public Safety, downloaded March 28, 2007. http://www.txdps.state.tx.us/administration/crime_records/chl/PDF/ActLicAndInstr/ActiveLicandInstr2003.pdf
78 *Conviction Rates for Concealed Handgun License Holders, Reporting Period: 01/01/2004 – 12/31/2004*, Texas Department of Public Safety, February 15, 2007.
http://www.txdps.state.tx.us/administration/crime_records/chl/ConvictionRatesReport2004.pdf
79 *Active License Holders and Certified Instructors as of 12/31/2004*, Texas Department of Public Safety, downloaded March 28, 2007. http://www.txdps.state.tx.us/administration/crime_records/chl/PDF/ActLicAndInstr/ActiveLicandInstr2004.pdf
80 *Conviction Rates for Concealed Handgun License Holders, Reporting Period: 01/01/2005 – 12/31/2005*, Texas Department of Public Safety, February 15, 2007.
http://www.txdps.state.tx.us/administration/crime_records/chl/ConvictionRatesReport2005.pdf
81 *Active License Holders and Certified Instructors as of 12/31/2005*, Texas Department of Public Safety, downloaded March 28, 2007. http://www.txdps.state.tx.us/administration/crime_records/chl/PDF/ActLicAndInstr/ActiveLicandInstr2005.pdf
82 Same references for each year as Table 5.9.
83 Victim Costs and Consequences: A New Look. Miller, Cohen, Wiersema. National Institute of Justice Research Report, US Department of Justice, January, 1996, Table 2, page 9. http://www.ncjrs.org/pdffiles/victcost.pdf
84 2003-2005 incident costs calculated using year-end inflation rates at Bureau of Labor Statistics, Inflation Calculator.
http://data.bls.gov/cgi-bin/cpicalc.pl
85 Tabulated from data derived from *Table 5: Crime in the United States by Volume State* for each year, Federal Bureau of Investigation. Email request for comprehensive Excel spreadsheet.
86 Compiled from 1992 and 2002 data, WISQARS Fatal Injuries: Mortality Reports, National Center for Injury Prevention and Control, Centers for Disease Control.
87 Compiled from 1992 and 2002 data, WISQARS Fatal Injuries: Mortality Reports, National Center for Injury Prevention and Control, Centers for Disease Control.
88 *Violence Among Family Members and Intimate Partners*, Section V, Crime in the United States – 2003, Derived from Table 5.2: Number of Incidents with a Violent Crime, page 342.
89 Ibid.
90 FBI Crime in the United States by Volume and Rate, 1984-2003.
http://www.fbi.gov/ucr/cius_03/xl/03tbl01.xls
91 Expanded Homicide Data Table 13 – Justifiable Homicide by Weapon, Law Enforcement, 2001-2005, Federal Bureau of Investigation. http://www.fbi.gov/ucr/05cius/offenses/expanded_information/data/shrtable_13.html
92 Expanded Homicide Data Table 14 – Justifiable Homicide by Weapon, Private Citizen, 2001-2005, Federal Bureau of Investigation. http://www.fbi.gov/ucr/05cius/offenses/expanded_information/data/shrtable_14.html
93 Brady Campaign State Report Cards Show State Legislatures Are Failing to Protect Kids from the Dangers of Illegal Guns, The Brady Campaign to Prevent Gun Violence, April 2006.
http://www.bradycampaign.org/facts/reportcards/2005/ (Use drop-down list to select each state's 2005 grade.)

94 Compiled from FBI , Table 4: Crime in the United States by Region, Geographic Division, and State, 2005-2006. http://www.fbi.gov/ucr/cius2006/data/documents/06tbl04.xls

95 Ibid.

96 The Brady Campaign to Prevent Gun Violence 2001 Report Card, January 22, 2002, Brady Campaign to Prevent Gun Violence. http://www.bradycampaign.org/facts/reportcards/2001/details.pdf cross-referenced with Table 4 - Index of Crime by Region, Geographic Division, and State, 2001-2002, http://www.fbi.gov/ucr/cius_02/pdf/02crime2.pdf.

97 The Brady Campaign to Prevent Gun Violence 2004 Report Card, January 12, 2005, Brady Campaign to Prevent Gun Violence. http://www.bradycampaign.org/facts/reportcards/2004/details.pdf cross-referenced with Table 4 - Index of Crime by Region, Geographic Division, and State, 2004-2005, http://www.fbi.gov/ucr/05cius/data/documents/05tbl04.xls.

98 Brady Campaign State Report Cards Show State Legislatures Are Failing to Protect Kids from the Dangers of Illegal Guns, The Brady Campaign to Prevent Gun Violence, April 2006, cross-referenced with FBI , Table 4: Crime in the United States by Region, Geographic Division, and State, 2005-2006. http://www.fbi.gov/ucr/cius2006/data/documents/06tbl04.xls

99 Table 1 – Crime in the United States by Volume and Rate per 100,000 Inhabitants, 1987-2006. http://www.fbi.gov/ucr/cius2006/data/table_01.html

100 FBI , Table 4: Crime in the United States by Region, Geographic Division, and State, 2005-2006.

101 Table 1 – Crime in the United States by Volume and Rate per 100,000 Inhabitants, 1987-2006.

102 Florida Crime Rates 1960-2005, The Disaster Center. http://www.disastercenter.com/crime/flcrime.htm

103 FBI , Table 4: Crime in the United States by Region, Geographic Division, and State, 2005-2006.

104 Division of Licensing, Concealed Weapon/Firearms License Statistical Report, 1987-1999, Florida Department of State and Division of Licensing, Concealed Weapon/Firearms License Statistical Report, 1987-2000, Florida Department of State. Reports must be ordered. Copies faxed to me by Marion Hammer, Executive Director, Unified Sportsmen of Florida.

105 Division of Licensing, Concealed Weapon/Firearms License Statistical Report, 1987-2001, Florida Department of State.

106 Division of Licensing, Concealed Weapon/Firearms License Statistical Report, 1987-2002, Florida Department of Agriculture and Consumer Services.

107 Division of Licensing, Concealed Weapon/Firearms License Statistical Report, 1987-2003, Florida Department of Agriculture and Consumer Services.

108 Division of Licensing, Concealed Weapon/Firearms License Statistical Report, 1987-2004, Florida Department of Agriculture and Consumer Services.

109 Division of Licensing, Concealed Weapon/Firearms License Statistical Report, 1987-2005, Florida Department of Agriculture and Consumer Services.

110 Federal Bureau of Investigation, Crime in the United States, 2000, Table 5-Index of Crime by State, 2000, page 77.

111 Federal Bureau of Investigation, Crime in the United States, 2001, Table 5-Index of Crime by State, 2001, page 77.

112 Federal Bureau of Investigation, Crime in the United States, 2002, Table 5-Index of Crime by State, 2002, page 79.

113 Federal Bureau of Investigation, Crime in the United States, 2003, Table 5-Index of Crime by State, 2003, page 83.

114 Federal Bureau of Investigation, Crime in the United States, 2004, Table 5-Index of Crime by State, 2004, page 87.

115 2005: Table 5-Crime in the United States by State, 2005. http://www.fbi.gov/ucr/05cius/data/documents/05tbl05.xls

116 Table 1–Crime in the United States by Volume and Rate per 100,000 Inhabitants, 1986-2005, Federal Bureau of Investigation. http://www.fbi.gov/ucr/05cius/data/documents/05tbl01.xls

117 Table 4.– Index of Crime: Region, Geographic Division, and State, 1995-1996, Uniform Crime Reports for the United States, 1996, Federal Bureau of Investigation, pages 66-67. http://www.fbi.gov/ucr/Cius_97/96CRIME/96crime2.pdf

118 Table 4.– Index of Crime: Region, Geographic Division, and State, 2000-2001, Uniform Crime Reports for the United States, 2001, Federal Bureau of Investigation, pages 68-69. http://www.fbi.gov/ucr/cius_01/01crime2.pdf

119 Table 4– Crime in the United States by Region, Geographic Division, and State, 2004-2005, Federal Bureau of Investigation. http://www.fbi.gov/ucr/05cius/data/documents/05tbl04.xls

120 Table 8.– Number of Offenses Known to the Police, Cities and Towns 10,000 and over in Population, 1995, Uniform Crime Reports for the United States, 1995, Federal Bureau of Investigation, page 119. http://www.fbi.gov/ucr/Cius_97/95CRIME/95crime.pdf

121 Table 8.– Number of Offenses Known to the Police, Cities and Towns 10,000 and over in Population, 2000, Uniform Crime Reports for the United States, 2000, Federal Bureau of Investigation, page 126. http://www.fbi.gov/ucr/cius_00/00crime213.pdf

122 Table 8.– Offenses Known to Law Enforcement by State by City, 2005, Federal Bureau of Investigation. http://www.fbi.gov/ucr/05cius/data/documents/05tbl08.xls

123 Bureau of Labor Statistics, National Census of Fatal Occupational Injuries in 2005, United States Department of Labor, August 10, 2006, page 2. http://www.bls.gov/news.release/pdf/cfoi.pdf

124 Freedom in the World 2007, Freedom House. http://www.freedomhouse.org/template.cfm?page=363&year=2007

125 *Corruption Perceptions Index 2006*, Transparency International, February 3, 2007.
http://www.transparency.org/policy_research/surveys_indices/cpi/2006
126 *GNI per capita 2006, Atlas method and PPP*, World Bank, July 1, 2007.
http://siteresources.worldbank.org/DATASTATISTICS/Resources/GNIPC.pdf
127 *2007 Index of Economic Freedom*, Heritage Foundation. Spreadsheet available, but too complex to include.
128 Rudy Rummel, *20th Century Democide*. http://www.hawaii.edu/powerkills/20TH.HTM
129 *Freedom in the World 2007*, Freedom House.
130 *Corruption Perceptions Index 2006*, Transparency International, February 3, 2007.
131 *2007 Index of Economic Freedom*, Heritage Foundation.
132 Graduate Institute of International Studies, *Small Arms Survey 2005*, Oxford University Press, Copyright 2005. Data from 2003 and 2004 received as PDFs in email from Tania Inowlocki, Publications Manager. Data also available for download at http://www.smallarmssurvey.org. Data from 2007 downloaded PDF at
http://www.smallarmssurvey.org/files/sas/publications/year_b_pdf/2007/CH2%20Stockpiles.pdf.
133 See corresponding references for Table 6.5.
134 See corresponding references for Table 6.5.
135 WISQARS Injury Mortality Reports, 1999-2003. National Center for Injury Prevention and Control, Centers for Disease Control. http://webappa.cdc.gov/sasweb/ncipc/mortrate10_sy.html
136 Table 4: Crime in the United States by Region, Geographic Division, and State, 2003-2004, FBI Crime in the States, 2004, pages 76-85. http://www.fbi.gov/ucr/cius_04/documents/CIUS2004.pdf
137 WISQARS Injury Mortality Reports, 1999-2003. National Center for Injury Prevention and Control, Centers for Disease Control.
138 Compiled from United States Crime Rates 1960-2005, The Disaster Center. http://www.disastercenter.com/crime/
139 Compiled from: Crime in the United States, 1999, Table 4 - Index of Crime by Region, Geographic Division, and State, 1998-1999, Federal Bureau of Investigation, pages 66-73. http://www.fbi.gov/ucr/Cius_99/99crime/99c2_13.pdf
Table 1 - Crime in the United States by Volume and Rate per 100,000 Inhabitants, 1986 – 2005, Federal Bureau of Investigation. http://www.fbi.gov/ucr/05cius/data/documents/05tbl01.xls
140 Compiled from United States Crime Rates 1960-2005, The Disaster Center.
141 Compiled from Crime in the United States, 1999, Table 4 - Index of Crime by Region, Geographic Division, and State, 1998-1999, Federal Bureau of Investigation, pages 66-73.
142 Compiled from United States Crime Rates 1960-2005, The Disaster Center.
143 Compiled from: Crime in the United States, 1995, Table 4 - Index of Crime by Region, Geographic Division, and State, 1994-1995, Federal Bureau of Investigation, pages 60-67. http://www.fbi.gov/ucr/Cius_97/95CRIME/95crime2.pdf
Crime in the United States, 1996, Table 4 - Index of Crime by Region, Geographic Division, and State, 1995-1996, Federal Bureau of Investigation, pages 64-71. http://www.fbi.gov/filelink.html?file=/ucr/Cius_97/96CRIME/96crime2.pdf
Crime in the United States, 1997, Table 4 - Index of Crime by Region, Geographic Division, and State, 1996-1997, Federal Bureau of Investigation, pages 68-75. http://www.fbi.gov/filelink.html?file=/ucr/Cius_97/97crime/97crime2.pdf
Crime in the United States, 1999, Table 4 - Index of Crime by Region, Geographic Division, and State, 1998-1999, Federal Bureau of Investigation, pages 66-73.
144 Federal Bureau of Investigation, Table 74 – Full-time Law Enforcement Employees by Population Group, Percent Male and Female, 2005. http://www.fbi.gov/filelink.html?file=/ucr/05cius/data/documents/05tbl74.xls
145 Federal Bureau of Investigation, *Crime in the United States, 2004*, Table 74 – Full-time Law Enforcement Employees as of October 31, 2004, Percent Male and Female, by Population Group, page 375.
http://www.fbi.gov/ucr/cius_04/documents/CIUS_2004_Section6.pdf
146 Federal Bureau of Investigation, *Crime in the United States, 2003*, Table 74 – Full-time Law Enforcement Employees as of October 31, 2003, Percent Male and Female, by Population Group, page 370.
http://www.fbi.gov/ucr/cius_03/pdf/03sec6.pdf
147 Federal Bureau of Investigation, *Crime in the United States, 2002*, Table 74 – Full-time Law Enforcement Employees as of October 31, 2002, Percent Male and Female, by Population Group, page 328.
http://www.fbi.gov/ucr/cius_02/pdf/02crime6.pdf
148 Federal Bureau of Investigation, *Crime in the United States, 2001*, Table 74 – Full-time Law Enforcement Employees as of October 31, 2001, Percent Male and Female, by Population Group, page 322.
http://www.fbi.gov/ucr/cius_01/01crime6.pdf
149 Federal Bureau of Investigation, *Crime in the United States, 2000*, Table 74 – Full-time Law Enforcement Employees as of October 31, 2000, Percent Male and Female, by Population Group, page 296.
http://www.fbi.gov/ucr/cius_00/00crime6.pdf
150 Federal Bureau of Investigation, *Crime in the United States, 1999*, Table 74 – Full-time Law Enforcement Employees as of October 31, 1999, Percent Male and Female, by Population Group, page 296.
http://www.fbi.gov/ucr/Cius_99/99crime/99cius6.pdf

[151] FBI, *Crime in the United States, 1998,* Table 74 – Law Enforcement Employees, Percent Male and Female, As of October 31, 1998, page 296. http://www.fbi.gov/ucr/Cius_98/98crime/98cius30.pdf

[152] FBI, *Crime in the United States, 1997,* Table 74 – Law Enforcement Employees, Percent Male and Female, October 31, 1997, page 301. http://www.fbi.gov/ucr/Cius_97/97crime/97crime6.pdf

[153] FBI, *Crime in the United States, 1996,* Table 74 – Law Enforcement Employees, Percent Male and Female, October 31, 1996, page 290. http://www.fbi.gov/ucr/Cius_97/96CRIME/96crime6.pdf

[154] FBI, *Crime in the United States, 1995,* Table 74 – Law Enforcement Employees, Percent Male and Female, October 31, 1995, page 283. http://www.fbi.gov/ucr/Cius_97/95CRIME/95crime6.pdf

[155] Federal Bureau of Investigation, *Crime in the United States, 1994,* Table 74 – Law Enforcement Employees, Percent Male and Female, October 31, 1994, page 294.

[156] Federal Bureau of Investigation, Table 25 – Percent of Offenses Cleared by Arrest or Exceptional Means, by Population Group, 2005. http://www.fbi.gov/filelink.html?file=/ucr/05cius/data/documents/05tbl25.xls

[157] Federal Bureau of Investigation, *Crime in the United States, 2004,* Percent of Offenses Cleared by Arrest or Exceptional Means, by Population Group, 2004, page 267. http://www.fbi.gov/ucr/cius_04/documents/CIUS_2004_Section3.pdf

[158] Federal Bureau of Investigation, *Crime in the United States, 2003* Percent of Offenses Cleared by Arrest or Exceptional Means, by Population Group, 2003, page 257. http://www.fbi.gov/ucr/cius_03/pdf/03sec3.pdf

[159] Federal Bureau of Investigation, *Crime in the United States, 2002* Percent of Offenses Cleared by Arrest or Exceptional Means, by Population Group, 2002, page 223. http://www.fbi.gov/ucr/cius_02/pdf/02crime3.pdf

[160] Federal Bureau of Investigation, *Crime in the United States, 2001* Percent of Offenses Cleared by Arrest or Exceptional Means, by Population Group, 2001, page 222. http://www.fbi.gov/ucr/cius_01/01crime3.pdf

[161] Federal Bureau of Investigation, *Crime in the United States, 2000,* Table 25, Percent of Offenses Cleared by Arrest, by Population Group, 2000, page 207. http://www.fbi.gov/ucr/cius_00/00crime3.pdf

[162] Federal Bureau of Investigation, *Crime in the United States, 1999,* Table 25, Percent of Offenses Cleared by Arrest, by Population Group, 1999, page 203. http://www.fbi.gov/ucr/Cius_99/99crime/99cius3.pdf

[163] Federal Bureau of Investigation, *Crime in the United States, 1998,* Table 25, Percent Cleared by Arrest, by Population Group, Offenses Known to the Police, 1998, page 201. http://www.fbi.gov/ucr/Cius_98/98crime/98cius21.pdf

[164] Federal Bureau of Investigation, *Crime in the United States, 1997,* Table 25.– Offenses Known and Percent Cleared by Arrest, Population Group, 1997, page 213. http://www.fbi.gov/ucr/Cius_97/97crime/97crime3.pdf

[165] Federal Bureau of Investigation, *Crime in the United States, 1996,* Table 25.– Offenses Known and Percent Cleared by Arrest, Population Group, 1996, page 205. http://www.fbi.gov/ucr/Cius_97/96CRIME/96crime3.pdf

[166] Federal Bureau of Investigation, *Crime in the United States, 1995,* Table 25.– Offenses Known and Percent Cleared by Arrest, Population Group, 1995, page 199. http://www.fbi.gov/ucr/Cius_97/95CRIME/95crime3.pdf

[167] Federal Bureau of Investigation, Table 1–Crime in the United States by Volume and Rate per 100,000 Inhabitants, 1986-2005. http://www.fbi.gov/ucr/05cius/data/documents/05tbl01.xls

[168] See Table 8.1 for corresponding references for each year.

[169] Derived from percents reported to police from Bureau of Justice Statistics, *Criminal Victimization* from years 2000-2004, U.S. Department of Justice. Access BJS reports at http://www.ojp.usdoj.gov/bjs/cvictgen.htm; FBI clearance rates, see Table 8.3 for corresponding references for each year included; adjudication data from Bureau of Justice Statistics, *Compendium of Federal Justice Statistics,* 1994-2004, U.S. Department of Justice, tables 2.2, 2.5, 4.2, and 5.2. Access BJS reports at http://www.ojp.usdoj.gov/bjs/fed.htm.

[170] Ibid.

FOUR HUNDRED YEARS OF GUN CONTROL . . .
WHY ISN'T IT WORKING?

CONTRAST MEDIA PRESS

ISBN-13 978-0-9817382-2-2

Printed in the United States
129292LV00004B/101/P